I0309372

NO PLACE TO BE BUT HERE

My Life and Times

by

Larry Mild

(An Autobiography)

Magic Island Literary Works • Honolulu, HI • 2019

Published by Magic Island Literary Works.

Printed in the United States of America by Lightning Source, Inc.

Interior book design by Larry Mild.
Cover design by Marilyn Drea, Mac-In-Town, Annapolis, MD.
Cover photos by Rosemary Mild

Library of Congress Cataloging-in-Publication Data:
Mild, Larry M.
No Place To Be But Here, My Life and Times by Larry Mild
(An Autobiography)
Mild, Larry M.
ISBN 978-0-9905472-1-1

First Edition 2019
10 9 8 7 6 5 4 3 2 1

Dedication

For my two terrific wives:

Hannah Joan Forsch Mild (of Blessed Memory)

Rosemary Pollack Mild

For our wonderful children:

Jacqueline Arlene Mild Lau

Myrna Lynn Mild Spurrier

Miriam Luby Wolfe (of Blessed Memory)

For our beloved grandchildren:

Alena, Craig, Ben, Leah, and Emily

Acknowledgments

We could fill an entire volume with the names of all the family members, dear friends, and acquaintances who are loyal fans of our books. You are all precious to us and give us the ultimate push to continue our writing. I owe special thanks to the following for their expertise, advice, feedback, and encouragement:

- My wonderful wife, Rosemary, who makes everything possible in my life.

- My loving daughters, Myrna and Jackie, who were my trusted first readers and family consultants for this book.

NOTE: A few photographs of ships, aircraft, and WWII slogan posters were included from the Internet to support my story. I appreciate the indulgence of those various sites, for I can't anticipate a broad interest and distribution of this work beyond family, friends, and community. All other photographs were taken by myself and family. Thank you!

Disclaimer

My personal history *is* as I remember it some eighty-six years after it began. I have always been bad with exact dates and precise names for those who shared time with me. If I mis-tagged a photo or mis-aligned an association or forgot to mention someone or something pertinent, it was surely not intentional. For these things I apologize and hope you will remember me with interest, fondness, and respect anyway.

Contents

Contents

§

Chapter 1

An Unexpected Beginning

Six years and three months after the arrival of my brother, George Leon Mild, a second delivery arrived at Grace-New Haven Hospital for my parents, John Mild and Hilda Eleanor Glueck Mild. The auspicious date was September 20, 1932. Some years later, that lengthy gap in sibling arrival time started me wondering whether I, Lawrence (Larry) Milton Mild, was a planned or an oops event. I also learned they were anticipating a Lois Mild, perhaps a second disappointment. Even so, I never felt there was a lack of love or caring among the four of us. Fact is, they didn't return me to sender. The separation in brotherly years soon labeled George "Big Brother Babysitter" and me "Larry the Brat," a status neither one of us ever wanted, but wound up experiencing anyway. A few days after my bursting on the scene, I traveled to a modest, pale green, two-story home at 157 Spring Street up in the hill section of New Haven, CT.

Passing the diapering, feeding, toddling, and preschool mischievous ages with flying colors, I emerged a shy, chubby, and tall kid who wore short pants in the summer and knickers and knee socks in the winter. Oh how I yearned to wear long pants like the big (older) guys. My size was always stout and my knickers were noisy due to the rubbing of corduroy on the inside of the legs. You could always hear me coming with my infernal *zizz-zizzing* sound. A rip or a stubborn stain in any article of my clothing, accidental or not, usually warranted a stiff scolding from Mother. Once past the Mommy stage, it was always Mother in the early years, because "Ma" and "Mom" were undignified, "sounding too much like a billy goat," she insisted.

I attended Horace Day Elementary School slightly over one city block away from home. The student furniture comprised row on row of attached folding seats in front of wooden, hinged, flip-top, desks supported by wrought-iron pod-like legs that were screwed to the floor. There was always a two-inch hole in the right corner of each desktop for an inkwell. Each row of desks and seats grew in size and height from the front of the room to the rear, to accommodate varying student packaging. So guess where oversized Larry wound up. Yep, in the last row lest my knees be squished and bruised. One might think this afforded a child some measure of invisibility during hands-raised class questions. Yep again, that is, when everyone among a sea of anxious hands knew the answer, but a definite nope when no one knew the answer. The last row became vulnerable then and I had trouble sometimes delivering the tough right answers. I had my share of bright and lucky answers too; I certainly wasn't a dullard.

The schoolrooms were spacious—wide with high ceilings and eight-foot-high windows. At least two walls were functional in each room. One of them was covered in bulletin boards and another in dusty wood-framed, black slate, blackboards that required routine washing. Chalk sat on a narrow ledge below the blackboards alongside erasers, whose cleaning required battering a pair together, so that the impact produced a massive cloud of chalk dust from both erasers. This cloud was both a source of humor when its dust reappeared on someone else's face and clothing or a form of punishment when it reappeared on your own puss. Some found the practice a good excuse to miss some class work. Others thought the assignment was a teacher's reward for good behavior.

Did I mention the earliest desktop peripheral—the glass

inkwell that occupied the aforementioned hole in every desk cover? They were delivered to each desk only during penmanship exercises and returned afterward. Yes, we actually used them with our wooden dip pens, a mere step above bird-feather quills and only used by show-off calligraphers today. Dip and scratch (from the noise they made) pens were five-inch, tapered wooden stems with a metal nib or pen point stuck in one end. I want to blame my growth spurts and poor small motor skills for the unintelligible mess that evolved from my penmanship classes. Teachers were not always willing to decrypt much of my scribbling, so my grades suffered for it even then. Being classroom-shy didn't help the grades any either. My shyness I attributed to my mother's strict discipline and her philosophy "Children are best seen and not heard."

Getting back to those eight-foot schoolroom windows. In second grade two of them came crashing in on our classroom due to the high winds of the great hurricane of 1938. Everyone knew there was a storm afoot, yet no one dreamt of its intensity. And who knew of the early storm warning systems that are in place today? Luckily, we were all hunkered down in a central hallway, with the doors to the surrounding rooms shut, so to the best of my knowledge, no one was injured. During the quiet of the storm's eye, my father came to the school to rescue me. I still have a child's faded vision of branches and leaves everywhere, but the uprooted trees lying across impassable roads and across sidewalks and yards stayed with me. Mostly, I remember the demise of a giant elm that once towered over the front of our house, graciously lending us its shade and cool. You see, only some theaters had air conditioning in those days, so nature's cool was quite important. This tree's roots continually tore up our front sidewalk and kept my dad busy cutting them back and patching the walk with concrete cement. Well, the tree finally had its measured revenge and tumbled straight across Spring Street, stretched to the opposite walk, and bent to rest on someone else's front stoop, a serious shoal to through-traffic. It could have fallen toward our house and devastated most of our home, but it didn't.

A lattice structure attached to the backyard boundary fence was always thick with grape vines. Late in the growing season my parents made a juice and sometimes a wine from the grapes and, at the end of the process, bottled it in our basement. I couldn't tell you much about either the grape or the wine, but my discovery of the bottle-capping device became a source of mischief for me. Put the cap on the bottle and pull down the lever. Pull off the cap with a bottle opener. Hey! This is fun—try another—and another—

157 Spring Street house in New Haven

until a whole carton of caps became a lost cause on the basement floor. After my mother's call down the stairs: "What are you doing down there?" and my casual reply: "Nothing"—I literally caught hell for my folly.

We lived on the first floor of the two-story, house on Spring Street and rented out the second floor. The house had a finished-floor attic which we used mostly for storage. One small window in its rear accessed a clothesline strung from the third floor to a telephone pole in the backyard. A screened-in front porch ran across the narrow frontage of the house. A door outside the porch led to the second floor, and a door inside the porch led to our dining room. Two smallish rooms shared the front of the house, the living and dining rooms. A door off the dining room led to the kitchen. To the left of the kitchen lay a tiny hall accessing two bedrooms and a lone bath.

We had a long cement driveway that ran the length of the house and broadened to the width of the property line beyond—ending with a four-car garage that we rented out. In my earliest memory we had a car, but for the life of me, I couldn't tell you its make and model. I must have been four or five years old when I climbed into its driver's seat and made-believe I drove it all over town. As with most of my mischief, I was caught red-handed at the steering wheel and heavily scolded for, would you believe it—breaking the car. To reinforce this accusation, the car was taken away the next day and never seen again. It was many years later that I learned that my mother had had a nervous breakdown and was no longer allowed to drive. She never drove again, and as far as I knew, my father never drove at all. He preferred public transportation which was mostly trolleys at the time.

Another white lie proffered by the family concerned my father's older sister, Aunt Fanny, who had a big white house on a hill in the Westville section of New Haven. Three words told all—she was a *cheek-pincher extraordinaire,* and my plump cheeks were just too much for her to resist. Most of the time I dutifully bit my lip and endured the pain, but on one occasion, she went too far, and I told her off in no uncertain terms. "That hurts! Get out of my house and don't come back!" She left the house, and I didn't see her for at least ten years afterward. I was led to believe this was because of my outcry. Again, many years later I learned the truth. My mother and Aunt Fanny had had their own skirmish on a totally different subject. The family did reconcile with my aunt some time after that.

Though these (the 1930s) were the years of the Great Depression, my father continued to work regularly, thanks to the carpenters' union hall and his reputation and persistence. Money was tight, but there was always food on our table, and our clothes were always clean and in good repair. But jobs were scarce. Many men were out of work, and due to the reigning culture of the times, women were restricted to a scant number of vocations. Beggars often came to the door for handouts. We did what we could.

Street vendors, a common sight in the 1930s, are almost unheard of today. A fish monger pushed a two-wheeled, wooden cart from behind, holding onto two wooden handles. Under the double-hinged wood covers lay the fish packed in ice. A pull-spring scale and tray, suspended from a pole arm, ensured good product measure, and a conical-shaped metal horn's tooting announced his arrival. A man with a smaller, hand-driven cart and a large emery wheel driven by foot pedals could sharpen scissors and knives or even repair umbrellas. Fresh vegetables came down the street direct from the farm on a horse-drawn wagon. Trails of horse poop in the street were common. And there were the rag men who bought scraps and leftovers from just about any project. They paid pennies, nickels, and dimes for weighed old clothes and metal scraps—even my father's old bent nails. The proceeds were always mine—my first access to personal spending cash. The largest personal allowance I ever received from my parents was 25 cents per week.

Aunt Catherine, my mother's younger and unmarried sister, lived with us from my earliest days in the Spring Street house until her marriage. Her bedroom was a small footprint alcove off the dining room, a space under the external stairs that led to the second-floor rented apartment. With room for a twin-sized bed and standing room only, my dad installed a built-in dresser under the bed and a pair of curtained glass doors for the thirty-year-old's privacy. It also had one curtained window to the outside. When I was approximately eight years old, she married Uncle Meyer Rubenstein, a fun and lively sort some years older than her. They lived in New London, an hour's drive from us. Eventually they had two sons, Richard and Lenny.

Afterward, I spent a few weeks each summer with them. One summer's day we all went swimming at a nearby pond—that is, they went in to swim, and I dangled my feet over the edge of a pier at one end of the pond. Uncle Meyer came back onto the pier and asked me if I wanted to learn how to swim. When I answered in the affirmative, he literally picked me up and dropped me into the drink. Why would he do such a thing? With the question sitting on my mind for a split second, I began floundering, my hands flailing, my chubbiness trying its best to contribute to my minimal buoyancy. Finally, I looked up at Uncle Meyer and saw him slowly, methodically, and repeatedly going through the essential motions of the crawl. It didn't take long before I got the message and began to follow suit. Using arms only, I reached the pier, and he leaned over and pulled me from the water. He apologized for the surprise launch and spent a good deal of time refining the arm motions and teaching me the kick. In one terrifying lesson, I had learned to swim.

Although many cooperative grocery markets flourished in the times, the concept of the supermarket remained somewhere over the horizon, a thing yet to come. More common were the small, independent, sole proprietorship and partnership businesses, i.e., the family business era. The interaction between seller and buyer was far more personal then than it is today. For example, my father used to take me a few blocks away to Meyer's Bakery (not my uncle) where, after a jovial conversation, the owner would take me into the back room to watch the crullers being twisted or the jellys and creams being injected into the donuts. We would always return home with a large (12-inch-round) flowered or seeded corn-rye bread or pumpernickel bread—best eaten with sweet unsalted butter. Sometimes there would be bagels or bialys in a second bag, another treat.

Not only the bakery, but the kosher delicatessen too. I wish I could remember that kindly man's name. Whenever I tagged along to the store, he came out from behind the counter to reward me with a small chunk of halvah—a ground almond cake. When it came time to purchase new dill pickles, he'd hand me the large tongs and let me bob and fish in the wooden barrel for them myself as he held the waxed paper to receive them. The salamis and pastramis were my favorite deli meats, and if I was lucky, he'd hand me a scrap from the overage. If my mother went to the dairy case, there was a chance she would buy some pot cheese, the main ingredient for my favorite, her cheesecake with the braided top. Pot cheese came in a large round wooden tub that faced forward on a tilt in the glass case and was dispensed with a large wooden spoon. Slightly drier, much airier (lighter) than cottage cheese, pot cheese made the best cheesecakes ever and yet is almost unheard of today.

Quintos Fireworks store, several doors away from this deli, was the site of a major explosion and fire started by the casual toss of a lit cigarette into the outside display. The ensuing fire consumed most of the surrounding block, but for some unknown reason and our good fortune, it had spared the deli.

The price of a loaf of Wonder Bread was 12 cents; a pound of butter, 25 cents; a half-pound of salami, 30 cents. A child's haircut was 25 cents, and an adult cut was 75 cents. A Saturday matinee cost the better part of a dime (9 cents), leaving you enough for a penny's worth of loose candy. Candy bars cost a nickel. Saturday matinee fare at the movies usually meant a pair of older double features or a single new feature and a string of short subjects (*Superman, Buck Rogers, The Green Hornet, The Three Stooges*, and three or four animated cartoons.) If you were lucky, sometimes a comic book, with the corner cropped to prevent resale, was thrown into the bargain. Adults had their own bargains on Tuesdays or Thursdays and could collect glass tumblers or even dishes and the like. Gas stations had their own promotional give-aways in tumblers and cups.

In the 1930s and '40s polio threatened the nation and, as yet, no cure had been found. Spending time in an iron lung to breathe and using double mirrors to see, was a very scary thing. People deserted organizations and clubs and avoided crowds. Kids wore camphor bags around their necks that stank to high heaven, but they did keep friends from getting too close. Even movie theaters suffered a decline in patronage.

Television hadn't arrived on the scene yet. Radio and newspapers were our main source of information and entertainment. Our main radio was a piece of maple furniture, standing at least three feet high and two feet wide; it stood in a corner between the upright piano and the sofa. The geometric floor space created by the confluence of sofa, radio, and upright piano was mine. I'd curl up there with my back against the sofa and my toes propped up by the piano. Smack-dab in the middle of the yellow radio dial was this big green evil eye, which was actually a tuning eye, an aid to sharper station selection. The narrower the eye's wedge-like beam, the sharper (more accurate) the tuning.

While my parents preferred listening to the news and President Roosevelt's Fireside Chats, I liked to listen to afternoon entertainment such as *Jack Armstrong*, *Henry Aldrich*, *The Lone Ranger*, and *Got-em-Tennessee*. Sunday night was always family radio night. The comedic fare began with *Jack Benny* and continued with *Edgar Bergen and Charlie McCarthy*, *Fred Allen*, and *Judy Canova*. My bedtime on school nights was still 7:00 p.m., so weekday evening radio was out of the question for me. On Fridays and Saturdays it was 8:00 p.m., so I was usually shuffled off to bed in mid-*Inner Sanctum*. I could hear the sound through the wall of my bedroom next door, but it was so muffled, I couldn't make out what was happening or even playing. The same was true in the summertime when the rest of my family sat on the screened-in front porch, and their voices drifted in through the open bedroom window. Boy, was I nosy! Was I ever missing something!

There were two houses next door to us on the left, one on the street and the other fifty feet behind it. Each of the two Catholic families living there had a son—one named Robert McCaulif and the other, Buddy Baker. They were my age and a year older. They never allowed me to be their friend, but it wasn't for the lack of my trying and, as time went by, I learned it was because they knew I was Jewish. In my early efforts to join their exclusive clique I was told I'd have to go through some hazing to prove my worthiness. The paddling, the tainted tasting, and the leg lock, wrapped around a basement stanchion, I endured, but I refused to swear on the Christian testaments or recite prayers from them. Needless to say, I did my best to avoid them thereafter. It was my first exposure to anti-Semitism, yet I don't know what made me feel so strongly about the ultimate price they tried to impose on my offer of friendship.

Perhaps it was my early Sunday School training at Temple Mishkan Israel. Looking back now, I'd say I acquired a fine Jewish education and strong Jewish identity. I'm guessing the temple was between five and six miles from our home—in other words, the other side of downtown. At one point my brother, George, and I frequently walked the whole way, stopping here and there to pick up his older classmate friends. When George was confirmed and had moved on to other Sunday activities, I rode the trolley to the end of the line and walked another two blocks to religious class.

End-of-the-line meant the trolley reversed direction without turning around, so the angled pole contacting the overhead wire at the rear had to be reined in, and the pole at the front let out. While the conductor did this, I often helped to reverse all of the seat backs, so the passengers could ride face forward. It was a job that made me feel useful.

I joined the YMCA primarily to be able to swim at their pool. It cost 25 cents a month to join, and I was assigned to a group of eight boys led by a Yale University divinity student. Right from the beginning everyone knew I was Jewish. We met twice a month for discussion, once a month to swim, and once a month for sports. At these discussion groups I learned a fair amount about the Christian religion without having to give an inch on my own faith. It turned out to be a decent learning experience. In fact, I acquired Bob Altier, Clark Caugland, and Louis Gramaldi as friends for the remainder of my time living on Spring Street.

In the summer of 1941 we moved from Spring Street to 211 Maple Street on the northeast corner of Brownell Street, a few blocks from the main artery of Whaley Avenue in western New Haven. It was a slate roofed, all white, three-story house in which we initially occupied the second and third floors and rented out the first floor. Later we rented out portions of the third floor. There was also a two-car rental garage—we still didn't own a car. All of the rooms branched off of a long hall that began with the bathroom at the rear of the house and ended in a house-wide living room. A kitchen and dining room lay to streetside of that hall and two bedrooms lay to the other side of it. The new neighborhood brought with it a fresh set of friends. I started Augusta Lewis Troup Junior High School (grades seven through nine) that fall. The new school district meant a fully integrated school, a novel yet broadening experience for me, for I had not encountered black students before.

211 Maple Street house in New Haven

I turned nine in September of 1941, the year the European rumblings began to reach our local media. Hitler was on the move and countries were falling before him. I knew this meant some dread to my parents, but I believe I was quite oblivious to these happenings. After all, I was just a kid. My awareness was something that would soon change.

Chapter 2

Immersed in the World War II Years

It was a Sunday, December 7,1941 and barely afternoon in New Haven when all our radio stations were interrupted to announce that Japanese planes were bombing Pearl Harbor in Hawaii. Most people on the East Coast had only a vague idea of where Hawaii was situated. A few days later everyone knew. I was listening to one of my radio shows in the living room when the announcer broke in with the terrible news. I rushed in to tell the rest of the family, who were still finishing lunch in the kitchen. In a matter of minutes the whole family huddled around the radio with me.

People were dying, but I hadn't any notion of how this would affect us personally. A day later President Roosevelt declared war on both Japan and Germany; thereafter they (and later Fascist Italy) were labeled the Axis Powers. At the time I wondered why the label and why the other two nations when just Japan had attacked us. My father and brother took the time to explain that Germany and Japan were at opposite ends of the globe, and a line between them constituted some sort of an axis. Also, the three powers were aligned by treaty, so the U.S. was bound to fight an expanded war in Europe as well as in the Pacific Ocean.

We found out soon enough how we were affected when Uncle Leo Glueck, my mother's youngest and fondest brother, wound up selected and inducted into the Army Air Corps in the earliest wave of the newly established draft. He left a store manager's position at Sears and Roebuck in Lynn, MA. Leo was my favorite uncle, never showing up at our house without some sort of gift from the store for us boys—a baseball glove, a football, and the like. He was one of the few members of close family who ever took us for car rides. One of my favorite places was the road by the airport to watch planes take off and land.

Uncle Leo Glueck

Typical U.S. B-24 Liberator bomber

Staff Sergeant Leo Glueck was trained as a radioman in Florida and was assigned to a B-24 Liberator bomber, flying out of a base somewhere in North Africa. On July 9, 1943 his plane was shot down over the Greek Island of Crete on the way to the Romanian (Floestian, sometimes Ploesti) oil fields, Hitler's main source of fuel for his panzers (tanks) and aircraft.

Leo was classified missing in action or simply MIA and declared dead a year later when nothing more was learned about him. As was the custom, my mother, who mourned him the most, replaced the silver star with a gold star ribbon that hung on our front door glass. That ribbon was again replaced with both a silver and a gold star when my brother, George, enlisted in the Navy a year later. He served through the war as a Fire Controlman Third Class aboard the *USS Bristol*, a destroyer, and thankfully came home safely. Blue stars denoted family members serving in the armed services. Silver stars denoted family members serving in the military overseas, and a gold star indicated the loss of their life.

Our country feared attacks on both the East and West coasts,

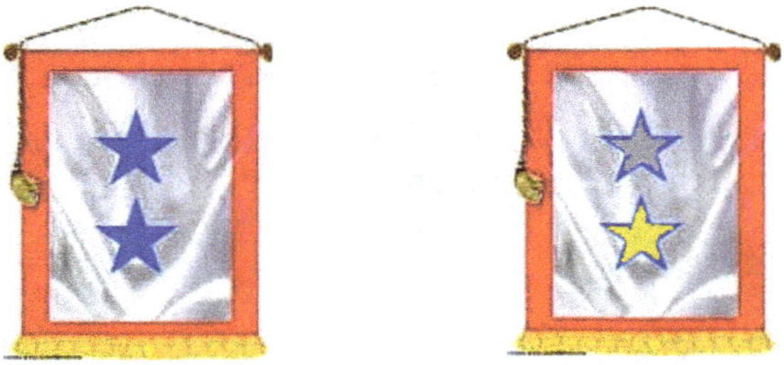

Blue, silver, and gold stars in the window

so our lives changed again. My father installed snug black shades on all the windows, so light would not leak out and reveal a city, a potential target to enemy bombers. There were citizen air raid wardens appointed in every neighborhood to roam and report lighting violations and to direct people to designated shelters, mainly basements of public buildings and schools, and finally, to assist in any attack emergencies.

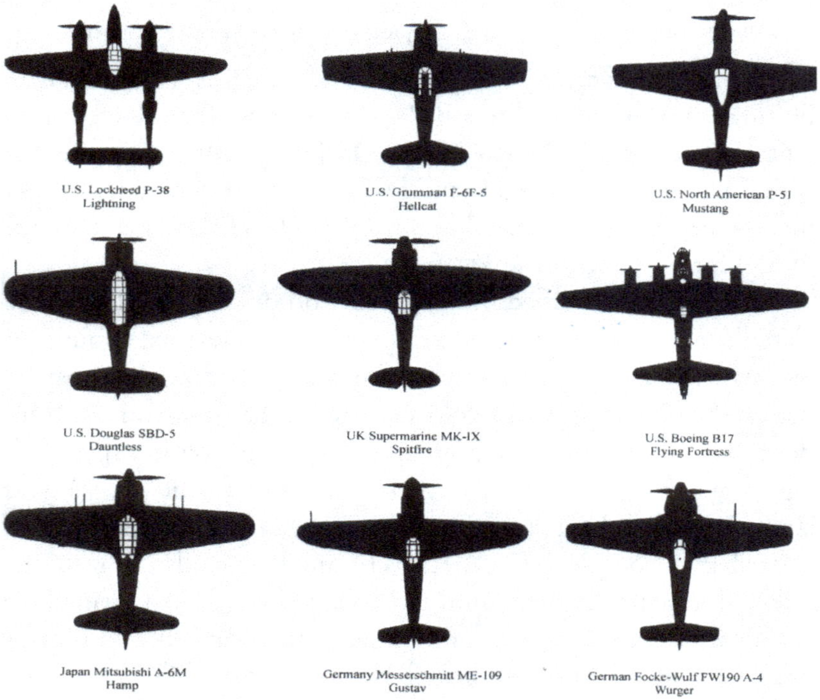

Typical WWII Aircraft Identification Posters

There were posters everywhere, revealing the bottom and side profiles (silhouettes) of both enemy and friendly aircraft. Most junior high students could discern, identify, and even name these planes as well as they knew the automobiles on our streets. I prided myself on this accomplishment as well.

The war was expensive, and the Government needed help financing it, so they sold multidenominational war (later called liberty and then savings) bonds to the public. Officials and celebrities held bond drives to promote the sale of these bonds. Students participated by buying 25-cent stamps weekly and dutifully pasting them in books until the $18.75 initial value had been reached. The $25.00, terminal, or redemption, value of those bonds was reached somewhere between seven and eight years later.

Like most of our neighbors, we followed the war effort through the newspapers and radio reports. We had a four-foot bulletin board in my bedroom that was covered over with a large National Geographic map of the European continent. Pins with tiny beaded heads had colors to denote the various Allied troop positions. A news short at the movie theaters called the *March of Time* brought the war home much the way television does today. No day went by without some reminder, There's a war on!

Posters were the thing, and mostly they conveyed slogan messages like—Uncle Sam Wants You!—Enlist Now!—A Slip of the Lip Sinks Ships—Buy War Bonds.

My father died at the young age of fifty-two in 1945. In some indirect way the war could partially be blamed for his death. Almost all seasoned wood—essentially plywood, planks, and framing studs—had been diverted to the war effort, especially to build Patrol Torpedo (PT) boats and military camp barracks. So while he used unseasoned scaffolding on a carpenter's building job, a key board bent, then broke under his weight, sending him into a two-story fall. The result was a broken leg and a severe heart condition. The leg mended, but the induced heart condition took his life two years later. He couldn't go to work after the fall. Of course, being overweight didn't help any. I was thirteen at the time.

Full employment existed, as the draft and enlistments continued to drain manpower on the home front. Housewives patriotically pitched in and joined the workforce, thus changing its makeup henceforth. The price of everything rose and scarcities existed in almost all goods and services. Government-controlled rationing and price freezing became the norm. Gasoline became the dearest commodity, so a square, two-inch lettered patch in the corner of the windshield revealed how much and how often you were allowed to buy it. The letters also denoted how essential to the war effort the vehicle and driver were. This also meant additional bookkeeping for the gas station owner, who had to account for what he, and now she, dispensed.

Foods were also rationed with butter, frying oils/grease, and butchered meats being the top priorities. Butter, oil, and grease were used to make munitions and explosives, and the meats fed an army and navy abroad with precious protein. Books of stamps were issued for every member of the family, and you separated your stamps and paid for those items you purchased with them right along with the going cash price. However, some things or cuts were hardly ever available. Unfortunately, greedy folks bypassed the system and dealt under the counter, growing a considerable black market that was hardly ever threatened by law enforcement. Patriots frowned on this sort of thing to little avail. Vegetables and fruits would have been a problem too, but many families grew Victory Gardens in any vacant space left on their property. We always had a flower and vegetable garden that ran the length of the driveway, so when the war came along, we just planted more veggies and relabeled it a Victory Garden like everyone else.

Recycling is hardly a twenty-first century idea. Tied ten-inch bundles of neatly folded newspapers were left curbside for pickup, as were cans of used and congealed cooking fats, and numerous other items. The leftover cans from canned goods were stripped of their paper labeling, washed, opened from the bottom as well as the top, stepped on to flatten, and boxed for pickup too. We also saved aluminum foil from cigarette packaging, as well as that from used food wraps, and pressed them into a ball for easy handling. As a member of a Boy Scout troop, we participated in the pickup process. Our troop leader provided the truck, and the scouts ran alongside the truck, tossing in the neighborhood pickup items. Other scouts aboard the truck did the stacking. These items were then dropped off at recycling centers.

I joined the scouts at age twelve, and in the three years that I was active, rose from Tenderfoot to Life Scout, one rank below Eagle. The uniform and the organized activities attracted me. Joining one of two Jewish troops in town, I went on long hikes, some as long as 14 miles—a round-trip to Mt. Carmel and the Sleeping Giant State Park. At one scouting jamboree I remember pitching a pup (one-person) tent and completing a drain ditch all around it, as required, just in time for the rain to keep me inside for most of the weekend. Who knew what camping was all about? I did learn to like it better when I went away for two weeks to scout camp in central Connecticut. We slept eight to a cabin and ate in a central dining hall. At camp I tried new strokes, honed the rest of my swimming skills, and learned all about canoeing and boating safety. I came away with my junior life-saving certificate and a number of merit badges. It felt good—I was finally good at something.

School, Sunday School, and scouting afforded me with few close friends, only friendly casual acquaintances. My efforts to improve my status were often shunned. I was still the chubby, shy, and awkward kid. However, I was slowly learning to work at being social. The new neighborhood provided me with the only close friends that I had known to date. The problem was that my two closest friends, Eddie Bailey and Moose (Malcolm) Alderman, went to private schools, while the others were a grade above or below me.

I have never been musically adept. In fact, one might say I was musically challenged. Don't get me wrong—I've enjoyed a wide range of music from jazz to opera all my life. We've even had season tickets to the opera for about twenty years. What I'm trying to convey here is that I play no instrument and I am monotonic when I try to sing. At Troup Junior High, we were required to attend choral class—to sing for the Christmas program, no less. It didn't matter if you were Jewish or any other kind of ish, you were required to sing. The teacher noticed I wasn't singing and shouted: "Lawrence, you're not singing." I tried merely mouthing my part in silence, but only got rebuked again, so I joined in with the class until I heard my name once more: "Lawrence, stop singing. You're throwing everyone else off key." I was familiarly known as Larry and preferred it that way. Lawrence was reserved for when I was in deep trouble at home or in school. A school day at junior high always began with the standing Pledge of Allegiance, followed by a Protestant rendering of the Lord's Prayer.

By and large, I have always been a pacifist, but I have also been called out on occasion—mostly to defend my excess weight. I managed to get the better of those situations a fair amount of the time. Name calling, I could walk away from, but tripping and shoving I couldn't avoid. Then sometimes anti-Semitism would rear its ugly head again. His first name was Joe and his last name began with a B, so I always referred to him as Joe-the-bastard, but not to his face, of course. I didn't want to antagonize him. He was taller and bigger than me and at least two years older than me. I tried to ignore his label of "Jewboy," but a few times he caught me alone on Elm Street when I was late walking to junior high.

The first time I hurried up when I saw him across the street. Letting out a string of cuss words, he crossed the street and shoved me down into a hedgerow. Each time I tried to get up, he'd shove me down again. My being full of scratches and bleeding and whimpering seemed to satisfy him, so he moved on. The next time I tried to hit back he beat the bejeebers out of me. I wound up with a split lip and a black eye for my effort. From then on I was never too late to walk with the crowd to school again.

With George away in the Navy and my father gone, I became the man of the house, destined to carry out the maintenance skills taught to me by my patient father. I took care of his tools to keep them efficient and tackled all sorts of carpentry, plumbing, and electrical repairs inflicted on the house. I imagine I saved the family a fair amount of money this way. Before my father's death, we had three additional rental houses that he had purchased in disrepair and had completely renovated. The tenants in the Edgewater Avenue house went off on vacation during the winter, turning off the heat entirely without draining the water pipes. As a result, the pipes froze and burst, devastating the house into a total loss. We sold off the other two houses when upkeep expenses exceeded the rental income we needed for living expenses. As cash became dearer, my mother went back to work as a saleslady in a dress store, a terrible strain for a middle-aged, heavyset woman to stand on her feet for an eight-hour day, but she managed to slow down the outflow of family savings.

At the age of thirteen I went to work as an usher in a neighborhood theater (the Westville) managed by Eddie Bailey's father. Being underage, he was kind enough to pay my salary via out-of-pocket cash. I learned much about movie theater operations, and when I became a junior in high school, I worked as lead usher at the Crown Theater in downtown New Haven, and then, as I became a high school senior, the assistant manager of the Lincoln Theater on the north side of town. This arrangement continued on the weekends during my freshman and sophomore years at the University of Connecticut. One of the benefits of all this was that, through a company affiliation, we were able to get occasional open seats at the famous Shubert Theater, where many Broadway shows got their trial start. For example, I got to see *Oklahoma* when it was still called *Away We Go*. The popularity of the song soon influenced the title of the show before it got to Broadway. There were a number of other shows, but none so famous and many never made it to New York. Often, after work on Saturday nights, I would stop on Oak Street for fresh bagels to enjoy on Sunday mornings. The Jewish bakeries would start up again as soon as Shabbat was over.

One of our Maple Street neighbors and a friend of my mother's was notified that her son died on the battlefield. He had been a ham radio operator and a member of the American Radio and Relay League (AR&RL). His kind mother offered all his radios, related parts, and a stack of the League's quarterly magazines to me, and I accepted. Although my first venture into the guts of a conventional radio ended up blowing a bunch of household fuses, I had already built simple radio sets consisting of a crystal, a variable tuning capacitor, a pair of earphones, a long wire antenna, and a coil of wire wrapped around an empty toilet paper tube. The crystal had a whisker attached that allowed you to tickle the rough face of it until you found a sensitive spot, and then you tuned the capacitor until you captured a station. My recent windfall had experiments galore documented in the AR&RL quarterlies, allowing me to learn a whole lot about electrical and electronic fundamentals, and thus became one of the most influential things in choosing a career for myself.

In the early Fifties, while I was away in the Navy, my mother sold the house and moved to Miami Beach, FL. In the process she got rid of many of my father's precious tools and, of course, the windfall radio stuff—all given away or sold by the pound. In the mid-Eighties I came across similar parts, particularly the four- and five-pronged vacuum tubes displayed in the Smithsonian. Many were worth thousands of dollars, according to a knowledgeable docent there. Oh well—easy come, easy go.

In April of 1945 President Franklin Roosevelt died of a hemorrhaging stroke in his fourth term in office. The president was beloved by a nation like no other before him. He had rescued them from the Great Depression and led them through WWII.

The war ended in 1945 with victory in May across Europe (VE Day) and victory in the Pacific against Japan (VJ Day) late in August. Both days warranted a good deal of celebration.

Chapter 3

The Immediate Family: My Rock

My Father, My Mentor:

John Mild

I have always regretted that we had so little time together. My father had suddenly passed away at age 52, just beyond my thirteenth birthday, and there were only so many years that I was mature enough to appreciate the sort of man, the kind of parent I had. I'm sure he gave me the most perfect start in life.

I am still today my father's child—inheriting his sensitivity, work ethic, and patience to teach. Although John Mild was a good father to both of his sons, and though my brother got to know him at least six years longer than me, I felt I had more of a special connection, a greater bond with him.

My earliest memory of him was a large man with a roundish handsome face, napping in a straight-back, armed dining room chair after a hard day's work. He would snore loudly, sometimes waking himself, and then with a peaceful grin, return to sleep. He somehow preferred that chair to an upholstered chair and hassock while we waited for my mother to serve supper. Dad wasn't much of a disciplinarian. In fact, he was more a source of solace after being scolded by my mother. His arms were always open to me. Looking backward now, I have the feeling that he was henpecked—the willing victim of his strong-willed wife. He much preferred a peaceful coexistence within his own home. I can't say that I ever witnessed an exchange of affection between Mother and Dad, although I'm sure that they shared mutual kindness and respect.

Dad having a drink at the bar with a West Point graduate friend, who later became Lt. General Shunfield and an American Red Cross executive

The weekends were our time to be together. On Saturday morning his two wooden toolboxes were brim full of hand tools, nails, and sawdust. You see, Dad was a skilled carpenter and builder, and neither the bosses nor the clients allotted time on the job for cleaning and sorting. That was my job. After removing, cleaning, and oiling all of the tools, I would drag a six-inch horseshoe magnet through the sawdust to attract all kinds of nails from the wooden sea and sort them by condition, purpose, and size. The badly bent ones were discarded in a small wooden barrel to be sold as scrap later. Those suffering from a slight curvature of the spine were subjected to correction with the tap of a hammer or squeezed straight in a bench vise. Brads and finishing nails found their way to one pile and common nails to another. Then, by size, every nail wound up in a coffee can designated from two-penny length to ten-penny and spike. All I know of tools and their safe and proper usage I owe to my father and his patient teachings. He taught by example and never scolded.

My father made a steady living and supported our family comfortably. In the early days he made most of my toys. A dowel and two pieces of shaped wood nailed together constituted a sailboat. Shaped differently with wheels cut from a broomstick handle, the wood became a race car. As I grew older, the toys became more sophisticated. Abandoned roller skates and a wooden box nailed to a 2x4 served as an excellent scooter. Baby carriage wheels and another wooden box emerged as a serviceable wagon, at least until I finally got a genuine red Radio Flyer wagon with removable wooden stake sides from Sears and Roebuck. That was a rare store-bought treasure for me.

My father, John Mild, was born October 5, 1893 in a small shtetl (Tarasta or Tarashcha) 65 miles south of Kiev, Russia, in what is now the Ukraine. His parents were Joseph (or Jaakov or Jacob or Israel in Hebrew) Malement (or Mild) and Ester Sobinefsky, according to my parents' May 1928 marriage certificate. Joseph, a coppersmith, died on the job, falling from a roof in Kiev. On May 26, 1903 Dad (a.k.a. Reesel) arrived in the United States with his mother and one sister, Fanny (a.k.a. Freidel) on the Dutch ship *Ryndam*. The ports of departure and entry were Rotterdam, Holland and New York, NY. and His older brother Sam{1884-1975} had arrived in the U.S. a few years earlier in 1897. The family name change from Malement to Mild was attributed to Uncle Sam, but poorly documented. His family settled first in Ansonia, CT and then moved to nearby New Haven. On June 24, 1929 Dad became a naturalized U.S. citizen (Certificate #2924631 issued in U.S. District Court, New Haven). See marriage and naturalization certificates below.

My father worked hard, lived frugally, and with his savings, purchased older, run-down homes to renovate and rent out. The Charles Morris Glueck family rented the second floor of one of these fixed-up homes at 242 Spring Street, not three blocks away from number 157 where I was reared. Dad, at age 32, married their 21-year-old daughter, Hilda Eleanor Glueck, on September 5, 1925.

The final memories of my father are tainted with guilt.

THE UNITED STATES OF AMERICA

No. 2924631

TO BE GIVEN TO THE PERSON NATURALIZED.

CERTIFICATE OF NATURALIZATION

Petition, Volume 43 Number 9870

Description of holder: Age, 35 years; height, 5 feet, - inches; color, WHITE; complexion, DARK; color of eyes, BROWN; color of hair, DARK BROWN; visible distinguishing marks, NONE

~~Name, age and place of residence of wife~~

(NOTE: AFTER SEPTEMBER 22, 1922, HUSBAND'S NATURALIZATION DOES NOT MAKE WIFE A CITIZEN.)

Names, ages and places of residence of minor children George 3. Resides at New Haven, Connecticut.

ORIGINAL

District of Connecticut ss: X John Mild (Signature of Holder)

Be it remembered, that JOHN MILD then residing at number 157 Spring Street, city of NEW HAVEN State of Connecticut, who previous to his naturalization was a subject of RUSSIA having applied to be admitted a citizen of the United States of America pursuant to law, and at a -------- term of the United States District court of DISTRICT OF CONNECTICUT held at NEW HAVEN on the 24th day of June in the year of our Lord nineteen hundred and 29 the court having found that the petitioner intends to reside permanently in the United States, and that he had in all respects complied with the Naturalization Laws of the United States, and that he was entitled to be so admitted, it was thereupon ordered by the said court that he be admitted as a citizen of the United States of America.

(SEAL) In testimony whereof the seal of said court is hereunto affixed on the 24th day of June in the year of our Lord nineteen hundred and 29 and of our Independence the one hundred and 53rd.

C. E. Pickett

CLERK, U. S. DISTRICT COURT (Official character of attestor)

DEPARTMENT OF LABOR

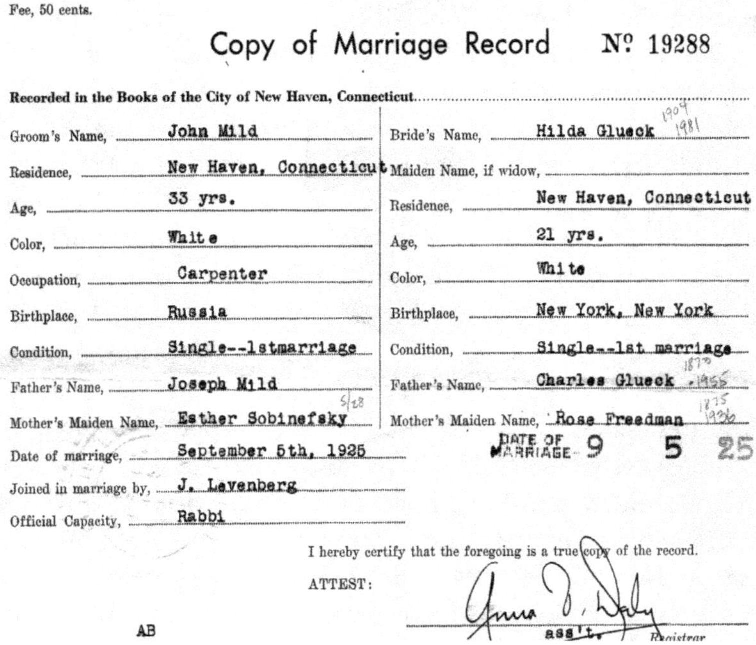
Fee, 50 cents.

Copy of Marriage Record No. 19288

Recorded in the Books of the City of New Haven, Connecticut

Groom's Name,	John Mild	Bride's Name,	Hilda Glueck
Residence,	New Haven, Connecticut	Maiden Name, if widow,	
Age,	33 yrs.	Residence,	New Haven, Connecticut
Color,	White	Age,	21 yrs.
Occupation,	Carpenter	Color,	White
Birthplace,	Russia	Birthplace,	New York, New York
Condition,	Single--1stmarriage	Condition,	Single--1st marriage
Father's Name,	Joseph Mild	Father's Name,	Charles Glueck
Mother's Maiden Name,	Esther Sobinefsky	Mother's Maiden Name,	Rose Freedman
Date of marriage,	September 5th, 1925	DATE OF MARRIAGE	9 5 25
Joined in marriage by,	J. Levenberg		
Official Capacity,	Rabbi		

I hereby certify that the foregoing is a true copy of the record.

ATTEST: Anna V. Daly ass't. Registrar

AB

That particular evening, November 25, 1945, he had scolded me for being fresh with him, and I never got the chance to apologize. It wasn't that the offense was so great. It was childish. Rather, it was the way I had left our parting. To make matters worse, on answering a call to nature, Dad had to pass my bedroom door, and just as he did, a heart attack took his life, and his form fell into my bedroom. I was still awake. I know he forgave me—he always did—the gentle, forgiving man that he was. The funeral and burial and mourning period hammered home how fragile our family relationships were. I missed my Dad sorely. He was only fifty-two years old. I had just turned thirteen at the time and I now had to become the man of the house. He was buried at Mishkan Israel Cemetery in New Haven, opposite his mother-in-law. I remember being told by George that Dad's mother, Esther (or Ester) Sobinefsky, was buried in either the same cemetery or one adjacent to it.

John Mild had three siblings, a brother, Sam, and two sisters, Fanny and Rose. Uncle Sam married Aunt Rose Nebb (originally Nebulinsky or possibly Neeb), who lived well into her nineties, and they had three children: Anita Mild married George Golson (originally Goldstein); George Curtis Mild (a Citadel graduate who became a lieutenant colonel in the USAF); and Bernice Mild Rothberg. At this time Sam, Rose, and all three of their children have passed on.

Anita Golson had three children: Ashley (married, living somewhere in Ohio); Brian (married to Michael Gross and living in Atlanta, GA); and Joseph. George Curtis Mild married Frances Henshaw and raised two children: Jane (adopted) and Cathy Curtis Mild. Bernice Mild married Mike Rothberg and they had six children: Go, Barry, Bobbie, Richard, Jean, and Sandy.

Go (Mildred Golda Rothberg) married Manny Nodar. Go had three children (by a former marriage with Stanley Morstein): Susan Celeste, who is married to Steven Saul; Ruth Ellen Nickens, who is divorced; and Debra Rae, who is married to Tony Sloss.

Barry (Barron Lewis Rothberg) married Harriet Schway. They have two children: Sandy (Sandra), who is married to Philip

Minnes, and Robert.

Bobbie (Roberta Jaye Rothberg) Christmas is divorced with one son, Sanford. Richard Irving Rothberg is also divorced with one son, Aaron. Sandy (Sandra Evelyn Rothberg) unfortunately died in a sky-diving accident.

The majority of these foregoing relatives live in the southern states, including Georgia, the Carolinas, Florida, Texas, and California.

Rose and Sam Mild

Mildred (Go) Rothberg Nodar

Ruth Nickens **Debra Sloss** **Susan Saul**

Barry and Harriet Rothberg, Larry and Rosemary Mild, Go Nodar, Sandy Minnes, Cathy Curtis Mild, Susan and Steve Saul.
Back row: Jackie Mild Lau, Bobbie Christmas, Brian Golson, and Michael Gross.

* * * *

John Mild's sister Fanny married George Grovit. They had two children: Mildred, who died in her late teens; and George Jr., who had a son slightly younger than myself. John Mild's sister Rose Mild married a furrier by the name of Al Joseph and they had four children: Lester, Harriet, Estelle, and Frederick. The only one I've ever met is Lester, who became a doctor at the Mayo Clinic.

* * * *

Mother, My Disciplinarian:

My mother, Hilda Eleanor (or Elinore, according to one document) Glueck Mild was born in New York, NY the 14th of May, 1904. She married my father at age 21. Early photographs depict her as a stout woman with a pretty face and glasses. The fact that she was an excellent cook and baker may have influenced the weighty figures supported by our entire family. In her later years, she trimmed down nicely in response to her threatening diabetes. It was that same cooking and baking expertise that drew so many of our family members to our house on most weekends. In my pre-teens and early teens I believe she was a slave to her own kitchen. There was always something good to smell and eat and feel guilty about later.

My grades were never good enough for her. I was always leaving a mess about the house, and I left so many chores undone. Guilty as charged, but when I heard, "Why can't you be more like your brother, George?" that hurt. I never did shake the good son, bad son label even as an adult. In fact, whenever I made a major decision, she would caution me to consult with George, the elder, first. Looking back, I never did anything so terrible as to warrant such a label. Don't get me wrong—despite these confrontations, there was still a whole lot of love between us. I did more than most teens to help out around the house. In addition, I went to work when I was too young to legally hold a job. When Dad died, we

Rear: Uncle Ted and Aunt Viola Glueck, Grandma Rose Glueck, Mother
Front row: George, Larry, and Dad

The Spring Street Milds

Meyer Rubenstein, Richard Rubenstein, Myrna Mild, Larry Mild,
Catherine Rubenstein, Lenny Rubenstein, Hilda Mild, and Jackie Mild

John and Hilda Mild

Hilda Glueck Mild

became even closer.

Hilda Glueck graduated from the Commercial High School wing of New Haven High School and went to work as a secretary for the Reo automobile dealership in New Haven in 1920. That ended when she married my father, and she didn't reenter the work force for the next twenty-eight years. As a younger woman, she was active in the United Order of True Sisters (UOTS), a Jewish ladies service organization in New Haven. She held offices in that organization, including the presidency.

Hilda Mild had two brothers and two sisters. The eldest, Josephine (Aunt Jo) Glueck Mischeloff, married Nathan Mischeloff and had two sons: Harvey Mischeloff, who was mentally disturbed and a very talented artist and a pugilist; and Jervis Mischeloff (an aerospace electrician), who married the same wife, Lillian, twice and had at least three children. The next oldest was Theodore (Uncle Teddy) Glueck (a private investigator for the Chrysler Corporation and a reserve FBI agent), who married Aunt Viola and had no children. My mother came next. Then came Aunt Catherine Glueck Rubenstein, who married Meyer Rubenstein (metal worker and furniture salesman) and they had two children: Richard Rubenstein (deceased), who married Mandy, and Leonard Rubenstein, who married Jo Ellen. They had a son, Scott Rubenstein, and possibly a younger daughter. Lastly, there was my mother's youngest brother, Leo Glueck, who was lost in WWII. He had also managed a Sears store in Lynn, MA. My mother's baby brother left no spouse.

Mother with Catherine Rubenstein

An interesting story about Uncle Teddy was that he was born in Germany while his parents were touring Europe. No one ever challenged the validity of his U.S. citizenship until WWII broke out and he became a reserve agent in the FBI. Many months of bureaucratic paperwork eventually settled that question for good.

My mother moved to Miami Beach a year after I entered the Navy. She got a job in one of the major Miami Beach banks as a check verifier. Unfortunately, she neglected her diabetes while gallivanting around with her lady friends in the evenings.

Diabetic retinopathy made blood vessels in her eyes burst, causing her to become legally blind with only a small amount of peripheral vision remaining in one eye. She could only see a few close-in shadows. Mother moved near to brother George in Washington, PA for awhile, but had to relocate closer to us when George moved because of a new job. She preferred to live alone, but required two phone calls daily. Any missed call was a capital crime. Hannah, my first wife, made one, and I made the other.

A visiting nurse filled her insulin needles and checked her blood once per week, and I came to clean and tidy a bit on weekends. In between, all the insulin shots were administered by herself, but she always welcomed the one shot by the nurse in a place she couldn't reach. She also cooked, cleaned, and dusted for herself. I put all the pictures and paintings back on the horizontal again, and the standing joke was that the water was running out of one of the tilted oils painted by my grandfather. We did her shopping and things ran reasonably well for a few years. Ladies from the shul across the street paid visits on Shabbat afternoons, and one even took her for haircuts occasionally.

Mother couldn't watch, but loved listening to baseball on TV and knew all of the players and their batting averages. In Washington, PA she was an ardent Pirates fan, but she became a big Orioles fan when she moved to the Annapolis/Baltimore area. Football proved to be too difficult a sport for her to visualize from an announcer's description. It was hard for her when the baseball season ended.

One night she fell getting out of bed and was never the same after that. The injury was slight, yet she feared falling again in the worst way. Since there was no one at home in our house during the day, we arranged for her to move to a nearby nursing home. After a rocky start Mother finally settled in. She even made a few friends. I tried to visit her there once or twice a week at lunchtime. This continued until another fall occurred while standing at the sink with her walker. This time she hit her head substantially and, when the initial trauma subsided, she no longer recognized us.

Things went downhill rapidly after that, and she passed away February 9, 1981 at the age of 76. We buried her at the Mishkan Israel Cemetery in New Haven in plot #214b on the west (Mild) side of the headstone next to my father. Her parents (Charles {1873-1955} Morris Glueck and Rose {1875-1936} Freedman Glueck) were buried earlier on the east (Glueck) side of the headstone. Just inside the main cemetery gate, the path splits. The Mild/Glueck headstone lies on the right side of the left-hand path, several headstones in.

* * * *

Brother George, Friends at Last:

We rarely horsed around the way most brothers of a similar age do. The one time that I do remember horsing around with him did not end well. The Spring Street house had a preserve cellar with shelves containing all the fruits, jellies, and vegetables my mother had preserved from the garden and trellises out back.

In reality, it was just another basement room with a wooden door. Unfortunately, that door was rife with protruding nails

Larry Mild

The Mild Brothers

Brother George (home on leave from U.S. Navy during WWII)

Larry and George (circa 1947)

George and Larry (circa 1970s). Where da hair go?

supporting outside-the-door shelving. In a mean-spirited moment, I tried to lock my brother in that room by shoving the door shut on him while he was inside. He resisted and one of those nails gashed, then ripped open his left forearm. As soon as he screamed, I released the door. Dad was at work and Mom was out of town for one of her UOTS conventions. The upstairs neighbor looked at George's arm and determined he needed stitches, so she wrapped the arm and took him to the hospital. George forgave me, but he was left with a lifelong battle scar for my foolishness. I caught hell from my parents when they got home.

It took far too many years for George and me to become true friends. In the beginning it was the sheer number of years that separated us, and then his tour in the Navy during the war years, followed by college and, finally, marriage. Early on, we shared a very crowded bedroom in the Spring Street house. George had a double bed, and two feet away, I slept in a twin bed. A copy of Gainsborough's *Blue Boy* hung in an oval frame over his bed and a plain armoire for our clothes sat at the foot of my bed opposite the only door. There wasn't a closet in the room. The pull string attached to the light in the symmetrical center of the room had a loop in it that hung over his bed. He sometimes would turn off this light with his big toe hanging in the loop.

George served in the Navy aboard the *USS Bristol*, a destroyer, during the war years. He was a Fire Controlman Third Class and served in the Pacific theater. He was witness to the frequent kamikaze attacks by Japanese suicide aircraft. The *Bristol* was assigned to escort the mighty *USS Missouri* into Tokyo Bay for the signing of the peace treaty to end WWII. Instead, the *Bristol* incurred damage while taking on mail from a tanker at sea and had to put in for repairs.

George Leon Mild married Millicent (Mitzie) Ruben in the early Fifties, and they went off on their honeymoon in their brand-new Pontiac Chieftain, a wedding gift from her parents. Upon their return to our house a short time after the honeymoon, and while George carried suitcases upstairs to our home, Mitzie confided in me: "Don't tell George, but I backed into a garbage can and put a small dent in the left rear fender. See there." She pointed at the offending dimple. I smiled sympathetically while she picked up some smaller items and headed for the stairs. George returned for another load, but not before confiding in me as well. "Don't tell Mitzie, but I scraped the front right fender on a pole in a parking garage." He indicated the tiny silvery wounds, and I pledged my secrecy. I remained mum to this day and at this writing almost seventy years later; however, I've always wondered whether either one ever told the other in all that time.

George Leon Mild and Mitzie (Millicent) Ruben Mild

George and Mitzie had a boy, John (Johnny, though mostly called Paco), and a girl, Catherine (Cathy), a few years later. After a number of career starts, Johnny eventually took over George's executive head-hunting business when he retired. John married Marsha and they had three girls: Ashley, Sydney, and Samantha, who, at this writing, are still single. Cathy has had a successful sales and management career in the food service business. Cathy married Tom Sexton and they had one girl, Stephanie, who, after graduating in bio-medical engineering (with honors), is currently pursuing a law degree.

I was still recuperating from my first heart attack when I learned that George was battling pancreatic cancer. The first prognosis gave him up to six months to live. He'd been complaining for some time that something was not right with him, but the doctors couldn't seem to find anything wrong with him. The next prognosis came as a shock to us: only three weeks to live.

Cathy Mild Sexton, Tom Sexton, and Stephanie Sexton

Ashley Mild, Johnny (Paco) Mild, Sammy Mild, Marsha Mild, and Sydney Mild

On the first day after my heart attack that I was allowed to drive, my second wife, Rosemary, and I drove to Fairlawn, OH to visit for the last time. I was glad that I did visit, because that next day he lost consciousness for good and had to be transferred from home hospice care to the hospice care facility where Mitzie volunteered her clerical services.

My daughter Jackie had flown in from Hawaii to be with Uncle George for his last two days. We visited at home and maintained a bedside vigil at the hospice facility. I couldn't stay for the funeral, but Mitzie sent us a copy of the rabbi's eulogy. He died on September 5, 2006 and was laid to rest in a veteran's cemetery about thirty miles south of his Fairlawn Village home.

* * * *

Grandpa, an Inspiration:

Grandpa, Charles Morris Glueck (1873-1955), stood 5'11", tall for his generation, tall from the perspective of a doting pre-teen, and taller yet from my adult recollection of this man who made such an intellectual impression on my life. I remember him in a white shirt, suit, and vest—a balding man with gray-white fringes, perfectly erect in posture, and a prominent yellowish mustache. The yellow tinting I assumed came from his pipe smoking—his only known vice. I remember trying to touch his mustache as a youngster, and he'd respond with a dog-like growling sound that would surprise me and put me off. Then we'd laugh about it. Even though we lived apart, he became my father figure at age 13 after my dad passed away. He visited frequently. At 72 Grandpa died in the early Fifties while I was on my way to Korea. I missed saying goodbye to him—telling him thank you. I had just broached another stage of parental appreciation. I knew only then what he had done for me.

My earliest recollection of Grandpa Glueck was on a summertime trip to Royal Oak, MI. At the time I was probably nine or ten. He chose the location in order to be close to his eldest son, my Uncle Teddy and wife, Viola. Grandpa lived in the country at a modest ranch house with an open porch that ran the width of the entire front. It sat hundreds of yards off the nearest street, and the rear grounds backed up to a schoolyard fence.

I mention this fence because I was able to reach the schoolyard by squeezing through a breach in it to join in some softball games with kids my own age and older. As was the custom, the Skins were pitted against the Shirts. Being chosen to play with the Skins, I hung my striped polo shirt up on the fence and proceeded to play for hours. That is, until my father called to me from Grandpa's backyard and returned to the house.

When I went to collect my shirt, it was gone. Someone had either taken it by mistake or had taken it to be malicious. I entered the front door with a faceful of tears and announced to the whole family, "I lost my shirt." Instead of being chewed out for the loss, I encountered a houseful of laughter. It was a joke that I just didn't quite appreciate at that age.

Uncle Teddy and Aunt Viola enjoyed camping out, so they had a family-sized surplus army tent that they loaned my brother and me. We decided to erect it in Grandpa's front yard. I helped with holding the poles while George pounded in the tent stakes with the hammer-head side of a hatchet.

Proud of our accomplishment, we stepped onto the long porch, I on the inside and George on the outside. Inadvertently, he swung the hatchet against one of a dozen or more wooden posts supporting the sloping porch roof. In doing so, he unleashed a nest full of angry hornets bent on revenge for disturbing their peace. George paid the price in multiple stings as he ran frantically back and forth trying to evade further stings. I ran alongside, oblivious of his woes, because I was so much shorter and thus hornet free, I guess. Mother fixed him up with some remedy, but the next few days were indeed painful for him. The next day he wondered why the hornets chose him and not me. I told him those were smart hornets—they knew who riled them up.

Grandpa's house was so countrified that his telephone number began with a Big Beaver (BB) exchange. It also had a peculiar toilet that sang unusual melodies. As the ceiling chest filled with water for the ensuing flush, poorly regulated water and air pressure forced to the ceiling in narrow pipes yielded a loud tone-modulating shrill. He didn't seem to mind these things, saying the house had character.

Besides Michigan, Grandpa also lived at one time or another in New York City; Mobile, AL; and Sarasota, FL—sometimes to be close to one of his children and other times to create some distance. He never seemed to argue about anything—he'd go silent instead.

His greatest loss was his youngest son, Leo. From the same photo that I included earlier, Grandpa painted a much larger image on canvas. To start with, the painting displayed an excellent likeness of my Uncle Leo in uniform, but as Grandpa grew older, his failing sight and an attempt to improve upon the painting distorted that likeness until it no longer reflected his son. It was like *The Picture of Dorian Gray* in reverse. Only in this case, it was love rather than evil that drove the distortion.

Though he grew up in Hungary and spoke most of the languages of Europe, I never knew him to speak with any kind of accent or abuse of the English language. I attribute this to the literature and newspapers he read as well as his willingness to join any discussion. He painted houses and rooms for a living and oils on canvas for an avocation. While I must confess that I take to other languages only under extreme duress, he instilled in me a love of literature and the arts and a will to study.

Invading my favorite reading haunt, our verandah rocker, he'd invariably discover me reading the forbidden comic book. Like so many of my young peers, I'd been seduced into reading mere pictures. Catching me red-handed, he'd trash the comic book and lead me off to the nearest library. His approach to selection wasn't entirely classical. He didn't say: "Go pick one off the shelf." Instead, he whet my appetite with his description of a favorite character or a tantalizing plot. I'd reel myself in without realizing I'd been caught. Dickens, Dumas, and Stevenson became friends for a lifetime.

I spent many a week and weekend with him in New York City just 78 miles from my Connecticut home. Each trip included one or more art museums. Grandpa used walking as both an exercise and a mode of transportation. At one particular age he had a stride half again longer than my own and distance limits which continually challenged me.

He would talk to me all the while we walked and visited in the galleries and libraries of New York. Stories of painters and authors ran through my head, though we never discussed brush techniques or writing schemes. Some 70 years later I'm still running to museums and art shows, and in my favorite recliner I can still enjoy my favorite authors. On rare occasions

Grandpa obtained special passes, which permitted him to set up an easel in a gallery, even one being renovated. He loved to copy miniatures of famous paintings on a larger scale with increased detail to which he would attach the original painter's name in one corner and his own in another, less noticeable, corner. *The Wheelwright's Backyard* hangs in the Metropolitan Museum of Art, and a larger copy sits on my living room wall, alongside *Boy with a Jug*, which is a self-portrait added to a copied magazine picture, done in the style and quality of Frans Hals.

Aunt Catherine wound up with a number of Grandpa's early sketchbooks where he'd practiced doing facial parts—eyes, ears, noses, and the like. Whenever I laid claim to boredom during my summer visits with the Rubensteins, Aunt Catherine would cut open a brown paper grocery bag and flatten it for me to draw on. One of Grandpa's sketchbooks and a pencil always accompanied the bag. I spent hours copying his facial exercises. I tried several times in my life to capitalize on that training but, alas, my true talents lay elsewhere.

I tried to pass his cultural legacy on to my own children—Sunday afternoon trips to the many national museums: the Hirshhorn, the Corcoran, the Phillips, the Renwick, and so many others that were free to the public in Washington, DC. Although the girls proved to be good students, they never found the same enjoyment of literature that I have.

Instead, Grandpa's legacy produced two fine artists: a sculptor with a Master of Fine Arts degree and commissioned work in two museums; and a ceramic sculptor and printmaker with a Master's in Art Education and a fine collection of surrealistic work. They are both prize winners in their respective fields and excellent teachers as well.

* * * *

Grandma Rose, Only a Glimpse:

Grandma Rose Freedman Glueck passed away when I was only four years old, leaving me without memories of what she was like. While I'd like to think she had a happy marriage with Grandpa, I don't remember him ever speaking about her. All I can find is that she was born somewhere in Hungry in 1875 and died in1936 at the all too young age of sixty-one. She is buried in Mishkan Israel Cemetery in New Haven next to Grandpa. My parents are buried on the opposite side of this same gravestone.

Mild gravestone

Glueck gravestone

* * * *

Grandma Ester, We never met:

Grandma Ester Sobinefsky (possibly Sivronofsky) passed away in May of 1928, four years before I was born, so I know even less about her. There are some document notations that she arrived in the U.S. at the New York port of entry with my father and his sister in 1906. According to my brother, she is buried somewhere in the group of cemeteries next to Mishkan Israel cemetry. I have never seen her grave.

Chapter 4

Weathering High School

Completing the ninth grade, I matriculated from junior high to high school in 1947. Throughout the three junior high grades, my small motor skills continued to haunt me—I was still a klutz everywhere except in metalworking, woodworking, and print shop. With some talent for visual perception and spacial conception, I liked mechanical drawing most, but my smudgy lines sometimes betrayed me. Geography, history, English, and art all interested me and I'm sure I acquired a good deal of knowledge in those subjects, but as I turned in handwritten papers in them, I continued to be penalized for my penmanship. My grades suffered because I was never much of a neatnick.

Then my saving grace found me, or rather I found it in a rubbish pile between two downtown buildings as I left work. It was a manual typewriter, not just any of the sort, but an accounting machine with a clumsy, two-foot carriage. What a pair, we two! Having never had a typing course, I began with the two-finger hunt-and-peck method and added a finger or two as I got faster and more proficient with the orphaned device. In a way, the typewriter added a characteristic style to my school papers that was clearly unique within my class. The machine was probably abandoned because of its hardened roller platen. I found that when you struck certain keys, and especially the "O" key (capital or not), they cut clear through the paper, leaving it distinctively full of holes—so much so that everyone knew when my work was about to be read by the teacher. No longer having to decrypt my terrible scribblings, teachers began to find favor with my work and even used it as examples. Needless to say, most of those grades went from C's to B's and A's. I still type with a thumb and two fingers on each hand (six digits altogether) and I've written ten novels, two textbooks, countless documents, and many school and work papers this way.

New Haven High School comprised three educational elements, housed in three separate brick buildings situated amid the Yale University campus. The first was Hillhouse High, the scholastic high school for those intending to go to college. It also supported the core subjects for the other two. The second was Commercial High for those choosing the secretarial and business vocations. The third element was Bordman Trade School, where those who worked with their hands learned their terrific skills. I had college ambitions, so I chose Hillhouse. Centrally located, New Haven High was the only high school in the city of a quarter-million; at least six junior highs and a number of middle schools fed into it. To avoid overcrowding, the school operated on a split-session scheme: juniors and seniors, 7:00 a.m. to noon; and afternoon: freshmen and sophomores, 12:30 to 5:30 p.m. The older students needed the afternoons off for committing to employment schedules.

When the weather was nice, I rode my bike the seven miles to the downtown high school. We took the trolley during inclement weather, using books of tear-out student-transportation coupons. Sometimes we had to stand because all the kids coming from Westville took all the seats. One piece of mischief many of the kids did while they waited was to put copper pennies on the tracks so that when the trolleys rolled over them, they would flatten out and grow in diameter. The steel pennies left over from World War II didn't work as well.

My bike was a conglomeration put together by myself from mostly cast-off parts that I found in the trash of a nearby new bike store. I somehow managed to recondition them into a usable state. The bent frame was once from a Raleigh English bike, so I had to match two thinner wheels, a hard seat, and a three-speed transmission to it. I did purchase a tire and two accessories for it—a head- and tail-light package, and a seat cover to cover the crack in the seat. The last thing I reconditioned for it was a speedometer. I acquired a full bicycle over a six-month period, ending in July between my ninth and tenth grade years. I spray-painted it a shiny black. It rode perfectly until you reached twenty-two miles per hour and then there was a slight wobble due to what was left of the bend in the frame.

I never really excelled in sports, but my close friend, Eddie Bailey, had an uncle who was a proficient tennis player, both patient and willing to teach him. This uncle competed in the city league. He didn't seem to mind if I tagged along to the courts with them. After all, Eddie would need someone to practice with. I played with an older, abandoned Sears racket that my Uncle Leo had once brought for my brother, George. Observing and then practicing with Eddie paid off in two ways. I became a pretty fair hand at tennis, and it became a lifetime sport that I enjoyed for the next sixty years.

Not being the fastest player or one with a long reach, I eventually stuck with playing doubles thereafter. Schools did not have free tennis courts then like many do today. Public courts in parks charged twenty-five cents per half-hour—not an exorbitant fee, but tough money for me to come up with. What I earned at the theaters went to helping at home, covering my few personal expenses, and into savings for college. We did discover beautifully manicured tennis courts just outside the famous Yale Bowl, a mile and a half from our house. We soon learned that they lay idle most of the time. We climbed over the eight-foot, chain-link fence with all our gear and played undetected for hours at a time. When we did see the caretaker's pickup truck heading up the winding access road, our gear went over the fence first and then ourselves. I still remember the caretaker shaking his fists at us as we disappeared into the thick of nearby Edgewood Park. Yeah, guilty as charged—we had trespassed on university property, but we did no damage and left no residue behind.

Within Edgewood Park there was a unique spot the neighborhood kids called Sandy Hollow. A little over three blocks from home, the hollow was our own neighborhood's special place never recognized nor challenged by anyone else. It was a tree-free landscape, flat at the bottom with rising edges on three sides of the perimeter, ideal for playing softball and touch football with fewer kids than normal team size. We usually played either sport with no more than four kids on a side. The rising edges of the hollow fielded all wayward balls. After being clipped in the ear by a hard ball, I avoided that game for good.

I did have a dream of playing guard in high school football in my sophomore year, but a barn-dance aftermath changed all that. I had been going on a number of dates by then, mostly one-timers, since I was still the chubby, shy kid, unable to come up with suitable conversation. I didn't have personal access to a car, so I had to rely on double-dating with either Eddie Bailey or Moose Alderman. Anyway, one summer night we went to a barn dance and Moose parked his car in a field surrounding the barn with scores of other cars. This wasn't a problem until it was time to go home. Someone had parked extremely close to the driver's door, rendering it inaccessible.

As I was already on the passenger side, I foolishly volunteered to reach across the front bench seat to release the emergency brake while Moose got in back of the car ready to push. Carelessly, I left my right leg stuck out of the front passenger door as I released the brake. Neither of us had accounted for the topical incline, and the car quickly rolled forward against an adjacent car, forcing our door hard against the calf of my protruding leg. I was trapped for some time until Moose mustered sufficient help to push his car backward while I, in all my pain, steered. This released my trapped leg and I immediately pulled it inside. At one point Moose had sufficient door space to enter the driver's side and start the engine. The pain continued through the night, and I couldn't walk normally thereafter. The front of my foot wouldn't lift when I raised my leg to take a step.

My mother took me to an orthopedist the next day who

failed to recognize that I had a classic drop-foot caused by the crushing and severing of the peroneal nerve just below the knee. After three expensive visits and treating it mainly for swelling, i.e., cold pack application and posturing my leg in the raised position, the doctor pronounced it a permanent condition and had me fitted for a brace. The device was essentially a very stiff spring riveted to a leather strap that fastened about my calf. The bottom of the spring was attached to a three-eighths-inch diameter metal dowel that slid into and snapped into place within a metal sheath planted in my right shoe's heel. The front of my foot popped up whenever I lifted my foot and flattened again when I put pressure on it. Oh, I had a practiced slight limp, which was hardly noticeable in long pants unless you looked twice.

I wore the brace for a little over a year with little incident. Sports were out of the question, but I did dance some. Eddie Bailey's cousin from Long Island needed a date for the Westville Country Club's winter dance, and I was chosen to be her escort for the night, doubling and riding in the back seat of the Bailey car. The cousin was very pleasant and we enjoyed dancing together. She hadn't noticed my limp or anything out of the ordinary so far. And then, as we passed the double doorway to the kitchen, I felt a *thud*—the spring had popped its rivet from the strap. I excused myself abruptly and, without explanation, darted through the doors to the kitchen, where I found a chef to come to my rescue. I borrowed his cleaver and used the flat backside to hammer in place the errant rivet atop his chopping block. With thanks, I returned to the dance floor and my bewildered date, who was still standing by the doors waiting. I wound up giving her less than the whole truth and somehow that satisfied her, although I noticed that she was somewhat quieter and less responsive after that.

After living with the brace and accepting it as a necessity for the rest of my life, I happened to accompany and wait for my mother at the office of her gynecologist. She introduced me to Dr. Cutler when they were finished. As soon as we started walking away, he stopped us and asked us to step into his inner sanctum.

We told him the story of the injury and treatment, and he shook his head. Dr. Cutler believed that the problem shouldn't be permanent, so he had his secretary phone and make an appointment with Dr. Poverman, a prominent neurosurgeon in town. I had the surgery to repair (effectively sew together) the damaged nerve endings and then went through nerve reeducation treatments three times a week. These unusual treatments consisted of a conducting foil-like band wrapped around my lower hamstring area and a padded probe, which explored crucial nerve nodes below the knees and all the way to the toes.

Both the band and the probe were wired to a machine much bulkier, but not unlike today's TENS muscle-pain machines with an array of dials and meters. It sent a charge to key motor nerves, exciting them to produce ankle, foot, and individual toe motion. My excitement in seeing parts of me move on their own overshadowed the sharp pain caused by each jolt. Six months later, I had a near-full recovery. From then on, I had a fully functional foot except that it took a little extra concentration to raise my right big toe. No football team, but I could swim and play tennis again. In the spring of my junior year, I lettered in varsity tennis. Who could ask for more?

I encountered two English teachers with Ph.D.s who had the distinction of teaching not only my brother, but my mother as well. Both abruptly announced that they remembered their names and proclaimed that they had higher expectations of me. Outside of them being a grumpy, unsmiling pair, I did learn quite a lot from them—memorizing poetic passages (especially Shakespeare) and handling stand-up vocal recitations that were not my forté. I had to re-read Shakespeare some years later in order to appreciate the Bard and his archaic English. I had the feeling that neglecting the plots and exploring his choice of every last word and its implied meanings was a little much for the high school student.

During high school I went on my first blind date. I had many other firsts with Ailene Snowe. A friend of my brother, Marty Wallenski, told me there was nice Jewish girl living a few doors down from him. He asked: "Would you like to meet her?" She turned out to be an easy looker with a round face and a slightly zaftig figure. Our first date was a movie that we walked to on Whaley Avenue, and no, I don't remember what was playing, but we did hit it off great. And she didn't mind walking to our future dates. Unless I found someone to double with, I had a lot of walking dates, even to her house for that date and a few subsequent ones afterward. We went for walks just to be together. The dates usually ended with a goodnight peck and later a hug was added. This was actually a female I found easy to talk with—the conversation seemed to flow easily for the first time in my life.

Ailene told me she liked biking too, so we planned a summer biking picnic out to Mt. Carmel Sleeping Giant State Park. We started out at eight that morning and arrived there by noon. By early afternoon we were relaxing on a blanket in a shady secluded spot. I wanted to kiss her, but feared I'd spoil our relationship. I took the chance anyway, and she responded so positively and so passionately that I was surprised—pulling my face down atop hers. From that date on we necked and petted every chance we could—joining her for babysitting jobs, movies, and back seats. We went steady for a little over a year before mutually agreeing to go our separate ways, but I remained grateful for all our firsts.

Some seventy years later than the event, I wrote about the following episode. I called it "Iced." It is a first-person description of what I was like then.

"There it's finished," I said aloud without realizing it. I took a few steps backward to admire my work. The white enamel paint had dried, and I'd just put on the finishing touch—a product decal—on perfectly straight. It happened to be a lidded plywood box fourteen inches square and almost chest high. A shoulder strap affixed to the middle and near the top of one side declared its portability, as if a thirty-pound insulated box could be so. The Styrofoam cooler wouldn't be invented for some years to come, so this is how I had to make do. The added decal presented an ice cream bar with a thin, delicious-looking, chocolate coating with one bite missing so you could see the inside.

A week or so into the transitional summer between junior high and high school, our ambition couldn't be stifled, nor could the ingenuity that accompanied it. My friend Moose and I had come up with a scheme to sell ice cream to customers relaxing on one particular sandy beach along the northern shore of Long Island Sound. It had the Native American-sounding name of Mamauguin. Counting on the idea that most people are inherently lazy, we decided to bring the treats to them. This meant hauling the heavy insulated box from blanket to blanket and chair to chair.

I built the portable box, and Moose cajoled his father into signing for the loaner freezer case that would reside in the garage of their summer home only two blocks from our targeted beach. We pooled our funds for a deposit, and the freezer case, fully loaded with consigned merchandise, was delivered by the local Sealtest distributor. The first day I rode the trolley from home with the box between my legs fifteen miles to the same beach. Sales were slow the initial day of business—we had to build trust in our clientele. By day three the box sold out and had to be replenished four times. It was hard work, but the money started to roll in.

Moose and I took two-hour turns walking the box across the mile or so beach, and business went smoothly for about one and a half weeks. While on one of my tours of the beach, I had stopped to make a sale. Then, in the midst of making change, I felt a hand on my shoulder. "You'll have to wait your turn," I said.

"I don't think so," returned the very deep voice of authority.

I dropped the change into the lady's hand and turned to face a blue-uniformed officer who demanded to see my retailer's license. I didn't have a store—why would I need a license? The officer corrected my misconception and directed me to follow him to his black and white cruiser. I later learned that ice cream sales had fallen off at the local grocery and sundry store several blocks away. They had sent a spy down to the beach who found out why and called the police. My box and I were taken to the police station for interrogation.

"What's your name?" the officer asked.

I told him.

"What's your father's name?"

"John," I replied nervously, "but he died last Thanksgiving."

"What's your mother's name then?"

"Hilda," I answered, shaking more with each question.

Where did I live and what was my last name and telephone number came next. I responded, and was told to sit on a wooden bench outside a row of offices with frosted glass doors. Soon a white-haired man with sergeant's stripes came out of one of those very doors and began to lecture me. The words sounded angry, but there seemed to be a glint of a smile behind his gruff tone. In my state I only caught the gist of what he told me. Afterward, I sat there on the hard bench for two or three more hours with nothing to do but squirm and worry. Was this my punishment? Would they let me go sometime soon? Would there be a fine or jail time?

On the other hand, the box sat there with nothing to do but drip and run melted ice cream from its imperfect seams. Air conditioning was not in general use yet, and the contents of my box could do no less than melt. No one seemed to notice until one of the officers hurrying down the hall slipped in the milky puddle. I received one awful glare from him as his knee and pants bottom were smeared with the sloppy mess. This really wasn't my fault—or was it? Would this tack onto my punishment, and would they put me into one of those holding cells overnight? Apparently not right away, for I was destined to sit for yet another hour.

At eight o'clock that evening the door to the station opened, and my distraught mother hurried in. She scanned the room and quickly located me on my bench. Immediately, she rushed over to where I sat and began scolding me. I'd never seen her so angry, but somehow I knew her wrath would be short lived. It usually was. Hearing the commotion in the hall, the sergeant leaned out of his door and asked my mother into his office. At the time I think I feared her disappointment in her son more than what the police had in mind for me.

I never knew all of what went on in that office, but I believe the sergeant must have waived the first offense fine of fifty dollars—an enormous amount in those days. As a result, my mother left a much calmer person. She was, of course, still angry over having to travel thirty miles round-trip on a warm trolley to bail me out of jail, as she put it. Grabbing the sleeve of my T-shirt, she led me out of the station and down to where the trolley stopped. She scolded me all the way to the stop, and then I absorbed the silent treatment all the way home.

For punishment I performed a slew of additional household chores such as shining Mother's considerable collection of brass knickknacks with bright-work polish. I took my punishment in stride. The freezer, a third full of ice cream, was returned to the distributor. Needless to say, the partnership dissolved, although Moose and I remained friends until college and military service sent us our different ways. For a number of years afterward I went on believing that I had caused my mother a great deal of trouble and embarrassment with the incident. But one day, when she thought I was out of earshot, I overheard her describing my entrepreneurial misadventure to a friend with no small amount of pride and humor attached.

Chapter 5

College Attempt: A Poor Start

I managed to graduate from high school in the class of 1950, and the ceremony was held at the New Haven Arena. As chance would have it, my brother George's college graduation happened on the very same day. Promising to be at my future college ceremony, my mother departed for Chicago and his ceremony. My grandfather volunteered to be there for me instead. Through some miscommunication, I couldn't find him in the audience afterward and went home to wait for him. Missing me there and having the wrong phone number, he decided to return to New York where he was living at the time. Boy, was he miffed. Boy, did I feel guilty, and boy, was my mother angry! It turned out to be a three-way fiasco.

I graduated with more than a diploma. I had acquired a bad habit, smoking. When you didn't know what to do with your hands or you couldn't think of something witty or profound to say, you lit up a cigarette and took another puff. That pack and a half a day habit lasted for the next twenty years despite quite a few attempts to quit in between. Roughly 200 students would spend their lunchtime and between-class times in an outdoor alcove behind the school. For some it was social, and for the remainder it was to grab a so-called much-needed smoke.

I was accepted at the University of Connecticut (UConn) and lived on campus with a roommate, Dick Wolfman, in a Quonset hut that was constantly surrounded by six inches of mud unless it was frozen solid. This male-only housing with its steel semicircular roof held eight student rooms with bunk beds and a two-sided desk with chairs. It was located in the boonies at the edge of the campus, easily a mile and a half from the nearest classroom or library. Dick became a good friend and we hung out together frequently. He was from the town of Milford, CT, just north of New Haven. We drifted apart after he started going steady with a girl he eventually married. I, of course, didn't have the cash to do much dating.

I had tapped into my savings to put together the $125.00 college tuition and a like amount to cover my housing at UConn, but I needed ready cash to cover meals and personal items. Yes, I still had my job managing the Lincoln Theater in New Haven on weekends, and that meant selling tickets, picking up film canisters/posters, and delivering them back to the distributor afterward, making night deposits, and getting film ads to the newspapers. This entailed a round-trip car ride from the college campus at Storrs, CT and New Haven, a trip requiring me to chip in for gas occasionally, so I needed more income. I answered a few babysitting ads, but that wasn't for me and it produced nowhere enough cash. I responded to an ad from the State Department of Audio and Visual Aids (AVA) to run 16-mm projectors during classes that didn't conflict with my own. This meant a lot of hustling across an extremely wide and sometime very muddy campus to get to these classes and my own classes.

Being at the AVA office in the middle of campus during November I saw someone inspecting films that had been loaned out to schools all over the state and decided that I could do that as well. There were several stations; there was always an empty inspection station, and I took advantage. The job entailed actually feeling for the sprocket hole imperfections in films and repairing them by cutting out the damaged frames and re-splicing the remainder. So, with a textbook in one hand and moving film in the other, I motored and braked the film from one reel to another with a foot pedal under the workbench as I sat by on a high stool. After extracting a damaged frame I made a film splice by removing an eighth-inch of film emulsion on both cut edges and applied cement to one edge. Next I put the two ends into a form with nodes that fit the sprocket holes, aligning both sides. The two edges were brought together with hinged top and bottom to make a bond.

I stopped the classroom projector work. As time went on, the projector repairs would sometimes get behind, and the kid who was always good at fixing things stepped in again. I was fully employed and, including my Air Force ROTC credits, a student carrying twenty-one credits. Way too much, and my grades suffered for it, but I got through the year without failing anything.

At the core of my class difficulties lay my two math nemeses, Analytical Geometry and Calculus. In freshman Analytical Geometry I managed to squeak by, but I couldn't quite get the sophomore Calculus. The professor was brilliant yet weird, and certainly not a teacher to very many. He simultaneously faced and wrote on the blackboard, starting at the window's edge and continuing around the room, across the door to the next board and on and on to bare wall by the end of the period. Dr. Bourne was always in the way of what he wrote, so that you saw the writing more than a minute after hearing his words. Because he continued to talk, it was hard to put what he said to what he wrote together, let alone get it on paper to analyze later. He used expressions like "Tweedle-e-dee to the Tweedle-e-dum power, as any fool can plainly see," and "George Washington's birth year" instead of the square root of three.

There were at least a dozen other expressions, but after so many years, I can't remember all of them. His homework assignments included tons of problems and the premise to incomplete proofs for us to finish. If it had only been *his* class grades, it wouldn't have been so bad. But four other parallel classes depended on what he might have taught me. Physics, Chemistry, Strength of Materials, and Statics all used the level of calculus he was supposed to be teaching. Thirteen years later I took two Calculus courses at Anne Arundel Community College in Maryland and suddenly the light turned on and I got two blooming A's for my trouble. Many thanks to you, Dr. Kinsolving, and a long raspberry for you, Dr. Bourne.

At the beginning of my sophomore year I learned that the student who ran the campus theater had graduated and left the job open. I jumped at the opportunity and gave notice to the Lincoln Theater in New Haven so that I went home only once a month afterward. The frequent travel was hard on me. The new job had me selling tickets and pre-boxed popcorn; collecting tickets; and running premium features from yesteryear. I had to alternate between two 16-mm projectors to provide uninterrupted and seamless movie viewing. I made a tiny dot in the upper right-hand corner of two film frames six frames apart. The first warned me to start the opposite projector, and the second told me when to flip the light shield to cover the opposite projector's light path. The audience was never aware of the dots, because only the trained eye knew where to look for them.

The really dumb thing was that I didn't slack off from the other AVA work and I was to pay dearly for it in grades. I wasn't failing yet, but to maintain a student deferment from my most vulnerable One-A draft status, I needed to have a better grade point average. Too late—I had two alternatives. I could wait for Uncle Sam to come for me and I'd wind up in the Army and its trenches—face to face with the enemy. Or I could join the Navy and do my part without seeing the face of my enemy. It was Spring 1951, and the Korean War had been raging for a little over a year—not a particularly good time to face the draft.

Chapter 6

U.S. Navy: The Making of a Sailor and a Mensch

In June of 1951 I left the U.S. Navy enlistment office in New Haven with the commitment that I would report to the local train station at 6:30 a.m. on August 31st for transport to the Navy's New York City induction facility. Because I had scored the maximum during the intelligence testing, and with my electronics experience, I was permitted to take the Eddy Test, an aptitude and ability exam verifying my suitability for fifty-two weeks of electronics training. This too I passed with flying colors—both a good thing and a troublesome thing, as I would soon learn.

A Third Class Boatswain's Mate from the enlistment office accompanied seven of us on the train and bus to the New York recruitment facility. We were told to bring only the clothes on our back. We shed our shoes and clothing until we stood in a line in just our skivvies (underwear shorts). The huge room was partitioned into examination stations. Approaching the first station, a sailor wrote a brand-new service number across my chest with a magic marker—in purple, upright to the writer, but upside down and troublesome to me, the reader. Arriving at each station I was ordered to recite this number. So, by the end of the seemingly endless number of stations, I knew my number for good. Every station had its unique physical exercise for me to demonstrate; or a general health check by medical personnel; or skin, hair, or fluid taken by lab people. There was always someone shouting:

"Name and service number?"

"Look away and cough!"

"Get down and give me five!"

"Get up from knees down—no hands!"

"Open wide!"

"Read back the last line you can make out!"

"Repeat back all the numbers you can hear!"

Apparently, I was declared fit enough to become an Electronics Technician Seaman Recruit (ETSR) with one lonely half-stripe, so I eventually found myself on a crowded overnight train from Hackensack, NJ to Camp Porter at the Great Lakes Naval Training station just outside North Chicago, IL After a haircut, a total head shave, and a delousing we were dubbed "skinheads"—bald and gray on top and humiliated through and through.

Those with infestations and dental problems were separated and treated and were destined to join later units. Afterward, white and blue dress uniforms were issued, along with dungarees (blue jeans) and chambray work shirts as well as skivvies. Peacoats, flat hats, white hats, and shoes were also issued in the closest approximate (but never quite exact) sizes. Then we received cloth ditty-bags containing all sorts of unfamiliar brands of toilet articles. Our high-top, heavy work shoes were known as boondockers. Our low-top dress shoes had to be literally spit-shined so you could see your face in them.

The boot camp principle, as I've often heard it said, was to take away all our God-given rights, privileges, and self-confidence until we earned them back one by one. As depressing as it sounds, I look back over seventy years later and think it wasn't as bad as it seemed then. We learned Naval history, shipboard geography and nomenclature, gunnery, precision marching, firefighting, swimming, survival skills, personal hygiene, self-defense, and much more in the thirteen weeks at boot camp.

It was called boot camp not because we wore the slide-in type boots. No, it was because we wore tan, stiff canvas boots laced up the double-cleated sides with the pants cuffs tucked flat and neat inside. They were always getting scraped and marked with shoe polish and dirt and needed to be scrubbed harshly with

a stiff brush and a strong detergent.

I found firefighting school most fascinating. The huge blackened concrete structures and compartments within were set afire, fueled with oil, and teams of four seaman recruits were fully charged with extinguishing the flames with a single powerful hose. It took four to point and stabilize this hose. Because the nozzle position was not only the most critical and dangerous, the team learned to rotate through the four very different hose-front positions without loss of control. Loss of control meant that the hose would break loose and squiggle all over the place like a bronco resisting his taming. Frightened abandonment was the number one cause of this loss. A water shutdown was the cure, but a shutdown meant lost time in fighting a dangerously growing threat.

We functioned in the classroom and on the grinder (drill field) and slept in barracks as companies and, as such, everything was a company competition. Slackers were treated poorly as competition points meant the possibility of liberty (four to six hours off base) for all or even worse, company discipline. That usually meant marching on the grinder at night with sixty-pound sea bags on your shoulder. Most of my company came from the tough Red Hook section of Brooklyn, so the innocent among us frequently suffered along with the wise-guy guilty. The recruit in the two-high rack (bunk) above me usually bounded out in the morning, pounding his sea bag with a flurry of jabs and hooks from both hands and toe dancing while sniffing his nose in peculiar patterns. He'd been a New York State Golden Gloves boxing competitor.

A company chief and scribe were selected from our recruits on the basis of past Naval Reserve experience. The two were tough, but fair. On the other hand, the Navy sent a veteran Boatswain's Mate First Class Petty Officer as company commander (the Navy's version of drill instructor) to make or break us. The "Dutchman" was the nicest name anyone ever called the short, stocky redheaded tyrant. Secretive, devious, malicious, and unapproachable were among his lighter descriptions. For those who ignored reveille, the wake-up bugle call, transmitted over the public address system in our barracks, the Dutchman spun a coke bottle inside of an empty GI or metal garbage can. The initials "GI" stood for "general issue," a term for military standard issue. The unique racket produced by the spinning bottle was said to be horrible enough to scare the bark off trees—a mean way to wake up in the morning anyway. Amusingly, during roll call, he would call one recruit with a twenty-letter unpronounceable, unspellable last name beginning with a C as "Jones." The intended recruit responded dutifully when he was called "Jones" in the middle of the C's. We called him Al.

Inspections were frequent and strict. Every article of clothing in your sea bag (including skivvies and sox) had to be rolled tight and secured with ¼-inch clothesline tied in square knots and laid out according to a predetermined inspection map. Discrepancies could lead to dragging your entire sea bag, contents and all, into the showers where all the non-color-fast clothing fraternized freely. It took much elbow grease and bleaching to restore their original coloring.

The uniform of the day, including color and whether peacoat collars were up or down, was posted daily on the bulletin board. We were stuck with this determination regardless of weather and temperature change. We stood watches in dress uniforms on a rotational basis. On land, this was the Navy's version of guard duty. At sea, it meant being a lookout or a helmsman or some specialist's extra duty that had to be maintained round the clock. In boot camp the watches rarely guarded anything worthwhile. We did have to stand them "at ease" with a fake piece at our side. If you called your piece a rifle, you were ordered to sleep with it that night.

One blustery cold night that November I was ordered outside to guard a dozen or so GI cans. It started to snow, and the wind raged up to the point where the can covers popped and flew everywhere. I managed to retrieve them, and like an octopus, I sat on one can and spread my limbs across several others. Even the weight of my piece covered two more. You can only imagine the chaos when the duty chief made his rounds and came upon my awkward situation. He immediately ordered me to stand at attention, upon which the covers began flying against the adjacent building. He helped me gather the covers once more and left me with these words of wisdom: "As you were, sailor."

Those with special skills were usually broken out of the company to assist in teaching the others. So when I passed my swimming tests early, I volunteered to help. Nope! They had enough volunteers. I got sent to mess-cooking (the Navy's version of KP) instead. It was late October and the waters of Lake Michigan were unkind when we had to jump 30 feet off a tower into a ring of fire and swim underneath until clear. We then had to remove our dungarees and tie knots in the legs and use them for flotation aids.

There was a resentment among my company colleagues about the designation emblems we wore with our single half-stripe on our left arm. While I never bragged or made an issue of it, others thought of it as some sort of elitist symbol and went out of their way to be offensive about it. My emblem was a helium atom (an electron in each of two offset orbits), but there were two other recruits in the company, promising them some sort of (clerical) schooling as well. Everyone else was destined to go to sea and likely to wind up chipping paint at least a year before earning the right to go to school. This was known as striking for a rating, or seeking a Naval occupation. At the end of boot camp everyone earned the second half-stripe, a Seaman Apprentice (SA). I entered school as an

Electronics Technician Seaman Apprentice (ETSA). Most of my former colleagues (SAs) were assigned to ships needing generic deck hands. I had to wait three weeks for the next starting class of

electronics school. *Time off,* I thought, for we had but a measly two, six-hour liberty passes in the entire thirteen weeks of boot camp. The longer time off never materialized—the Navy had other plans for all those awaiting schooling of any type.

We were sent to the receiving station barracks and sent on work details each weekday. The usual details were routine make-work: loading, unloading, and cleaning, but there was always the dreaded rail detail. This involved sliding a heavy quarter side of beef along a rail inside a boxcar, lifting it off its rail-car hook, and carrying it 50 feet to another hook inside the reefer (freezer) warehouse building. The number of trips back and forth seemed endless as the lot went to feed hundreds of companies at the three boot camps (Dewey, Downs, and Porter) and many Class-A major service schools. Talk about sore bones at the end of the day. I spent three random days on the rail detail.

I obtained a 48-hour liberty pass two of the three weekends while assigned at the receiving station. The third was a duty weekend where I stood two watches in the building lobby. There were really only two liberty choices: after a train ride from the burg of North Chicago outside the west gate, either downstate to Chicago or up to Milwaukee, WI. The latter offered tours of the famous breweries, with samples, while the former offered the USO with free snacks, drinks, and girls. We spent the night sleeping on the rail station benches. After all, our monthly pay had just gone from $78 to $126 with our second half-stripe. I tried both cities and found that servicemen were welcomed in both.

While the Great Lakes Electronics school was included in the naval base, its front gate led to the Illinois city of Waukegan of Jack Benny fame. Classes were organized into twenty-six, two-week sessions. We were tested at the end of each session. If you failed one session, you could repeat it for a better grade. Fail twice and you were sent to sea. We went to class seven hours a day in six-, and then later, five-day weeks. We had one to two hours of homework each night. Only core electrical and electronic subjects and math were taught. There were no electives included—not literature, nor history, nor geography, nor foreign languages. The average attendee already had two years of college, so the competition was fierce. Our class had six Marines (mostly victims of the only drafting of Marines in their history) and fifteen sailors. One of our early instructors was an ex-professor from the University of Chicago who had worked on ENIAC, one of the earliest vacuum-tube computers.

The first few weeks were spent on electrical and electronics theory. Using Ohm's Law and other network laws, we solved for unknown values of resistors, capacitors, and inductors in a variety of practical circuits. In a lab class we built bare-bones, super-heterodyne radio receivers that picked up all the local commercial stations. One student couldn't seem to get his receiver to work until, accidentally, he elbowed it onto the floor where it blasted everyone audibly. He took a lot of joshing over that.

We usually had a ninety-minute lunch period and at least half of that time was spent playing cards, specifically, bridge. I never rose out of the ranks of the beginner, but I kept trying because it was expected. We did have a table of sharp players who could have played masters-level bridge.

As the weeks progressed, we tackled functional and wave-shaping circuitry and added vacuum tube, transistor, and diode theory. The labs began to include more and more shipboard equipments and systems. Soon we were into communications theory and transmitting and receiving equipment; antennas, transducers, and arrays; then radar, navigation, sonar, and depth-finding systems. The labs included internal signal tracing and troubleshooting theory as well as practical diagnosis and corrective measures, including parts replacement and alignment procedures. The most profound statement to come out of the troubleshooting labs was: "Yeah, I found it—the fuse is shorted!" Of course, all good fuses are shorted until they are blown (melted) open from overload.

Just about the time we'd reached sonar classes, the liberty passes were running from midday Friday to midnight Sunday, a sort of reward for making it this far through school. Many arrived in Monday's class sleep-deprived and/or hung over, tending to periodically nod off. The instructor's revenge was to sneak up on the sleeping sailor with two GI can covers and slam them together with a major clang over his head. This experience proved to be quite uplifting and impressive for the victim and surely humorous for the rest of the class.

With a good number of Chicago liberties behind us, we began to know how to exploit the system. A whole weekend's hotel expense would be shared by up to eight sailors. We literally separated the beds and furniture to accommodate everyone's sleeping arrangements. Two slept on bare springs, two more slept on the mattress on the floor, another on the upholstered chair and hassock, another on folded blankets on the floor, and so forth. Even the bathtub in some cases. Just before noon on Saturday and Sunday, we would cruise the hotel halls outside the ballrooms looking for wedding and Bar Mitzvah receptions and other lavish events. There was always a generous participant who took pity on lonely servicemen in uniform, and they would invite us to join the festivities and meet the young ladies in their party. We enjoyed the food, drinks, and dancing. Besides, we met all kinds of future dates this way. We kept a "Do not disturb sign" on the room's door for the whole weekend and returned the room to pristine condition before leaving. We also kept our eye out for events at local synagogues and churches. Almost any free event with girls attending attracted us.

Liberty in Milwaukee was a bit different. We toured the several breweries by day and attended George Devine's Million Dollar Ballroom by night. Major orchestras and bands appeared nightly with the accent on Polish music (polka and schottische). The ballroom was the size of a football field. A raft of tables, chairs, and bars selling drinks filled the balcony that surrounded the open chandeliered ballroom below. The music was loud and terrific, and I soon learned all the dances and many of the drinking songs. Single girls down from the Wisconsin farms to work in the city frequented the ballroom, especially on weekends. There were twice as many gals as guys—the kind of odds that sailors liked, and they were not governed by strict, no-date USO rules. I had many a fine time there and had many intimate dates as a result.

The last ET school session dealt with radiac theory and radiation measuring devices. We learned about electromagnetic pulsing (EMP) and atomic energy radiation—sources, shielding, and radiation patterns. Working with a model city made of wood and a re-locatable source and various elemental shields, we used Geiger-Muller counters to determine safe-level locations for human operations. We were to be the sole responsible technicians for radiac safety aboard ship.

We were graduated from ET school with a third half-stripe as Seaman Electronics Technicians (ETSN). Our next duty assignments were based on our collective test grades. In the upper third, I managed to capture the last shore-based assignment at U.S. Naval Air Station, Pensacola, FL, where naval aviators were trained. I was further assigned to the Naval Transmitting Station at Chevalier Field for the next thirteen months. In addition to maintaining a dozen or so multikilowatt transmitters at the station, we repaired and replaced equipment from Chevalier and all seven of the outlying airfields' control towers in an adjacent electronics repair shop.

Standing duty in the transmitter building meant patching control of the big transmitters to the various control towers or local communications centers. Some were manually tuned and others were automatically tuned to preset frequencies. The transmitters were spaced several yards apart around the inner perimeter of the huge brick and glass building. Covered channels cut into the concrete flooring afforded the space for interconnecting cables to reach the control console in the middle of the room where all of the patching took place. A fearless family of felines also used these channels for privacy, and once we even discovered that a batch of kittens had arrived inside one of the channel sections.

A bunk room in the building allowed at least one of those standing watch to sleep. However, when one of the big transmitters went active, the fluorescent light tubes flashed with each keystroke or voice transmission, thus illuminating the entire bunk room. Removing the fluorescent tubes from their sockets didn't stop the tube gas from ionizing and radiating light. If we wanted any sleep, the tubes had to be removed and stowed in closed drawers.

There was a generator driven by a large diesel engine in the basement of the transmitter building—an engine so large that it had to be turned over and started by a car-sized gasoline engine. The arrangement restored building power whenever base power went down. Starting, engaging, and shifting power sources were complicated and often tricky, but anyone standing watches in the building had to be qualified in this regard. Because the equipment was considered such a valuable asset to the Navy, we also stood these watches with live sidearms, the standard Navy Colt 45. We had to qualify on the firing range every six months, and many a boring watch was spent field-stripping this weapon.

Each transmitter had its own antenna lead-in, which passed through a glass window hole and a copper lightning horn upward for a specified antenna length to an insulator attached to a cable running up to a strong-back cable stretched between two of the three 400-hundred-foot towers surrounding the building. I mention this because, during one inspection, the very new base communications officer (a full commander) wanted the lightning devices polished and their gaps set uniformly. No amount of arguing would convince him otherwise, so the task was accomplished as ordered. The horn part of the device is a short length of copper tubing bent to a critical angle. The second part of the device is set apart from the horn by a precise gap and tied directly to the building's grounding system. Normally the horn part conducts the transmitter power to the antenna, but should the antenna engage a lightning strike, the lightning bolt, which travels in straight lines, would shoot downward, jump the gap to part two, the ground system, rather than follow the horn inside and damage

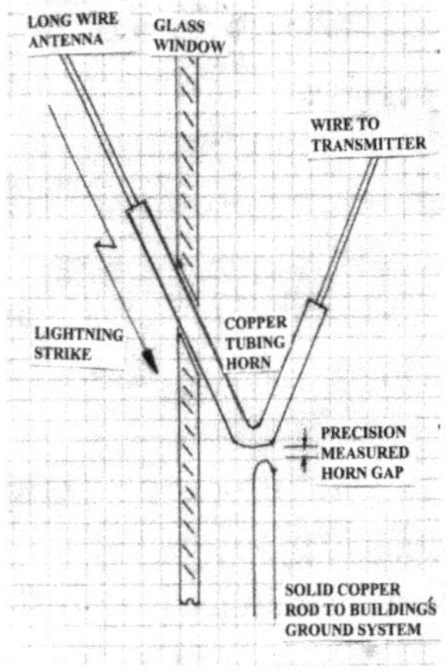

Horn Gap Arrester (Simplified)

the transmitter.

Pensacola is rife with thunder and lightning storms, especially during the spring and summer. It was my luck to have the duty during the very next such storm after the horns were disturbed. I was asleep in the bunk room when it started, and my duty mate was at the console. It was like being the target of Fourth of July rockets. The flashes were coming from every which way, leaving big burn spots and shallow pits on the concrete floor wherever they bounced. The noise from the shearing strikes added to the accompanying thunder to make them sound terrifying. The other sailor miraculously made it to the bunk room and the two of us hid behind the bunk room door until the storm ceased. The damage to the equipment was minimal—mostly burn spots in cabinets. Three transmitters needed to have all the components in their final output stages replaced.

Angry with us for having to find funds to repair his mistakes, the communications officer doubled the size of the watch and tripled the frequency we had watch. Everyone groaned over this loss of liberty, especially the married men who lived off base. He also had the gall to bring his ship-to-shore radio in for repairs. He imposed on a sailor to repair it for him and demonstrate that it worked again, but before he could get it reinstalled in his private cabin cruiser, someone else would install another faulty component. After several tries, he finally had to take it to town and pay to have his radio repaired. However, our revenge was not complete until his commuting scooter was found one morning at the top of one of the antenna towers. Apparently, his manic outbursts in his other communications sections led to his expeditious transfer out of Pensacola. My conscience was clear—I had nothing to do with the revenges.

Eventually, I passed the exam for Third Class Petty Officer and earned my first Crow and Chevron. I became an ET3c on May 16, 1953 and, as a result, would now become a crew leader. The problem was that I didn't have a civilian driver's license, and I needed one to attend the Navy's driver school. A friend taught me to drive in one of the Navy's pickup trucks within the parking lot of our immediate facility. When I thought I was proficient enough, I went into town and purchased a used 1940 Oldsmobile coupe. I studied the Florida driver's manual and practiced driving and parking off base in a low traffic area until I was ready. I got the Florida license on the first try and immediately applied for the Navy driver's school. I took the final driving test in a 1½-ton stake truck and had to drive it forward and reverse in a pre-programmed zigzag pattern and parallel park it as well. I passed, but soon learned that I had to qualify to drive the mobile broadcasting station truck, which was an armored truck chock-full of communications gear, and pull and (heaven forbid) back up a serially connected generator trailer and fuel trailer as well. After many tries I finally qualified. This communications array would be used in case the main transmitting station was damaged or abandoned.

The 1940 Olds didn't last all that long. It burned nearly as much oil as gas, and I had to cut a hole in the floorboard to wrestle and operate the transmission levers. The fenders had machine screw and sheet metal patches. It got me to Miami Beach a few times (Mother had moved there in the meanwhile) and to Mobile, AL where my grandfather had moved to be close to his eldest daughter, Josephine. I traded the Olds in for a 1946 Plymouth that wasn't in much better shape.

Jimmy Petit, a Second Class Aviation Machinist Mate, was newly assigned to our unit, and we became good friends. He'd also been a tail gunner on a plane that was shot down over North Korea. A prisoner exchange had gotten him out of a POW camp in Korea, and this was as close as he could get to his Rome, GA home. He surprised a base bank teller by asking for eleven applications for thousand-dollar U.S. savings bonds from what was left of his accumulated back pay. It was Jimmy who suggested we work on the Plymouth at the base's hobby garage. There, at the hobby garage, I discovered an immobile 1941 Plymouth, and I bought it as well. Little had changed with the Plymouth's design throughout the WWII years. We stripped both cars down, including the engines, transmissions, and universals, before rebuilding a hybrid machine with the best parts from either year's car. The result wasn't a perfect car, but it proved very serviceable transportation for the next 100,000 miles.

We drove to Jimmy's parents' farm near Rome, GA one weekend in his old 1949 Ford. On Saturday he gave into an impulse and traded in his car for a 1950 Harley-Davidson. He drove it up, down, and around his father's pastures for the rest of the day, learning the ways of the two-wheeler motorcycle. That night we went to a local dance in town. He danced all evening while I only managed a few turns on the floor with the fringe girls. If they didn't want to dance with me, they stared me down. I later found out that the locals didn't take to strangers in that part of the woods. Besides, they danced kind of strangely there too. It was sort of a quick-stepping number with your coupled hands moving through a 45-degree arc with each step while you spun circles on the floor. I had never experienced anything like it before. The next morning, after a grand breakfast, we set out through the woods to see his father's liquor still. Expecting to see a few coils of copper tubing and a pot of brew boiling over an open fire, I was surprised to find a modern still with copper and stainless steel components looking like they belonged in an ordinary modern kitchen. It was quite an operation.

That afternoon he continued practicing on the Harley, only this time, with me riding behind him. We needed the practice too, because I had to get used to leaning just so much into the turns and fighting the urge to always stay upright. An hour or so later I became a solid co-passenger. Around five that afternoon we took off down the road toward Pensacola. Soon darkness overcame us, and we had to turn on the Harley's lights. Simple? No! The motor began to sputter and tell us that it was near to quitting. There was a short in the lighting system. Turning the lights out cured the engine problem, but left us in the near-dark of an almost full moon. He flashed on the lights to alert oncoming cars, but as we left the country roads for the more traveled highways, this became more and more impractical. After a few dangerous close calls we convinced a local farmer to let us store the Harley in his barn until the following week. From there, we hitchhiked back to base, arriving only slightly late the next morning. When our story was actually told, nothing came of our lateness. He rode back to the farm the following week on the back of someone else's "iron hog" to retrieve the newly acquired Harley.

In fact, as Jimmy's interest in motorcycles increased he began teaming more with the six to eight other bikers assigned to our electronics compound. One or more of them had stooped to snitching gasoline from the mobile broadcast unit's fuel trailer until the loss was noticed. Then the new and more tactful communications officer put out a memo saying: "The high rate of evaporation of gasoline has exceeded scientific proportions. Let a word to the wise be sufficient."

Occasionally, I dated girls I'd met at bars. A few of them worked at the local paper mills. But none that interested me. I tried several times to interact with the Jewish community in Pensacola and attended Friday night services. It was as though I was shunned—I spoke with no one, and almost no one approached me. I did meet and become friendly with a Jewish Coast Guard couple that lived in the lighthouse facility adjoining our west gate. In fact, after I got to know them better, they furnished me with a key to that gate. We spent a few Sunday mornings in a boat changing batteries in buoys and fishing with lines over the side for red snapper. I gave them whatever I caught because I just didn't care to eat fish. They were a fun couple to hang out with and usually sent me back to the barracks with something home baked.

On the subject of fishy things, every six weeks or so some ETs in the group would pull daylight crash boat duty. Two AVRs, 63-foot aircraft rescue boats, sat alongside the pier opposite the operations building. They were high-speed boats designed to pull fledgling pilots from the sea quickly before their wreckage sank beneath them. The pilots practiced "touch and go" landings at marked-off areas of Corey Field and, when they were ready, they tried the real thing on moving aircraft carriers out in the nearby gulf. A small building on the pier housed an office and a lounge with recliners and cots where the crews waited. When an alarm sounded, the duty boats were already moving by the time the last man was aboard. In minutes these boat were at top speed headed toward the crash scene.

On most days when the touch and go's were not active, the boats would lie idle. But on one Saturday morning, when I was called to crash boat duty, I found the crew receiving a group of brass in sheep's clothing: the Chief of Naval Air Basic Training, his aides, and guests, and they weren't going on crash duty either. Instead, it was a planned fishing trip. We were out in the bay for nearly five hours before returning to base. The catch was stored collectively in communal ice chests aft. The largest fish caught belonged to a member of the permanent crew. When he went to retrieve it, the fish was gone, taken by one of the brass and unashamedly photographed with it.

Normally, my job as a crew leader kept me pretty busy. I drove a pickup truck, usually with another technician, to the control tower facilities at the many outlying fields and either repaired radio equipment on site or replaced it and carried the troublesome unit back to the shop for further diagnosis and repair. On occasion, I'd pick up a special assignment over at Ellison Field, where they trained helicopter pilots. This field was not officially commissioned yet, nor had it been fully funded either. Most of the equipment was a generation behind and supported by spare parts from the Navy's equivalent of an equipment dump.

My part in these assignments was to pick up an air controller person and drive out to the end of a bayou, where we'd set up a portable control tower (with all the necessary equipment in the bed of my pickup truck) for training purposes. I read while they, in headsets, sat on tall stools with binoculars and granted permission for multiple helicopters to move about a map grid—like chess pieces on a chessboard. I had to admire these air controller types because of the confident way they handled their job. The job was made more complicated when you consider that this map contained many bordering chessboards with all of the included hazards.

The thirteen months passed quickly, and I was ordered to the naval base at Norfolk, VA to pick up my ship, the *USS Oak Hill*, LSD-7. Oak Hill was President Monroe's home in Loudon County, VA. The LSD stood for Landing Ship Dock and had nothing to do with the hallucinatory drugs of the same initials. The number seven indicated that she was old—WWII vintage. In fact, I would later learn that she had been loaned to the British for two of those war years and returned afterward. As an LSD, she could ballast down and flood her amidships well-deck with sea water (like filling a huge bathtub) so that up to three large Landing Craft Utility (LCUs) might drive in through her rear floodgates. LCUs were capable of car-

***USS Oak Hill* Landing Ship Dock, LSD-7 (My first ship)**

rying the largest military tanks. The LSD then pumped out all of the sea water in order to transport this payload to an amphibious assault beach anywhere in the world. A helicopter deck spanned the rear of the well-deck to land that type of aircraft or, in some cases, carry more amphibious assault vehicles. The *Oak Hill* was armed with a five-inch .38 caliber gun forward, followed by two twin 40mm and four twin 20mm antiaircraft guns. She could ride the seas high to avoid torpedoes or ride deeper for extra stability in rough weather. Her flat hull and minimal keel made a great slap

Landing Craft Utility, LCU-41 entering the well-deck of *USS Oak Hill*

each time it met the ocean. Not ideal for sleeping, I assure you, and many's the night I wound up with sore limbs as a result.

I reported aboard ship, remembering to first salute the flag aft and then salute the Officer of the Deck (OD) next. I dropped off my personnel records and received my bunk assignment, an upper rack in crew's quarters right below the five-inch gun. My bunk comprised a one-inch, steel-pipe rectangle with rounded corners and a reinforced sheet of canvas stretched across it with clothesline laced around the pipe through grommet holes in the canvas. A three-inch mattress covered with what everyone called a fart sack came next, followed by a sheet and blanket. The two high pipe racks folded on hinges attached to vertical (deck to overhead) stanchions. A pair of chains hung from the overhead (ceiling) supported the side opposite the hinges. There were approximately fifty men assigned to this crew's compartment. Being senior, I chose the upper bunk. I felt the upper bunk was preferable, as you didn't have to view the sag and bulge above you, and it was light and roomy enough to read. I soon discovered another unique thing about this bunk position—it was directly below the first vent after the ship's bakery ovens. The wafted aroma of fresh-baked bread greeted me every morning.

I met briefly with the division officer, who was also the communications officer, and then, after changing into work clothes, I reported to the lead electronics technician (ET). He was a short-timer ET2c who would not be going to sea with us as his enlistment was up. He introduced me to his current crew, consisting of two seamen ETs and an ET3c who was junior to me, based on time seniority. This meant that I would be leading the ET gang by the time we went to sea. This also meant that I had to learn my new equipments quickly and determine their readiness. I found that most of them needed some essential work, and there were even some signs of neglect, so I went to work, garnered the respect of my new crew, and put them to work as well.

Sixty days later, when we finally put to sea as a squadron of amphibious ships, our electronics were in much better shape. We headed for the Mediterranean Sea to join the Sixth Fleet, a two-week journey. We were greeted with my first sight of France: three-foot-high letters painted on the rocks at Gulf Juan, halfway between Nice and Cannes—"U.S. GO HOME!" The division officer was so pleased with the lack of equipment downtime that the ETs were removed from standing all deck watches on the condition that any and all repair efforts would continue round the clock 'til finished. The agreement was that, as long as we had no equipment down and one ET remaining on board, the rest had liberty while in port. I had open gangway for the rest of my shipboard experience, because I had never failed an operational readiness inspection.

Topless bathers and especially topless boaters on the French Riviera were a common sight, which caused an immediate rush to use the Fire Controlman's optical range finder, a 3D telescope device. Once the inevitable traffic problem was noted by those in charge, the close-up images were shut down and left to memory and what the naked eye might otherwise chance upon.

I was disappointed in the quality of the coarse, stony beaches of the Riviera. The ship put a few small Landing Craft Vehicle/Personnel (LCVP) over the side to run sailors with liberty to a local dock called a fleet landing. Unfortunately, a twelve-hour liberty pass put a sailor with limited resources on shore at 10:00 a.m. with little to do in a strange place. Some swam, some walked around taking in the local sights—such as they were. A few got stuck with

Shore Patrol (SP) duty while the rest wound up drinking beer in local pubs.

Typically, the six-ship squadron(s) would spend three-day weekends in port; depart for ships' drills, squadron maneuvers, and joint operations at sea; then return to shore at other Mediterranean ports such as Barcelona, Marseille, Algiers, Nice, Genoa, Naples, Piraeus (Athens), and Izmir.

One Sunday morning, after pulling into Algiers and taking on fresh produce and eggs, the crew was promised a rare breakfast treat of steak and eggs. Bowls of the local eggs were put on the table, supposedly soft-boiled, to start before the eggs-to-order would follow. Initially, there was no indication that anything was wrong. Then, when the first egg was cracked open, a terribly acrid and foul odor filled the mess compartment. A second, third, and more only increased the stench until most of us bailed out of the mess compartment for relief. It took three big fans over an hour before the compartment was habitable again. After jettisoning the eggs, our treat was reduced to powdered eggs and steak.

The ship's recreation officer arranged a tour of the Casbah with a Cook Tours guide for the following day. As we waited in a square for the tour to start, a young (maybe 13-year-old) local boy ran around the corner of a building at the edge of the square and arbitrarily approached me. He had, under his arm, a meter-square rug with a scene of a lion devouring a man's head woven into it. He wanted ten dollars for it. I got it for five, and those around me agreed that I had gotten a bargain. A few minutes later, a local gendarme appeared at the edge of the square and spotted the errant salesman. He blew his whistle and chased the boy right up to the Casbah gate and stopped abruptly there. The guide explained that no police were allowed in the Casbah by agreement, as it was a self-ruled entity.

The tour took us up and down thousands and thousands of steps bounded by stained white walls no more than a yard apart, past openings in the walls into some of the most poverty-stricken, crime-ridden, foulest hovels in the world—and through surprising palace-like chambers lined with exquisite tiling, exotic tapestries and other works of art. I came to the conclusion that these were two diametrically opposed cultures that fragilely lived together and were feared no end by the outsider. The most striking thing was that this place had the audacity to govern itself.

In Barcelona, we toured cathedrals and churches as well as carried on the usual port activities. The most striking thing about this city was the total desertion of the populace during most of the afternoon. A large proportion of the businesses were closed, and when evening arrived everything livened up again. Shopping in Spain appeared to be quite different. Shops carrying similar wares were grouped together in clusters. Hats here, shoes there, jewelry elsewhere, and so on. After wandering around the shops for hours, I bought a dark purple lace mantilla (shawl) for Mitzie's birthday (George's wife).

In Izmir, Turkey we happened upon a park, hosting a world exposition. We visited the displays of a number of countries. Soon we discovered the Russian exhibit tent. Following a short debate as to whether we should enter, we decided to venture in anyway. As soon as we sailors (in uniform) were spotted, a light came on behind us and a cameraman followed us through the entire exhibit. Our perception of what we saw was that these appliances, household conveniences, and assorted gadgets would have existed in American homes a good twenty years earlier. We regretted that the film taken of us might be used in Russian venues to say: "American sailors marveled at Russian genius."

Naples, Italy had its medieval castle. A display of the day, month, and year, all done in a flower arrangment, greeted you as you exited the waterfront area. There was a glass-enclosed galleria for very high-end shopping and vias for regular street shopping. We saw an extraordinary number of police dressed in a wide variety of fashions, including colonial police dressed in tricornered hats, jodhpurs, and tall black boots. Of course, any Italian port drew extra interest in the houses of ill repute. There was always a sailor who claimed to know the way there.

Whenever we were in Italian ports, there were approved salesmen allowed to enter the mess compartment to sell their wares from catalogues. I bought an Austrian pendulum clock for my mother. I also bought two cameras, a Swiss Zeiss Icon, and a German Agfa Carat (35mm, f2 lens).

In Piraeus, the port for Athens, Greece, we made the rounds of many historic monuments, including the Parthenon, during the day. The nightclubs were filled with Uzo and lively dancers in traditional costumes. I met a young British girl from London who allowed me to buy drinks for her in return for conversation. Four hours later she admitted to being married to a Greek sailor at sea. She was alone and lonely. It was an invitation I couldn't refuse, and it was a fun interlude for me.

At the end of seven months in the Mediterranean, we sailed home to Norfolk, VA. With the exception of a small USO facility located in a third-floor apartment, I found the city extremely unfriendly to sailors. I don't remember dating anyone the whole time I spent in Norfolk. One bar after another was banned to the military by the brass when repeated fighting and bilking incidents were reported. Shortly after our return I drew shore patrol duty in the most notorious section of town. But I had to attend a two-hour lecture on the preservation of order, the optimum manipulation of the nightstick, and a number of legal aspects before I could serve as an SP. With the exception of one small altercation that began with the exchange of "Swab Jockey" and "Jarhead," things went well after I sent the sailor on his way, leaving the Marine behind.

On various deserted beaches on both sides of the Atlantic Ocean, we staged full amphibious assaults with multiple squadrons, but without the live ammo and explosives. As ETs, it was our job to set all of the boat radios to preset command frequencies, and check them out in the boats before returning to the ship. The boats would assemble at the line of departure (LOD) and await their turn to advance.

Several months later the ship received orders to change its home port from Norfolk to San Diego, CA. We were to sail to

General Quarters drill aboard the *USS Oak Hill*

Panama and cross the canal to the Pacific Ocean. The news got mixed reception, especially bad with the married homeowners, but we did learn that our cars were to be transported in the ship's now-dry well-deck. After an eight-hour liberty in Colon, a very small and poor city with dirt streets and no air-conditioned bars, we sailed toward the Gatun locks under our own power and drove into the first of two locks. As soon as the gates closed behind us, heavy hawser lines were tossed from the four quarters of the ship and secured to four towing "mules" running on rail tracks on either side of us. These bulky rectangular machines stabilized the ship in the center of the lock while it flooded or drained to the level of the adjacent lock or body of water and towed the ship from lock to lock to Lake Gatun when the levels matched.

Most of the time in the U.S. Canal Zone we experienced sunshine and extreme heat, but we were also there during the summer monsoon season. Every so often we saw the densest rainstorms—like pouring solid water in front of your face for maybe thirty minutes, and then only minutes after it stopped—bone dry, no evidence of the rainfall except for the lush rain forest seen ashore. We sailed across the lake under our own power and entered the Chagres River. We then followed the lush, jungle-covered shores to the Miraflores locks, which cleared us in similar fashion through to the Pacific Ocean and the port of Balboa, where the other half of the crew had their liberty.

The ship followed the Central American coastline from the Panama Canal Zone up to Acapulco, Mexico. Here we discovered a resort full of beautiful beaches that received sun only one part of the day due to the close-in, but high cliffs. There was a morning and an afternoon beach, and if you dallied too long at the first, you'd wonder where the people went.

As luck would have it, I drew Shore Patrol duty again, this time at a bar outside a resort hotel. I believe the name was Hotel Las Predos Americanos. It was famous for high rock leaps over a hundred feet into the ocean. The landing depended on a tidal pool being full or shallow at the time of landing, so timing was of the essence and this grew audience crowds, photos, and movies. That night a First Class Electrician's Mate from my ship had gotten sloppy drunk and noisy—so noisy that he'd drawn warnings from the bar's manager and hotel security before one of them called the local police. I happened on the scene just as the local policeman arrived. I huddled with the manager, who spoke a pretty fair English, and he convinced the policeman to allow my shipmate to use the john while they determined his fate. I accompanied him into the men's room and we both went through the opposite door to the street that I'd used earlier.

I paid a taxi driver to drive him to the fleet landing and nowhere else. I retraced my steps, stood just outside the john door, and waited. The policeman eventually got impatient, and when he found me, asked where the sailor was. I pointed at the door. Inside, of course, there was no sailor. He swore at me, shook his head, and walked off. My shipmate had gotten back safely and was grateful enough to reimburse me for the cab fare. Rotting in a Mexican jail is not what he had in mind.

The *Oak Hill* put into the port of San Diego in late July 1954, and for some unknown reason we were berthed at the 22nd Street piers. We could walk right off the ship into the city's downtown streets. West Coast weather seemed strange to me. You could swim in the afternoon, yet by nightfall you needed a heavy coat. Our liberties took us as far north as Los Angeles and Hollywood and as far south as Tijuana and Ensenada, Mexico. In Tijuana we visited the jai alai stadium and marveled at the open betting scheme, where the betters shouted out the bets at a standing man who wrote everything down on little slips of paper. It was a fast and exciting sport, but betting was not for the sailors' salaries.

In Ensenada I parked my Plymouth on the main street late in the afternoon, and a youngster immediately approached me for a handout to guard my parked car from theft and vandalism. Foolishly, I sent him packing, and we headed for the nearest bar with rare air conditioning. The bar was packed, but there were extra chairs at our table. Soon two good-looking, young Americans asked to sit with us. They claimed to be the sons of a macho famous film star and one of them had the exact face to prove it. They left several hours later without paying their bar bill, a considerable one at that. It took almost all the cash we had to buy our way out of there. They had been drinking premium hard liquor, whereas we had been slowly nursing our cheap Mexican beers. To top the evening off, we found a live poisonous snake on the driver's seat of the locked car—the mysterious revenge of a young street entrepreneur. We hauled it out with a stick, but wondered how he got the snake in without unlocking the car.

Local liberty meant returning to crashing church and synagogue functions to meet young ladies, as the hotel strategy didn't work as well in San Diego. At one Lutheran church they asked too many questions about our religion and began a proselytizing mission with me as a target. Even the girl I'd been dating went to work on me, so I hightailed it out of there in a hurry.

In December of that year I learned that I had received my second chevron, effective January first. I was now an ET2c with only eight months of active duty left. The captain of the *Oak Hill* invited me to dine with him in his cabin one noon in an effort to retain me. He offered me a shot at the Navy's version of Officer's Candidate School (OCS) if I would re-enlist immediately. All I had to do was pass the physical and he would recommend the appointment. I thanked him, but turned him down, saying that I wanted to try college once more. He never spoke to me again, but managed a wave as I left the ship for the last time. I turned and saluted him out of respect and walked down the gangway.

Shortly after receiving my new rating, I received orders assigning me to the *USS Lenawee*, APA 195, an amphibious troop transport capable of landing almost 4,000 troops and equipment on an assault beach with Landing Craft Mechanized (LCMs) plus Landing Craft Vehicle/Personnel (LCVPs) also known as Mike and Peter boats, respectively. I replaced a retiring

***USS Lenawee*, Amphibious Personel Assault Ship APA-195**

Warrant Officer as the leading Electronics Technician aboard. I now had two Third Class and two seamen technicians in my electronics crew. In the overlapping weeks I became friends with the WO and even visited him at the Point Loma Transmitting Station, his last duty station before retiring. I remember swimming in a pool there, normally used in cooling powerful transmitting tubes.

Several weeks passed and our ship and others moved to the Marine Corps Base at Camp Pendleton in Oceanside, CA, where we filled the troop compartments in the hold with 2,800 soldiers of the Third Marine Division. The *Lenawee* put to sea upon completion of the loading and headed for Sasebo, Japan, where we stayed long enough for each watch section to have liberty.

The *Lenawee's* Electronics Crew (I'm embarrassed—no names, sorry!)

The *Lenawee* put to sea once more, and this time, we headed for Inchon, Korea, where we would off-load the Third Marine Division troops. As we pulled into this Korean railroad center, we saw the battle-worn soldiers of the First Marine Division hunkered down along the shore buildings next to the rail tracks. These men had not seen the States in three years, but they were now going home. We were bringing their replacements. Unloading and loading took several days and the ship was made ready for sea again.

Our payload was now 3,700 troops, almost a thousand over design capacity. Their racks (similar to ours) were six high in the cargo hold. Their pieces (rifles) and their duffles, containing all they owned, were strapped to their racks. The hold soon smelled like a gymnasium—only much worse from too many, too close. Once a day, one company at a time came to the main deck for exercise. Three times a day they came to the mess compartment for meals, only the benches were stowed within the tables, and the tables raised so that eaters had to stand to eat. It was quicker that way and one troop meal almost ran into the next in order to get everyone fed on time. Sadly, this was all we could offer American fighting men who had been living in foxholes in a strange land.

Several Marine radiomen volunteered to help out in the ET shop so they might see a little more daylight. Four of them slept on tabletops in the shop, and one slept on the floor rather than return to the six-story hotel below decks. They were a big help to me, and I was glad to help them. When they weren't busy, they were card players; pinochle was their game. They played until they were exhausted and could sleep.

When the ship got within 400 miles of the West Coast I received an okay to raise the Long Beach, CA telephone operator. We offered the Marines the opportunity to call home in the States with this arrangement. They lined up around the main deck waiting their turn. The commanding officer ordered someone to monitor the calls so they could key-out anyone giving out our exact position. The few turns I took at this were pitiful, in that most of the five minutes they were allotted were spent in crying and stilted conversation. We had problems with interference from striking tuna fisherman breaking into our frequency. Finally, the commanding officer took the microphone and explained who we were and what was happening. It worked, and the frequency became totally ours. Three days later we dropped off the Marines and returned to San Diego.

Upon returning, I discovered that my car had been broken into and some tools and a camera stolen. The car itself was intact. Originally, I had enlisted in the Navy for three years. Not long after, an act of Congress added what everyone called Truman's year, making it four total. That was amended some time later into an eight-year service obligation—requiring four more years in the Naval Reserve.

Six weeks after returning to the States I was transferred to the receiving station in San Diego for mustering out of the active Navy. I was appalled to find that sailors, even senior petty officers, were assigned menial tasks, such as sweeping streets, while awaiting their individual discharge dates—such an indignity. My own release into the Naval Reserve occurred on August 30, 1955.

Chapter 7

College: A Second Chance

It was August of 1955. After four years active Navy I received an honorable discharge and transferred into the Naval Reserve for another four years. I was released at the San Diego receiving station, and I and two other vets drove my vintage-hybrid Plymouth sedan cross-country to Miami Beach in sixty-one hours. It was nonstop except for multiple gas, rest, and food stops plus an oil change. One drove, one slept, and one navigated. We shifted every three hours. My mother was now living in Miami Beach. My ultimate goal after a week's visit with her was to return to UConn for another chance there.

As a returning veteran, I was given first opportunity at campus housing. I chose the fourth floor of a university-owned fraternity house. The frat wasn't large enough to support the entire building, so they needed to rent out the extra space. I can't even remember the the frat's name, but the brothers were friendly enough and usually invited me to their parties where you paid for your own beer. I went to one and stayed away, politely declining thereafter. The parties were rowdy and loud and too expensive for my taste. There were a number of incidents at the other frats as well. The university thought so too, so they banned drinking on

campus altogether. The frats struck back by pasting stickers over all the "No Parking Anytime" signs, so they then read "No Fun Anytime."

My roommate was a South Korean Army major on exchange from his country. He was also a multi-sport athlete, so between our two busy schedules, we saw very little of each other. I had a little mustering-out cash, but that was dwindling ever so quickly. The Veterans Administration was remiss in reimbursing us for our tuition and housing and their monthly allotment checks. The first check arrived the last week in November, and I was down to my last can of beans (or maybe it was Spam by then). Luckily, the building had broad window sills, which a number of us used as outdoor iceboxes in the cold of winter for treats sent from home and Mother.

My brother, George, and family lived in western Pennsylvania, and I drove from school to spend Thanksgiving weekend with them. I measured the necessary gas money I'd need to get there and back, but an unexpected repair, a flat tire, drained my wallet to the point that I had to leave my wristwatch behind at a turnpike gas stop in trust of repayment. I had to borrow money from George in order to reclaim my watch and pay for the gas to get me home. I paid him back out of the second monthly VA check. Other than that, the weekend was a success. They treated me to a *Holiday On Ice* show and a club dance.

On the advice of my academic counselor, I had to retake freshman Analytical Geometry and Qualitative Chemistry before he'd approve more engineering subjects. I had a hard time learning to study again and, surprisingly, trouble in chem lab, where we dealt with unknown yet clear solutions. I found it to be lengthy testing procedures of measuring and provoking reagents to find an answer that always seemed to elude me. There was a wee bit of satisfaction in getting it right a few times. I was rarely able to finish within the allotted time.

I met Enid Bogner at a Hillel meeting one Friday evening after Shabbat services. She was a teaching assistant in the English department who was from Miami, FL, and I was a year older than her. Enid was a physically attractive woman with light brown, almost blond hair and brown eyes. And I thought I'd finally found an intelligent conversationalist with plenty of charm. Since returning from service so many of my dates had seemed immature and even silly. It had been hard to find someone with common interests, although even I wasn't sure what those might be yet. Looking back, I wonder—was it my attitude?

Enid and I had one or two dates and then one really warm Indian summer's day, we went for a ride in the countryside surrounding the campus. On one winding, one-lane road, we came across a seemingly deserted pond. We parked beside it to admire the scenery and then one of us looked at the other and there was a nod in response. Yup! We went skinny dipping—in cold, refreshing water for about thirty minutes. Then, in the middle of drying off, we saw a pickup truck racing across the open field toward us on the other side of a wire barrier fence. Needless to say, we scurried back into our car half-dressed and rapidly drove away. In the rear-view mirror I saw a farmer with what looked like a shotgun in one waving hand. We stopped a ways away and finished our dressing, hee-hawing all the while at the experience.

We had a few more dates, and then both of us decided it was not the time in our lives to become serious. We did remain friends and, during winter break, she arranged a share-the-driving ride to Miami.

My first semester back yielded an A, two B's, and the rest C's, not alarming—yet. Academics and hard work made for a tough combination in my case. I vowed that I would try harder in the second semester. Having a car now, I wanted to live off campus for the second semester. I thought I would be better motivated away from all the tempting action. Besides, I needed a job to keep me going and one that paid considerably more than AVA or the university, for that matter. I believed my chances would be better in the town of Willimantic, CT. My first priority was to find a place to sleep and then look for a job. I answered a newspaper furnished-room-to-rent ad at the Herman Davis home and found the second-floor room with its own stairs to the rear hall and outside more than acceptable. Herman and Ellen Davis were even Jewish.

But the real bonus turned out to be that Herman Davis was an electrical contractor in need of help for a wide variety of tasks. He liked my military electronics experience. I hauled and stapled Romex cable through newly constructed homes, and after a few days on the job, he had me wiring terminal boxes. We wired machinery at two well-known thread factories. I learned how to service refrigeration units at two breweries. And then there were the normal renovation and expansion jobs as well. He even had a contract to maintain the city's traffic light system.

Me outside the Davis home in 1956

As a Korean veteran, I had first choice at selecting classes and their schedule times, so I wound up bunching them into three days, keeping the remainder of the week free for work. Herman had pull with the electricians' union and the state licensing board and was able to get my military experience to count for work experience. After a wee bit of coaching and an easy test, I had my journeyman's permit to do wiring, subject to inspection by him, a master electrician.

Many's the evening the two of us came home late and tired and Ellen Davis would have me in for dinner. Once she caught me heating up a can of Spam under the hot water tap; then the invites became more frequent. Herman, Ellen, and their thirteen-year-old son, Georgie, became a second family to me. Herman was not a young man and his doctor had told him to slow down. The redheaded, round-faced man was short, heavy, and a veteran of two heart attacks. Just before I left them, he called me aside and told me that Georgie wanted to be a musician (trumpet), not an electrician. He not only offered me a no-cash partnership in his business, but would help me obtain my master's license. A very generous offer, and once more in life I had to wonder about the path not taken.

At the end of the second semester my grades remained the same, covering the A to C range equally. Unfortunately, with C's in Calculus and Chemistry, my counselor told me he would not allow me to continue in the engineering program. He recommended that I transfer to something else or leave school altogether. I began to look for work. With my background, I knew that I could qualify as a field engineer, which was paying pretty well at the time. I interviewed with Raytheon and RCA. I accepted the offer from RCA and left school.

Chapter 8

Hannah: First Love, Wife, and Best Pal

During the winter break of my last year at the University of Connecticut I wanted to visit my mother in Miami Beach, but I was having car trouble. Enid Bogner, who I wasn't dating any longer, arranged with a friend attending Lowell Institute in Massachusetts to drive four of us to Miami Beach. It was during this break that I met Hannah Joan Forsch. A co-worker of Hannah's at Burdines department store just happened to live in the same apartment-hotel as my mother, and they arranged my blind date with Hannah without my knowledge or consent. By the time I got wind of the plan it was too late to back out, and, boy, was I glad I went on that date! I was so impressed with her that I wound up seeing her almost every night for the rest of my stay in Miami Beach.

Hannah was a sophomore in early education at the University of Florida in Gainesville. We went to movies, stopped for drinks, went for strolls and even managed to play tennis a few times at a local park. She was a very pretty, slightly full-figured girl with a terrific personality and beautiful eyes and smile. Her conversations were engaging and interesting and she liked almost everything I was fond of. What more could a guy ask for?

Hannah Joan Forsch

Herta Forsch

Eventually, I did get to meet Hannah's mother, Herta, but missed meeting her father, Sigmund. Her parents owned a men's haberdashery called Sig's Men's Wear on Washington Avenue, half a block from Lincoln Road. Herta was a frugal, no-nonsense, no-frills, stern woman with an oval face and sharp tongue, but she turned out to be generous and loving, as I learned in the passing years.

A photo I took of Hannah in Miami Beach

When it was time to return to Connecticut, Hannah and I had made a pledge to write to each other. Over the spring break Hannah had made plans to visit her Uncle Justus and Aunt Ida Seidenberg, who lived in New York. Would I drive over from Willimantic and meet her there? Would I!

Hannah the majorette

I did meet her in New York, and we were inseparable for the whole two weeks. I rented a room four blocks away, but spent only sleeping time at the room. We did some movies, met some of her family, and necked under an overpass in Fort Tryon Park. Before our interlude ended, I had proposed, and she had accepted. Looking back, it was certainly a whirlwind courtship. As yet, I had no prospects of a job. The RCA offer didn't come through until after classes ended in May.

In June of 1956 I entered RCA's Government Services, Field Engineering School at Cherry Hill, NJ. I moved from my room in the Davis home to a rooming house in Delaware Township close to the six-week school. The students were all graduates of military Class A Electronics schools. Some even had bachelor's degrees in electrical engineering. The teaching method was unique in that the students became teachers to the other students. It was necessary to prepare lesson plans and teaching aids for presentations as well. The classes alone comprised a forty-hour week, so all the preparatory work had to be done on our own. I taught a half-day and rotated with the others as students. I graduated with honors and the knowledge that I was doing something that I liked. This was my life's field. After graduation, RCA assigned me to their field office at the naval base in Norfolk, VA.

By now Hannah and I were writing letters almost every day. We agreed that Labor Day weekend and, specifically, the first of September would be our wedding day. With only a few days to call my own, I moved to Norfolk and took a three-room furnished apartment without a lease. I figured we'd have a temporary place to stay while we looked for something better together.

Our Norfolk facility belonged to the Commander Service Forces, U.S. Atlantic Fleet or COMSERVLANT as it was called. RCA had an office in a brick building at the end of Pier Seven on the main naval base. We had a supervisor and a little over a dozen engineers from RCA, Philco, GE, Raytheon, and others sharing the building. It was a forty-hour week with overtime pay, if authorized.

Hannah and Larry relaxing at Fort Tryon Park, New York City

Mostly, we answered troubleshooting calls from U.S. naval ships in port, but occasionally, one of us would be flown to a ship at sea. The troubles or problems were generally those equipment failures and shortcomings that had stumped the onboard technicians—"the real stinkers" so to speak, where they failed to solve and sometimes even recognize the problems. Periodically, a team of engineers would go aboard a ship and inspect all the electronic gear for combat and operational readiness and then stick around to help fix all the deficiencies afterward. We had overseas teams riding with the various fleets at sea as well.

Friday, August 31, 1956 (Labor Day weekend) arrived on time and I went through my checklist. I had already sent the paperwork for my blood test and marriage license to Hannah and my bag was packed. I had even cleaned and spruced up the apartment. Saturday, the first of September, was my wedding day, and the plan was for me to fly to Miami via Washington, DC. I took off work at noon Friday to shower and change and get to the Norfolk airport for a four o'clock flight to DC. As I sat in the waiting room, I thought everything was going beautifully. Wrong!

The plane to DC had engine trouble, and the predicted forty-minute flight now wouldn't even land until 8:30 p.m. My connecting flight was taking off at 7:55. The 11:32 p.m. flight was oversold by at least 15 percent. There were more heavily oversold flights the next morning, but the earliest confirmed seat for the two-hour, fifty-minute flight to Miami was two in the afternoon. Was I to miss my own four o'clock wedding?

The troubled flight made it to DC, and I headed straight to the Eastern Airlines desk only to find out that my connector had left and there was no change in future flight prognoses. What did happen while I was still standing at the desk, a twentyish young man checked his standby status on the 11:32 flight. I overheard the attendant tell him he had moved up to number two. It was now a little after nine—time for a gamble, so in front of the desk attendant, I turned to the young man, told him my plight, and offered twenty dollars for his standby seat position. His head tilted slightly, so I doubled my offer. The attendant sympathized, but claimed she didn't know if that was possible. In the end, however, she considered my situation and swapped the two names in the number two slot. Both the attendant and the young man assured me that there was no guarantee there would be two or more cancellations. I'll never know whether the young man needed or wanted the cash or whether he simply cared about what the consequences would do to my plans.

I assume God wanted this marriage as much as I did, so He created at least the necessary two no-shows. I flew to the desk when I heard my name. Although the flight was late taking off, I nevertheless had an aisle seat on it. I deplaned in Miami just before three in the morning of my wedding day. Hannah and her father were waiting for me just beyond the arrival gate. They had been waiting since the original 9:45 p.m. arrival time. Hannah jumped at me and I hugged and whirled her around. Her kisses were wet because she'd been crying—understandable, since she was worried, tired, and suddenly made happy.

Hannah's engagement photographs

Soon, I realized her father was standing there watching all this. I introduced myself to Sigmund (Sig) Forsch, who I thought must have been the most patient, most obliging and loving father ever to have waited up half the night with her for my arrival. My first impression of the smiling man next to me was purely physical—a short, heavyset man with a round, uneven face and longish black hair covering over a bald spot. I was soon to learn there was much more to Hannah's dad. He was a learned man with a mastery of several European languages; one who kept up with world events; and a complete gentleman who valued his family. We picked up my bag at the luggage turnstile, and the three of us walked hand in hand to the street. We caught a cab outside the airport and they dropped me off at my mother's apartment-hotel, where I slept a nervous sleep until almost noon.

The rabbi conducted the wedding service in his study under a hand-held chuppah. George stood up for me as best man while his wife, Mitzie, and my mother looked on. Hannah's closest friend, Elaine Gross Jacobson, stood up for her as maid of honor, and Sig gave her away. Herta—her mother, her Aunt Lydia Haack (Herta's older sister) and her husband, Uncle Cy Haack, also looked on. The beautiful service ended with my stepping on a plastic glass as we all shouted *Mazel tov*! Two more of her friends joined us as everyone retired to a hotel restaurant for a wedding dinner. We spent our wedding night at a local hotel and flew to Norfolk the next morning for a one and a half-day honeymoon.

On our first night in the Norfolk furnished apartment, two slats supporting the bed springs and mattress broke amid our extracurricular activity, and everything dropped to the floor—the two of us sliding and rolling sideways and downwards against the outer bed frame. At first we were stunned, but then we started laughing. We laughed so hard that Hannah wound up crying. As I comforted her, she confessed that when she laughs that hard, she always winds up crying. I dismantled the wooden bed frame, and we spent the rest of the night with the springs sitting flat on the floor. On the way home from my first day of work I purchased three healthy wooden boards to replace the broken slats and one other from the other end of the bed. The sofa was so collapsed that we stuffed it with newspapers to bring it up to height and bought cushions to make it sittable.

Sig, Herta, Hannah, Me, and My Mother

Elaine Gross (maid of honor), Hannah, Me, Mitzie, and George (best man)

One thing led to another, and we decided to look for another, but unfurnished, apartment. We found one nearby and purchased a queen-size bed, a dresser, a bridge table, two folding chairs, and a recliner before we moved in. We added a settee some months later. The new apartment had a kerosene space heater, but because it was on the second floor, we burned a half-gallon that whole winter. The people downstairs had a baby and managed to keep themselves warm and us cozy as well.

Marriage Certificate (Katuba in Hebrew)

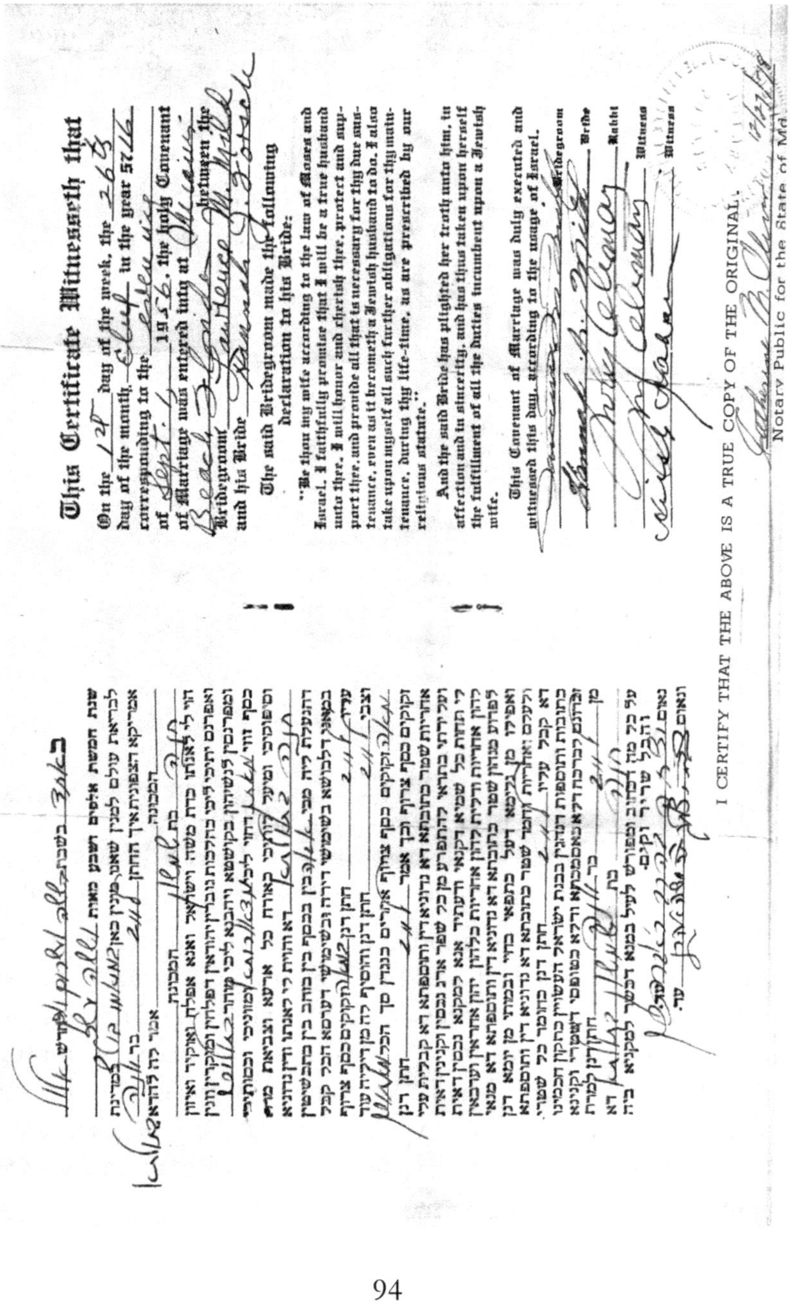

This Certificate Witnesseth that

On the 1st day of the week, the 26th day of the month Elul in the year 5716 corresponding to the ____ of Sept. 1, 1956, the holy Covenant of Marriage was entered into at Miami Beach Florida between the Bridegroom Lawrence M. Mild and his Bride ____

The said Bridegroom made the following declaration to his Bride:

"Be thou my wife according to the law of Moses and Israel. I faithfully promise that I will be a true husband unto thee. I will honor and cherish thee, protect and support thee, and provide all that is necessary for thy due sustenance, even as it becometh a Jewish husband to do. I also take upon myself all such further obligations for thy maintenance, during thy life-time, as are prescribed by our religious statute."

And the said Bride has plighted her troth unto him, in affection and in sincerity, and has thus taken upon herself the fulfillment of all the duties incumbent upon a Jewish wife.

This Covenant of Marriage was duly executed and witnessed this day, according to the usage of Israel.

Bridegroom

Bride

Rabbi

Witness

Witness

I CERTIFY THAT THE ABOVE IS A TRUE COPY OF THE ORIGINAL.

12/27/78

Notary Public for the State of Md.

We're hitched

Our multiyear car was beginning to show its age with repairs that far exceeded its worth. We traded it, and for a mere $500 more, we bought a sharp-looking, used, Mercury sedan. What we didn't know was that the transmission was about to go south two months later. I was sitting in the barbershop when Hannah walked in to tell me she couldn't get the car to shift. Back at the parking lot behind the apartment I tried to shift into gear for forty-five minutes before it accidentally happened. Holding the clutch in, I told Hannah to climb into the passenger seat, and we drove to a nearby Plymouth dealer in second gear, bravely facing two traffic lights on the way. Luckily, we got our $500 back on the Mercury's trade-in. We drove away that afternoon with a brand-new (our first) two-tone gray 1957 Plymouth, fadd-ish big fins and all. What a bargain. We left behind less than $2,000 cash in the exchange.

In October we tried to attend High Holy Day services at the synagogue four blocks away. In the foyer we were told that all seats were sold, paid for, and reserved. Even though there were several empty rows, we were told we could stand in the back. When we asked for a prayer book, they wanted us to pay twenty dollars to rent two books. We left, deciding we would try a different shul next year, one that offered a welcome to strangers, rather than the cold shoulder we received.

One night in that November we came out of the movie theater in the middle of a thundering downpour. We raced for the car, unlocked it, and got in. I heard two car doors close, only Hannah was not sitting next to me. When I looked farther, out at the next car, there she was, sitting in an identical car, obviously a popular model. She had unlocked it as well, using an identical key to mine. Our personal belongings indicated that I sat in our car. She found strange belongings in that car so she abandoned it for our car. Wow! What's the chance of that or is it one key opens all?

In December Hannah decided she was tired of being tied to the tiny apartment all day with nothing to do. She wanted to look for a job against my wishes. She insisted and got a sales clerk job at Rose's department store only three blocks away. That's where we bought the recliner and settee. In January I was given an office aboard the *USS Amphion*, AR-13, an auxiliary repair ship docked at Pier 3, where I continued to do similar work. Ships needing all kinds of mostly minor repairs and updates tied up next to repair ships in groups, connecting to each other via hull gangways. Major repairs and overhauls were done by the Portsmouth Naval Shipyard just across the harbor.

Hannah and I before the party began

When New Year's Eve arrived, we were invited to a smallish party given by our downstairs neighbors. I can't seem to remember their names—somthing with gold or green in their names. I do remember they were a nice military couple from Baltimore. Hannah never liked the taste of hard liquor, but something possessed her that night. After the other guests had left, she and the hostess decided to find out what being inebriated was all about, so they set to the task and attacked what was left in each of the open bottles. When they were finished, I managed to get Hannah upstairs and to bed. Hours later, she awoke and went to the bathroom to upchuck. Having this god-awful headache and hangover, she decided to wake me.

She shook me and cried, "My head hurts! What can I do?"

My not-yet-awake response was "Tinfoil."

"Tinfoil?" she questioned.

"Yes," I said. "Tinfoil. Go wrap your head in tinfoil."

I'm not sure what happened next, but I sure heard about it the next morning. I don't know where my response came from or even if tinfoil would actually help, but it took a few days before both of us could laugh about it.

We made two auto trips to see Hannah's relatives—the Seidenberg clan—in New York that spring. We stayed with Aunt Ida, Uncle Justus, and their son Jeffrey (Jeff) in their four-room flat in the Washington Heights section of New York. Three of her relatives lived across from each other, with windows facing, and within shouting distance: Justus and twin brother Manfred (unmarried); Friedie (married to Selma and had a daughter, Judy); and Hugo (married to Miriam and had a daughter, Denise). Lydia

Friedi, Hugo, Ilsa, Ida, Jeff, Lydia, Manfred, Herta, Justus (All Seidenbergs)

Haack (married to Seymore [Cy] Haack and had no children); and Ilse (married Max Arensberg and had a son, Danny) were the remaining siblings of Herta Seidenberg Forsch, Hannah's mother. Four of these men were butchers in a firm catering to the city's finest restaurants, so we always came home with a care package, a good-sized carton of the best cuts of meat money could buy. They were a kind, loving, and giving family.

Sig had two brothers living in the New York City area: Alfred Forsch, who married Erna and had son Arnold and daughter Marcia; and another brother, Eugene Forsch, living on Long Island (married to Toni and had a daughter Annette who had two sons, Jeff and Steve Pribut. Sig also had a sister, Bertil (or Bertle), who lived with her husband, Louis Guenzburger, on a dairy farm just outside Binghamton, NY. We met them once, stopping on our way back from a Canada trip. They had two unmarried sons—Peter, who spent his life wed to the farm, and Albert, who retired from the U.S. Army as a lieutenant-colonel.

Many of the New York relatives were WWII Holocaust survivors with stories they hesitated to tell and tattooed numbers on their forearms. I can only repeat what I've heard as I've remembered it. Hugo spent the war in a fake chimney in Belgium, coming out onto the roof only at night to have food thrown up to him from a window. His wife, Miriam, worked as a maid for a German

[From a much later time]
Denise, Steve, & Michael Frenkel; Nuru Chinoy, Me, Judy Seidenberg (Back row)
Ilsa Arensberg, Ida Seidenberg, and Rosemary (Front row)

SS officer's family with the employer's full knowledge that she was a Jew. Priorities? Their young daughter, Denise, was hidden in a nunnery school. The Seidenberg twins escaped from one of the lesser camps of Auschwitz and made it to England, where Justus met his wife, Ida. The escape was made possible through heroic sacrifices made by sister Lydia Seidenberg Haack. There are more such stories, but they are too fragmented to repeat here.

Hannah was born April 3, 1937 in Frankfurt am Main, Germany to newlyweds Sigmund Forsch and Herta Seidenberg Forsch. Hannah was named after her maternal grandmother, Johannah Kaufman (married to Josef Seidenberg). Hannah's father, Sig, had the foresight to anticipate the Nazi rise to power when most of the stores he customarily sold sweaters and dry goods to refused to buy from him anymore. Hannah was only four months old when Sig left to make his way in the U.S. Herta brought Hannah to New York six months later. Sig found employment in Bethlehem, PA, and the three moved there for the remainder of the war.

Sig was also instrumental in bringing some of the Seidenbergs to the States. His employer loaned him the tremendous sum of $100,000 as guarantee money to bring Herta's relatives here. He moved the money from bank to bank for each application to make it appear as though there was many times that sum. In the end the money was returned to the employer. The man was a saint. If I only knew his name, I would mention it here. When Sig decided to move to Miami Beach a few years later, the same man staked him to a start for his Sig's Men's Wear business.

Sigmund Forsch

Sig was born October 16, 1903 in Ettenheim In Baden, Germany. He became a U.S. citizen February 9, 1944. Herta was born August 1, 1903 in Brandobeandorf, Taunus, Germany. She became a citizen on May 14, 1945. As a child, Hannah automatically became a citizen under her mother's papers, but that was not enough for her. Because of her being teased by

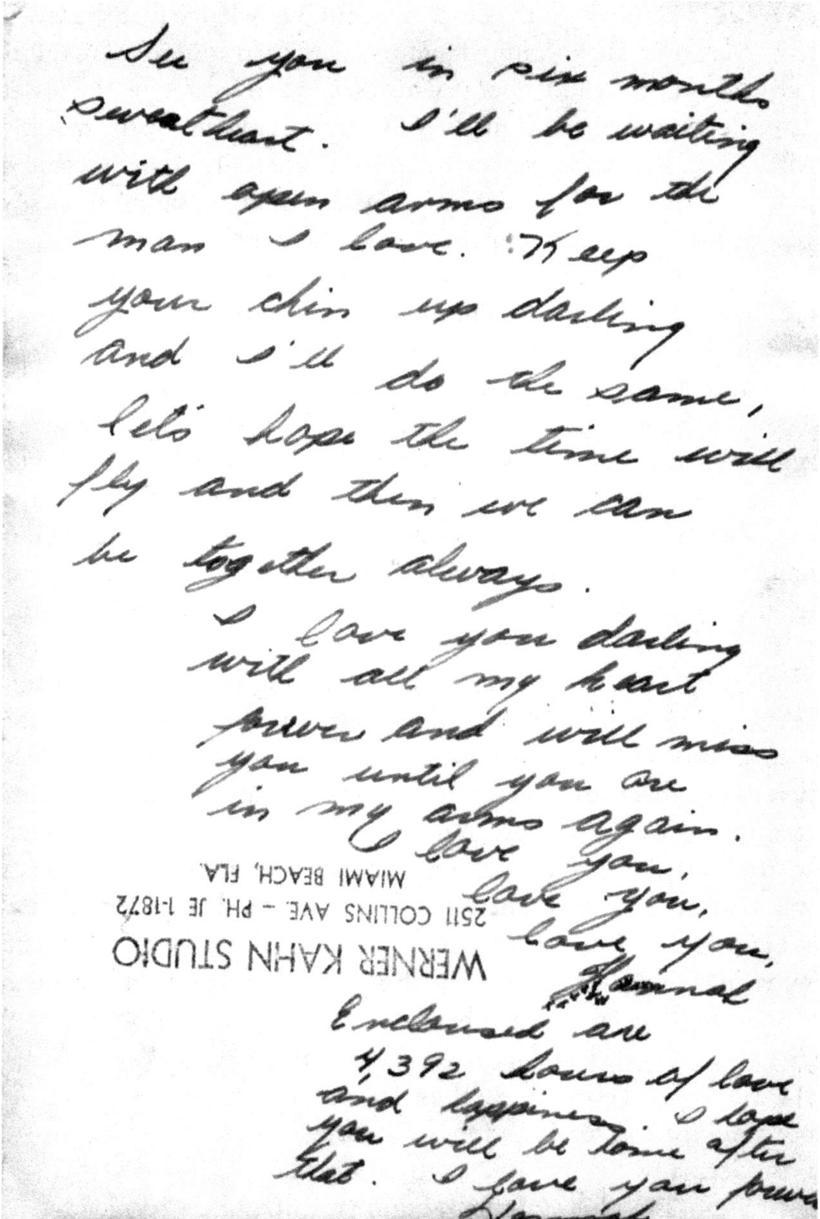

See you in six months sweetheart. I'll be waiting with open arms for the man I love. Keep your chin up darling and I'll do the same, let's hope the time will fly and then we can be together always.

I love you darling with all my heart forever and will miss you until you are in my arms again.

I love you, love you, love you,
Hannah

WERNER KAHN STUDIO
2511 COLLINS AVE – PH. JE 1-1872
MIAMI BEACH, FLA.

Enclosed are 4,392 hours of love and happiness. I hope you will be home after that. I love you forever
Hannah

Hannah's special love message

schoolmates as a Nazi during the war, she wanted her own citizenship papers. They were issued on May 14, 1947.

In July of 1958, the *USS Amphion* was ordered to join the Sixth Fleet (COMSIX) in the Mediterranean Sea. Shortly thereafter, I was ordered to follow the repair ship to COMSIX. I was told to purchase officers' khaki uniforms and given field engineering insignia to sew and pin on. My overseas tour was to last six months before I would be returning. Hannah was furious and decided to close up the apartment and return to Miami Beach and her parents for the duration. I joined her for two weeks of leave before I flew out. We stayed with Sig and Herta, so while the two-weeks time spent was very pleasant, it was still no honeymoon. When I actually left Miami Beach, Hannah gave me a photo of herself with a special love message on the back of it.

Two weeks R&R in Miami Beach for the two of us

I was one of fifty or more passengers who flew to the Mediterranean Sea via Military Air Transport Service (MATS), stopping in Bermuda to drop off a passenger and spending the night. We flew to Lodges in the Azores next to refuel and drop mail. Then we landed somewhere north of the Italian Naval Shipyards at Livorno (known as Leghorn to American sailors), and from there we traveled by jeep through Pisa, where I saw the famous leaning tower, and through Florence (Firenze), where I saw Michelangelo's famous statue of David—outside in the street, of all places.

There were at least two dozen field engineers diagnosing

electronic equipment problems with the U.S. Sixth Fleet at that time. Rarely were they all aboard any single ship at one time. The nature of our work never really changed; however, we were always on the move. Some of the engineers preferred the overseas assignment for a number of reasons. A bunch were dodging U.S. income taxes; several were dodging alimony payments; a few enjoyed a variety of mistresses; and still others enjoyed the sheer adventure of just being there. The smallest number of us were there because we had to be. When in uniform, we were considered equivalent to a lieutenant senior grade (two gold stripes at the cuff). We slept and ate with the officers in the wardroom areas. We boarded and debarked boats with ranking officers first.

Sometimes we changed ships the easy way by walking across a pair of gangways. Of course, there was always a boat ride between ships. Other times we wore a harness and were lifted off the pointer's chair of a gun platform and swept away by a helicopter and taken to a carrier or an airbase. The most complex transfer was called a "highline." A small projectile, with a lightweight line attached, was shot by a special gun across and over the top of the second ship. Heavier and stronger lines, then hawsers were successively pulled across and attached to booms at the side of the ship. Then a string of a dozen sailors on each ship manned those lines, so they were kept taut even though the ships were independently moving up and down while the space between them varied. A small single-

Typical highline transfer between two U.S. Navy ships

seater cupola suspended by pulley from the main hawser traversed the space while being pulled by separate lines and another string of sailors. Having done this twice, I can attest to its scariness; however, the helicopter lift was even more nerve-racking. Sometimes trains and jeeps were also involved in getting us where we had to be.

The *USS Amphion* was anchored in the Livorno harbor, and I was taken out to her via small boat. After a few days in port we put to sea once more and spent several days in various ports from Barcelona, Spain to the French Riviera to the Italian Riviera to Naples. Then we repeated the route servicing ships as we encountered them. One of my first roommates aboard the *Amphion*

was the squadron chaplain (I can't remember his name). A few weeks after I arrived, he decided to take a train ride to Venice (Venizia) for the weekend and asked me to join him. I jumped at the opportunity. The train ride took us through dozens of long tunnels in the Apeninne Mountains. We walked the entire weekend and saw the Grand Canal, the Bridge of Sighs, St. Mark's Square (Cathedral and unique bell tower), the Doge's Palace, and the famous glass factory. It was a fascinating weekend, and I came away with two small oil paintings and a tiny blue vase inlaid with fused gold. I decided that half the world's pigeons live in Venice.

One evening while the ship was in Barcelona, I discovered that one of the local police chiefs had been invited to dinner in the wardroom by the ship's public relations officer. By coincidence, the U.S. Consulate in Barcelona had invited all the off-duty officers aboard to a bash and dance at the consulate. When the table had been cleared, only two us remained in the wardroom—the police chief and myself. He was short, athletic-looking, and a sharp, natty dresser, with prominent bushy eyebrows that moved as he expressed himself. I started the conversation, and as he was anxious to practice his English, we swapped anecdotes and drank coffee until it was time for him to go several hours later. I can't say whether the man's charm or his interesting policing stories influenced me more, but some forty years later I used this man's image as a character in a three-book cozy mystery series. Oh yes, I almost forgot to tell you: the man's name and title was Chief Inspector Garcia Garcia Garcia. He explained that one Garcia, his father, had married into another Garcia family, a common name in Barcelona.

During my first highline transfer, the payload beneath me contained Asian flu vaccine to be further disseminated to the destination ship and many other ships in the fleet. The irony here is that, within the week, I had acquired the Asian flu myself. I had just reported aboard the cruiser *USS Salem* and found an empty stateroom, where I slept for three days and nights straight. No one knew where I was. I finally improved enough to resume my work without contaminating anyone else.

We resumed our Riviera schedule, and it was then that I dreamed up the idea that Hannah could follow me from port to port like some band groupie. A decent hotel wasn't all that expensive. As a noncombatant attached to the military we would both be eligible for medical and Naval Exchange privileges. My pay level certainly would support this. Her parents were strongly against it, as they had narrowly escaped the Holocaust themselves just before WWII, but Hannah liked the idea and persuaded them to let her go.

I met Hannah at the Barcelona airport on a Thursday evening, and we checked into a local hotel for the weekend and the start of a much-deserved Riviera honeymoon. The two of us were out walking on Sunday afternoon when we got the bad news. Hostilities, labeled "the Lebanese Crisis," had broken out, and the fleet was ordered to sea to lie off the coast of Lebanon to take on

American evacuees or even land troops, if necessary. So much for the honeymoon. Many of the married servicemen attached to the Sixth Fleet had wives and homes among the more frequent ports, so I made arrangements with a young lieutenant aboard one of the ships for Hannah to stay with his wife in Naples while we were gone. His wife was glad for the company and Hannah would help with the groceries.

Hannah told me that during her stay with the lieutenant's wife, they had encounters with her voyeur landlord. The man found endless excuses to come to the door to view the two pretty American ladies. On one such excursion, he'd open the door and measure how far it was open. Then he'd reset the door to another position and measure it again. He was an older and very polite man, so they tolerated his shenanigans at least a few times a week.

At the time I was assigned to the *USS Alameda County*, a Landing Ship Tank (LST-32) that had been partially converted to an Advanced Aviation Base, a support ship for a land-based airfield. For the duration of the crisis I was stuck on the ship in Souda Bay, Crete, surrounded by mountains that harbored an airfield on top of a mesa-like peak. Although previous fleets found the bay extremely untenable in the past, the biggest battle fought while I was there was to keep the mountain goats from eating the ship-to-field communications lines.

As soon as the crisis was over, I was offered a unique position. It had been decided that the *Alameda County* was to undergo renovations at the Italian shipyards in Naples to fully complete its conversion to an Advanced Aviation Base with the designation AVB-1. However, it was too costly to send the ship back to the States for this. The Sixth Fleet needed a civilian knowledgeable in communications to manage these renovations. I was Larry-on-the-spot and got the job.

There are twin hills in Naples—the Posillipo and the Vomero. We found a furnished apartment in the Vomero section of Naples, only neither of us spoke enough Italian to negotiate a lease, so with the help of a neighbor who spoke both German and Italian,

Hannah managed to get the job done speaking in German and the neighbor translated while I remained the bystander. The apartment was one of four on the second floor of the building at uno-cento-quaranta-cinque via Francisco Cilea (145 Francisco Cilea Street).

We had to put a *dieci* (10-lire coin) in the slot for the elevator to take us up or down, otherwise the stairs spiraled around the elevator. Our apartment opened into the dining room, a table with eight chairs for socializing with two windows, drapes, and bare walls. Down a short hall, the bathroom and kitchen were on the right while the bedroom was on the left. All of the rooms were large and paved in wall-to-wall marble. There was no central heating, so the routine was to cover yourself with mountains of quilts and blankets during the night and, upon awakening, reach out and light the kerosene heaters next to the bed and run like the dickens for the bathroom, taking one heater with you and leaving the other behind to warm up the bedroom.

With our language limitations, most of our friends were from the military. Many of them found that they loved the hand-carved Italian furniture, so it was always on order to be finished sometime before they left, as the Government would pay the freight. If you asked them what they were using in the meantime, the answer was usually "Early American Orange Crate." A carton of cigarettes, cheaply obtained from the ship's store for 80 cents, was the main unit of barter throughout the city, but the U.S. dollar remained golden with the locals. We purchased a blanket and a number of trinkets this way—shame on us.

Cooking was by bottled gas called P-B gas. One night we had the Chief Damage-Controlman Dan Denver and his wife to dinner, and Hannah had put up a leg of lamb for the meal. We served drinks while we waited. Hannah kept checking the oven to make sure the meat wouldn't burn and then she got suspicious; something was wrong. When I checked, I found the flame out and the oven somewhat less than hot. Conclusion: the P-B gas must be empty. We called the company, and they promised immediate delivery. Meanwhile, our guests were getting smashed. I stuck my head out the kitchen window looking for the delivery and finally I saw a bicycle with two tanks slung over the back wheel. An hour later we served the meal and saved the day. We poured plenty of coffee during dessert to make sure our guests got home all right.

I usually rode to work with Dan, and he sped around in a big old rusty Chrysler like a bulldozer down the super-narrow streets of Naples. People would grab their kids and jump out of the way. On one of our trips to the shipyards, he stopped for a traffic light and his muffler and tailpipe continued down the hill for another half-block. We always got to work on time, but I was never quite sure that all of me arrived at the same time.

The name Societá Esercizio Bacini Napolitano was emblazoned across the shipyard gates, although we did see the name Cantieri del Mediterraneo on several documents. A few leftover Nazi pillboxes (concrete WWII defense armaments) were still on the premises and a few of these even bore spray-on swastikas. Each morning out at the front gate unskilled workers were chosen from the assembled crowd by an under-boss standing on the back of a flatbed truck pointing—"You, you, and you" (in Italian, of course). When anything was to be lifted or toted, cheap day labor from this pool was preferred to ordering in a small crane or forklift.

After the ship was driven into a basin (dry dock) and cradled (supported by wood beams), all the water was evacuated from the basin, leaving the ship high and dry on its cradle. A gangway was fitted between the edge of the basin and the ship so workers had ready access and the ship's crew could live and work aboard. When all of the hull work was completed, the basin was flooded again and the cradle removed. Because the ship's engine was still under repair, the ship had to be towed to another pier by a tug, only the tug ran over its own tow line and severed it in the middle of Naples harbor. It then took three tugs to tame and nudge the wild *Alameda County* into her proper berth.

Most of my direct work had to do with the adding of additional communications equipments with mountings and antennas to support them. We replaced some navigational gear as well. I had to sign off on other ships' repairs and replacements, but relied largely on department heads and leading chiefs for their special expertise. As a bonus, I did learn how to weld, but to this day I have never had to use that skill again.

My efforts at the Italian language were crude, but I soon learned to convey my meanings effectively. Despite this, I was assigned an interpreter, who followed me everywhere. Raphael's English was only slightly better than my Italian, and he had no vocabulary in the technical, so I gave him small make-work assignments to keep him out of my hair. He called me "Senoré Cap-i-tan." This tall, strapping man with a bushy head of gray, almost white, hair wore shabby pinstriped coveralls every day. Then, one day about halfway through the project, he missed a few days of work. Next thing I knew, he showed up in a spiffy new suit complete with white shirt and bow tie, announcing he'd won the national football (soccer) pool, a sizeable sum. He'd come to tell me he was leaving his job. A week later, there he was again in coveralls standing outside my office: "I hada to splita da winnings dodieci (12) ways. Nota so much, hey!" And so I inherited Raphael once more.

Raphael wasn't the only technical problem. All the blueprints were furnished in American (English) units such as pounds and inches, whereas the Italian workers were used to kilograms and centimeters. In addition, there was a difference in industrial standards for pipe sizes and threading and hardware (nuts, bolts, and screws) size and threading. Needless to say, much work was rejected on the bases of not fitting or not mating. They even tried to get some jury-rigged hybrid fittings past me.

Some months earlier a Hong Kong salesman, offering Scottish wools and fine tailoring, gained authorization to come aboard the *Amphion* while in port. Since the price was right, I had him measure me for a new suit. Two weeks later the prepaid suit was delivered by mail. It seemed to fit okay, but a strip of the cloth bolt end was visible at the edge of the pants pockets. Oh well. Weeks later I bent over and a bottom seam parted by several inches. A Naval Exchange tailor replaced the inferior threading and the suit was usable again. In Naples a new problem developed. The trouser zipper jammed permanently. Hannah dropped the suit off at a dry-cleaning and alterations shop a block down the street from us and explained she wanted the trouser zipper replaced. She told me the man examined the zipper, shaking his head all the while, but he agreed to take on the job. Hannah picked up the suit, and when we examined the trousers, we found all traces of a zipper were gone—buttons and buttonholes were in its place. Zippers had replaced buttons on all American men's trousers several decades before. This was intolerable. The suit was given away.

There was no hiding that we were not locals. Whenever Hannah entered the grocery and produce store a few doors down the street from us, the owner's wife would remove or at least turn the pricing flags and labels so they couldn't be seen. Hannah would make her selections and ask for the bill. The woman would total a price more than twice the going rate and hand it to Hannah; whereupon, she would turn the little flags around again and arrive at her own total and pay that amount. The woman didn't seem to object, but over the many months we shopped there, she never stopped trying to overcharge us.

One day, as we returned from shopping on the 121 Bus, the driver had to stop prematurely to allow the big unruly crowd from the soccer stadium to cross the street in front of us. The Naples team had defeated Rome for the first time in several years. The delay seemed endless so we decided to get off and walk the rest of the way home. On the way we passed a school and, in the yard and on the fences surrounding it, were oil paintings. Apparently, it was a fundraiser to benefit the school and the artists as well. A 48- by 24-inch oil painting of Lake Como in northern Italy stopped us cold, and we had to have it. "But it's too large," I complained. "How will we ever get it home?" Seeing he had a sale, the seller removed the thumbtacks surrounding the frame and loosely rolled the canvas into a neat two-foot column. A mailing tube and postage were all that was now needed.

Several weeks later a friend sent an artist friend she knew

over to visit us. We bought a second painting from him. This time it was of a grandfatherly Italian man lighting his pipe while an all-ears child waited to hear his story. The artist was Alexander Fisher, a very pleasant Austrian Jewish man and a Holocaust survivor. We showed him the Lake Como painting and, by coincidence, that artist turned out to be a pupil of his. Both paintings hang proudly in our living room today, alongside works by my own grandfather. Many years later I used the Como painting as a cover design for one of our short-story books after basing one of our stories on it.

We considered being in Italy at this time of our lives a great opportunity to broaden our horizons, so when a bimonthly paycheck arrived, we didn't mind spending a goodly portion on travel. We saved very little during our stay. We explored the ruins of Pompeii; took a tour boat to the artsy Isle of Capri and a smaller boat into the dark caverns of the Blue Grotto; rode trains to Rome, parading about the Roman Forum and dozens of fountains; motored to the Amalfi coast, soaking up the scenery; and absorbed museums everywhere we found them.

Hannah at the Roman Forum

On one of our trips to Rome we took in an American film at a local movie house. It was *Love in the Afternoon.* The comedy was spoken in English and subtitled in Italian, which gave us a few seconds headstart on just when to laugh. The neighboring patrons were bewildered and began to stare. We thought it was pretty funny.

Occasionally, street singers would ply this Vomero neighborhood, and sometimes they would serenade romantically right outside our kitchen window. Our favorite was "Santa Lucia." The winter was one of the coldest in recent years in Italy, so it was strange to see children running around in the snow wearing mere short pants. The neighbors were friendly, but didn't speak much English, so our conversations were pretty much limited to *ciao, buon giorno, buona sera, buona notte, and bene grazie.*

Most of our neighbors shopped specifically for each of their daily meals, as refrigerators were still pretty scarce. We had one, but it was rather small. When we bought local produce, it had to be scrubbed and then soaked for an hour in a sink full of water with a generous helping of bleach thrown in. This was a necessary precaution, because produce in Italy generally was grown with animal (possibly human) fertilizer. The butcher shop hung meat from a hook in front of the store and unrefrigerated cheese came in sixteen-inch rounds, showing green mold where wedges were cut from it.

Toward the end of 1957 my tour with the shipyard was drawing to a close. Hannah returned to the U.S. on the 15th of December, and I returned one month later. On New Year's Eve preceding 1958, I literally watched Naples burn. It seems they have a tradition, at least in the Naples region, of saving all their old furniture and wood trash for this event and setting it afire in the streets. At first it was pretty to see the thousands of small fire lights all over the city of two hills, but then a shroud of dark smoke came down and smothered the city from view. I suppose having so few wooden structures gives them the confidence to even attempt such an event.

The MATS trip back was not uneventful either. We took off from Rome and headed west over the Mediterranean Sea. We weren't airborne long when we heard that a commercial tanker had rammed a Spanish freighter and was spilling oil on the sea. We came across the site, and after viewing it from the air, we were ordered to circle the spot until an American destroyer could take over the rescue mission. Hours passed, and we used up too much fuel to continue our flight much farther, so we landed at a U.S. air base at Nouasseur near Casablanca, Morocco. We soon learned that no flight out was scheduled for nearly a week. At the officers' club bar that evening, I struck up a conversation with a British pilot, a commander, who informed me that he was leaving on a bus for Sidi Slimane, another U.S. air base just outside of Rabat the next morning. He also told me that there were daily MATS flights out of there. My orders to return to the States were official with some level of priority, so I would have no problem getting a flight at any U.S. airbase. I joined him the next day at the base bus terminal, but I grew nervous when I saw that the windows were covered with armor plating. I was informed that Moroccan revolutionaries had tossed grenades onto a bus just one week earlier, killing eight aboard. I got on board anyway and viewed a lengthy piece of the country of Morocco through a narrow slit in the armor plate. Of course, we arrived safely in the Rabat area. Airborne once more, we stopped in Argentia, Newfoundland to refuel, and then on to Washington, DC and Andrews Air Force Base. I flew commercial to Miami, and Hannah met me at the MIAD airport with the car. A week later we drove back to Norfolk to resume our life there.

Chapter 9

Our Precious Children

Arriving in Norfolk at the end of January 1958, we soon found a one-bedroom, second-floor apartment on Painter Street and emptied all our furniture, such as it was, out of storage. We got stuck with a telephone number that was one digit removed from one of the local delicatessens and were inundated with many of their intended calls. We kept telling the callers the correct number, but that wasn't very effective. It slowed to a tiny few when we started accepting orders: "Yes, that's two knockwurst, one pastrami, and one corned beef"—and not delivering. We weren't all that bad—just frustrated, creative, and a wee bit naughty.

Up to this point we had been using a second-hand TV set whose front screen was so transparent that you could see through to the filament glow inside the CRT tube. As an employee of RCA, I was entitled to a half-price discount on unused, year-old appliances. Another 10 percent was offered on electronics in addition, so we picked up a bargain 19-inch TV at the local RCA warehouse. All was fine until I carried the boxed unit from the car up the stairs to our apartment. I didn't feel the pain even then—not until I bent over to wash the mud off our tires the next morning. I heard the cracking sound and I couldn't straighten up again. I sat down in the passenger's seat, and Hannah drove me to the hospital's ER two blocks away. The doctor diagnosed it as a back muscle sprain. It took a prescription and a week on my back to recuperate. I lost a week's work in the process. So where did the savings go? I think this was the beginning of my chronic lifetime back problems.

***USS Tidewater* AD-31, a destroyer-type repair ship**

Returning to work, I was assigned to the *USS Tidewater* AD-31, a destroyer tender—a repair ship specializing in destroyer-class ships. The *Tidewater* was berthed at Pier 21 at the so-called Army Piers in Norfolk. The work was essentially the same, but the parking presented a unique problem. A rail siding at one end of these piers terminated in a grain elevator that dumped its contents into the holds of commercial cargo ships for international destinations. A rail siding at the opposite end of these same piers terminated in a coal elevator that dumped its contents into the holds of other commercial cargo ships bound for who knows where. It was a choice of having a thin coating of white (grain) or black (coal) deposited on your car every day. You had to get up before the roosters in order to get a parking space in the middle lot and, even there, you'd get a touch of gray when the wind blew in circles.

Generally, the engineers chose to lunch at the same places, so we usually had at least a hundred years of very current repair experience sitting at our table. Most of us were very familiar with the suites of equipments aboard U.S. ships in general and destroyers in particular. If any of us came up with a sticky set of symptoms, someone in the group surely had seen them before and had the diagnosis and solution for them. We solved many problems over the phone and even some over the radio. It was a sharp group.

One of my particularly interesting special assignments was

to a relatively new supertanker to change a depth finder's transducer, which protruded from the bottom of the ship's hull. I had a technician with me in an airtight compartment pressurized to equal the external water pressure on the hull. We loosened and removed the bolts to the transducer's mounting plate, removed the old damaged transducer, and set it aside. We were now looking down through the hole to the ocean below. Scary. It was kept from us merely by the compartment's pressure (and a bit of yours truly's faith). We secured the replacement transducer over the hole with new seals and released the compartment pressure. This type of transducer converts electrical energy to sound in water and the reverse as well, so it is able to transmit sound into water and receive return or rebounding sounds too. Yes, we felt the pressure in our ears, but it wasn't bad enough to affect us except for a mild headache afterward. It was an open-mouth solution to equalize the pressure inside and out.

The other interesting thing about this special assignment was that this supertanker was skippered by Captain Edward Beach, who had written the book *Run Silent, Run Deep* when he was a commander and a skipper of submarines in the WWII wartime Pacific. His several books also made it to the movies.

Hannah became pregnant with our first child sometime during the beginning of February right after my return. She was

due the beginning of November. We were delighted with the prospects. We became friendly with an engineer whom I had shared an office with aboard the *Amphion.* Ben Kinnish was going steady with Irene, and we had them to dinner a few times. He married her a few months later. We doubled up several times, taking side trips to Williamsburg, Jamestown, and Monticello—all in Virginia. On one of these trips we learned that Irene was also pregnant and due a few weeks after Hannah.

By now, the months had ripped by, and spring and summer were gone, and it was October. A new replacement candidate for the Sixth Fleet was needed. As the choice rotated among the engineers and fell upon them, four engineers up and quit RCA. The last of these was newlywed Ben, and he wrangled a position with a firm called Chesapeake Instrument Corporation in Shadyside, MD. Now I was one away from being chosen, but as far as I knew, the man in between would go. He'd already accepted the assignment. Safe for now, but at that point, I saw the handwriting on the wall—it wouldn't be long before I'd have to go again. Oops! Not with a new baby on the way. The following weekend I drove to Shadyside and interviewed with Ben's new boss. I got the job and gave RCA three weeks notice. I drove back the next week and put a deposit down on a second-floor apartment at Ten Oaks Manor on Burnside Street in the Eastport section of Annapolis, MD. Ben and Irene were living in the next building over.

While still on the job with RCA, I came home from work on the 3rd of November 1958 and found a note on the door. "The contractions are so close now, I'm walking over to the hospital delivery room (two blocks away at the end of Painter Street). Grab a bite. Don't hurry, you've plenty of time yet."

No hurry? Eat? No way! I ran all the way to the hospital. As I got there, the doctor was giving her a shot to speed things along, and I was banished to the fathers' waiting room. Jacqueline (Jackie) Arlene Mild was born a few hours later. I was the father of a beautiful baby girl. Hannah's mother came and spent the first two weeks helping out the new mother. Five weeks later we moved to Annapolis, and I started work one day later at Chesapeake Instrument Corp. The baby was named for her grandfather John Mild and her great-grandfather Adolf Forsch. Rabbi Rosenblatt at the Orthodox synagogue (Kneseth Israel) made the naming official. To this day I fail to see the connection to Deena Rena, her Hebrew name.

I carpooled to work with Ben and two other people, Ralph Clooley and George (?). Ralph and his wife, Betty, had the three of us and our wives over for a party six weeks later in December. Ron Darby, another co-worker, and his wife, Millie, were also there. Jackie had her bottle and slept through the evening, but nervous Hannah was in the bedroom every few minutes checking up on her. We made some fast friends that night. Almost sixty years later we are still friends with the Darby family. We became a lot closer to the Kinnishes too, but Ralph died a year later, only a month after passing an Air Force reserve physical. Ralph and Betty had two children of their own and two foster kids they'd raised since infancy. Betty remarried and went to live in New York State, but the state of Maryland would not let her keep the foster kids.

Our closest friends in Annapolis lived across the hall from us. Don and Jo Gormley became our friends for life. Don was a chemical engineer working at the Naval Engineering Experimental Station (NEES) across the Severn River from the U.S. Naval

The Milds and Gormleys some years later

Academy. Jo was an RN. They had a daughter Nan (Nanette) who was a few months older than Jackie. Soon after we met, they built a house in the Eastport section of Annapolis, but that distance never affected our friendships. It was a rare day that the two ladies didn't come in contact—either in person or by phone. Through the years every member of both families became firmly enmeshed, and it's mostly true even today as I write this, although Don and Jo have passed away in recent years.

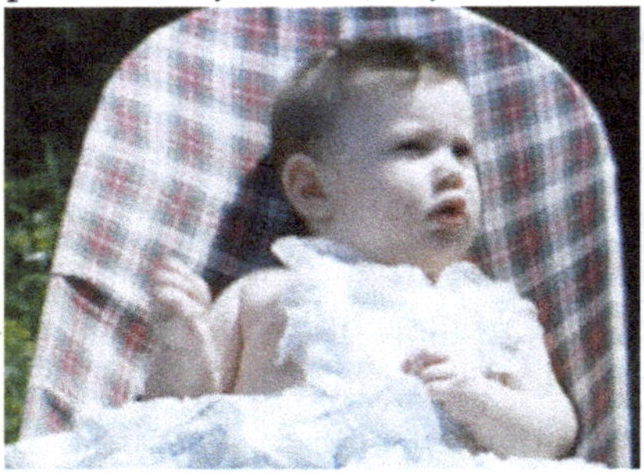

Jackie in old-style car seat

Rub-a-dub-dub Jackie in a tub

I plunged into all kinds of new work, winding up in a circuit design lab making amplifiers, filters, and electronic switches. We actually built these things in the lab, first from the calculated formulas and then on to optimizing and determining component tolerances. We tack-soldered the components together end-to-end until the circuits looked like some monstrous spider. Packaging came later.

The company manufactured underwater transducers used in sonar applications, such as for submarine hunting, depth sounding, and general sound analyses. I took a company-offered course in oceanography taught by a Naval Academy professor.

We had about thirty women in our assembly line, manufacturing what we called "Lollypops." It was a lollypop look-alike, a round ceramic disk sandwich mostly covered in rubber and dangled from a length of coaxial cable. It was a part of a sonobuoy dropped into the water by helicopters to listen for submarines. Its manufacture required the use of many chemicals—some adhesives and some cleaning agents. When 50 percent of the women on the assembly line began to experience multiple menstrual periods in a single month, they became furious. Toluene, a cleaning agent, became the leading suspect. Open jars of it were then banned, and only special dispensers were permitted afterwards. Success! The ladies were relieved of their extra burdens.

One of the ways to determine the quality and effectiveness of transducers was to measure the frequencies and amplitudes of their resonances, their hot performance spots. A professor of electronics from the Naval Academy came up with an idea to make these critical measurements with an instrument he called a Vector Impedance Locus Plotter (VILP). I was assigned to this project and implemented it exactly as he envisioned it. The method worked beautifully, although it did proliferate some minor internal component resonances (fakes) along with the real ones belonging to the measurement sample. We had the drafting department package it. Because of the number of vacuum tubes involved, it was big, klutzy, requiring a great deal of cooling, and the fans (attached to a vibrating rear panel) were extremely noisy. Instead of redesigning the device in a smaller, more rigid package using low-power transistors, management decided to market the device as it was. I took the device to the Harvard underwater systems lab and had to disconnect the fans while I lectured so they could hear me. I took the device to a convention of the American Acoustical Society with the same problem. There were many other potential customers, but with its high price tag, I doubt whether we ever sold even a dozen of these devices in the end.

I worked on another project with a mechanical engineer designing decoys. The first was a small boat that presented the profile of a much larger craft. Supposedly, it would sit idle in the water until an enemy radar activated its engine and controls. Then it sped off and maneuvered in a typical ship's wartime, zigzag, evasive steaming pattern. During the testing phase, we took the decoy out onto the Chesapeake Bay and put her through her trials. We used buoys to mark the safe outer boundaries of the decoy's path. Every so often there were illegal rubberneckers who got too close and then found themselves being chased by a driverless boat. We had a radio-controlled engine-kill button for that purpose, but it did mess up a lot of good testing.

We did meet a number of bay watermen out for their daily catch of oysters, clams, and/or blue crabs. These were real drinking men. The amount of alcohol consumed in the name of keeping warm was phenomenal—at least two fifths per man per day. I have to admit it was a hard life for them. Most were friendly, usually waving when passing and generally eager to strike up a conversation.

The second decoy was a battery-operated device that could be ejected through the garbage disposal unit of a submarine and make sounds like a sub, allowing the launcher, a real sub, to sneak off while running silent. I had to listen carefully to an awful lot of tapes to learn what real subs sounded like. I designed electronic circuitry to sound like propulsion, cavitation (the noise a maritime screw makes when it strikes water), galley sounds, and motor hums. Then I added a varying mix of white and gray noise generators. The result was pretty close to what the tapes sounded like to me.

Ben and Irene bought a lot and built a home in Southdown Shores, a new community about a third of the way from Annapolis to Shadyside, where we worked. Hannah and I talked over the possibility of building there as well. In the meanwhile, we had attached ourselves to Congregation Kneseth Israel (KI), the synagogue in Annapolis, and we had become active in many of the Jewish organizations, so we didn't want to get ourselves too far from these things, yet shortening the daily ride to work did sound attractive. So we eventually bought a double lot, comprising a triangle, and consulted a builder. Soon after we contracted to build, Hannah became pregnant for the second time.

The house plan was for a pre-cut, three-bedroom, single-story rancher finished in mahogany-stained cedar shake and re-used colonial brick. We set the house to face the front corner of the triangle and put in a semicircular drive stretching between the two adjacent streets, Wendlyn Way and Stepney Street. The builder preserved most of the trees on the lot. My mother contributed to the landscaping. Aunt Lydia loaned us part of the down payment. When we tried to pay her back, she insisted that the money go toward buying an air conditioner.

Some years later we purchased two additional lots, so that we now owned half of the larger, triangular-shaped block. When I cleared the new addition (i.e., cut down the wild brush and burned the waste), I contracted poison ivy all over my body from the smoke fumes. The lot looked great. Me? Well, that was another story, but a rash lesson well learned.

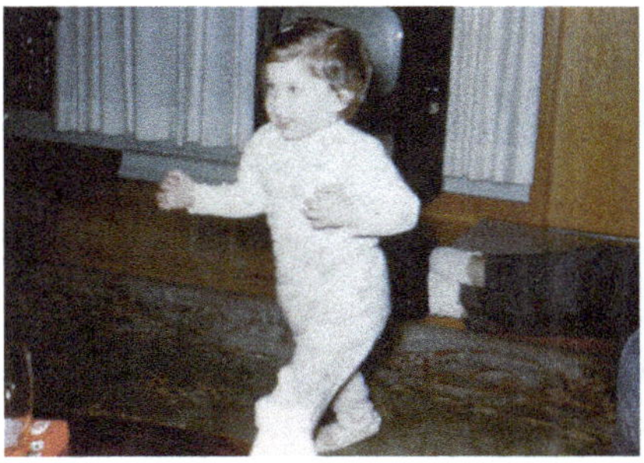

Jackie's first steps at the Kinnish home

Jackie decides to wash her trike

We moved into the house, and on her first visit, my mother's first reaction to our living in a wooded area was: "Why did you have to move into such a wilderness?" There was a rather large poplar tree with two major trunks coming out of the ground near our back door. It was a nice shade tree, so Hannah often put Jackie in her playpen under it for her nap in the nice weather. One day while Jo Gormley was visiting, she put Nan down to sleep next to Jackie. Sharing coffee and gossip in the kitchen, the two mothers heard a loud, sharp, cracking noise, followed by a thunderous thud outside. The two ladies rushed through the door to discover that the poplar now had only one trunk. The other trunk, and at least sixty feet of tree, had split and fallen away from the playpen and its precious contents. It had landed across the street, partially suspended from the power and telephone lines. The two infants were unharmed and sleeping as though nothing had happened. The mothers counted their blessings, and Hannah called the power company, who came and cleared the lines. They also cut the trunk into movable pieces and I finished the job, cutting, splitting, and stacking the pieces into firewood. We gave the firewood to the neighbors.

Some years later we had another tree come down at the edge of our property. It severed a neighbor's telephone line and came to rest on their electric power lines. Edith Waller was on her phone when it happened and couldn't figure out what had happened until we knocked on her back door and told her. The tree slid along the siding, but didn't even scratch the house.

One of Jackie's earliest babysitters was a teenager named John Aubuchon, who grew up to be a radio news anchor and then a White House news correspondent. His parents, Navy Commander Bob and Marion Aubuchon, lived across the street, and we were friends. At one point Bob announced that he had been reassigned to the Chinese equivalent of our Bureau of Ships for two years. He had a homemade 14-foot fiberglass boat and outboard motor that needed looking after while he and the whole family were in Taiwan. I agreed to take care of it, not realizing what a burden it would be. We wound up using it only sparingly—mostly for crabbing, but every time it rained, I had to go down to the dock and bail it out. I bought a frame and cover for it, but it was no match for windstorms. I was glad when they returned for more than one reason.

The community of Southdown Shores had two docks running out into Beard's Creek, which emptied into the South River and eventually into the Chesapeake Bay. The wide part of the creek was popularly called Southdown Lake. Community boat owners moored their craft along the outside perimeter of the two docks. Wooden frames covered in quarter-inch hardware cloth (metal wire squares) lined and connected these docks to afford a jellyfish-free area for the kids to swim in. The kids could then compete in swimming events with other waterfront communities. Hardly anyone seemed to mind the murky waters or muddy bottom until it came time to maintain the framed screens. The kids found them gross.

On April 4, 1961 beautiful Myrna Lynn Mild arrived in our lives. There was no note this time, and I had the pleasure of driving Hannah to the hospital. We parked Jackie with the Gormleys for the next few days. I even took the week off from work. Myrna, a wonderful baby in her own right, was named after Hannah's paternal grandmother, Minna, and my maternal great-grandmother, Lena. In Hebrew it was Minna Leah. Again, we had Rabbi Rosenblatt and Cantor (affectionately "Rev") Hammer make the naming official in the synagogue. Herta arrived to spend time with the new mother and to help out in general. Instead, she took over completely and bossed me around no end. The worst part was that I was good enough to hang diapers (outside in the "fresh" air at her insistence), but she wouldn't let me hold my own child and bond with her. Well, needless to say, Herta and I came to words, and there were things neither of us should have said. We kept the row from Hannah and the baby, but it took a few years to smooth "them ruffled mother-in-law feathers."

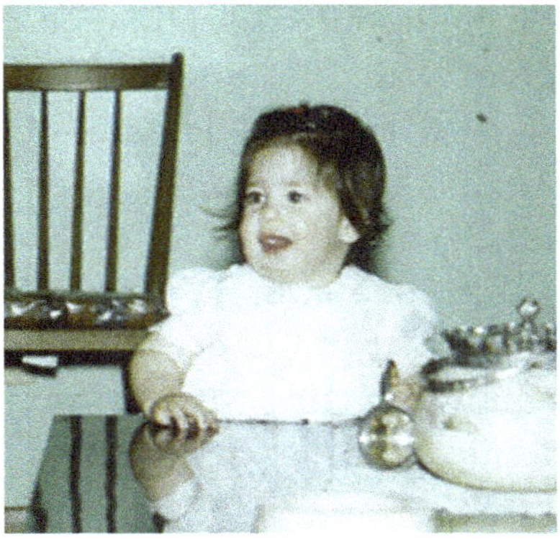

Myrna at little table

Myrna's first birthday party

We always had a supply of chicken necks in the freezer for bait in catching crabs off the piers. Fastening a cord to the neck and throwing it overboard, one could tease a crab into a metal net on the end of a pole. A few hours of this sport would lead to a pot full of crabs which Hannah steamed on the kitchen stove. There was a precise, efficient, and yet laborious method of extracting or picking the crabmeat from the rest of the creature. When the kids were small we did all of the picking for them, so that there was little left for ourselves. Many times we would go and purchase a store-bought bushel of the critters, spread newspapers on the picnic table, and dump the load on top of it. In any case, corn and burgers would supplement the meager fare.

Snow covering Southdown Shores—our house seen through the trees

One wintry week in January, with snow still on the ground, Bob Aubuchon (president of the community association) and Hannah (treasurer of the association) walked throughout the neighborhood selling memberships and shares in building a new swimming pool on donated land. The Southdown Shores Country Club opened its gates on the very next Fourth of July. Both of our children took to the water and became good swimmers. In fact, Jackie held a countywide record for the ten-and-under butterfly stroke one year until year-round swimmer Brenda with her yard-wide shoulders, moved to the community. Both Jackie and Myrna

Three matching swimmers on our front stoop: Myrna, Cathy Mild, and Jackie

took the Red Cross lifesaving courses and became lifeguards when they were in their late teens.

Two tennis courts were added to the country club the next year, and both Hannah and myself took up the sport once more. Hannah managed to capture the ladies competition while I stayed in the top three men. I also took advantage of my company's purchased time at a local racquet club. When that club went under, I joined the Big Vanilla racquet club with five work colleagues and played lots of doubles. As that group shrunk, we took on other club members. I played there for almost a dozen years. My partner and I won the summer league doubles two years running. On all-you-can nights I'd play from 7:00 p.m. until midnight. Two hours later I'd sit up in bed with cramps in every part of my body. I loved that game and miss it *sorely* today.

Some years later Hannah and I agreed that having a fireplace in the basement would be nice. We had just solved a chronic basement leakage problem with a tunnel and sump system, and I had paneled the main room and put in a drop ceiling, overhead lighting, and electrical outlets. A wall separated the main room from my workshop and a laundry room. We were already spending a lot of time in the basement watching TV. We contracted a neighbor, Joe Gomoljack, to put in the fireplace. He was a carpenter, builder, and brick mason. When he picked up a sledgehammer and went at a foundation wall, my heart was in my throat. At any rate, Joe did an excellent job, and we got a lot of use out of it. Many is the day we watched a football game with a nice warm log fire going.

When both children had started school, Hannah began to look around for things to do. Hadassah was looking for a new and younger president, and she accepted and was confirmed by popular vote. She came home that evening to announce that she had been elected president of Hadassah. The first thing that came out of Jackie's mouth was: "Mommy, are we going to live in the White House now?" Hannah found her perfect job in the strip mall just outside our community. She began as a receptionist to Dr. Bill

Barnett, an optometrist, and when he saw her ability with numbers and organization, he quickly promoted her to office manager. She was soon doing the bookkeeping for both of his offices,. When he became treasurer of the Maryland State Optometric Association, she did the books there too—acting as a virtual treasurer. Hannah kept finding failure-to-post-payment errors (by other employees) in his books, and would offer him the opportunity to pay her in errors found instead of her salary. Sadly, he refused. Years after that she even went to school for a semester to become a certified optometric assistant. In fact, she worked for him until she passed away—until then, a long and pleasant association.

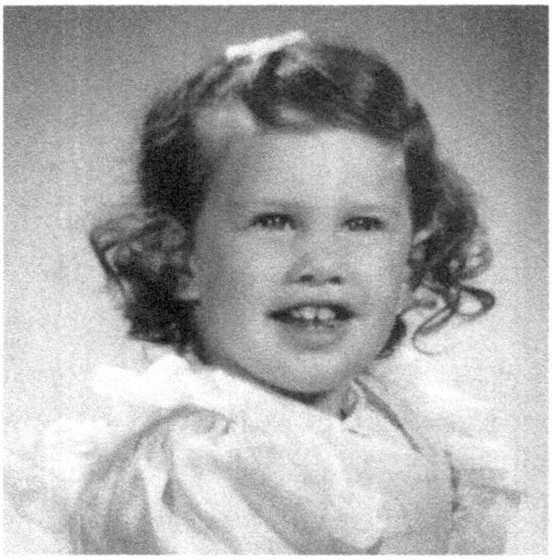

Jackie

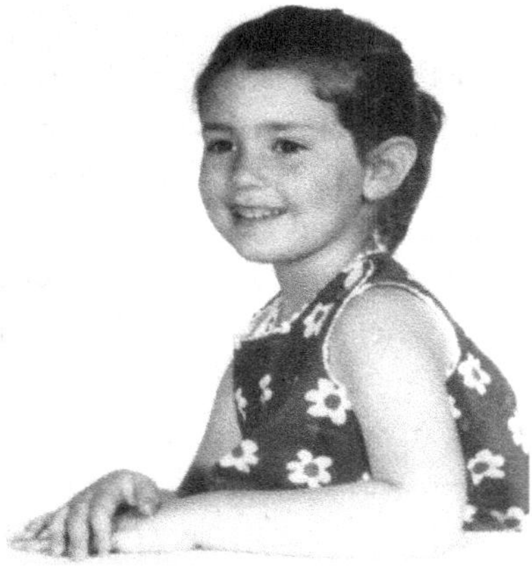

Myrna

With Hannah working most weekdays, she continued to use a cleaning lady twice a month to help with laundry, ironing, general housework, and keeping an eye on the kids once in a while. Her name was Gloria. One day when Hannah walked into the house, preschool Myrna complained that Gloria wouldn't let her have any of the neat green Kool-Aid that she was drinking. Not stocking anything the likes of Kool-Aid in the house, Hannah began to suspect Gloria was into our crème de menthe. She marked the level of that bottle and others in our liquor supply as well. Sure enough, the levels changed after Gloria's next workday. After that, we boxed up our entire supply and stashed it at a neighbor's house when she was due to come. Strangely, her attendance dwindled after that to the point where she was no longer reliable, so we severed the arrangement.

We drove to New York every two or three months and every year to Miami Beach over the winter holidays. During the late spring and summer of 1962, the financial outlook for Chesapeake Instrument was in decline. Contracts were being terminated, and it looked as though the firm was up for sale. I spoke with a neighbor, who was also the personnel director for a local firm called Electro-International. He had me come in for an interview, and I got the job. The down side of the job was that I had to commute every day to Washington to the Navy's Bureau of Ships on the main mall. The increase in pay seemed to make it worthwhile. My past naval equipment experience made me a valuable asset to the Bureau's Central Training Division (CTD). I was a civilian contract employee of the Navy once more. Our particular office was full of contract engineers from at least four different DC Beltway firms. One of the engineers had been a radioman/gunner on one of the few planes making it aloft during the December 7th Pearl Harbor attack. A single civil servant supervised our group. He kept trying to recruit me as a civil service employee. I would have been willing except that the pay grade offered wasn't up to snuff.

The Bureau awarded contracts to technical firms for new equipments, designs, and services. Our task in the CTD was to determine the type, cost, and scheduling of training needed to operate and maintain these state-of-the-art equipments months and even years before they were ever delivered to the Navy. We also contracted for the training, training materials, and aids. This meant we had to be in contact with the Bureau's equipment engineers and the design engineers at many of the manufacturing firms providing those equipments. In addition, we had to review and approve all aspects of training, from generating procurement specifications all the way to implementing delivery of training materials and monitoring classroom lectures.

What I liked most about the job was that I was learning all about the latest technologies—working with Operations Command and Control Centers (computers and digital science), submarines (antennas and communications techniques), and correspondence (the politics of smoothing the mail through a hierarchy of bosses). Initially, I found the correspondence part the hardest. The daily mails brought us all kinds of inquiries. Our responses carried the authority of the Bureau's chief and the signature of one of the assistant chiefs of the various departments, so each outgoing letter had to make it up the many levels of command before it was signed and sent, all of this within five business days of the inquiry's receipt. If any level of command disagreed with any part of my response, it bounced back to me for change. The response had to please every level, even those with diverse opinions. The process was time-consuming and sometimes difficult, but I soon learned the prickly points of those above me and got the mail out on time.

Parking in the district proved to be quite a problem, so I managed to find and join a carpool. One member, a captain who later made admiral, was one of the assistant bureau chiefs, whom the driver of the day had to wake (by phone) and pick up. It was worth it, because he had a reserved parking space inside the Bureau compound. Admiral James Stillwell was also noted for leading the investigation into the super-deep implosion of the *USS Thresher* (SSN-593). Two other members were engineers in the submarine propulsion section of the Bureau. A fourth was a Navy chief petty officer (CPO), who worked at the Bureau of Medicine (BUMED) a few blocks down from our buildings. I was the fifth member of the pool.

Toward the beginning of November in 1963, I began having my usual cronic sinusitis. It got so bad that I resorted to a popular brand of antihistamine four times a day just like the package said. I wasn't familiar with this kind of lozenge, so I continued for several days, until noting that I was getting periodic headaches. I stopped the antihistamine lozenge, but the headaches continued cycling in and out anyway. These headaches built up in intensity and lasted nineteen hours and then subsided for the next five hours. The nasty cycling went on for many days until I consulted a doctor who decided to hospitalize me so I could be tested for the cause.

Sure enough, they found that I had an uncommon allergy to antihistamines rather than the usual allergy to histamines. It took a number of additional days for my body to metabolize the antihistamines in my system, and this required an extended stay in the hospital.

On the twenty-second of November 1963, President John F. Kennedy was shot, so I spent a lot of time watching television from my hospital bed. As it turned out, I became a witness to the live televising of Jack Ruby killing Lee Harvey Oswald, Kennedy's killer. The camera followed Oswald as he was being taken into custody. Being live TV and totally unexpected, I heard Ruby's curse words, the shots, and the surrounding turmoil on the unedited sound track. Later reruns of the scene used commentator voice-overs instead.

In January of 1964 the Navy's Surgeon General of the U.S. released its report warning the public of the harms of smoking. Our carpool CPO had prior knowledge of its contents, and we were made privy to much of it while carpooling during the preceding month of December. The media had also gotten hold of some of its contents. It was so scary that I pledged to give up a bad habit that had plagued me since early high school. On New Year's Eve 1965 I was one of ten people at a party table. Nine took the pledge to give up smoking, and curiously, the one abstaining person was an MD. Go figure.

I was already in bed that first wee morning of January when Hannah came in with a plastic bag filled with my two favorite pipes, a half-carton of cigarettes, and a slue of cigars. "Are you sure?" she said. I responded in the affirmative and listened while hearing the cabinet door under the sink open and slam shut. Gone, I thought, but I was wrong. A year later she presented me with the same bag, saying: "I guess I can throw these things out now." She had kept them, thinking I might change my mind, as I had done so many times before. I didn't change my mind then and I've kept my pledge for well over fifty years now and have no intention of ever smoking again. Hopefully, no damage had been done.

Our semicircular driveway was always lined with flowers in the warmer months. The first to come up were the yellow daffodils. Hannah had this running competition with Fred Boetcher across the street as to whose would bloom first. One year Hannah purchased a bunch of fake ones and stabbed them in the ground in the plot along the drive just before the actual bulbs did their thing. She watched from behind the living room curtain when Fred came home. He saw the full blooms immediately and started to scratch his head when he saw nothing in his own flower bed. He crossed the street, touched the sham flowers, and then looked up at our house smiling; whereupon Hannah opened the door and waved to him. They both laughed about it for years to come. It was thanks to Fred that he wrapped her arm in a magazine and drove her to the hospital when Hannah broke her arm some years afterward. She had received a call from work and, in her hurried exit from the house, had tripped on a mat and fallen off the front stoop.

Our neighbors had a plethora of multicolored Chesapeake Bay retrievers, but none roamed the neighborhood freely. When Joe Gomoljack's dog got loose late one Friday afternoon and plowed through another neighbor's flower bed, that neighbor called animal control and had the retriever locked up. When Joe came home from work that evening, he discovered the dog gone and a note from the irate neighbor. Joe's trip to the canine hoosegow proved useless, because it was weekend policy not to release animals after four on Friday. Joe was even ready to pay the fine on the spot, but policy prohibited it. Joe's next door neighbor was Sergeant Ed Lyons of the county police. The two of them had planned to go hunting together with the retriever over the weekend. As soon as Ed heard the story, he said: "I arrest dangerous criminals, and they're out on bail before I can return to my police routine—and one harmless, mischievous dog has to be caged up for the whole weekend?" The next morning Ed obtained a court order, freed the dog, and drove it home in the back seat of his police cruiser.

It was cold, windy, and snowing outside one March afternoon, so Hannah and I decided to paint the living room. The two of us had talked about it for some time. We'd already purchased the paint and ancillary supplies, and we weren't about to go anywhere in that kind of weather. The job took longer than expected—afternoon had stretcched into evening, and we turned the room lights on. Outside, the temperature had gotten much colder, and the heavy snow, accumulated on the power lines, turned to an even heavier ice, a burden those lines couldn't take. Suddenly, in the middle of a long wall with my roller, the lights went out, leaving us with a dilemma. Stopping would have left a streak in the wall's surface. I finished the final wall with Hannah aiming two flashlights at the wall.

Snow at the Edgewater house

Our immediate neighbors around the triangle were a very social group. Once in a while they'd block off two side streets of the triangular block with benches and sawhorses and hold a block party. One neighbor, a Navy weatherman who was also a pilot, would fly to Maine in order to earn his flight pay. He'd return with a crate of live lobsters. Added to that were local raw oysters, clams, and crabs bought by the bushel basket; and silver queen corn from the Lyons' tobacco field directly behind their house. The corn, lobsters, and crabs were steamed in pots over the stove. The clams and oysters were steamed under a beer-soaked blanket on hot rocks that had been in a fire for hours. We—a pilot, a builder, a policeman, an engineer, two teachers, a Navy commander, and their whole families—moved their picnic tables from their yards to the middle of

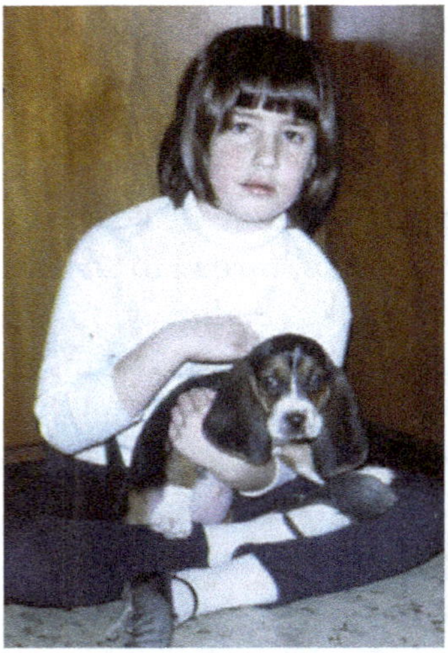

the blocked-off street.

In the beginning, our pets were limited to goldfish in little plastic bags brought home from school carnival fundraisers. On a visit in Miami Beach, Uncle Cy Haack bought us a whole aquarium outfit to house the tiny critters. He also bought tropical fish, so we had to give away the original incompatible goldfish. However, the fish didn't last that long. Serious pets came later and, oddly enough, brother George was always responsible. On one trip to visit George and Mitzie, he took his Cathy and our girls to buy a hamster for Cathy, only my girls came away with their very own hamster in a cage. Later the girls named it, of all things, "Hammy." All the way home from western Pennsylvania, Hammy lay still on her back in the cage with her four tiny feet in the air. We weren't even sure she was alive until we hit home. Hammy turned out to be a vicious biter, so Hannah got stuck with the care and feeding of this pet rather than the kids. To clean the cage Hannah put it in the bathtub and lured Hammy out with a carrot stick. A carrot stick in the clean cage lured the creature back into the cage. She lasted a little over two years and then we fitted her into a deluxe cigar box coffin. The girls said a few words and buried the box in the woods at the side of the house.

When the girls were seven and nine, brother George announced to us that their tricolored French basset hound by the name of Raleigh had happily been given out to stud for the pick of the litter. Would we be interested in that pick, Raleigh's puppy? Hannah knew that it would be a lot more work for her, but the kids were so ecstatic we could hardly refuse. On Valentine's Day we received a phone call from the air freight office of one of the airlines—they had a package for us. When Hannah and I got to the air freight dock, our gorgeous black, tan, and white puppy was out of her shipping cage; three attendants were playing with her. When we got her home, it was love at first sight—all four of us.

We named her Penny for her hound's scent, though her rightful name would be Penelope "Pit-stop" Mild. That first night in the kitchen, we had her chasing after a tennis ball. She tried to run after it, but kept on stepping on and tripping over her beautiful longish ears and tumbling head over heels, crashing into the kitchen cabinets—not once, but dozens of times, to all our amusement. She had many talents, including the ability to pick her own tennis ball from a whole bagful dumped out onto the floor. She played soccer goalie in the doorway like a pro, using only her nose to stop and return the ball. Penny could sit up vertically straight on her rear with her hind and forelegs out in front and beg.

She loved the outdoors, but we couldn't let her run free, because she'd take off after the first scent she picked up and be gone for who knows how long. She would eventually return, but we'd always wonder what she'd do if she ever caught up with her prey. We knew that dead squirrels repulsed her, but live ones were fair game. About 20 feet of rope tied to an anchored stake gave her a huge circle to run in. She rarely tested the perimeter except when the two cats from across the street decided to torment her. They'd walk just outside the circle, knowing Penny couldn't reach them. It drove Penny nuts and put a strain on her long leash.

I had made a cylindrical hanging lamp and two matching benches to line the floor-to-ceiling living room corner windows. If Myrna saw me coming home from work, she'd cry out to Penny in her most excitable voice: "Daddy's home! Daddy's home!" Penny would then leap up onto the front bench and claw away at the window and horizontal frame until I came in. When that piece of wood shrunk by a third (I had refinished it a number of times), I had to scold Myrna to refrain from getting Penny so excited. To tell the truth, I actually missed the exuberant homecoming greeting after that.

We had Penny for about five years and, as far as we knew, she was strong and healthy. But Myrna came home one day and found Penny sprawled out next to her bed and could not awaken her. She called her mother at work crying. Hannah came home and took Penny to the vet. The vet pronounced her dead, but without an autopsy, he couldn't give us a cause. We decided that an autopsy wouldn't change the fact that Penny was gone.

Not that it was a pet, but a beautiful male, red-headed, woodpecker took a fancy to our rancher house. Actually, it wasn't the entire house, but a small spot in the high northwest corner of it. It wasn't so much the rat-a-tat noise of it, but the damage to the house—he'd already gotten through the cedar shake to bare wood. I patched it several times with wood putty and painted over the spot, hoping that would do the job. Only when I included a product called Bird-OFF in both the putty and paint was I effective. But that wasn't the end of the fray. Woody got his revenge by moving to the rain gutter just outside and above our bedroom window. He pecked at the insects living there, and his beak made a terrible noise against the metal beneath them like a jackhammer in the streets. To make matters worse, Woody usually went to work much earlier than we woke up, especially on weekends. He forced me to hose out the gutters on a regular basis. Fortunately, Woody moved on to someone else's home or maybe a nice juicy tree loaded with goodies.

We tried growing vegetables in the spacious backyard. Our record year followed a trip to Amish country. We made a number of trips to the Reading, PA clothing outlets and an awesome, two-some, romantic trip to the Pocono resort area. Such trips took us through Amish country, and on at least one occasion, we tarried long enough to explore their culture and purchase packs of their hearty seeds. That year we had an all-round bumper crop. All of the other serious attempts at vegetable farming resulted in a fair crop share—just in time for market veggies to be at a lower price than ours. So what about our hard work or the outlay for sprays, fertilizer, and pole supports? Why bother? Besides, our neighbors the Lyons grew vegetables in the fields among their tobacco plants, and they often left some at our back door.

Meanwhile, the girls were growing like weeds and their school grades were fine until Myrna bumped into the more sophisticated math, mainly word problems. To make matters worse, she neglected to tell us until report card time. I worked with her and tried to teach her a few of the tricks I used to handle problem reading. The girls had tried violin lessons in elementary school only to prove they were not musicians. In high school Jackie turned out to be the big reader and Myrna read only when she had to. Today the reverse is true. Myrna has read all our books. Jackie hasn't the time for reading novels with all her other activities.

Penny taking the girls for a ride

Both girls have an affinity for the world of art. They were always technically superior for their ages and very appreciative of what they saw. We took them to the free museums in Washington, DC on many Sundays during the clear winter months. Perhaps we influenced them to a degree in that they both chose careers related to art.

Soon it was time for Hebrew lessons and Bas Mitzvah preparation. Twice a week Hannah shuttled the kids to Reverend Hammer's Hebrew class at Kneseth Israel synagogue. Rev was strict, lovable, and effective. The girls were reluctant only because it cut into their free time. The boys in their class usually had individual Bar Mitzvahs, but the girls were Bas (sometimes Bat) Mitzvahed in class-sized groups. On inclement weather days, practice took place in the form of a telephone recital.

Most of their teenage classmates lived in the Admiral Heights section of town, a virtual ghetto of Jewish kids with pre-cemented cliques and close interrelationships. Our kids were among the outsiders and had trouble fitting in. Unfortunately, one child's unkindness feels like downright cruelty to another at that age. I know this from my own lonely youth. Jackie's Bas Mitzvah came first, and during the last months of her preparation, she managed to trip over a rope in gym class and break her leg. She had a fiberglass cast and even swam with it in the pool, causing many ooohs among the pool-siders. By the week before the big event, Jackie had accumulated such a menagerie of multicolored artwork, trivia, pink flowers, and signatures all over her cast to the point that the other Bas Mitzvah parents proclaimed the cast to be inappropriate. The snooty remarks had been unnecessary, because the cast came off two days beforehand. Myrna's Bas Mitzvah came off with a lot less hullabaloo. Both affairs were wonderful, and we were extremely proud of their accomplishments.

Next came driver's licenses. Jackie got hers first and, with her newfound independence, joined B'nai B'rith Girls (BBG) and Young Judea, a strongly Zionist organization promoting *aliah* (a move to live in Israel). She attended weekly meetings and even went two summers to Camp Tel Yehudah, a Young Judea camp in (upstate) Barryville, NY.

I found it rather unusual that both girls formed close connections with many of their junior and senior high school teachers, even to the point of calling them by their first names. I would never ever have called any of my teachers by their first name even if I knew them. It just wasn't done in my time.

During the viewing of a Holocaust film in one of Jackie's World History classes, two of the boys jeered the prisoners in stripes, saying, "The Jews got what they deserved. They killed Jesus." Then the teacher asked the question, "Who really killed Jesus?" Jackie stood up in the class and gave the historically correct and responsible answer: "The Romans killed Jesus." When she finished the details, the majority of her class cheered her on. The teacher offered an apology and lit into the two boys before going on with her class work. Jackie boarded the school bus that evening to a round of applause and a few pats on the back and "Way-to-go"s. I was so proud of her when she came home and told us about this experience. I attribute much of her enthusiastic response to her Camp Tel Yehuda preparation.

Jackie played softball in the neighborhood league, and both girls played high school tennis doubles. We followed them around from school to school like true boosters, and Jackie and her partner made it to the countywide tournament one year. I usually left work slightly early those days and made it up the next day to attend these matches. Both girls, of course, swam competitively for the community swim teams.

A tornado smashes the rear window of our Dodge Dart

While Jackie and Myrna were at one of their Young Judea meetings one Sunday afternoon I received a call from Jackie to come to the synagogue quickly. Someone had broken the rear window of our Dodge Dart she had parked by the side door. All the way there, I am thinking it's a hate crime. It turned out to be a tornado that had chosen the path between the synagogue and the apartment building next door. It had taken the porch off Rev Hammer's house across the street and shattered some local windows. We cleared the glass out of the car into a wastepaper basket and vacuumed it out afterward. Our insurance didn't cover the replaced glass, so we paid out of pocket.

Rabbi Morris D. Rosenblatt and his wife, Esther, had a house across the street from the synagogue, next door to Rev Hammer. One evening in 1985, after *Maariv* prayers, the rabbi was crossing the street when a hit-and-run driver in a white pickup truck hit and killed him outright. From the distance, one witness saw the truck hit him, but didn't note the plates. Another witness said they saw such a white truck in the parking lot of a nearby church, watching while the police attended to the crime scene. The killer was never brought to justice—although there was a probable suspect with no substantial evidence.

After Rabbi Rosenblatt died we paid a shivah call to his family. During that visit, Esther, the rebbitzin, took Hannah aside to ask for a favor for a good friend of hers from the congregation. The elderly friend had recently lost her husband, a retired, high-ranking military officer, who had always handled all the family finances. The friend had never resolved a checkbook in her entire life. Would Hannah take the woman under her wing and teach her what she needed to know? Of course, Hannah took on the challenge and was gratefully appreciated.

Over the Jewish High Holy Days we often took one or two Jewish midshipmen (from the Naval Academy) home with us from services for meals and home hospitality. When our girls were of a dating age, a few of our guests tried to reciprocate by dating them. Most dates were short-lived, but Jackie, now a high school senior, continued to date only Rick Lowell from York, PA. The girls attended many of the academy affairs, football games, and dances. For the Army/Navy game one year Jackie and Rick painted our car full of slogans with temporary (tempera) paints. But when it came time to go to their senior proms, Jackie chose not to go to hers, and Myrna chose a childhood friend, Eddie Lyons, Jr., the policeman's son from across the street. They remained just friends.

Senior year was also a time for scouting out colleges. A career counselor set Jackie on a career-oriented track to be an architect, so Hannah took her to Carnegie Mellon in Pittsburgh for admissions testing and interview. They were willing to accept her into an arts program, but not into their architectural program. When Hannah took her to the architectural school at the University of Maryland, it was a mutual acceptance based on SAT scores. Jackie graduated high school with the class of 1976 and went on to her first year at the U. of Maryland. Myrna graduated with the class of 1979. She wanted to teach art at some advanced level, and Towson State University seemed to be a good fit for her. She had no problem gaining acceptance there. We altered our telephone exchanges to accommodate toll-free phone calls to both girls and spoke nearly every day. We picked them up any weekend they wanted to come home, and that was frequent.

Meanwhile, Midshipman Rick arranged for us to meet his folks up in their York home. Little did we know this was a ploy to get Jackie alone to pop the marriage question. The question hit inexperienced Jackie like a ton of bricks. Rick was tall, nice looking, athletic, smart, and came from what appeared to be a decent Jewish family. Besides, he was about to embark on a solid new career as a nuclear submarine officer. When she consulted us, we asked her if she loved him, and she replied that she liked him a lot and liked being with him. Was that love? Love enough to undertake marriage? We couldn't answer that for her. That was her answer, not ours. Looking back, perhaps we should have pursued this question a little further.

Pressured by Rick and acceptance by both families, Jackie finally responded favorably to his proposal, and a wedding was planned at Kneseth Israel that June, following Rick's graduation and commissioning as a naval ensign. It was a grand occasion with 150 guests attending and Rabbi Rosenblatt officiating. Sisterhood catered for the most part, and we embellished where we could. A hired school bus took our relatives from their hotel on a tour of Annapolis, winding up at the rehearsal dinner site.

When they returned from their honeymoon, Rick was temporarily assigned to a naval mapping facility in Suitland, MD while awaiting Nuclear Preparation school. This allowed Jackie to finish another semester at Maryland. Then they were off to Orlando, FL for his schooling there. I actually cried seeing Jackie off.

During the six months in Orlando, Jackie took courses at a local liberal arts college. From there they went to Nuclear Reactor school in upper New York State. During that time, Jackie worked as a draftsman for a local architect. Rick rounded off his training with a short tour at the submarine school at Groton, CT. At the end of all that training he was assigned to a submarine at Pearl Harbor, HI and Jackie accompanied him there as well.

The newlyweds were able to get government housing in Ewa Beach on the south shore of Oahu, just west of Pearl Harbor. It was a three-bedroom place with a screened lanai and a large grassy backyard. A sandy beach and a wooden bench were directly across from their house. Rick rode to work at Pearl Harbor by boat from a pier only a few blocks away. When we first heard that they were going to be in Hawaii, we telephoned our friends Ron and Millie Darby, who had been living there for fifteen years. Coincidentally, our phone call interrupted their twenty-fifth anniversary party. The whole Darby family confirmed that they would look after our kids, and they sure kept their word. In fact, Jinny Darby, their same-age daughter, and Jackie became fast friends.

We visited the kids in Ewa Beach twice. On one of these occasions, time-zone lag caused us to awaken at four in the morning and we opted to wait for the sunrise on the bench across the way. We had a clear and unobstructed view of a flat horizon looking due east. At the precise moment of sunrise we were treated to a rare (at least for us) phenomenon, a bright flash (more like an explosion) of green light lasting only a fraction of a second. It took us by complete surprise and only later did we find out that the flash was due to sunlight refraction over the horizon.

On the first trip to Ewa Beach we complained a wee bit about sleeping on a lumpy, pull-out sofa-bed, so on the second trip, Jackie borrowed a water bed from the Darbys. While the night was warm, the bed was cold and damp to the touch, and after we sloshed, heaved, swayed, and rippled for several hours without any meaningful sleep, we went back to the much preferred sofa-bed to finish off that first night.

During our many phone calls to Myrna at Towson State U, Hannah would often ask her what she had for supper, and she'd cleverly reply: “Unidentified meat clumps.” In the past she usually talked about any of the dates she’d had, but recently, that subject hadn’t come up. We didn’t know whether she wasn’t dating or just not talking. Toward the end of her second semester at Towson, Myrna came home one weekend and defiantly announced: “I met a non-Jewish boy and I love him and I’m going to marry him no matter what you say.” It sure was a mouthful to swallow. We had friends whose son married out of the faith, and they disowned him. I’ve always wondered who they punished more with such an act—the son or themselves. We asked if they had considered all of the ramifications of a mixed marriage. She claimed they had.

“What about children?” we returned.

“We’ll let them decide when they’re old enough,” was her reply.

“How old is he?”

“He’s a junior, so he’s probably a year older than me.”

“Are you planning to convert?”

“Of course not,” she replied.

“Is he willing to convert to Judaism?”

“No, he’s Lutheran,” she answered.

“Would he agree to a Jewish wedding?”

“Maybe, I don’t know.”

“What about his parents?”

“They’re ex-military, Army, I think.”

“We mean what do they think of this marriage?” I asked.

“I don’t know, but I think it’s okay with them.”

“Well, if you’re sure that’s what you want, we’ll accept him.”

“What’s his name?”

“Tim, Timothy Spurrier and he’s a Communications major.”

We met Tim, and he made a nice impression. He proclaimed his love for Myrna, so we began to plan a wedding with two stipulations. One, he had to be gainfully employed prior to the marriage, and two, he had to allow Myrna to continue her education.

Tim graduated that May and took a job in sales for a franchise photography firm. Soon after, we met his parents at a restaurant in Baltimore's Little Italy and found them a charming couple. His father, a large man, was also named Lawrence and called Larry. The Spurrier family had settled in Edgewood, MD after retiring from the Army. Larry and Harriet Spurrier took to us right away. Unfortunately, some time before Tim graduated, his father died, and we attended the funeral.

Meanwhile, we found a marriage hall on the Baltimore Beltway and began our search for someone to marry them. No rabbi would marry a non-Jew without at least a promise of a conversion or of child-rearing in Judaism. We finally found a cantor licensed to do the job. The wedding was another grand affair with about 100 guests—this time fully catered by the hall. At this point we were empty-nested. One low light of the affair was that our neighbor Marion Aubuchon fell and broke her leg while dancing.

Shortly after the newlyweds returned from their honeymoon Tim switched jobs. He became the tennis professional at a tennis club in Hagerstown, MD. They took an apartment halfway between his job and her school at Towson on U.S. route 40.

Tim and Myrna Wed

The Wedding Party

After Myrna graduated from Towson, Tim took a tennis pro job with a much larger club in Hagerstown. I was an unhappy dad. It bothered me no end that they were getting farther and farther away from us.

Please excuse the fact that I digress here and travel to the present, for I feel that I have not adequately described our kids. I have always known that we have raised two wonderful children, who have grown into two exceptional women, each in her own inimitable way. I see them as kind, friendly, loyal, and always helpful. While Jackie seems to be more chatty and slightly more socially proficient—always welcoming the newcomer and sometimes the stray, Myrna is more cautious in making and trusting friends. I believe this is due to a stinging betrayal among one of her childhood friendships. That kind of thing always hurts. I have always enjoyed the girls' company and, today, look forward to our weekly dinner dates with as much of the whole family as is available.

Sure, they both have grown an inherited talent to express and explore themselves in the wondrous world of art, but they have found uniquely original and personal ways to do this. Inherited? Certainly not from me. I do not have any particular talent in the arts, but perhaps my grandfather's talent still runs boldly in their blood. I have found my niche writing stories. But my daughters have won many awards, prizes, and stipends for their creations. I take pride in knowing they have made their mark in the world of art.

The family helps celebrate my 86th birthday

Jackie prefers the genre of sculpture, working in wax, clay, plaster, wood, wire, glass, and bronze. Today she does bronze commissions, mostly real and fantasy animals, and rents a workshop in Kaneohe, HI. Although Myrna has a wide body of work in ceramic surrealism, much of her recent art has been in animals and print making. She does bring some of her former surrealism into her dabbling in bronze, as she takes advantage of Jackie's bronze classes and workshops. They continue to turn out more art every time I see them, often entering juried shows and winning prizes.

Another thing both girls share is a natural affinity for teaching their art skills to children—not only their own, but classrooms full of kids over many years. They have encouraged excellence for the talented; enjoyment for the mediocre; and hope for the hapless—including those with ten thumbs. Both girls have developed strong opinions, weighing advice cautiously and avoiding dissuasion at all cost.

Myrna and Tim have done an excellent job in raising their three children on a forty-five acre horse farm in rural South Carolina, teaching them all about animals, farming, and home care and giving them the life experience that goes with it. The Spurriers have moved on since, but the youngsters have grown into wonderfully sensitive and caring adults.

Jackie and Rodney raised their two children in Honolulu's wooded Palolo Valley, and they have done a superb job in producing two terrific young ladies. Their multicultural public school groundings have given them insight into the needs of others, which may have steered both into careers of physical therapy.

Both Jackie and Myrna have gotten past some serious medical issues, and thank God they remain trim and reasonably healthy today. Jackie is the taller and possibly more athletic. She still swims a mile in the ocean and takes a master swim class and attends Jazzercize classes regularly. Myrna enjoys walking, hiking, swimming, and boogie-boarding with the rest of her family.

Myrna is the more playful and enjoys all sorts of games. She even apes my punning skills. Jackie is more serious and often generous to a fault. The way I see it Jackie tends to get her looks from Grandmother Herta's side of the family; whereas Myrna definitely looks like a Mild. Of course, there's a bit of Forsch and Mild in the both of them. Sometimes I smile when I even see a bit of myself in each. Above all, they are loving sisters in every respect.

My beloved girls: Jackie Mild Lau and Myrna Mild Spurrier
The best a father could ask for

Chapter 10

Hannah's Courageous Struggle

After a little over two years of commuting to Washington, the whole idea became stale. Also, I wanted to try going back to college to improve myself and my earning power. I began to look for a slot back at the firm's Annapolis office. I finally found what I was looking for and I returned to Annapolis. The company did a lot of equipment/systems compatibility and vulnerability testing and studies. In order to conduct these functions properly one had to know how these complex electronic equipments actually worked. My new job required me to: study technical manuals and analyze schematics; interpret the physical circuitry and controls to make that detailed determination; document it for the engineers doing the testing work; and prepare the final reports to the customers. In fact, I was also responsible for the technical and grammatical proofing of the final reports. My past in military equipment and theory served me well once more. Not only did I do this type of work for a number of years, I began to learn the testing and studies side of the work as well as all the associated specifications. I was now working for Honeywell (which had bought out Electro-Interational) in its Signal Analysis Center in Annapolis.

When an invitation to bid arrived in-house, involving a large, six-of-a-kind, digital system for a Defense Department customer, I was the only one available with all of the qualifications to head up the proposal effort. We got the contract, and I led the project and its several extensions to fruition successfully. From then on my title changed to senior project engineer. The title came with a welcome raise, and I successfully designed, manufactured, documented, and delivered many more systems and equipments to a wide variety of defense and commercial customers.

I designed a system for the Picatinny Arsenal in New Jersey that tested the pre-launch readiness of production-line missile batteries, simulating all the severe current-draining functions expected of these batteries. The system had to be programmable to accommodate a variety of missiles and their batteries in a harsh environment of multiple large (many amperes of) current drains of varying durations over the life of a missile. For example, imagine the huge amount of current necessary to operate the latches holding the stages of a missile together. Normal magnetic and similar reprogrammable memories are highly vulnerable in those environments, so I designed a limited-function computer that used diode memory cards. A single diode tied to a voltage represented a logic one bit, whereas a diode tied to ground (zero volts) represented a logic zero bit. Using medium-scale, hard-logic modules, my computer accessed thirty-two bit rows of these diodes via either consecutive or complex addressing techniques. Every one of the thirty-two bit positions was tasked with either an action or a test function or an alternate address (dependent on some test position result) or a timing function to the next step.

I also participated in a number of Defense Department studies. One of these had to do with the arrangement and placement of electronic equipment in smallish U.S. Navy shipboard and submarine compartments. Honeywell did a lot of compatibility testing in screen rooms to determine an equipment or system's suitability in proximity to other electronic devices. This data was compared to almost arbitrary limit curves furnished by Government specifications. However, other than to identify and fix potentially problematic sources and targets of radiated and conducted excess electromagnetic noise, this mountain of recorded data had lain idle. A Navy study was underway by a group of professors at Penn State University to solve such compatibility problems by committee, using basic physics relationships on a one-by-one problem basis. I proposed a software program using actual compatibility test data, proposed distances, and the same physics relationships being used by the committee. This would give them the best overall predictive look at new electronic spaces. The results would be presented in matrix form. We ran some samples and proved that the task was feasible, but one of the professors, noting that I was the only one on the committee without a doctorate, convinced the Navy coordinator to squash the entire project. Curiously, one of his graduate students got hold of one of my papers and published an article in *Microwave Magazine* citing my work. His professor was furious.

In February 1965 I enrolled in Anne Arundel Community College (AACC) in Arnold, MD. My UConn transcript yielded little and after so many years, my goals seemed so far away. I took two and three courses each semester to whittle down the requirements for an Associates Degree in Business Administration, and as a challenge, I even conquered Calculus this time. I did well with my other subjects, and especially took to Accounting where I aced both final exams. I graduated Magna Cum Laude, earning that degree and honor in June of 1968 with a grade point average of 3.79. Hannah and I attended the graduation.

In the Fall of 1968 I enrolled at American University. I traveled to downtown Washington, DC (a fifty-minute drive) for the first year until the evening school moved to the main campus in northwest DC (a seventy-minute drive). I took two ninety-minute course sessions each Tuesday and Thursday. My grades were all A's and B's and with the exception of two C's, I was pleased with my overall progress. One of the C's was in statistics, where I had allowed my Calculus to grow stale. The other was in Economic Geography, where I had disagreed with the professor's philosophy on a final exam.

I had another professorial disagreement in one of my computer science classes, and it did drop me from an A to a B. On my research term paper I described the process of digitizing mechanical and electrical schematic drawings. My professor said he liked my well-written paper, but claimed the process was "pie in the sky"

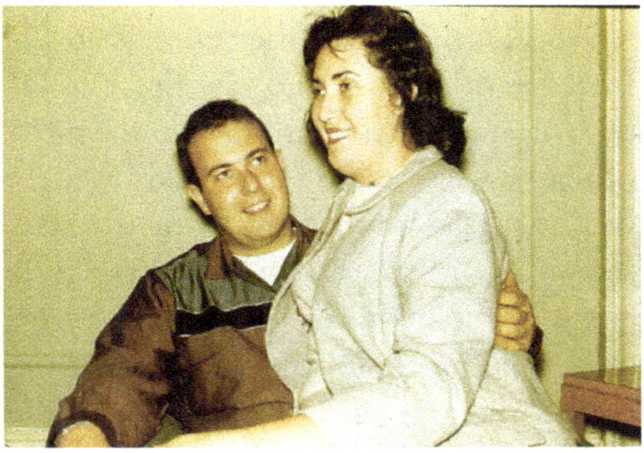

SNUGGERY
1665

and gave me a C on the term paper. I went to him afterward to explain that my company was under contract for just such a process. He wouldn't listen, but did give me a B for the course. I was majoring in Information Systems Management, so I was a bit ticked, to say the least.

These were the Vietnam War years and, on one occasion, a group of anti-war protesters broke into and took over our classroom. The professor asked them politely to leave and then, not wanting to initiate any violence, stepped aside. One of the protesters guarded the door, so we listened to an anti-war lecture for the rest of the session whether we wanted it or not.

During finals that same year, I approached Ward Circle at the edge of campus and saw that the DC police had cordoned off the entrance to the campus. Smoke filled the air and fresh canisters of tear gas were being launched by the police. Even though it was Business Law, my last final for the semester, I continued around the circle and headed home. I received a telephone message the next day rescheduling the final, but when I showed up to take the exam, the professor said I had already cinched the A. Did I want to take the exam anyway? I smiled and walked out thinking, Why hadn't he put this choice in his phone message?

I wound up with a high grade point average, but not high enough for honors this time. In December 1971 I earned a Bachelor of Science Degree in Business Administration. I did not attend my own graduation this time. Why? I attended night school and had no colleagues for more than a single semester and I wasn't up for a bunch of speeches. I worked hard, but I have to give credit where it's due—Hannah and our teenage kids enabled me the opportunity and the study time.

I developed a close working camaraderie with Joe Green, who had an office next to mine at Honeywell. He was a physicist with over sixty major patent credits to his name. We spent a lot of time at the blackboards in either office discussing unique ways to obtain, separate, measure, and display electromagnetic phenomena. We called it chalk-talk, and I usually wound up designing a specific instrument as a direct result. In November of 1979 we each had peer technical papers accepted at a week-long Government symposium held at the Lawrence Livermore Labs just north of San Francisco. We took our wives along and expanded the trip to include both weekends. Our papers were a great success and withstood the peer question and answer periods afterward. My paper led to a hardware contract based on the paper's concept. The ladies shopped and sight-saw while we attended, and a good time was had by all when we were together. We concluded that San Francisco was a cold and expensive city.

Our first indication that something might be wrong with Hannah's health came to us in 1980 rather stealthily. Dr. Mike Monias, Hannah's gynecologist and a close family friend, announced to us, in a low-key fashion, that he had found three tiny suspicious spots in the ovaries area. He thought that it might be nothing, but he wanted to wait six months and see if they might change in size. Whether that six months would have made any difference in the ultimate diagnosis and treatment, no one knows. Herta, Hannah's mother, believed that it was crucial and harbored ill feelings toward Mike ever since. Six months later the spots had grown sizable and rapidly, so Mike did the surgery and removed all of the cancerous growths that he could find and, once she healed from the surgery, he turned her over to doctors at the Johns Hopkins Oncology Department for prophylactic radiation and chemotherapy measures.

In that time there was no way the doctors could determine how far the tentacles of the cancer had reached, so many of these treatments were considered preventive. I went with her to some of the radiation treatments, at least as far as the waiting room. It was there I learned that cancer was unprejudiced and impartial in selecting its victims. I saw elderly, unable to leave their beds—babies in carriages—tots barely able to walk—athletic-looking teenagers—young adults—a prisoner in manacles—and including every ethnicity imaginable. During the first phase of her chemotherapy treatments, several of her friends drove her up to Baltimore and Johns Hopkins Hospital. Then those routine chemo treatments no longer seemed effective. Anything more sophisticated required hospitalizing.

Prior to her first hospitalization, Hannah received word that there was trouble in paradise—Jackie's marriage had reached a crisis. We had already used up my vacation on an earlier trip to Hawaii where we had learned only of minor complaints—not terminal material. Hannah flew back to Hawaii to try and solve Jackie's marital problems. Rick had become unhappy at work and had become depressed and withdrawn at home, taking much of his problems verbally out on Jackie, who was still attending classes at UH. He no long participated in Jackie's favorite activities of hiking and swimming.

Months before our vacation visit, they had moved to another place—from Government housing at Ewa Beach on the leeward side of the Island to an A-frame house within an idyllic garden at Laie on the windward side. The purpose of the move was to give a boost to the marriage, but all it did was create grist for the mill and slowly move toward the eventual divorce. Before returning home, Hannah did all she could to support Jackie in solving the more immediate problems, but the course for divorce was inevitable. Rick transferred to a sub in Seattle, WA and moved there as well. Jackie stayed in Hawaii, and soon the divorce was final.

Over the next five and a half years there were three long hospitalizations at Hopkins and there were remissions and good times too. But the remissions were all too short. When the earlier drugs failed, the oncologists brought out the exotic and experimental ones—drugs so new we both had to sign consent forms before they were administered. Many of these drugs lowered immunity to unheard-of diseases most of us won't ever catch. An example of this was an autotoxic drug, which caused her to lose her hearing. No, not a high- or low- or middle-frequency loss that can be helped with a simple filtered-frequency hearing aid—but a combing effect, where closely adjacent frequencies across the spectrum might be 40 decibels (a factor of 100 times) apart. Amplifying the lower level and the adjacent higher level created an unbearable, screeching high. An infrared device attached to the TV helped to bring the diverse levels closer, but not enough. When my mother went blind, I had wished it had been her hearing, so I could have done something about it. I was an electronics engineer, wasn't I? Then this type of hearing problem attacked Hannah and I was struck totally dumb. Initially, her deafness only aggravated her other problems, but she eventually taught herself to lip-read.

Another example of a rare disease she somehow picked up was Guillain-Barré Syndrome. She could hardly move, and her pain was so excruciating that they had to put her in bed full of warm sand and continually recycle her blood through a cleansing machine before returning it via intravenous tubing. She also had a respirator mask over her mouth, so communication was near-impossible. One of the nurses came up with a placard with a few basic pictorial messages that she could point at, but from her point of view, the placard fell way, way short. In fact, some time afterward, Hannah designed her own more functional placard for the next patient and gave it to that nurse. I hope the improved placard or a better one is used today. The Guillain-Barré Syndrome also passed in the ensuing weeks, and Hannah returned to her regular hospital bed once more.

Another one of the drugs, which the nurses labeled "Shake and Bake," caused a high fever and intense shivering, but it was designed to protect where the body's immunity failed. Neither blankets nor fans would give her any relief. Yet one more drug caused her to lose all her hair. Then there were the drugs that prevented her from eating, so she had to be fed intravenously. In fact, there were times when she had as many as four IVs going at once—tubes going every which way—a bunch of dosimeters, clicking away, measured every drip going down those tubes. The nurse would change her bag, and Hannah would ask whether the bag contained steak and baked potatoes. It was their little joke. I can only admire that kind of courage.

In addition to all the IVs, the floor-roaming phlebotomists drained blood daily for testing until her selected veins couldn't stand it any longer and began collapsing. Searching for a substantial vein involved painful multiple pricking and exploring. The longer Hannah stayed in the hospital the more difficult it got. There was one particular nurse who not only had a magic knack for needle insertion, but a genuine kindness and a saintly disposition. The other nurses called her Sister, so I assume she belong to a Catholic order of some kind—although I never saw her wearing any kind of habit. Months after Hannah had passed, she called me twice to see how I was doing. I believe that's kindness well beyond the call of duty.

My daily routine was wildly hectic while Hannah was hospitalized, but I felt my complete support was essential to her morale. Besides, there was nowhere else that I'd rather have been than with her. I went to work an hour early, took a ten-minute Cup-a-Soup lunch, and left work at three every weekday. I drove the forty-minute drives to and from Johns Hopkins Hospital every day. On weekends I was there well before noon. Each night I'd leave sometime after eight when the nurses shooed the rest of the visitors out of the building. I'd take my supper from the cafeteria to her room and we'd eat together, even though hers came in a tube much of the time.

Spouses of oncology patients were given tokens for the meters in a much closer parking area, and I took advantage of this benefit. One day I shut off the car engine and temporarily stuck the car keys in my sweater pocket. Then I bent over to pick up the Sunday paper, which had slid to the floor on the passenger side. While I bent over, the keys slid out and fell to the floor without my knowing it. As soon as I had locked and shut the car door, I reached for my keys and discovered they were no longer in the sweater pocket. I was about to put them in a safer place. I could see the keys staring back at me from the floor, but I couldn't get to them.

Inside the building at the reception desk, I had asked to use the phone to call a locksmith and somehow wound up explaining my foolish accident. The male receptionist reached under the desk for a long, thin, flat strip of notched metal, and followed me out to the car. He slid the metal down next to the window glass, caught the latch mechanism in one of the notches, and pulled it up to unlock the car. I told him that he had made it look easy. He shrugged his shoulders and said: "Shades of my shady youth." He was smiling. He wouldn't take money, so I thanked him profusely. Another day, almost a year later, I left the hospital after visiting hours were over and couldn't find the car where I had left it. I went to the reception desk to report a stolen car. Again, they came to my rescue.

Miraculously, the police had caught the thief, and the car was towed to a compound at the edge of Baltimore. I caught a cab to this compound and soon learned that I had to pay $220 to bail out my car. That accomplished, I moved on to the next obstacle on the list. The thief had used a screwdriver to punch out the passenger door lock and to punch off the ignition lock face. Without the ignition lock face in the way, a screwdriver can be inserted through the hole to turn the switch. I had to buy a ten-dollar screwdriver from the compound manager in order to drive home that night. I wondered how many screwdrivers he sold in a year. To make matters worse, when I had the ignition and door locks fixed, it turned out that the insurance would only pay for the damaged locks, so from then on I had separate keys for the ignition, each of two separate side doors, and a glove box. The trunk key did match the driver's door lock.

Two months later I received a notice of a trial for the thief who stole the car. I went to juvenile court to be a necessary witness. I arrived early and sat in on a number of cases before mine. I noticed a print of a famous painting on the wall to my left—an older boy was carrying a younger boy on his back. The caption beneath it read: "He ain't heavy, he's my brother." When my case came to order, I was ushered out into the hall—a witness shouldn't be influenced by other witnesses was the policy. In the hall I met the young policeman who had arrested the car thief. He had spotted two youngsters leaning on a car parked at the curb while he was on foot patrol. Believing they were up to no good, he approached to ask for identification. Meanwhile, one of them hurried off in the opposite direction. The policeman followed and when he put his hand on the boy's shoulder, the boy spun around with a gun pointed directly at the officer. The policeman said he didn't know what came over him, but acting on pure dumb instinct, he actually grabbed the gun out of the boy's hand safely. He apprehended the boy just as the car pulled from the curb with the thief driving. By a strange coincidence, a police cruiser had turned the corner at that moment and blocked the thief's getaway. They had seen the policeman pointing at the car.

The thief was charged with two counts of car theft and breaking and entering a school gymnasium—and damaging and looting lockers there. However, the policeman and I were the only pertinent witnesses who showed up that day in court. I gave my testimony and left, learning that the magistrate's decision and sentencing would not happen that day. Six weeks later I received a court notice that the thief had been released after a tongue lashing and time served. What a waste! I'd lost a day's pay, the bail money, and screwing fee the comprehensive portion of the insurance, and endured a lot of inconvenience and stress while the sixteen-year-old thief got off with only a few weeks served.

In the remission following one long-term hospitalization, we planned a trip to Ottawa and Montreal, Canada. Hannah and I drove to Albany, NY and stayed overnight in a motel. We met George and Mitzie the next morning and left our car there with the motel manager's permission. George did the driving, but whether the spouses or the brothers sat together, Hannah could not read anyone's lips and, as a result, she couldn't take part in any conversations for long periods of driving. These seemingly endless drives brought her to tears. We did have a wonderful time touring the magnificent Canadian government buildings and old-town historical sites in Ottawa. In Montreal we visited museums, galleries, and the underground shopping malls. The city streets remained alive and seemingly safe until well after midnight, earning it its title of "the Paris of the new world."

In Honolulu, our daughter Jackie was finding life lonely after her divorce While hiking on the Isle of Kauai with a girlfriend, she stumbled into Rodney Lau, an accounting major at the University of Hawaii at Manoa, where she was now an art major. The two groups shared a campsite and roasted mountain-stream prawns over a fire while they cemented a more permanent friendship. Months later, they became a loving twosome and, eventually, she moved in with Rodney.

During one of Jackie's visits to see Hannah, she was asked whether she loved Rodney enough to marry him. She responded yes, but said, "That move is still down the road in our planning." Then Hannah told her, "If you're going to marry him anyway, I want to be there and see it." So, we traveled to Hawaii and, on the side of a mountain called Round Top (part of Mount Tantalus), Jackie and Rodney were married by a judge, a close friend of Rodney's father, Gym Lau. His mother, Gladys Lau, and Rodney's siblings and families were also present. Despite the clouds and threatening rain, the marriage turned out

Rodney and Jackie's wedding day

We joined the bride and groom on the mountain

The mothers in the wedding party: Gladys Lau, Hannah, and Herta

to be solid and fruitful over the years. A reception was held at a nearby Chinese restaurant. The Lau family was Chinese and not Jewish, but this didn't seem to matter one bit to anyone, as Rodney had already consented to bring up any children in the Jewish faith. Rodney proved to be all the things that Rick was not. Hannah got her final big wish, and we returned to Annapolis and Baltimore for more treatments.

During her last remission, it became clear that death was around the corner regardless of how she felt at any given time. One evening in bed, Hannah and I both started a crying jag that lasted about ten minutes. She stopped first and began to wipe her face. I couldn't understand it, she was actually smiling now. I stopped too.

I'll never forget what she said next.

"We can go on crying for what little time I have left, or we can cherish and appreciate every precious moment God is willing to give us."

Her hand went to my cheek, and she brushed away a tear with her thumb.

"I agree," I replied. "Let's not waste them."

"No more crying?" she said. "Promise?"

"Promise!" I assured her.

I kept that promise, at least until I stood at her covered

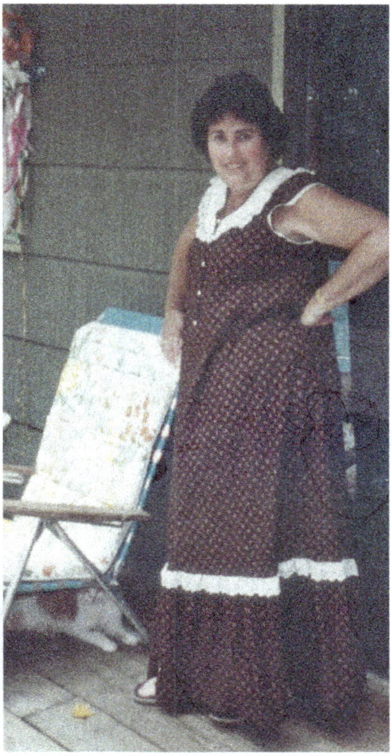

4867 FT.
ABOVE SEA

gravesite, and then I couldn't hold it back any longer. I was even scolded by a friend for breaking down during the recital of the memorial Kaddish. Naturally, that didn't help my feelings one bit—our Hannah deserved every loving tear I shed. She was the finest and bravest soul on God's earth, and she was so full of love for all of us. Myrna was there, but Jackie had returned to Honolulu and her Rodney only a few weeks earlier, and it would have been a hardship to be there so soon again. It was more important for her to have been there while Hannah still lived.

At some point Hannah had realized that her doctors could do no more for her and that death loomed just around the corner. The death of Rabbi Rosenblatt, a man we both knew and loved, created a problem for her. The new rabbi, the first in a succession of several, knew nothing about her. This was unacceptable. How could he deliver her eulogy? What could he say? She went to visit with him on several occasions to get acquainted. As a result, he spoke beautifully, though briefly, at the Kneseth Israel funeral.

The children visited her whenever they could. I learned later that on one particular visit when both girls where there and I was not in the room, Hannah had a serious talk with them. She was afraid for me. She understood that I wasn't the type of person who could be alone for very long. She wanted me to find someone worthy and eventually remarry. In fact, she had instructed some of her friends to be on the lookout for me. She wanted the children to encourage me to find a new life and trust and welcome my decision. All I can say is today, they have carried out Hannah's wishes and mine in accepting Rosemary in the warm way they have.

Hannah passed away at Johns Hopkins on January 28, 1986 while holding my hand. She had spent the last few days heavily sedated for her pain and in extreme discomfort, so I had been sitting next to her bed in silence for some time. An attached monitoring machine informed me when her time had come. The monitor had also brought hospital personnel into the room, so I kissed her on the lips for the last time and left her to get out of their way. I remember the lips were cold, stiff, and blue. I had to release her fingers from mine as I slipped away. The last image of her face was tired, bland, and looking almost angered. This was not the true image of that terrific wife, best friend, and mother I shared so many wonderful years with. This was not the image I wanted to remember. It took so very, very long before I could capture her true image once more. The mind plays so many dirty tricks on us.

A memorial service was held at Kneseth Israel synagogue, and I believe there were over 200 people in attendance. Several neighbors spoke or read notes during the service. One even made reference to the Challenger space mission that had blown up soon after launch earlier that day. Beautiful notes came from many of the relatives in New York City. She is still a part of my life today, and I think of her often, even over thirty years after she left me.

Chapter 11

Rosemary: Second Love, Wife, and Best Friend

In January of 1986, in the middle of funeral arrangements, I had a second peer technical paper accepted for a Government symposium in Florida. I could not attend, so a colleague, Harry Lee, presented the paper for me. He had a paper of his own to present as well. By his assessment, my paper was well received.

Hannah had been taken from me, and our girls had removed most of her personal things, dividing up her jewelry, sharing mementos, and leaving the house all too empty, too quiet. I wasn't spending hours cruising the roads, dodging traffic to Baltimore and back, nor was I sitting at her bedside working hard at being cheerful. I've tired at playing cards and board games. They are reminders of terrible declining times and I approach them sparingly and with caution even today. As a result, I found all this extra *me time* on my hands, so I began taking hour-long walks each evening through the neighborhood to take the edge off my loneliness. It took many months before I could open my eyes each morning and not expect to see her form on the other side of the bed. It was like starting your day with disappointment—every day.

Friends Marty and Sheila Litzky

A number of months later I tried dating. I was clumsy about it, and the two I tried were uninspiring and not worth repeating. In October of 1986, just when my loneliness was at its lowest, I received a phone call from Sheila

Litzky. She and husband Marty were close friends of Hannah and me for over twenty years. Sheila said she had someone I should definitely meet. Her pronounced pedigree was: "She'd be a good friend, if nothing more." I agreed.

Sheila promised to call Rosemary Wolfe, a divorcee for nine years, and let her know I would be phoning. I called Rosemary the next evening to introduce myself, and we settled on a 6:00 p.m. Saturday dinner date.

On the appointed date I arrived fifteen minutes early in case I had trouble finding 120 Kennedy Drive in Severna Park. Not wanting to ring the doorbell before she was ready, I read my newspaper to kill time. Apparently that had made some kind of favorable impression on her, so she came to the door to invite me in. One of the first things I learned from her was the fact that she'd known Sheila and Marty for over twenty years, and others in our inner social circle as well. Now the question arose: why hadn't we met before? We tore through all of the Litzky special occasions and found that either one of us was out of town or otherwise engaged for each event, but the marvelous thing was that we knew so many of the same people.

Needless to say, our conversation never lacked for content the entire evening. At one point on the way back to her place, I informed Rosemary of my plan to write a novel when I retired. Learning of her own literary and editing background, I asked if she would assist me. She surprised the dickens out of me with a prompt and decisive yes. After all, we had just met a few hours earlier. Wow! I was thoroughly in sync with and highly attracted to this bright, chatty lady with a cute figure, so I didn't want to mess things up. As a result, I limited my kissing to a goodnight peck for the first few dates.

We dated regularly after that, sometimes twice a week. When I finally took her in my arms after nearly a month she wondered why I took so long. Who knew—I hadn't much recent experience in dating. Once that happened, it was literally hard to keep us apart. We became inseparable and intimate soon afterward. In

Rosemary Pollack Wolfe

Rosemary at her father's desk

early December I took her to a Redskins football game. I had been sharing two season tickets with the Litzky family for a number of years. I showed up at Rosemary's front door with a burgandy and gold corsage, the Redskins' colors. I so thoroughly indoctrinated her into watching professional football that she eventually became an avid fan. Now we both look forward to Sundays, Monday nights, and even added Thursday nights during the football season.

That fall Myrna and Tim moved in with his mom in Edgewood, MD. They each had left their jobs to pursue master's degrees. The move to his childhood home would save them food and lodging and provide company for his mom. Shortly after the football game date, Harriet Spurrier, Tim's mom, invited the two of us up to their place to celebrate Chanukah. I wanted the girls to meet Rosemary in the worst way. I guess what I really wanted was their approval, but Jackie's turn would have to come later. Rosemary charmed everyone the way that I thought she would.

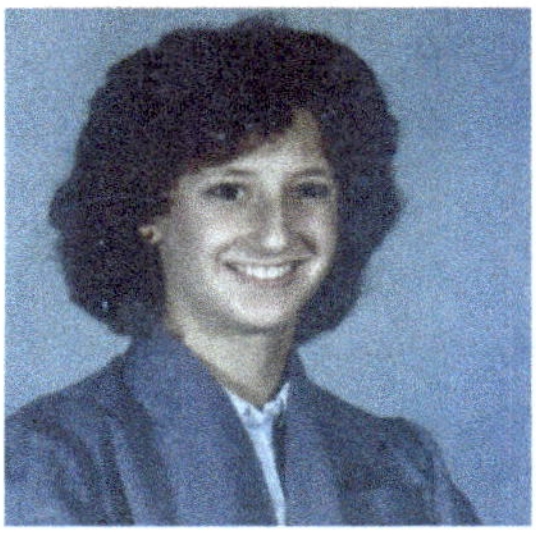
Miriam Luby Wolfe

I had learned on our first date that Rosemary had a daughter, an eighteen-year-old college freshman away at Syracuse U. in upstate New York. The first time I met Miriam was when she came home for Thanksgiving week. That night she virtually filled the room with her presence. She immediately captured my attention and held it for the next several hours. I believe that she wielded this captivation intentionally.

She was so natural and so wonderfully explosive. It was the highest level of exuberance born of a need to share—to share her life's experiences and discoveries with those she loved. It was a level of animation and energy that could not be contained, for she would simply burst for the lack of its expression. Miriam was a new experience for me. I had never met anyone quite like her.

This energetic and animated enthusiasm extended to every surface and limb of her long, lean, ever-dancing frame. She never stood still, not even for a solitary moment. Her shoulders, arms, and hands covered almost as much space as her feet as she swiftly and gracefully darted about. I found it hard work for my eyes to follow her. Her warm and laughing smile drew you to listen, and you dared not let go for fear that you would miss some of the charming and interesting things she had to say. My being there, a total stranger, had not inhibited her in the least.

I began to spend more time with Rosemary, including some overnights, so that by the time Miriam arrived home, it had become quite routine. I won't ever forget my first overnight with Miriam across the hall. Once there were at least two closed doors between our bedrooms, the ever-ramping sounds of Ravel's *Bolero* escaped from her phonograph and penetrated the master bedroom. We found it both humorous and, unfortunately, sad. Needless to say, when we got through giggling and analyzing, we were both inhibited. Perhaps that was her intent. We'll never know.

Over the holiday break while Miriam spent time with her father in Virginia, I took the time off work to visit Herta in Miami Beach, so Rosemary was really alone. I sent flowers and called from Florida. Not wanting to upset Herta, I called Rosemary on New Year's Eve from a public phone on the beach boardwalk. Rosemary informed me that she was rehabbing from minor foot surgery and was currently sitting in a Wendy's franchise with girlfriend Donna Bennett. She had received my flowers. Miriam's reaction to the flowers: "Marry him, Mom!"

By the end of January I was certain of my feelings for Rosemary. I asked her to join me on a trip to Honolulu to visit Jackie. I even told her she could come as my bride. It sort of slipped out without any planning, but I really meant it. At first she was hesitant, saying she needed her valued personal space. She told me togetherness twenty-four hours a day for two weeks was a little much for her. I was deeply disappointed. However, after consulting with her father in Milwaukee she relented, and so I purchased round-trip tickets for the two of us.

On Valentine's Day I invited Myrna and Tim to join us for supper in Annapolis. I didn't realize how big a night that was, so, without making reservations, we had to make the rounds of a half-dozen better restaurants before having to settle for Fudruckers and super hamburgers. The weeknight before Rosemary and I were due to leave for Honolulu, I had tickets for the Kennedy Center musical *Les Misérables*. I left work early to pick up Rosemary at closing time at Williams and Wilkins Publishing House where she worked in Baltimore. We rushed down to the Kennedy Center in Washington, DC, only to be turned away from multiple parking facilities, one after another. By the time we had found parking and had entered the theater, the show had started and we were forced to wait (with about 100 others) for seating until the first act had finished. We enjoyed the show, but could have done without the tumult, especially the night before leaving on such a big trip.

Our 2nd date to Old Town Alexandria, VA

Rosemary at a Hawaii hotel

We spent two glorious weeks like two peas in a pod in Hawaii and never once did Rosemary complain of her space being violated. We stayed with Jackie and Rodney, and they lent us their second car to circle the island of Oahu, taking in all of the major sites, especially my favorites like Hanauma Bay, the Pali cliffs, the east end rocky coast, Foster Gardens, the Honolulu Academy of Art, and the Valley of the Temples. We swam at Kailua Beach and took walks and played tennis at Ala Moana Beach Park.

On the middle weekend, Jackie and Rodney joined us for a tour of Volcanoes National Park on the Big Island of Hawaii. We stayed overnight in a Hilo hotel. We saw both Kilauea and Mauna Loa erupting, steam vents spewing sulfurous steam, colorful rifts, and trails of past damage due to lava flow. She never did have to rely on her backup plan of taking solo walks to preserve her precious space.

Rosemary had only two weeks of vacation, while I had planned to stay for the third week to spend more one-on-one time with Jackie. We took Rosemary to the airport, and I literally came to tears when her plane took off. During our time together, we agreed to a November 22nd wedding. She had put away all of her mental reservations. We were ready to make plans.

I moved in with Rosemary at her place, 120 Kennedy Drive, Severna Park

When I returned home, I began to spend even more time at her place. Rosemary and Miriam had two pets—Hoppy, the orange and tan striped cat with a mind of his own, and Midnight, a shy, lovable, all-black dog mix without a trick to her name. Before I came along, the two pets each had their own bedrooms. Midnight slept on a cot in a bedroom Rosemary used for her office, but Hoppy slept in a padded box on the floor in his own, otherwise empty room and abused much of that flooring with his calls to nature. But I did come along and, in preparation for our combination of households, I tackled the difficult task of refinishing that floor by removing what was left of the former finish through sanding and then applying several coats of fresh shellac. The pets, of course, were relegated to more appropriates spaces after that.

The next task was to tackle an undivided, unfinished basement, functional only from the standpoint of the washing machine and laundry tub and otherwise storing abandoned boxes. I laid out and affixed 2x4-inch framing studs on the floor and ceiling beams; spelling out a large 22- by 12-foot rectangular recreation room with a 3-foot-deep closet; a 10- by 12-foot bedroom; a 12- by14-foot laundry room; and a 6- by12-foot furnace and storeroom. I added vertical 2x4-inch studs to the horizontal frames and framed in three doors and the staircase to the first floor. Next, I nailed furring strips to the concrete walls before I paneled all of the framed walls. Then I put in a drop ceiling, fluorescent lighting, and power outlets. I enlisted Rosemary's help for laying down the tiled flooring. By the time we had tiled the recreation room and started the other areas, we had become experts and realized we should have started the other areas first. At one end of the laundry room I built a workbench and established my workshop with table saw, drill press, and vise. All of this work kept me pretty damn busy for most of that spring and summer.

At the end of the spring semester, Rosemary and I drove up to Syracuse to pick up Miriam and bring her and all of her dorm belongings home. I had no idea how much stuff can be accumulated in a single semester. My poor Honda Accord was so gorged to the gills that the half-open trunk had to be tied down, and Miriam sat squashed in the back seat holding up piles of stuff around her, blocking the rear window view. She was home for the summer, and I got to know my future stepdaughter pretty well.

My Honda Accord often served as the arena for our discussions. While we were bringing Miriam home from Syracuse, she suddenly blurted out: "My friend's older brother is an alcoholic and he's really destroying her family. The saddest part of this is that he's a brilliant student—he's a senior—and quite charming when he's sober. But she says he's really mean when he drinks. He breaks things and calls her up at two in the morning crying in his beer. I feel so sorry for her. She's asked me, so I go along with her to Al-Anon meetings to give her moral support. The meetings are incredible. I was shocked at the number of professionals there—doctors, lawyers, teachers . . ."

I ask Miriam why the guy doesn't go to AA. "He doesn't have to continue drinking," I told her.

"Alcoholism is a disease, Larry," she argues. "Not everybody can just quit."

I counter with an argument of my own. My first wife died of cancer. She would have given anything to live even one more day. She wasn't given a choice. This guy has a choice to turn his life around and refuses to do so. Why should I feel sorry for him?

Miriam protested. "You have to have compassion for people. Not everybody is strong."

Miriam became loving family long before I walked down the aisle with her mother. To be sure, my marriage to Rosemary would be a difficult transition for her. She felt she had to compete for her mother's affection and attention, and yet it was still her wish that we wed. Although we lived under one roof only for that one summer's length and a couple of semester breaks, we began to know one another. We both sensed that this was an ongoing process. I was not her father, nor would I ever try to be. She already had a father, a stepmother, and a stepbrother living in Virginia. I applied for the position of very special friend, and I'd like to think she accepted that.

Miriam talked endlessly on the telephone while pacing through four rooms of the house to the extent that the tethering phone cord would permit. If we'd had a cordless or cell phone like today, there'd be no telling how far she would wander. She left her mark throughout the house in the form of doodles. She virtually obliterated any unguarded Post-it or note in sight, often obscuring messages that still had pertinence.

There just wasn't anything we couldn't discuss, and more often than not, we were on opposite sides of varying subjects. She was an incurable optimist, seeing the world's imperfections and needs as being extremely clear to her. She meant to be a part of its fixing too. With all the fervor of a college freshman, there were no gray or mitigating areas in delineating right and wrong. We were on our way to a Society of Professional Journalists (SPJ) holiday party at the H.L. Mencken House in Baltimore. In the car, a heated debate nearly boiled over. Rosemary had been in an accident and had been cited for reckless driving. Fortunately, the case was dismissed—the other driver and arresting officer didn't show up in court.

Miriam was incensed. "Mom, you didn't deserve to get off like that. You were guilty, you should've been punished."

"You know, Miriam," I interjected, "your mother actually did get punished. She got three points on her license and eleven stitches in her head."

Miriam frowned, unconvinced that justice had been served. She seemed to set even tougher standards for her mother than she did for the rest of the world.

She pursued knowledge and understanding with an insatiable thirst. Every few days there was a new stack of books in her arms to be read. This she did till the wee hours of the morning, sometimes till three and four, as evidenced by the light from under her door. It was as if she knew there was so much to take in, but so little time to do it in. There were rehearsals and plays that summer and swimming and tennis too. I remember one night, the three of

November 22, 1987 Marriage Katuba for Rosemary and Larry

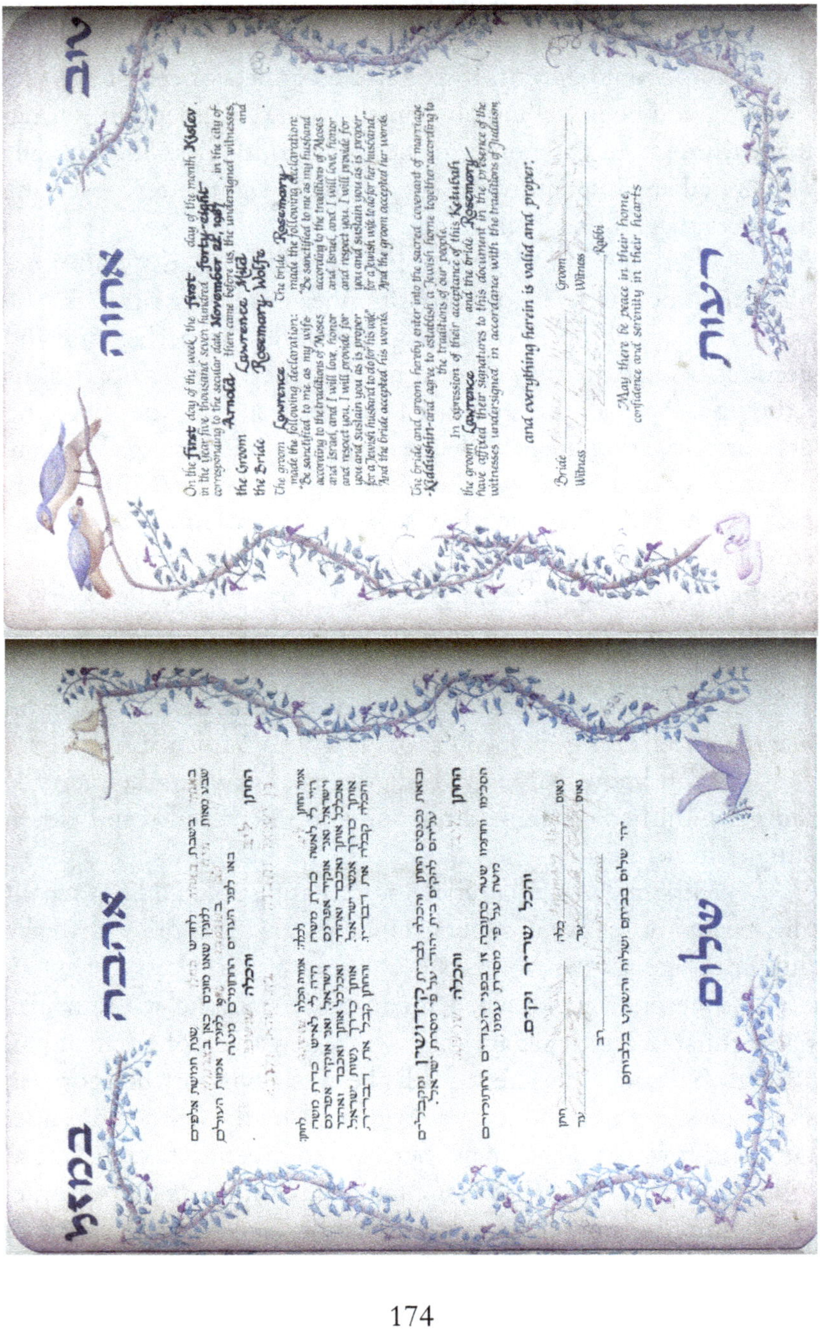

A Glorious Wedding Day for Rosemary and Larry

us went to play tennis at the community college and discovered the overhead lighting was hungry for quarters. After the first set, we ran out of quarters, so Miriam and I sat against the net on the ground in the dark while Rosemary went to get more change, another opportunity for one-on-one time. However, her friends filled most of her time.

She was a happy, friendly person to be around. When she bounded down the staircase with her light-colored and tightly curled locks bobbing up and down, I had a strange feeling that she touched hardly a stair in the descent. There was something about the way she moved, a nod, a tilt, a shrug, a stance or a glance that was all Miriam. That something belonged to her. Some of it, not all, can be seen in photographs, and that belongs to us always.

I finally put the Wendlyn Way house up for sale. The agent and I agreed on a reasonable price. On every trip to Kennedy Drive I brought some of the smaller things from the Wendlyn Way house. One particular trip I conveyed some wall paneling on the roof of my car and while crossing the Severn River Bridge, a major wind gust caught the top panel and folded it in half. The piece broke off and sailed into the river. I had to stop on the bridge and retie the lot more securely. Each night that I spent at home I cleaned out all the excess things unworthy of moving. I asked the girls about cleaning out the things they had left behind. Jackie, living so far away, gave me the grand go-ahead to dispose of all her things, including the bulky architecture projects stowed above the drop ceiling in the basement. On the other hand, Myrna avoided a physical response to all my warnings for more than two months, so, using my own judgment, I put many of those things out with the rest of the trash. Upon hearing about this, Myrna accused me of "throwing out my past." I was indeed a bad dad. She hadn't really missed those things in the several years she'd lived away, so she recovered quickly enough.

By the end of summer, I had a buyer, but it would take another six weeks before we would go to settlement. I made a plan view map of the rooms in the Kennedy Drive house and scale-sized furniture squares to see what would fit and what would not fit in the rooms. I engaged a friend's (Dave Earle's) moving firm. By the time they dropped off the furniture, I had an exact place for every stick of it. Of course, Rosemary and I had to give up some things and move a few other things around as well.

Fall came, and Miraim returned to Syracuse, using a friend to convey all her dorm goodies this time. November followed October, and the wedding was upon us. Rosemary's widower dad, Dr. Saul Pollack, who was a prominent Milwaukee psychoanalyst, came for the occasion. Jackie, Rodney, Myrna, Tim, the Litzkys, the Beers, and a few other friends were also in attendance. Miriam had returned home for her Thanksgiving break. In fact, she sang our way down the aisle with such feeling that tears came to my eyes and a lump to my throat that affected my participation in the ceremony. She and her two new sisters, Jackie and Myrna, embraced our marriage wholeheartedly. Rabbi Robert Klensin, a neighbor and friend, officiated the ceremony at Temple Beth Shalom in Arnold, MD where Rosemary belonged. We had a modest reception at a local restaurant. Five couples, friends, chipped in to give us a hotel room at the Philadelphia Marriott, for a two-day, honeymoon wedding present.

Dr. Saul K. Polack (R's dad) and me

Ann and John Pollack (R's brother)

Miriam returned again in December for her next holiday break. I was flabbergasted by her strenuous schedule and abundant array of friends. Her correspondence list resembled a corporate mailing list. When I came upon her in the midst of her holiday note-writing, I foolishly suggested that she could be briefer. She replied, "No I can't, they're my friends!" Indeed, these were deep and hearty bonds she shared with so many friends. She openly cared so much about them too. I believe she gave and took in precisely the right amounts. It was a formula known only to her. I called it Miriam's gift.

In February Rosemary and I returned to Hawaii to visit Jackie and Rodney and to take a more extended honeymoon than the weekend in Philly. A travel agent friend of Rodney's arranged for a condo on Maui over the middle weekend, only when we arrived, there was no reservation, and it was Ironman Triathon weekend, and there were no rooms or condos to be had. I pleaded with the manager of the place where we were supposed to stay, and she put us in touch with a condo owner, who planned to be away for a few days. The owner agreed, and we rented a gorgeous two-bedroom, kitchen, living room/dining room condo with a side view of the pool, a rear view of the ocean, and the tip of Molokai Island. Our three-day trip coincided with arrangements by Rosemary's dad, who was renting a Maui condo with friends just down the road from us.

We were on our way out to dinner that first night when I cracked a pun, as I often do, and her father wouldn't allow me into their car until I promised not to pun again. It was his little joke that he was offended by puns. In fact, on later visits following an accidental pun, he would calmly pull his airline tickets from his suit jacket pocket and make an oral note of the time and date of his departure. "It's time to go home," he'd say. He was actually a kind and generous man, but an extremely formal gentleman—he never wanted to be caught without a tie and jacket. After all, he was a doctor. Several years later, while visiting him in Milwaukee, I put on a truly conservative aloha shirt to go out to breakfast. He insisted on a dress shirt, tie, and jacket before we could be seen in public. You'd have to love the man and, of course, I did.

By the time we left Honolulu the following week, Jackie was pretty sure that she was pregnant with her first child. It was expected in September. Oddly enough, Myrna informed us, two months later, that she was due in November.

Miriam's announcement was quite different. She wanted to do her fall junior semester abroad just as her mother had done in Switzerland (her entire junior year) while attending Smith College. Miriam wanted to go to London in her pursuit of musical theater studies. Rosemary gave her approval a few weeks later. Miriam applied for the slot and, soon after, learned it was hers to have. We drove up to Syracuse to see Miriam perform in a show during the Spring semester. It was a quickie, two-day round trip that included a dinner with all her roommates.

Sometime during that same Spring semester Miriam had auditioned for a singer/dancer position at Darien Lake State Park in upstate New York. She not only got the job but made arrangements with another girl in the show from North Carolina to room and board with a family in nearby Corfu, NY. This meant that we'd be seeing her for only a week or so at the beginning and end of the summer.

Miriam at Darian Lake Amusement Pk.

All my girls at Myrna's graduation from Towson State U.

Summer came quickly and, with the two of them missing each other so terribly, Rosemary flew to Corfu for a weekend. She took in all of Miriam's musical performances during the days, and the two of them stayed in a motel for two nights. Rosemary returned with a flock of pictures. Years later I would see actual videos of her performances, which were quite professional and good.

I traveled to England on company business toward the beginning of August. It was to field-test someone else's faulty theory of how one of my own devices actually worked. The fundamental purpose of the test was doomed before I even left the States. It was not designed to perform that particular task. I spent some time in London and York and then a week at a base in northern England. I hadn't realized how short the nighttime was at these latitudes. I had to cover the hotel's window drapes with my raincoat to make the room dark enough for me to sleep. The trip was expensive even though the company reimbursed me for most expenses. Knowing that Miriam would soon be headed for London in the Fall, I didn't cash in a hundred and fifty dollars worth of my British currency when I returned. It would be unrestricted spending money, a gift, until she established her regular banking needs. I also purchased an oversized wallet to carry the larger currency.

The last week at home before Miriam left for London passed in a hectic flurry—shopping, visiting relatives and friends, packing, etc. Rosemary was exhausted by the time she dropped Miriam off at the airport on her way to work. It was only a day later that the succession of transatlantic phone calls began. The first was to say she missed her mother, and the second was to inform her that the wallet containing the British currency and the stack of Traveler's checks from her mother, had been pick-pocketed from her purse hanging over the back of her chair in a London restaurant. After calming and cautioning her, Rosemary furnished her with the necessary check numbers so Miriam could replace the checks at the American Express office in London. We later found out that Miriam also kept in touch with many of her stateside pals, such that one of the monthly phone bills topped the $500 mark.

Miriam's letters were newsy, full of classroom assignments, apartment notes, classmate trivia, museums, local history, and the many sights she encountered. They were frequent and so full of her interesting and sometimes poetic observations, a knack she had developed on her own. We looked forward to them and learned a lot from them. More letters described a class field trip to Amsterdam and Paris, a day trip to Oxford, and a week in Wales with a friend.

Jackie gave birth to Alena Grace Lau on the 21st of September 1988 at Queens Hospital in Honolulu. We were thrilled to be grandparents. Auntie Miriam called her from London to congratulate her and heard Alena crying in the background. Myrna gave birth to Craig Timothy Spurrier on the 13th of November that same year at an Essex County hospital near Baltimore. We now had two grandchildren—a boy and a girl.

Grandparents with Craig

Grandpa with visiting Alena

One of our most treasured possessions, adorned with a teddy bear on the front, is the card Miriam sent us for our first anniversary:

> **"Dear Mom and Larry**—It is unbearable to be here when what I want to do is to wish you a beary, beary HAPPY ANNIVERSARY! I couldn't be happier for you. You both have taught me a great deal about love, and you have an equal partnership that most marriages never achieve. The success of your marriage is not due to luck or chance: you both are extraordinarily giving individuals, which helps you to compromise when necessary. The harmony you have achieved in your relationship spills over into my life, and I'm very grateful for that. You are both such special people. You deserve the best that life has to offer. And you have found it—in each other. May your relationship continue to blossom, and change, and grow forever. —All my love, **Miriam."**

To send us this card, she had to reach the point where she no longer agonized over the prospect of feeling abandoned, of losing her mother. Did she reach this point easily? Absolutely not.

December 1988 brought the holidays, Chanukah, and

then Christmas. On the 21st I had left work early to attend a party at my boss's home. Myrna and family were at a time-share condo in Ocean City, MD, and Rosemary was still at work when she received Myrna's 3:00 p.m. phone call. A few answered questions later Myrna established the intended timing for Miriam's flight home for the holidays and that her plane was in jeopardy. She had learned this from breaking news on the television.

Rosemary rushed home and turned on the TV in time to hear news anchor Dan Rather say: "The plane (Pan Am Flight 103) exploded at 31,000 feet over Lockerbie, Scotland." Between unresponsive calls to Pan American Airways and the Syracuse program office, Rosemary called my boss's home and discovered I had already left the party. I was never much of a party person. I walked in the door at 5:30 that evening not suspecting the tragic news. I found Rosemary sitting on the steps and crying, with four couples, close friends, milling about the living room and dining room.

I got my explanation in a hurry, but there were so many things left in doubt for all of us. Was she actually on that plane? Did anyone actually survive the crash? Did they have any remains? What caused the explosion—was it an accident? The rabbi called me and wanted to come over. Rosemary told me: "No!" In her wish to extend her disbelief, she thought the rabbi's presence would confirm Miriam's demise and make it all real.

I took another call in the kitchen from a woman who started the conversation by saying her children had just come in the door. This broke me up and, in a rush of tears, I said: "Count your blessings, you still have children." I couldn't continue. I hung up the phone. To this day I don't know who it was, but I feel sorry for my mistreatment of the unknown woman. She didn't deserve my tirade. Marty Litzky found me sulking in the kitchen and asked if he could help. I told him of our plans for the three of us to fly to Miami for a two-week vacation. He volunteered to cancel the reservations for me.

After midnight that night Rosemary got through to Pan Am and they confirmed that an M. Wolfe was on the manifest. At eight the next morning a Scottish policeman declared there were no survivors. All hope for Miriam had dissolved into none. Without a body, a memorial service was held at Temple Beth Shalom and, amid hundreds of attendees, Rabbi Klensin did himself proud with Miriam's eulogy. They came from all over the East Coast and the Midwest—friends, relatives, and the curious. I met her father and stepmother for the first time that day and I extended my condolences to them.

Over the next two years, we received thousands of letters—many teaching us something more about Miriam that we didn't know. Quite a few carried a common message: that Miriam had somehow bonded with them and changed their lives for the better. Pictures and videos of the exploded plane on the ground and its remembered victims in the media drove home the ugly facts of the crash. I wrote an op-ed piece on ways to prevent these disasters for the *Baltimore Sun* and U.S. Senator Barbara Mikulski had it read into the *Congressional Record.*

We learned that Miriam's body was found on December 24th and days later identified with the help of fingerprints and personal items Rosemary had sent along to the FBI. Miriam's father and stepmother went to Dulles airport to receive her closed remains. Later that same day we received them at the funeral home in Severna Park. Originally, I hesitantly volunteered to make the facial recognition, but Rabbi Klensin came to our rescue. He affirmed that it was indeed Miriam and told us that we shouldn't be burdened with that despoiled memory of her. I purchased two more cemetery plots adjacent to where my Hannah lay. On January 9, 1989 her parents and stepparents laid Miriam to rest at Kneseth Israel cemetery with a private burial service.

Up to this point Rosemary had remained somewhat stoic and brave with only occasional outbursts of grief in the presence of friends and relatives. In private it was another story. Without interfering with her rightful need to mourn and grieve, I tried my best to console Rosemary, but sometimes she withdrew from me, repeatedly saying: "You don't know what its like to lose a child. You can't." She was right, I couldn't, exactly, but I had lost both parents and a life's mate for twenty-nine years over long and deteriorating periods, so I thought I, better than most, had some idea of what it was like. She disagreed. I cried for Miriam too, but I hadn't invested twenty years in her rearing from womb to college like her mother. There were more than a few times when she pushed me away to be alone, saying, "You just don't understand, you can't." I thought I was losing her. I fought through those thoughts and I'm glad that I did. We got past those saddest of times and wound up with an even stronger marriage.

Soon after the crash, remnants of bomb materials were found amid the widely spread wreckage. This launched the largest international investigation ever, involving the Scottish police, Scotland Yard, the FBI, Interpol, and the local police forces of many of the twenty-one involved nations. Little by little the hint of terrorism became a reality, and the investigation intensified in that pursuit.

In the months to follow we drove up to Syracuse and over to Virginia and DC for meetings, briefings, protests, and memorials. We received flags from President Reagan at the Executive Office Building and sympathetic words personally from two U.S. Secretaries of State (Reno and Powell). We pushed to have Miriam's personal things returned.

Rosemary started writing about Miriam. It began with turning her daughter's résumé into a press release that very day it all happened. Rosemary had been writing and editing for most of her adult life. She had been an assistant editor for *Harper's Magazine;* a copy editor for Williams and Wilkins' various medical journals; managing editor for *Chemical Times and Trends;* an engineering writer for Westinghouse; and the author of a half-dozen or so feature articles for the *Baltimore Sun* newspapers. Certainly, she was no stranger to the written word.

When Miriam's personal belongings began to trickle in, Rosemary found she had a treasure trove of original source material, enough to write a memoir about her. Letters, daily diaries, class papers, short stories, poems, news articles, and notes were at her disposal. In reading these things, she began to learn so much more about her daughter, some things she never knew. She even confessed having some guilt about prying into Miriam's inner thoughts. A strong sense of duty hung over Rosemary. The world needed to know who Miriam was and what marvelous things she had accomplished in her twenty short years. Someone had to write about her and who better than her own mother? So she began writing in earnest.

But there was a problem to be solved first. Rosemary had always written both objectively and subjectively, but had never put her *own* emotions to the page before, so her several attempts at an introduction came out flat and noncompelling. She realized this herself and agonized over it. I sat down over lunch one day at work and roughed out an introduction for her. She began to see how to grab the readers and draw them into Miriam's life. From then on

she wrote and wrote. For eight and a half years she wrote, and in 1999 Fithian Press published *Miriam's Gift: A Mother's Blessings—Then and Now.* My only contribution to the book was the short bit about my impressions of Miriam, my whole-hearted encouragement, and many lonely nights watching TV by myself. We didn't know it then, but Miriam's story was not quite complete. That would come years later.

In the time that followed, both pets met their end. When Hoppy the cat challenged a neighbor's large dog for his supper, he wound up on the short end of the argument. The neighbor was kind enough to spare us the burial details. Midnight, the dog, was constantly attracting fleas, despite all the pills and collars Rosemary attempted. When the fleas started to appear on visiting baby Craig, she decided it was time for Midnight to go back to the SPCA.

Early in 1989 Rosemary and her ex-husband, Jim Wolfe, entered into a lawsuit against Pan American Airways. A lawyer friend, Abel Merrill, referred us to the New York legal team of

Kriendler and Kriendler, specialists in airline disasters. On July 10, 1992 Pan Am was found guilty of willful misconduct, and all the Pan Am 103 families received a modest settlement. Pan Am had failed to X-ray unaccompanied baggage and/or search inter-airline baggage, including the bag containing the bomb; failed to use properly trained personnel in screening baggage; failed to carry out advertised and paid-for security measures; and failed to disseminate U.S. State Department bomb warnings to passengers.

Also in 1989 the families of the Pan Am Flight 103 victims banded together—at first for the return of personal belongings, and later to lobby Congress for better airline security. A newsletter called *Truth Quest,* representing the group, is still being disseminated, although much less frequently today. In November of 1990 Congress passed the Federal Aviation Security Improvement Act and it became law. The nation soon became aware of the changes this law brought about.

By mid-1990 we learned that both of our girls were pregnant for the second time. Myrna gave birth to Benjamin Lawrence

Our five grandkids: Alena, Craig, Ben, Leah, and Emily

Spurrier on September 19th. I thought it curious that Ben and Alena's birthdays had hugged each side of my September 20th birthday and that Miriam's was only six days away. I believe that each of my first cousins on my mother's side were also born on the twentieth of different months, and that brother George was born on the nineteenth of June.

Jackie gave birth to Leah Michelle Lau on the 4th of April, 1991 (Myrna's birthday) Another curiosity is that Leah's birthday closely follows Hannah's birthday of April 3rd. I regard all these curiosities as positive omens, even though there isn't a superstitious bone in my body—at least I haven't found one yet. Myrna's youngest, Emily Hannah Spurrier, arrived May 20, 1998.

At work I was asked to do my first computer-aided design and computer-aided engineering (CAD/CAE) project. The company, now Alliant Techsystems (a Honeywell spin-off), had acquired a major contract to build the controls for a super-speed, ten-channel, video recorder with interchannel synchronization and digital bit error correction. The company hired four young engineers and drafted me, the only digital design engineer currently at the facility, for the job. We attended two weeks of special CAD/CAE training at a facility in Rockville, MD, just north of DC.

My responsibility was to design and build the digital synchronization card. Its function was making sure that less than one picosecond of time difference existed between each of the recorded channels. The CAD/CAE library of components contained schematic representations of real functional components with all of their physical connection points shown. We took the components from the library and placed them on the computer screen. When all of our components were there, we made all of our point-to-point, electronic (functional) connections, resulting in one large schematic for each of our 18- by 12-inch, five-layered, printed-circuit boards.

At this point we applied computer-generated signals to the card's input and monitored testing points throughout the schematic version of the card to see if any changes were required to achieve the required outputs. In this way we created a test model for the finished product as well. Once we were satisfied the schematic complied, we physically placed computer-converted library components with their fingerprint images, i.e., their physically true connection points, on a fully scaled representation of the card. Now the computer was able to physically wire all of the interconnections by printed circuitry track with only a few manual interventions. The result was five printed-circuit drawings, which were sent out to become manufactured PC-boards, with the five layers laminated into one thick board and interconnected via computer-drilled, plated-through holes.

Components were inserted into computer-drilled, plated-through holes and soldered in place by passing the loaded board over a wave of molten solder, lifted from a solder bath ultrasonically to precisely immerse and make all the necessary connections. The boards were tested individually using the same test model employed to check the schematic version. A system test model was used to test everything as a unit. The project was a success, and we delivered twenty systems. This work was a far cry from the lab-intensive work I began my career with some thirty-odd years prior.

There had been a number of management and, yes, even firm name changes in the many years I'd been at this location. We usually briefed new management upon their arrival and in progress meetings. In my opinion, only a scant few managers were qualified for the job. I had to laugh when one of my former technicians told me he had a phone call from one of our former operations managers asking him what we actually did there in Annapolis.

Another of my peer engineering papers was selected for a Government symposium at the FBI's headquarters, the J. Edgar Hoover building in DC. Shortly afterward, I was promoted from senior project engineer to principal engineer. Then I returned to my signal analysis work. The arrival of my birthday in 1993 meant something entirely different—retirement.

Reflecting on my two wonderful wives, past and present, I oddly come to a wild observation about them, which I'd like to

At the FBI headquarters podium delivering my peer paper in Washington

call "the solder connection" and "the big round button." Hannah and Rosemary have both been exciting, attentive, faithful, and loving wives and companions, and I would surely pick each of them out of a crowd any day of the week. If I were privileged to meet them in an afterlife, I would choose them both. Don't tell me that I'd have to make a choice—I'd still need and want them both. However, I might note that the two of them differed in many respects—differences that helped shape my life at times when it required notable sculpting.

Aside from my love, respect, and companionship; Hannah needed absolutely nothing from anyone, including me. She functioned independently, developed strong opinions, exhibited a forceful will, exuded reliability, and was willing to tackle anything. She was neither bossy nor demeaning nor intrusive by any means, but she could wade into almost any task, see what had to be done, take charge, and do it right. Hannah inherited this uncanny talent for adding up a long column of figures three times and getting the same total each time, a task she relished, and one I envied. So Hannah managed our finances for the most part, always knowing what bank had the highest interest rates and pitching in equally at tax time. I had this knack for accounting, but a penchant for making careless mistakes on tax forms—blame it on poor penmanship and the lack of a computer. She could wade into a child's birthday party (ours or someone else's) and turn chaos into entertaining games.

Hannah was also mechanically savvy, and the following is an example of what she was capable of. Jackie and Myrna wanted to use a portable 45-rpm phonograph that Hannah had since her college days. It rotated, but for some reason it wasn't producing sound when the needle met the record. I was asked to look at it, but over a number of weeks I was busy with overtime at work and night school studies and I was bushed when I got home. Then, when I was ready to fix it, she told me she had taken care of it on her own, and it no longer needed my attention. She had taken apart the case and, after finding a loose wire, heated up my soldering iron and soldered it in place. Even her knowing where the wire had to go could have been problematic. It seems that I had married a techie after all.

On the other hand, Rosemary's technical gene is missing or at least suppressed, although I must say she has managed her computer with some degree of success. She repeatedly tells me: "You have to outlive me because I can't handle the four TV remotes, let alone the computer updates." Yes, there are times when the computer or the television misfires or she can't find where she saved something or "I've never done that before." Then her balding white knight on his charger rides to her rescue and wipes away the tears. "What did you press?" she'd ask. "The big round button on the Prime Fire remote," I'd tell her. To tell the truth, I don't dislike the role of Mr. Fixit—I've always been good at finding solutions. I've spent most of a lifetime doing it for a living. That's what an engineer does.

Then there's the vacuum cleaner incident. Rosemary rushed past me to my tool drawer and withdrew a hammer.

"Where are you going with that hammer?" I asked.

"I can't get the vacuum cleaner to go from floor to rug any more so I intend to discipline it."

"Put the hammer away and bring me the vac," I responded.

She did. I tinkered for a few minutes and handed it back to her with the lever allowing both the rug and hardwood floor settings.

"All fixed?" she asked.

"Yep."

"Would I have broken it with the hammer?"

"Probably," I answered.

One day Rosemary said that her sponges didn't last long before discoloring. "I can't get them clean no matter how often I rinse them." I suggested a bit of bleach might help. A day later she thanked me for the bright results; however, several days after that she complained that the sponges decomposed when she picked them up. When I asked how much bleach she added to the water, she responded, "What water?" I just smiled.

Rosemary's background in literature and art far exceeds my own, and her ability to make sense of my writing is excellent. She's a stickler to a style manual and, of course, *spelzz* much better than I do. Whereas I shrink from corresponding and telephoning, Rosemary lives for them. We spend a lot of time conversing and discussing things, and then there's that love of doing crossword puzzles together. We once loved tennis and travel and still share pro-football (especially the Redskins), *Jeopardy, Nova,* and *Masterpiece Theater* (on TV), opera, and theater. I can't think of a more perfect companion for me.

I have never met anyone kinder than Rosemary. Her charity lists are enough to make any checkbook a challenge to balance, and going out of her way to give rides to shut-ins, especially to Temple, is putting it mildly. She is always bringing food and dental items to the food bank. Rosemary's concern for my well-being is deep and genuine. She is always offering something to soothe and comfort my current, frequent, and plentiful ailments. Who could ask for more?

Chapter 12

Gains and Losses

The year was 1993. Myrna, Tim, and the two boys moved to Molokai, HI. Myrna and Tim had obtained state teaching jobs there. She wanted to be closer to Jackie, and Tim wanted to be a year-round outdoor athlete. Rosemary felt deprived and depressed, anticipating the loss of having the kids nearby, but now the two of us had even more reason to vacation in Hawaii. As long as Rosemary and I had been working, we'd stretched our two-week trips into three, but with retirement in hand, that visit could now be three months or more. A snowstorm greeted us getting off the plane in Maryland after a three-month stay the following year, so little by little our time in Hawaii got stretched into spending the entire winters there—approximately six months—from October through March. We actually wound up snowbirding it for over twenty years.

The longer Honolulu stays prompted us to search for a condo apartment to rent, so during one of our earlier stays, Rosemary and I walked around a few key neighborhoods until we came to the Princess Leilani building on Kanunu Street. We found an "Apartment for Rent" card on the bulletin board with a phone number. We called and made an appointment for the next morning with Michi Naruo, the owner. Our meeting was a success. The owner was a charming, trusting lady in her early seventies, and she eagerly rented us a portion of her furnished condo that included one bedroom, a bathroom, a living room, a dining room, and a well-equipped kitchen. A simple handshake and no lease was required. She reserved another bedroom, bath, and dressing room for her infrequent Honolulu visits, as she spent most of her time in California with her husband. Apartment 403, with its huge lanai, faced Kanunu Street, and the only disadvantage to living on such a low floor was that the traffic noise and car exhaust soot forced us to keep our sliding doors shut. Most years we rented a minivan to drive around the island.

Rosemary kept friendly with Michi by always remembering to include a cheery note with each rent check, and occasionally she would get a nice reply. Michi died a few years later, requesting that everyone wear purple, her favorite color, to her funeral. Her adult children rewarded our friendship with a favorite candy dish of Michi's. The rent checks then went to a daughter in California and Randy, her son, became our rental agent. Randy had us sign multiyear leases with a rent increase and new terms, because we would henceforth have the entire apartment at our disposal.

Within a year of arrival on Molokai, Tim was run off the road while riding his bicycle and assaulted by an irate, drunken local. Tim was beaten up as well. He recovered from his injuries with a short hospital stay, while the *haole*-hating local drew a two-year prison sentence. As it turned out, Tim taught at the same elementary school where the man's own child attended. When the errant local learned about this, he said that he wouldn't have done it if he'd known Tim was a teacher. Wow! What screwed-up thinking—it's okay to beat up strangers if they're not teachers. In fact, we later learned Tim wasn't his first victim.

When visiting the Spurriers in their home across the street from the ocean, we stayed in the Hotel Molokai about a half-mile away. With the island not being in the mainstream of tourist attention, the shoreline across from them was a treasure trove of seashells. Offshore, a shallow, muddy-bottomed shelf of turquoise water extended a half-mile or so, ending in dark blue-green ocean. In that ocean channel beyond, humpback whales came from the Arctic seas to spawn. Watching for breaching whales proved to be an exciting pastime.

The island, shaped like a hotdog in a bun, had but two

small supermarkets, one traffic light, no movie theater, and very few other amenities. With an unspoiled floral and unique rocky coast at the east end and white sandy beaches and a mountain at the west end, a solitary highway connected the island's beautiful ends. The high north-central portion of the island featured some of the world's tallest cliffs, overlooking the Kalaupapa Peninsula and Father Damien's former leper colony.

At night, the lack of bright city lights afforded the clearest views of the heavens above that I have ever seen. We'd lie back on pool lounges every night before turning in and soak up the constellations.

The sprawling Hotel Molokai was indeed quaint. Its restaurant servers were all *mahus*, Hawaiians who embody both male and female spirit. Our room had what Rosemary called "the resident gecko," a small, green, wall-walking lizard who makes smacking noises that sound like kissing. One thing our room did not have was any sort of clock. One evening before leaving the island, we wanted to be sure to wake on time to make an early morning flight back to Oahu. At the desk Rosemary asked for a wake-up call at six-thirty. Since the hotel was not equipped for automated wake-ups, we assumed that the desk clerk had turned away to obtain a clock. At that very moment a wild gamecock crowed loud and clear. Rosemary and I had this mutual thought: the clerk was going to hand us one of those colorful roosters to take back to our room. Our joke. Of course, he handed us a small wind-up alarm clock instead. As a note, wild gamecock fighting is illegal in the islands, but it is also quite prevalent anyway. Tiny A-framed wildfowl houses with tethered fowl can be seen on all of the islands.

Previously, the worldwide investigation into the Pan Am Flight 103 bombing had progressed to the point where, in 1991, the U.S. had indicted two Libyan intelligence agents, Abdel Basset Megrahi and Lamen Khalifa Fhimah, for the infamous deed. The big problem there was that Moammar Gadhafi, the Libyan leader, shielded these killers from being extradited until an agreement was reached in1998 among Libya, the United States, and the United

Kingdom. This agreement specified that the indicted two would be tried under Scottish law using five Scottish judges in the neutral country of the Netherlands. The chosen site was Camp Zeist, a former U.S. Air Force base there.

The trial began in May of 2000 and concluded in January 2001 with a guilty verdict for Megrahi and a not-guilty verdict for Fhimah. As there is no death penalty under Scottish law, Megrahi received a twenty-year prison sentence without the possibility of parole. Testimony had proven that a small piece of the bomb's timing board was part of one that Megrahi had purchased in Switzerland. It was also proven that clothing he purchased in Malta was used to disguise the tape recorder containing the bomb.

Although it was strongly believed that Fhimah's professional association with the Malta-based airline enabled him to bypass normal luggage scrutiny and put the baggage containing the bomb-laden recorder on the plane, the corroborating evidence was considered too circumstantial. This was despite the fact that it was proven the two were in close contact on the day the bomb suitcase was planted. Although we survived several anxious trial appeals, each of them was later denied.

The bomb suitcase traveled from the island nation of Malta to Frankfurt, Germany, where it was transferred without the required interline scrutiny to Pan Am Flight 103. The bomb then traveled to Heathrow in London, where the plane took on more passengers. The same plane took off again, headed for New York and, this time reached the critical altitude that triggered the bomb's timer, which then counted down to detonation over Lockerbie, Scotland. There were no survivors.

Rosemary and I traveled to Camp Zeist to sit in on the trial for a week. We had been following the trial quite closely beforehand. A special and secure computer website provided not only daily transcripts of every word said at the trial, but summaries and translations as well. There were video facilities set up in New York and Washington for the families to view trial proceedings. We kept our trial summaries in loose-leaf binders for most of the trial.

At Camp Zeist we discovered that the prisoner holding facility had all the comforts of home, including prayer rooms, specially prepared Muslim meals, television, and pleasant decor. Even U.S. prisoners are not treated that nicely. The courthouse had strict security measures in place with armed guards everywhere. Visitors in stadium-style seating viewed the main courtroom through a thick, bullet-proof glass window. A similar window at the rear of the visitors' room separated us from the United Nations observer team. The visitor area on the left was roped off for the defendants' families. Of course, separate restroom facilities were provided for them and the victim families to prevent spontaneous clashes.

Inside the main courtroom to our right sat the four judges and a chief judge on a raised, polished-wood podium with a jeweled silver scepter and Scottish shield on the wall behind them. At the start of each court day the judges paraded in, ceremoniously carrying the scepter. The desks inside were arranged in a four-tier semicircle; the near group belonged to the defense while the far group belonged to the prosecution. A wide aisle separated the two groupings. Although we never counted them, there had to be at least thirty people in the room, mostly legal types. The prisoners were in the top tier closest to the glass barrier. Documents and evidence items were shown to the visitors via television screens.

The portion of the trial that we witnessed considered the legality of a business partner opening a commercial desk belonging to Megrahi to obtain the date book that would closely connect the two prisoners—a pickup at the airport, mutual living arrangements, shared meals, and meetings on the day the suitcase was put aboard the Malta flight.

It rained the entire time we spent at Zeist, so there wasn't much of a chance to see the surrounding area. Some of us walked to town in the rain anyway. Other family members in attendance at the trial joined us for dining, socializing, and comparing notes. I especially appreciated the basket full of Dutch mini-cheese rounds for breakfast each day.

After attending court all five days that it was in session that week, a train ride took us back to Amsterdam. Not realizing first-class travel included a meal on the train, we purchased sandwiches and drinks in the rail station prior to leaving. Twenty minutes into the trip, our carry-on meal eaten, a waiter in a white coat pulled a table out of the wall next to us and set it with a white cloth, china plates, and dinnerware. How were we to know—it wasn't covered in any of our French lessons.

After two years on Molokai, the Spurriers sought more opportunities and a better education for their children than the smallish island could afford. So they looked for new teaching jobs on the Big Island of Hawaii. That's right—Hawaii, HI—is that any different than New York, NY? They found teaching positions there, but they soon discovered that the public schools were lacking in many respects, and the existing private schools were not progressive enough. This gave them the impetus to open their own private school on the Big Island.

Starting with twelve children in an empty storefront, Waimea Country School soon flourished and grew, so they had to find additional space. They rented a house and second storefront, hired additional teachers, and it wasn't long before they were serving all the grades, kindergarden through eighth. Over time, there were even a few celebrity kids in attendance. The school and Spurrier home were located in Waimea, high on a foothill of Mauna Kea (White Mountain). To distinguish this Waimea from others in Hawaii, many of the locals called it Kamuela, which is Hawaiian for Samuel, honoring Samuel Parker, one of the largest ranchers in the U.S.

The first Spurrier home there was a rented duplex rancher that sat smack-dab in the rear of a cul de sac, which afforded them a fairly safe play space for the kids. A few years later they bought a one-owner house that had belonged to a Japanese family who visited their school children in the U.S. only twice a year for a week. As a result, it was in great shape.

We visited them on the Big Island for all of the long holiday weekends during our winter stays. It was great to be able to be a part of their lives and watch the grandkids grow. One of the larger resort hotels on the Kona coast near Waikoloa served our needs nicely, as we could bring the kids down to swim, dine, and play tennis and Ping-Pong with us. I would mention the hotel's name, except that its name, layout, and ownership have changed so many times.

On occasion we brought visiting guests such as Jo Gormley and daughter Mara. Another time we brought John and Ann Pollack. Once, when George and Mitzie came, the hotel gave us the concierge suite, because we had so many sleep-over credits. Over the years we covered many of the Big Island restaurants and sights. We went back to Volcanoes National Park and the black sand beaches several times.

Jackie had left her job as art director at the Boys and Girls Club of America and became an art teacher at the Linekona Center of the Honolulu Academy of Art, teaching both adults and children. She also did contract work for the Artists in the Schools program, using student help to create beautiful ceramic 3D murals on outer school walls.

When her girls, Alena and Leah, reached the ripe old age of two and a half, Jackie enrolled them in ballet. Her two girls were quite adept at it. Whenever Rosemary and I were in town we tried to relieve Jackie of getting the girls to and from ballet class, preschool, and later gymnastics, and much later, high school and track. Of course, we attended recitals and meets when we were able—like grandparent groupies should. We enjoyed every minute of being with them.

Rodney, fresh from becoming a Certified Public Accountant, hired on as a contract employee of the Department of Hawaiian Home Lands, a state government agency geared to provide housing loans to first-time homeowners of Hawaiian blood; provide accompanying infrastructure; and manage resources. He soon discovered that, due to some past disaster (flooding or fire or maybe even gross neglect), the records of existing loan payees comprised only those actually making monthly payments. Computer records were completely nonexistent. Rodney set to work to first computerize everything and then resolve all outstanding loans.

Because of his efforts to successfully restore order from near chaos, the agency chiefs sought to hire him as a government employee. However, Rodney wisely chose not to hire on at entry level as the salary system required. The chiefs were so determined to have him that they were forced to go to the legislature and get a law passed to hire him at a more appropriate level. Many years later, he rose in the system to become the Administrative Services Officer of Hawaiian Home Lands, with presentation responsibilities and accountability to the state legislature. We are extremely proud of him.

With the Waimea school thriving, Myrna informed us that she was pregnant again and Emily Hannah Spurrier arrived on the 20th of May 1998. Growing up, Emily was surrounded by animals. The school had started an animal care program and, as time went on, the Spurriers somehow acquired backyard ducks, sheep, rabbits, guinea pigs, and birds.

Emily bottle-nursing a lamb

Emily walking an alpaca

Computers have alway held such a fascination for my grandson Craig that he soon began following Julia, the Waimea Country School's computer specialist, picking her brain and watching her every move until he became quite a computer whiz on his own. He read everything he could on the subject of computers, even dissecting old discarded computers. At one point he and Julia started

Hawaiian Hosting, serving a fair number of online email accounts. Today, Craig owns that firm outright.

As a student, Craig turned out be extremely bright and quite an accomplished reader, so he soon became bored with classroom work. However, he was self-disciplined enough to pursue his high school diploma online from the Krista McCullough Academy. In fact, starting at age twelve or thirteen, he completed this course ahead of time in three years. By the age of fourteen he had enrolled at Aiken Technical College.

Waimea was actually a horse town in many ways. The Parker ranch, at one time the largest privately owned ranch in the U.S., actually surrounded the town. The Spaniards had brought horses and cows to the island a few centuries earlier. Because the early Hawaiians didn't eat beef, the cattle multiplied too quickly. One of the ruling kings hired John Parker to manage them, but Parker had to go to Argentina to bring back cowboys, called paniolas.

When ten-year-old Ben acquired a few free horseback-riding lessons, they spurred him on to beg for more of the same. Our birthday gift led to several additional lessons. We got to watch his riding lessons at the beautiful North Kohala Ranch, located on a steep slope running down to the ocean and overlooking the neighboring island of Maui. The indoor riding facility at this ranch was first class, with crystal chandeliers, and even the horse stalls were decorated with polished brass lamp-heads and fixtures.

Ben was a natural, so the Spurriers purchased a horse named Barbi and a small plot of grazing land they hoped would become the next site of their school. Then they bought Peaches and Jett, a second and third horse, so the rest of the family could ride along with him. These horses started Ben on a path that would eventually lead him to equine reining and cutting competitions and a number of trophy belts and ribbons at regional horse fairs in his later teens. Even a world championship was in his future.

In 2001 the Spurriers made a plan to consolidate their school and give it some sort of permanence. They had scouted out a piece of grazing land earlier and envisioned the construction of a classroom building. When fund-raising schemes were mentioned, many of the tuition-paying parents rebeled against the idea, seeing the school merely as a here-and-now measure to educate their kids—an alternative to the much-lacking public school system. They had no vision for the future, nor any desire to help finance it. As a result, dissention among the parents turned ugly. The growing hard feelings led the Spurriers to give up the reins of the school and move to South Carolina's horse country in 2002. Barbi, the horse, was flown to California and trailered the rest of the way. Peaches and Jett, the lesser horses, were sold to singer-songwriter Kenny Loggins before they left.

Chapter 13

On Writing: A New Endeavor

I finally wrote my letter of departure from Alliant Techsystems, gathered up my technical books and other personal belongings, and left work for home for the last time in September of 1993. My work books were included because there was a chance of doing consulting work for some of my former long-term customers. There were friendly lunches with a number of my technical cronies over many years after my retirement. But the consulting part never really blossomed, for as soon as the extra time appeared on my hands, the Hawaii novel mentioned on my first date with Rosemary drew all of my writing attention—even though neither Rosemary nor I had ever written any fiction before.

The emerging novel writing was slow, dull, and awkward at first. The initial Hawaiian *pidgin* title, *Murdah Is Fo Ewa*, was so obscure that no Mainlander *haole* would realize that Ewa was a community on the south shore of Oahu or that the Hawaiian word *haole* meant "without breath" or, more typically, "foreigner." Caucasians didn't greet each other in the ancient traditional Hawaiian way of blowing in one's face, so they were treated as outsiders.

Setting the promising novel aside, I joined Rosemary in writing our own separate essays. There was a need to hone my writing skills more before going on to longer fiction. Rosemary was already successful in submitting and publishing essays and articles in local newspapers and magazines on a frequent basis. I had no such publishing experience. All there was to rely on was my technical writing—equipment technical manuals, technical proposals, and peer technical papers. The two of us even joined a literary critique group that specialized in essays; we picked up all sorts of tips on improving our writing. Some of the group were members of the Maryland Writers' Association, and suggested the two of us might benefit from that association as well. We did join and remained members in good standing all the years we remained in Maryland.

Right up until the time *Miriam's Gift* was published in 1999, nearly all of Rosemary's writing time had been devoted to her book. I waited and waited for her help on fiction writing, sometimes even impatiently. However, she did keep what she called her Hawaii diary—really a never-ending collection of anecdotes, customs, and facts that grew with each winter's visit. Meanwhile, I had been working the Hawaii novel once more and hammered out a plot with a working title of *Rainbow's Reach*. The story was still choppy, way too long, and needed quite a lot of work. I set it aside for another, shorter, project while waiting for Rosemary to finish her memoir.

In 1995 the two of us joined another Maryland critique group, more suited to the long fiction and novel genres. The group met once a month, and three of the nine members would read chapters from their work in progress each time we met. We endured this for about a year before deciding the critiques were too slow in coming, and too little was covered: thus, there was hardly any continuity after a three-month wait. Also, there were too many genres represented and none of them were mystery or memoir. We had to look elsewhere for help. The engineer in me began to rile: there must be some analytical breakout of this mystery beast, an overall blueprint and a set of components with hand-holding instructions for assembly.

The Odyssey program at Johns Hopkins University (JHU) advertised a writing course with a well-known novelist. Rosemary and I took two semesters with Fabienne Marsh in a scheduled classroom, with other students, and did learn quite a lot about descriptions and characters and plotting. Following this, we made Fabienne a proposal: Would she meet us one-on-two to critique just our work in progress? We agreed on the terms, and she arranged a meeting room seven stories below the entrance level in the JHU Milton Eisenhower library—down where the dusty tomes are kept. I believe the effort we put in that room had a major effect on our ensuing work. We both benefited.

Saul Pollack, Rosemary's father, passed away in 1991. Before his death he had given Rosemary a secret list of malapropisms that his longtime housekeeper and cook, Dorothy, had uttered casually in his presence. Her amusing misuse of words in the English language usually conjured up other pertinent meanings. It was his intention that we submit the list to *Reader's Digest.* When I listened to the myriad of Dorothy anecdotes that Rosemary related, I thought all this material would make a wonderful fictional character, much too good to waste on a fifty-dollar submission prize. She agreed. I'd been toying with some mystery ideas, so I sat down and began a mystery novel that featured characters who resembled Saul, his Dorothy, and (confidentially) some of Rosemary's aunts and cousins.

Saul became Dr. Avi Kepple, Dorothy became Molly, and Dorothy's malapropisms morphed into malaprops and then mollyprops. But needing a detective for the story, I recalled Chief Inspector Garcia from Barcelona, Spain, whom I had met forty years earlier aboard ship. I turned him into Paco LeSoto, a retired Baltimore police detective, filling in as a part-time policeman for a small fictitious town on the western shore of the Chesapeake Bay called Black Rain Corners. It was fictitious only because I wanted to change the scenery—a large plantation-style mansion atop a sheer cliff overlooking the bay.

I finished the first draft just as Rosemary put her memoir to bed, so this was to be our first book. At this point our responsibilities became clear. I was the more devious, so I would manage story plot. Rosemary had an eye for detail, so she would take my characters and scenes and build on them until the characters had believable personalities and the scenes were plausible, if not actually recognizable. For example, she chose the Stan Hywet house in

Akron, Ohio as a model for the interior of the mansion. My partner-in-crime-writing also attacked my overly wordy verbiage with a vengeance. Together, we had a great deal of fun working out the details of the mansion's secret rooms and how they were accessed.

Locks & Cream Cheese was published in 2001 by Publish America, Inc. The rear cover blurb read as follows:

Paco LeSoto, a dapper retired detective, and Molly Mesta, a witty housekeeper-cook, team up as an endearing pair of sleuths. They encounter murder and mayhem among the residents of Black Rain Corners, a quaint Maryland town on the shores of the Chesapeake Bay. A million-dollar painting and a jeweled antique key disappear from Marche House mansion. Hidden rooms, locked doors, and dead bodies embroil the town's elite Historical Society in sizzling scandal. Trapped in the web of suspicion are a psychoanalyst, an alcoholic gambler, a mob enforcer, an iron-pumping gigolo, and an art dealer from the Orient. Paco and Molly expose the mansion's terrifying secrets and fall in love.

* * * *

The reviewers used words like: "an enjoyable, mind-bending mystery. The characters are extremely vivid and likeable, and the classic locked-door corpse story finds a totally new twist"; and "a one-of-a-kind upstairs-downstairs story, and it happens here on the Chesapeake Bay. I loved the book."

The publisher did absolutely nothing to promote the book, so in 2000 I bought a book on Hypertext Markup Language (HTML) and absorbed what I could about it. I'd programmed in other computer languages at school and work, so this was not all that foreign to me. My first project was to build a website to publicize our books. Our twelve-year-old grandson Craig, already a whiz at these things, obtained "magicile.com" for our domain name and critiqued my efforts upon my completion of the site. Unfortunately, the "magicisle.com" domain was already taken by some Honolulu-area gym. Craig was now so proficient with computers and websites that the underaged lad took the webmaster's exam in his father's name and passed it.

My next project was to convert the book's text to a Kindle format for e-readers. Whereas today there are many automatic conversion programs to do this, they were either too expensive or not readily available then. I inserted the HTML characters into the text manually. Even with the auto conversion programs I use today, some manual touch-ups are still necessary to achieve professional-looking formats.

Having some small success with our first published book and loving its characters, I roughed out the plot for a second book, a Paco and Molly sequel, based on a Collette tour of the National Parks out West. We had taken that tour in 1997. I reversed the day-to-day order of the trip to accommodate the plot. Rosemary loved the idea and jumped into the project. *Hot Grudge Sunday* was published in 2004 by Publish America, Inc. The rear cover blurb read as follows:

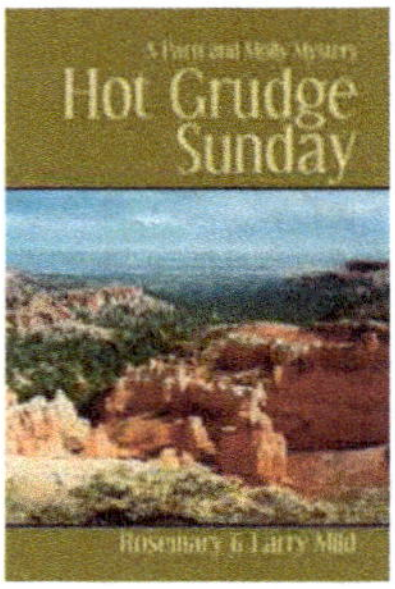

Inspector Paco and Molly, the endearing sleuths who fell in love in *Locks & Cream Cheese*, board a Vermilion Tours luxury bus for a blissful honeymoon out West. But conspirators and bank robbers sour their adventures through Yellowstone, Zion National Park, and the Grand Canyon. Each day dawns with a spine-chilling accident—on the Snake River; at Old Faithful; in a posh hotel bed. But are they accidents?

The perils and pranks seem to target Ray Symington, a ruthless, womanizing corporate vice president, who is leading his salesmen and their wives on this tour. Fearing for his life, he turns to Paco and Molly for help. They'd rather smooch than sleuth. But when they themselves—and other fellow travelers—also become victims, they start digging and uncover murderous schemes as spectacular as the Rockies and Lake Powell. They want to stop the attacks. But will they be too late?

* * * *

The reviewers used words like: "....a delightful action-packed ride. The story is full of surprises, and kept me riveted. I'm already looking forward to Molly's next adventure."

Believing there was at least one more story in the Paco and

Molly murder mystery series, I set to work on the plot for the third book, based on two sets of twins. One could guess that I was greatly influenced by a few of the Gilbert and Sullivan plots. Rosemary joined me in being quite a fan of the two operetta geniuses. We especially liked accompanying Carol and Tom Allen, our Towson friends, to the Bryn Mawr School in Baltimore to enjoy a summer performance of another one of their operettas. Once we tossed the ideas around, Rosemary contributed quite a lot to this plot, as well as her character and scene development. *Boston Scream Pie* was published in 2008 by Hilliard and Harris. The rear cover blurb read as follows:

The roiling blizzard toys with the overweight Chrysler. The momentum leads to impact: a crunching of metal and glass. Caitlin Neuman awakes from this nightmare, wondering if it might be a harrowing memory—she's the lone survivor of a crash that killed her parents and twin sister years earlier. Or could the nightmare be an eerie insight into some family she's never met? She engages relentless Detective Paco LeSoto and his clever wife, Molly, to find out the truth. Their investigation takes them to the family of Newton Boston and yet another set of twins. Newton discovers that his sexy blonde bride, Delylah, is a real piece of work—with three deceased husbands and two adult children who churn up plots to sabotage their new household. When a bizarre death rocks their beachside home, the clues point to murder.

* * * *

A sampling of what the reviewers had to say:

"It's not often I hate a character from the first line I read, but Delylah is one of those. By page eight you know she is a cold-hearted, conniving bitch. A charmer of a novel with interesting and despicable characters."—*The Baryon Review of Books.*

"This mystery sparkles and shines and if there is such a thing as a V.C. Andrews 'cozy' you will love it!"—*Feathered Quill Book Reviews.*

"**We have added** *Boston Scream Pie* to our recommended reading list."—*Suspense Magazine.*

* * * *

Rosemary and I made the mistake of aging the Paco and Molly characters much too rapidly, so we figured that a fourth mystery featuring them would not be plausible. Thus, the Hawaii novel, much labored over and now well-polished, emerged from the dust once more and begged to be finished. The 140,000-word *Rainbow's Reach* was cut by 10,000 words and renamed *Cry Ohana, Adventure and Suspense in Hawaii—ohana* meaning "family" in Hawaiian. *Cry Ohana* was published in 2010 by Publish America, Inc. The rear cover blurb read as follows:

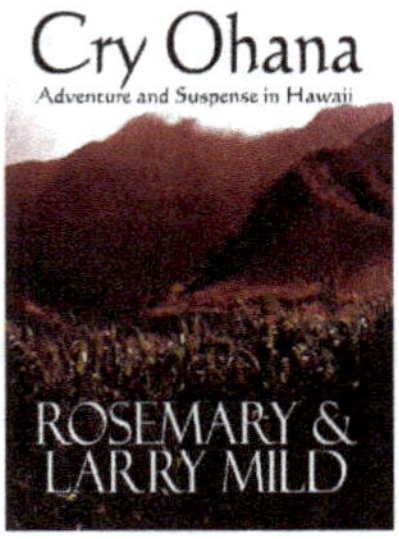

When Hank Pualoa drives drunk, killing his beautiful wife, he tears apart his Hawaiian family (o'hana) and leaves the Islands in shame. His children thrive with their grandmother until twelve-year-old Kekoa witnesses the murder of Big John, his loving uncle. The murderer stalks him, plotting to kill his only witness. Kekoa flees, plunging into a hand-to-mouth life in the sugarcane fields, the Chinatown streets, and as a baker's helper to a Japanese couple. A stray black Lab becomes his only friend. He's lost his sister, Leilani, to a foster home, where she falls in love but yearns for her family. And will their father ever return?

Cry Ohana vibrates with local color and breathtaking scenery. But danger lurks everywhere—at a Filipino wedding; at a Maui resort; and amid the Big Island's volcanic steam vents. Blackmail and betrayal erupt as the family struggles to reunite and bring down the killer.

* * * *

A sampling of what the reviewers had to say:

"The beautiful setting, engaging characters, and lively plot combine to bring readers a story that is literally difficult to put down. The 405-page novel deftly moves between the characters and their stories, concluding with a satisfying finish. It is an engaging story of tragedy, hope, and unconditional love."**—Edie Dykeman, Editor,** *Bella's Online Mystery Books.*

"This is an action packed story that will keep the readers guessing whether there will ever be a happy ending. The setting is beautiful and tells a story of Hawaii's customs and scenery that add a lot to the story."—**happyruby,** *Internet Book Database Reviews.*

"**....Cry Ohana took** me on a tour of the Hawaiian Islands and introduced me to their diverse ethnicity. The characters were easy to get to know – wouldn't mind meeting those resilient kids."—**Mary Ann Smyth,** *BookLoons Mystery Reviews.*

"***Cry Ohana* is** a choice pick, highly recommended."—**Margaret Lane,** *Midwest Book Reviews.*

"**I was hooked** from the very first page....there is plenty of suspense, intrigue, blackmail and betrayal. The characters are very easy to connect with. The descriptions of Hawaii are excellent. Adventure and suspense make this a book you won't want to miss."—
Readers Favorite.com—*Cry Ohana, Adventure and Suspense in Hawaii*, 2011 Gold Award Winner, Fiction - Mystery.

"**. . . . such a compelling** story. They mix into the tale a rich Hawaiian culture with Hawaii's ethnic mix of different people. Chase scenes and plot twists abound in this exciting story. We are given murder and blackmail as well as human pathos and drama in abundance. *Cry Ohana* is an exciting and poignant story rating a 9 of 10 on the Weaver meter." —**Sid Weaver@***Mainly Mysteries.*

"**Cry Ohana vibrates** with local color . . . I loved this story! The authors write with such eloquent detail, you can almost feel the island breezes and see the breathtaking scenery. I've been to Hawaii numerous times and lived there as a child, so I was familiar with many of the places described. This is an uplifting story of family and love, as well as being an extremely suspenseful novel with a very satisfying ending."—**Tanzey Cutter,** *Fresh Fiction Reviews.*

* * * *

With the indictment, trial, disposition, and multiple appeals of the bombers and the many additional memorials dedicated to Miriam, Rosemary felt that her first memoir, *Miriam's Gift*, told only half the story that needed to be known. She returned to writing about her daughter and *Miriam's World—and Mine* was published in 2012 by Magic Island Literary Works, our own brand, with the following rear cover blurb:

"I plan to sing and dance my way through life, become internationally famous and live happily ever after," Miriam Wolfe wrote in her high school yearbook. But her dreams ended brutally in December 1988. Returning home from a Syracuse University semester in London, she died in the terrorist bombing of Pan Am Flight 103 over Lockerbie, Scotland.

Join her mother, Rosemary Mild, on her jagged journey from the grief of losing her only child to renewed courage inspired by Miriam's legacy of love, humor, idealism—at age eleven she wrote to President Jimmy Carter, advising him on how to save the environment. *Miriam's World—and Mine* leads us through two decades up to the present, revealing the saintly people of Lockerbie; the stalwart Pan Am families who spearheaded a law for improved airline security; the investigation by the CIA, FBI and Scotland Yard. And the harrowing trial of the two bombers. Most anguishing of all is the convicted Libyan bomber's release, truly a betrayal of the 270 Flight 103 victims. Even today, how can a mother let go of anger (and should she?), when governments value politics over the lives of our innocent loved ones?

But wrapped around these nightmares, you'll find comfort and joy—optimism undefeated—in the array of families' memorials: scholarships, sculptures, a baseball field, and the Syracuse University Remembrance Quilt.

Finally, curl up with Miriam's wisdom and wit in her entertaining stories, poems, diaries, and essays.

* * * *

One reviewer had this to say:

"**Reading about Miriam** has had a very big effect on my life—I really carry her wisdom with me every day now. I had gotten away from seeing the joy of each day and she has restored my spirit. What a fabulous legacy." **—Kate White, Editor-in-Chief, *McCalls*, 1993.**

* * * *

No Place To Be But Here

After *Locks & Cream Cheese* we began to market our books in a small way—the only way we could. Major newspapers and magazines won't review books published by small and independent publishers. A hometown paper, such as the Annapolis *Capital*, was kind enough to run a feature article on us as coauthors releasing a new book, but steered clear of any kind of review. Even hiring a publicist couldn't help break that barrier. A publicist could, however, get us online, blog-style reviews, but a publicist would cost thousands of dollars and, at this point, we weren't sure enough about the sellability of our work.

We turned, instead, to selling at book signings—anyone who would have us. There were bookstores, book clubs, craft fairs, and community/alumnae/religious/civic associations. With its bagel on the cover, *Locks* sold well at local bagel shops. At all of these venues we'd sit at a table with a pile of books and a sign, MEET THE AUTHORS. A single day's return varied from ten to thirty-five books. A three-day weekend might yield more than seventy books. It's a lot of work and hard on the voice when you have to hawk your books for hours on end, but it is fun mixing with people. We'd ask: Do you like to read? And do you enjoy a good mystery? These questions drew in many of the sales, but we still had responses of another sort—such as: "I don't read." "I don't have time to read" and "I have enough mystery in my life." Can you imagine a mother with an eight-year-old in tow, saying, "I don't read"?

At one unfortunate signing at Border's bookstore, the manager convinced us that they would handle all the sales and they would give us a full check for the proceeds. We invited friends to the store who would have bought directly from us otherwise. We sold twenty books that day, and when it came time for payment, the manager informed us that the check would have to come from Corporate. Well, after several months of nonpayment, Borders bookstores went belly up, leaving us high and dry. We applied to the auditors as a viable creditor and were refused due to the size of our claim. Horsefeathers!

Attending the more informal gatherings, Rosemary and I gave prepared back-and-forth spiels from scripts and answered questions afterward. One of the most frequent questions was: "How do coauthors write?" Several presumed that each of us wrote alternate chapters. As difficult or ridiculous as that may seem, some books have been written that way. For example, *The Rule of Four* was written that way by seniors at two different universities. Our method is quite different, as you will soon see.

Writing is neither all joy nor all toil. It is more a complex mix of the two, yet writing is what I seem to do best, especially given my age and circumstances. I am extremely fond of the one-on-one discussions with Rosemary on story ideas and details, which range from the ridiculous to the beneficial. In time, something pertinent usually arises out of the topical batting back and forth, and I write a five to fifteen-page statement of work to capture these gems. I prefer the statement because I personally find outlining far too restrictive and formal. It seems to demand adherence—some loss of plot freedom.

Upon mutual agreement, I begin the most enjoyable portion of our coauthoring partnership, the first draft. That draft and the story plot are my responsibility, since Rosemary has dubbed me the more devious of the two of us. While the first draft continues to preserve the general intent and concept of the statement of work, it invariably tends to deviate from its story flow and sometimes even its order. This is due in part to the emerging strengths and weaknesses of our characters and the research facts imposed on the plot. It is these variances that provide the fun of not fully knowing where the plot will lead me and how the characters will fare on the way.

A second draft provides a continuity check, seeing that all of the necessary parts are included and making sure that the document is much more than just readable. My characters are the characters essential to carrying out the plot. They are thin on traits, and for the most part, are lacking a complete personality. My scenes are sometimes missing components needed for the reader to correctly envision the time, place, and mood. Often an additional scene may be required to bridge two events or to set up the next scene's arrival. For these maladies I call upon my partner in crime.

Now it's Rosemary's turn to take my second draft and build upon it. She applies a new pair of eyes, a reader's perspective and an editor's judgment for detail. By the time I complete a 250-page first draft, my characters are as well known to me as relatives and friends. I easily recognize them by name, deed, dress, and personality. There's a comfort level in knowing this when I pass my second draft on to Rosemary. So I'm surprised and somewhat annoyed when the next draft comes back to me and there are strangers moving through my original plot: Stan, Phil, Louise, and Joy?

"What happened to my buddies: Ralph, Bill, Jill, and Harriet?"

"Well," my wife replies, "the character just didn't act like a Ralph to me, so I made him Stan."

"And Jill?" I ask.

"Her name sounds too much like Bill, so I made her Joy."

Rosemary has a valid answer for each name change, so now I have to introduce myself to four new characters. Usually, I try to defend my choices, but in the long run, we iron out the third draft with her choices.

We write at different paces, and so, more often than not, we are working on different projects at the same time. I might be a whole novel ahead of her. This means that when she interrupts me to ask about one of the characters, I have to reply, "Who dat?"

* * * *

Well, after Rosemary has done her job in producing the third draft, she performs the sanity check on the overall work by producing a fourth draft. It is number four that I see next and it is then we negotiate. Not everything either one of us has written pleases the other, so we negotiate for the best of both writers to emerge. The changes elicit new ideas and angles and those too are negotiated into being—or not. Once all of the changes are incorporated into a fifth draft, we now have the makings of a novel. All that remains for the manuscript is proofreading to make it submittable. Each of us reads this draft front-to-back, back-to-front, and line-at-a-time several times before reading aloud to each other.

Marketing a manuscript is perhaps the most distasteful, yet most important, part of the writing effort. Superlative telephone, written, and emailed queries must be generated and executed to persuade agents, editors, and publishers to consider your work. Then you wait and wait and wait some more. Most often you hear nothing. Sometimes there is a rejection slip and, rarely, the sought-after acceptance.

One gloomy afternoon I was feeling low, way down after a few too many rejection slips. So I picked myself up by writing the following tongue-in-cheek piece:

Hello! I am Manuscript, a neglected one at that, and whether you know it or not, stories like mine have feelings, meaning, and purpose. My creative parents have endowed me with certain of their finest attributes, and I have an obligation to convey these to my readers. Despite my eagerness to please and inform, I am also bound to endure a long and arduous journey.

One doesn't easily forget the anxiety of being suppressed in the dark recesses of a mind—mulling, gestating, and waiting for a life on paper, or at least a trial at lip service. During my struggle to exist, I'm called many things; finally, I'm baptized with a working title. My initial exposure to the monitor is terrifying. I'm in my first draft and shaking. My prenatal experience is filled with disruptive punctuation, spelling, rephrasing, and annoying forethoughts and flashbacks. Then, emotionally torn from my birth printer, I arrive in complete innocence, all eight-and-a-half by eleven inches and twenty-pound bond of me. If I am not perfect, how can this be my fault? I had nothing to do with my origins. In fact, I appeared on the purest of blank pages made from humble rag and mere pulp.

I crave my parents' affection. Do they think me precious and commendable? If I'm rejected, what will become of me? I could be thrown in drawers to jaundice away, shelved to gather layers of dust, locked up in loose-leaf binders to serve some guiltless sentence, crunched and mutilated beyond repair in deep round baskets, and utterly abandoned for eternities.

I survive, but there are worse travails ahead for the likes of me. My pages are deemed worthy to travel to one or more meccas of literary processing gurus—there to be judged, not only for gems of wordsmanship, style, content, or cohesiveness; but mostly for the possible wealth and privilege I can generate in the publishing field. My touted attributes and my parents' pedigrees are included in many initial query letters to addressees obtained on websites that vociferously solicit submissions of my particular phylum, family, and genre. I try to contain my emotions when I see these letters eliciting only a modest number of form letter responses—a few with invitations to submit in the future and a considerably larger number to effectively take a literary hike. I'm further insulted when the message is "My stable is full" or "We're not taking any new clients until the next millennium" or "We are no longer accepting submissions of that genre." Those negative responses make me wonder why they are still soliciting on their websites. Yet the affirmative few turn a bright new page in my life.

What happens next? I'm forced to lose weight, shed numerous words, and even endure a physical makeover. My margins need to be girdled to accommodate some ideal figure. My header is messed with and my footer is stepped on or truncated. My pagination requires a new location. And all of these hoop jumps are the result of fickle cosmetic forces called submission guidelines that are specified on very differing guru websites. These same guidelines warn against simultaneously submitting my cloned siblings elsewhere, even though the decision on my submission may take more than a year. Good grief! At that rate, we'll all be in the Great Filing Cabinet in the Sky before very many gurus can be queried. Only a writer who believes in the tooth fairy complies with that one.

With mixed feelings, my cloned siblings and I finally leave home for the first time, but not alone. Accompanied by an SASE, a cover letter, and an acknowledgment-of-receipt postcard, I am slipped into a manila envelope, sealed into darkness, and stamped abruptly on one shoulder before being dropped altogether in some postal receptacle. Getting there is grueling—thin air, rough handling, more stamping, and finally, I'm deposited in someone's IN basket. My package is opened, and my cover letter perused by one or more recent English majors of school-teacher proportions, who make the first-level decision—either I'm someone they'd love to read or not. The nots are redirected toward the dreaded "slush pile," unopened, but not quite refused ... yet. There's the slim chance that I'll see sunlight again if another first-level decider wants a look before automatic rejection time. The pile containing my cohorts and me is picked over periodically, and if I haven't been orphaned from my SASE, I am returned home to Momma with a rejection slip. Otherwise, I am listed as dead and sent to the Potter's Field of manuscripts. All the while, my parents eagerly await word of their beloved offspring. The non-replies hurt most.

But wait! A publishing house pronounces my plot fit, of sound meaning, and full of promising dollar signs. Apparently, I also have enough luck and talent to get past first readers, editors, marketing sages, and executive councils. And so my creative parents are offered a publishing house contract. I'm so excited I can feel the words pumping through my sentences. Wow, a promise that a lowly member of the Manuscript family like me being promoted to Book! And with covers too!

When the initial excitement wears down, I find that I have been sold on the block like some slave with neither basic nor extended rights. I learn that I'll be indentured that way for years to come. I'm to serve in darkness, not knowing my actual publication date, nor any other milestone in my development. I have no approval in how my appearance will be altered. Suddenly, emails and phone calls go unanswered. Have I been forgotten? Or worse, lost? What has become of me?

One day, my text, clothed in a fixed format, arrives for proofreading. My parents examine me line-by-line and my faults are duly noted, repaired, and transmitted back in record time. Weeks pass, and an out-of-nowhere cover design turns up. Not exactly what I had in mind, but I can live with it. Hey, I've got an ISBN number and a price tag now. And my parents' names, they're in large print. That's got to mean something. Still no publication date yet.

That is, until a package finally finds its way to the front door. Undressing me from my plain brown wrappings, my parents find a revelation within. I have my arty covers and hundreds of printed pages. I am dedicated and acknowledged as well. I am truly Book!

* * * *

Chapter 14

Publishing: Our Own Brand

We learned quickly that even the smaller publishing houses take advantage of their authors. Our typical royalty was just a few pennies over one dollar per book. The two of us did almost a year's work, and the publisher, who did nothing to promote the book, reaps all the profit. Their so-called author's discounts (30 and 40 percent off retail price) were also a sham.

As an experiment, I went online and purchased a recent (but not new) version of *Adobe InDesign* publishing program for $100. We became our own publisher—now able to convert and format typical word processor text into ready-to-print copy for any commercial printer. It took only one person (me) about sixty man hours to format and proof a book, so why does the publisher take the lion's share of the profit? Printing, shipping, handling, self-marketing, and taxes were now our only costs. There were three things that gave rise to our next mystery.

One, our attempt to insert our alter egos, Simon and Rachel (in *Locks & Cream Cheese*) into our forthcoming mysteries didn't quite work. So we created Dan and Rivka Sherman as ourselves at middle age. Her name was Sarah at first, but Rivka left no doubt that she was Jewish. I found I could easily morph the couple from engineer and editor into booksellers in the Olde Victorian Bookstore in Annapolis.

Two, I have always been fond of books that give readers the chance to solve numerous clues right alongside their favorite sleuths. Perhaps I was inspired in this manner after reading three of

Dan Brown's books—that is, *Angel and Demons*, *The Da Vinci Code*, and *Inferno*.

Three, while looking for something of historical value to base a mystery plot on, I stumbled across a picture of Johannes Gutenberg's fifteenth-century press and a printed page featuring an enlarged and hand-illuminated first character. What if a fictitious character named Gerheardt Koenig were to create a whole set of enlarged font molds to replace the tedious sketches and inkings performed largely by monks by hand? We now had the makings of a mystery novel.

Death Goes Postal was published in 2013 by Magic Island Literary Works, our own trademark publishing house. We contracted Lightening Source near Nashville, TN to do our printing. We chose them because: one, they were owned by Ingram—the largest distributor of English language books in the world; two, they gave us access to bookstores via catalogue; three, they had a large online presence; four, they did an excellent printing job—clean, evenly dark, well-aligned print. The rear cover blurb to *Death Goes Postal* reads as follows:

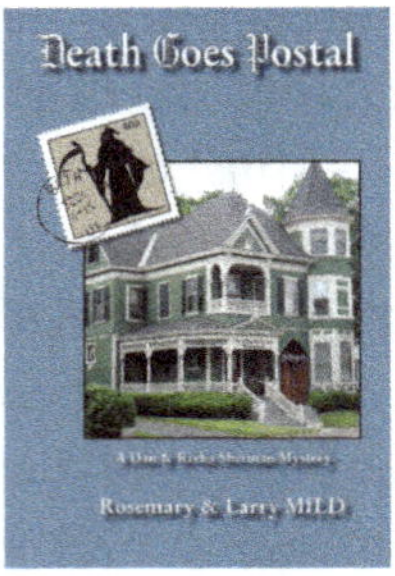

Daniel and Rivka Sherman have given up successful professional careers to become the owners of The Olde Victorian Bookstore in Annapolis, Maryland. Rare fifteenth-century typesetting artifacts journey through time to the present, leaving behind not only their original innovation, but a horrifying imprint in their wake: mugging, robbery, kidnapping, and murder. Professor Abner Fraume, brother of the bookstore's former owner, possesses these artifacts and gives his life to protect their whereabouts. A greedy colleague poses as one of several newcomers to a literary critique group sponsored by the bookstore. The villain leaves a trail of destruction in Bath, England; Annapolis; and the Deep South.

Dan and Rivka risk life and limb solving puzzles to locate the hidden artifacts and unmask the manic-depressive suspect behind the crimes. The conundrum's path involves the Internet, a young lad's term paper, the U.S. mails, the FBI, and Scotland Yard. Is it any wonder that Death Goes Postal?

* * * *

A sampling of what the reviewers had to say:

"**.... a young boy's** term paper, the U.S. Mails, the FBI and Scotland Yard all become a part of this delightful mystery. Death Goes Postal is a fun new addition to the mystery field."—**Mary Ann Smyth,** *BookLoons Mystery Reviews***.**

"**I liked the** historical aspect of finding the artifacts, and the international intrigue with robbery, muggings and murder. Death Goes Postal is a unique, new look at cozy mysteries set within a bookstore environment, and with two likeable sleuths (and a bookstore cat named Lord Byron) was a very enjoyable read."—*Cozy Mystery Book Reviews.*

"**The newly created** characters are interesting, and the bookshop makes a great base for new mystery stories. The pace of this story works well as does the unique way clues are presented to Edythe and later the Shermans. The authors provide clues in such a way that readers can also try to solve the puzzle, which is a fun way to keep them engaged in the tale. One interesting technique the Milds use for this book is that the killer is known from the beginning, but the suspense is still taut and the storyline intriguing. Fans of the authors and their previous mysteries will enjoy this new series."—**Edie Dykeman, Editor,** *Bella's Online Mystery Books.*

"***Death Goes Postal*** is a terrific bookstore mystery that is ironically made fresh by the six centuries old typesetting artifacts. The whodunit is fun to follow as readers, Dan and the Feds believe Kravitz is behind the dangerous crimes, but do not know who in the mystery writers' club he is (though you would think that would be relatively easy to find out). Fans will appreciate this engaging whodunit."—**Harriet Klausner,** *The Mystery Gazette.*

The year 2013 was important for us. We now knew we could publish on our own without going to a vanity publisher. We are henceforth "Independent Publishers," known as "Indies" throughout the industry. A much bigger chunk of the sales could now be ours. As a result, we bought back the rights to all three of the Paco and Molly mysteries and *Cry Ohana* as well. We redesigned the covers to the mysteries and bought back the rights to the *Cry Ohana* cover because we liked it so well.

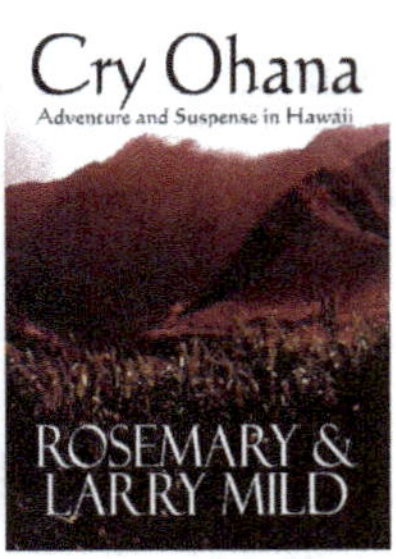

In that same year Rosemary and I published two short stories in *Mystery in Paradise,* an anthology featuring thirteen all-Hawaii authors. The anthology was sponsored by a group of authors from Sisters in Crime/Hawaii and not the organization itself. Our stories were entitled "The Joss at Table Twelve" and "Adrift on Kaneohe Bay." The following year, 2014, the two of us collected a book of eight short stories of ours that had been previously published in an online quarterly magazine (or e-zine) called *Mysterical-E*. We published *The Misadventures of Slim O'Wittz, Soft-Boiled Detective* in 2014. We did not send out review copies because of the expense and the fact that the stories had been published before. Each story features the same private eye, Slim O'Wittz, who is best explained in the following back cover blurb:

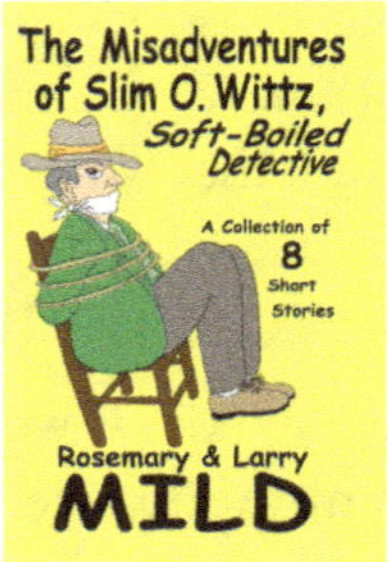

You're searching for hard-boiled private eyes? Go see Sam Shade, Flip Marlowe, or Mike Slammer. Should you desire a completely anal policeman, there's Adrian Schmonk. But if you're in need of a truly soft-boiled Private Investigator, you turn to me, Slim O. Wittz. I'm rarely in charge, frequently behind the eight ball, and seldom paid. In spite of all that, my case record is remarkably shaky.

I'm one of them old-fashioned private eyes. Yeah, I'm a dinosaur, a shamusaurus, a tossback to the gumshoes of the nineteen thirties and forties. Dames? I prefer mine over easy—both my eggs and my women. Mostly,

I investigate embezzlers, gamblers, runaways, unfaithful spouses, and the meshuge kind too.

* * * *

Rosemary had been writing and collecting her essays long before I ever met her, and when she finally stopped to analyze what they were all about, she discovered an amazing connection with her strong-willed mother. *Love! Laugh! Panic! Life with My Mother* was published in 2012 by Magic Island Literary Works with the following rear cover blurb:

Don't we all have mixed emotions about our mothers? But how many of us have a mother like Rosemary's—multi-talented, yet super-tough to live with? Luby Pollack was a widely published journalist, popular book author, and even an artist of sorts. She sometimes had a daunting role to play. In the delivery room during Rosemary's birth, her psychiatrist husband ordered her not to make any noise during labor—it was "unseemly for a doctor's wife." Rosemary Pollack Mild started to write a book strictly about herself, but that didn't go so well. She discovered that Mother popped up on every page. Looming. Encouraging. Warning. Always the Protagonist, the Star, the Heroine, the Antagonist, and sometimes the Villain from the viewpoint of a loving but ornery daughter.

* * * *

By the time the year 2015 rolled in, the two of us had written a goodly number of original short stories on a variety of subjects. Some of the stories reflected our own experiences in foreign lands—tales from our world travels, acts we'd seen or overheard, something even *you* might have said or done. *Murder, Fantasy, and Weird Tales* was published in 2015 by Magic Island Literary Works with the following rear cover blurb:

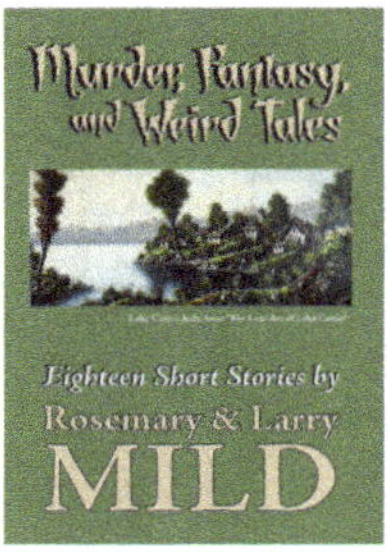

Compulsion! *Murder, Fantasy, and Weird Tales* explores the strange obsessive compulsions gnawing away within most of us. Whether to commit murder, dream wildly, or just wander out of the box, we're all tempted. But who acts on these wild urges and why? Perhaps you have already put one toe in to test the waters. Do you dare to go any further? Meet "The Novice Killers," the "Hits and Misses,"

the "Fantasizers and Dreamers," and the "Art Lovers." Join them as they venture into these forbidden realms.

* * * *

We chose vengeance as the theme for our second Dan and Rivka Sherman mystery. Just as we opened the first in Bath, England, we again drew upon our former travels in England to open this mystery in London. We added a love story between Fenton and Heather to play off the main plot. In our anxiety to publish early, our first proof was so full of typos that we engaged a friend, Diane Farkas, to proofread our text. We had just looked at the galleys one too many times and read over the top of our own typos. Finally, *Death Takes A Mistress* was published in 2016 by Magic Island Literary Works, with many scenes in a synagogue. The rear cover blurb read as follows:

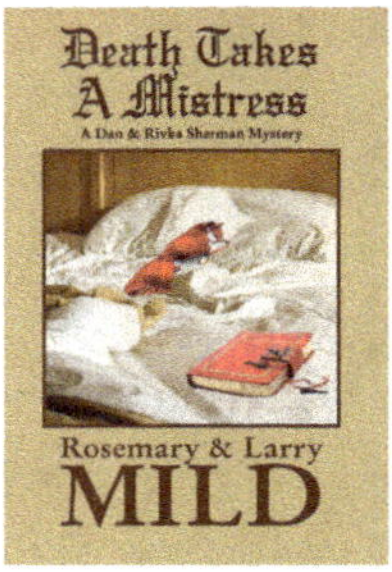

After twenty-three years, the daughter of a mistress seeks revenge from the murderous lover who killed her mother and deserted her at age three months. Ivy, the daughter, follows the cold case clues from London, England to Annapolis, Maryland where she discovers her father and killer belong to one of four families. But which one?

Ivy seeks employment as a clerk at The Olde Victorian Bookstore where she finds friendship, advice, love, and caution from Dan and Rivka Sherman, the booksellers. The Shermans use their old connections at Scotland Yard to obtain Ivy's mother's diary, but it is soon stolen. Will they get it back? Does it contain the clues they need? Will Ivy cause fear and havoc in the four families—enough to put her own life in jeopardy?

* * * *

A sampling of what the reviewers had to say:

"**.... the mystery critique** group had less of a showing this time around, allowing Dan, Rivka, and Ivy more opportunity to solve the mystery on their own. I liked having fewer hands in the pot, so to speak, as it kept the storyline a bit tidier and easier to follow. Although, it was nice to see those familiar faces again, including that of the store cat, Lord Byron. One of my favorite additions to this book was Ivy's mother's diary and how they used it to figure out who her father was. It was an interesting concept and led them astray a few times, only to help them get right back on track. *Death Takes A Mistress* was a funny and engaging cozy mystery set in my favorite of places, a book- store."—*Bitten By Books*, **the review site with a bite.**

"**If I only had four** words to describe *Death Takes A Mistress* they would be "what a fun book". It reminded me of a whodunit of days gone by with an interesting plot peppered with a host of equally interesting characters.

"This was the first book I'd read by the authors and my first introduction to their sleuths Dan and Rivka Sherman. They run a bookstore which I felt like I was actually in and snooping around. They are likeable, well developed characters who I'd like to read more about in the future.

"The secondary characters in this book were also well developed. Some were more likeable than others but all had an interesting story to be told which kept me turning the pages. As the story progressed I found myself reading on trying to figure out who Ivy's father was and if he had, in fact, murdered her mother.

"The setting of this story is great too, and I liked the subplot of the mystery writing group. As with all fun whodunnits, there are some clues that lead you off track and a good sprinkling of humor.

"During the last five chapters or so I kept reading to see if I figured out correctly who the guilty person was. It had a satisfying ending and a nice closure for Ivy. It has left me eager to see what the authors have in store next for Dan and Rivka. If you like a classic whodunit, I think you'll enjoy this one." **Four Stars**—*Stephanotis,* **www.Long and Short Reviews.com.**

"**The second Dan and Rivka** Sherman cozy is a super cold case mystery (it went frozen twenty-three years ago) wrapped inside a family drama as Ivy learns what matters in life, how fortunate she has been with people caring for and about her, and that revenge is insignificant. The keys to this fabulous tale are the amateur sleuthing seems genuine and Ivy keeps the storyline focused as refreshingly the prime player." **—Reviewed by Harriet Klausner,** *The Mystery Gazette.*

"This is the second in the Milds' Dan & Rivka Sherman Mystery Series. It reads fine as a stand-alone novel, with just enough references to the first book in the series (*Death Goes Postal*) to pique my interest but not give away the plot.

"*Death Takes A Mistress* is a delightfully twisted tale of intrigue. Every time I thought I knew who the killer was, a plot twist would make me second-guess my conclusion. I didn't know for sure until the final chapters, which makes the mystery lover in me very happy.

"The characters were fun and believable. Even secondary characters like the woman who rents Ivy a room have personalities that made me connect with them. The bad boys that weren't all bad and the good boys who are actually bad are exceedingly well done and true-to-life. I am looking forward to reading more books by the Milds." —*Laura Hartman,* **reviewer.**

— —

Also in 2014, Rosemary and I published "Seeing Red," a wickedly funny Valentine's Day story, in the *Homicidal Holidays* edition of Chesapeake Crimes. This was an official anthology of Sisters in Crime in which we are still faithful national members. We are members of the Honolulu and Chesapeake chapters as well. I am what is commonly known as a Mister in Crime.

It would be extremely difficult to explain how we came to write the third Daniel and Rivka mystery novel without you first learning about a piece of my inheritance and understanding what it has meant to the two of us. I thought it best explained the way it appeared in the preface of that book called "My Sacred White Elephant."

My Sacred White Elephant: Many of us possess something out of the past for which we have never found a practical or decorative place. Maybe it's a gilt-framed picture of a great-great uncle, a bewildering trinket, an ugly vase, or a haphazard stamp collection. Or it may be a trunk stuffed with such items—all deteriorating, occupying space, but guarded by the concept that this item is precious and should be kept in the family, even though no family member recalls exactly why.

My own white elephant is a rare holy book passed down from my maternal grandfather to my mother and then to me. *Sefer Menorat ha-maor* arrived at our house in a flimsy, white department store gift box nestled in tissue paper. This edition is written in Yiddish, the language that predominated among European Jews at the end of the eighteenth century when it was printed. *Sefer* means book. The English translation of *Menorat ha-maor* is *The Candlestick of Light*. It was originally written in Hebrew in the fourteenth century as a moral and religious household guide for Jews in the Middle Ages.

One of the most important books of its time, it is filled with biblical topics and rabbinical interpretations on righteous living; a compilation of sermons, anecdotes, and tales drawn from both written and oral Jewish law and ethical teachings.

I cannot read Yiddish. The *Sefer Menorat ha-maor* sat in my house year after year deteriorating. In 2008 I opened the gift box, gently lifted the book out, and placed it on the table. Small brownish flecks of the heavy leather cover fell off. Carefully opening the cover, I found neat script on the flyleaf: dates ranging from 1803 through 1836, along with names I did not recognize—births, I presumed. The edges of the yellowed pages had turned brown as well. They were brittle, too brittle to continue in my care. The projected extent and cost of restoration were beyond anything I could manage. Sadly, in its condition, I could not display this fragile holy book in the place of honor it deserved. I sought professional help. After consulting with a cantor and three rabbis, my *Sefer Menorat ha-maor* was carefully packaged and sent on its way to Cincinnati, OH, for curator evaluation at the venerated Klau Library of the Hebrew Union College-Jewish Institute of Religion. On page xii is a description by Dr. Dan Rettberg, of blessed memory, who attested to the book's authenticity. Its permanent home is in the Klau Library's Rare Books Collection. It was my honor to donate it. *Sefer Menorat ha-maor* inspired me to create the basic plot for *Death Steals A Holy Book.* Forgive me for taking a few literary liberties with its condition, content, and monetary worth for the sake of the story. —— **Larry**

* * * *

In order to better understand what gems of wisdom the fourteenth-century author Isaac Aboab had written, we needed an English translation. After almost a year of searching, Rosemary located and purchased a copy of *Menoras Hamaor* in a Brooklyn, NY religious bookstore. Rabbi Yaakov Yosef Reinman had indeed translated the original *Candlestick of Light* or, as he called it, *The Light of Contentment.* When we sought his permission to use quotes of wisdom from his translation, Rabbi Reinman challenged the religious point and purpose of the book. I had to convince the good rabbi as follows:

> "In all honesty our book does not have a strict religious point, nor was it ever intended to. Our book is a traditional mystery, a work of fiction truly inspired by our growing knowledge of *Menorat ha-maor* and of our Yiddish version's eventual journey and donation to the Klau Library. It is certainly moral and ethical in that the guilty are punished according to the laws of the land, and all religious practices mentioned are treated with respect. The selected quotes are used therein to match applicable misdeeds found within the chapters."

Rabbi Reinman finally relented and gave his permission. We sent him an autographed copy of the finished and published book that included a credit to him and his book on the copyright page. We also wrote an addendum to the preface as follows:

"In the long-standing Jewish tradition of seeking and passing on the wisdom of the ages, we have excerpted quotes from the holy text to include as chapter heads in our mystery text. The reader may notice that we give the source of the quotes as *Menoras* with an "s." Larry's donated Yiddish copy of the *Sefer Menorat ha-maor* spells *Menorat* with a "t": the Sephardic, or Spanish, spelling. The quotes we have chosen are from the recent English translation (1982), with *Menoras* ending in "s": the Ashkenazic, or Eastern

European, spelling. (Capitalization and hyphenation also vary between the two titles.) Be assured it's the same book.

—— **The Authors**

Finally, *Death Steals A Holy Book* was published in 2017 by our own Magic Island Literary Works. The rear cover blurb reads as follows:

Reluctant sleuths Dan and Rivka Sherman yearn for a tranquil life as owners of The Old Victorian Bookstore in Annapolis, Maryland. But when they inherit a rare, ancient manuscript, they find themselves embroiled in a firestorm of deceit, thievery, and worse. *Death Steals A Holy Book* places the Shermans and those closest to them in peril once again. Israel Finestein, renowned restorer of old books in Baltimore, has just finished his work on the *Menorat ha-maor,* "*The Candestick of Light.*" His life is brutally snuffed out and the book disappears. What makes this text so valuable that someone is compelled to kill for it? The true value of the Shermans' rare gift lies in its gems of wisdom—as a guide to righteous living for Jews in the Middle Ages.

Two Baltimore detectives uncover a puzzling number of suspects. Is it the controversial woman whom Israel plans to marry? The rare book agent who overextended himself in the stock market? Israel's busybody cousins who resent his changed lifestyle? Or the wayward lad who thinks a gun is the way to big bucks?

* * * *

The reviewers had the following to say about it:

"**Loved it!!** One of the best books I have read this year. I feel honored to have been asked to review it. This is the 1st book I have read by Rosemary and Larry Mild. I will definitely be on the lookout for more of their books. *Death Steals A Holy Book* made me stop and think. Could this happen? Has it happened? I believe something like this has already happened. Thank you to the Milds for a really wonderful story." —**Reviewed by Tess at** *Goodreads.*

"***Death Steals A Holy Book***" provides a clever plot and additional story lines, an unusual set of characters and some twists and turns.

The authors provide the reader with a taste of Jewish culture and use short quotations from "*The Candlestick of Life*" to introduce each chapter. These touches make for a richer and more historically interesting read. For those who enjoy a cozy-style mystery, this book will provide a pleasant diversion. **—Reviewed by Jane Schulz**.

"I love this unlikely crime fighting duo. They are wily when on the hunt for clues, but sometimes Dan forgets to feed the bookstore cat. Rivka gets irritated with Dan but never for a minute doubts him or stops caring for him. They are the old couple that have been together through thick and thin and their loving relationship is obvious to the reader. The Milds have crafted these rich characters that develop more with each book. I liked them before and love them now like a couple of kooky next-door neighbors." *Five Stars*, **Reviewed by Laura at Goodreads.**

"Husband-and-wife mystery novelists Rosemary and Larry Mild have created a tightly woven, cleverly plotted and supremely suspenseful tale in *Death Steals A Holy Book*. Resplendent with action, intrigue, wit, and a to-die-for cast of characters, *Death Steals A Holy Book* is bound to delight." **—Reviewed by** *Bookish Pleasures.*

Another unofficial anthology by a select group of Hawaii authors from Sisters in Crime/Hawaii was published in 2017 with the title *Dark Paradise, Mysteries in the Land of Aloha*. This time our two stories were "Tsunami" and "Snake Lady."

The idea for a story called "Unto the Third Generation" had its roots in an essay I started in the early days of our writing. The original intent of this story was to travel cryogenically to a future generation and find out how our descendents solved the world and domestic problems of today. The premise was that two brave souls would endure cryogenic suspension and travel to the future to avoid a pandemic illness. The essay was shelved for more than twenty years. I was experimenting with another science fiction story idea in the fall of 2016 when I ran across the essay once more. It was just what I was looking for, so I partnered the illness with

Signing at a Malice Domestic convention

Signing at a Baltimore bookstore

Signing at North Beach, MD craft fair

An iguana visits the North Beach fair

Signing at Neil Blaisdell Center Craft Fair, Honolulu, HI

a universal food product that attempted to abolish world hunger and came up with the plot for *Unto the Third Generation, A Novella of the Future*. It was published in 2017 under our own brand. The cover blurb read as follows:

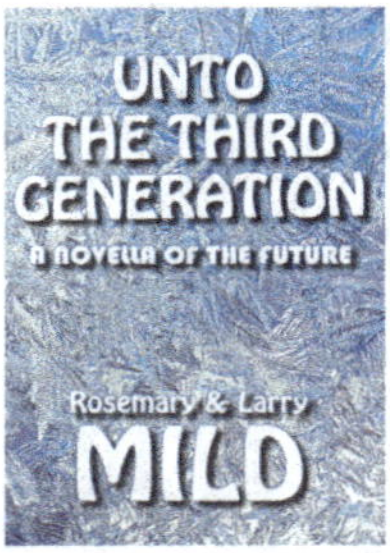

Rosemary & Larry's science-fiction tale will chill you to the core. Two young people, unaware of each other's existence, volunteer to become cryonauts—physically frozen in a life-suspension experiment. Leonard Tall-Chief, a high-steel worker, and Francine Mapleton, a waitress, postpone their destinies for untold generations.

The year 2039 would be unremarkable except for two world-shaking events. The first marks a giant breakthrough for the well-being of all mankind. For once, no man, woman or child will ever go hungry again. Everyone will benefit from partaking of this discovery. But should they? The second event poses a threat to the human race itself—a disease that tortures, teases, and ultimately kills. Will it spell the end of all human life?

It will take three generations before these two events clash. And when they do, the futures, the very lives, of Leonard and Francine are at stake.

* * * *

Because this book was only a novella, we didn't want to spend the money on review copies, but those fans close to us have said they enjoyed the book.

Cry Ohana, our most popular seller, stirred a movement among our fans to ask: What happened to the *Ohana*, the families, of the original epic? At this writing we have just released the sequel. The cover blurb reads as follows:

Honolulu Heat, Between the Mountains and the Great Sea—the long-awaited sequel to *Cry Ohana*—brings back the same Hawaii families that readers so warmly embraced. With fiery emotions, they face new torments, take on exotic challenges, and find new loves.

Leilani and Alex Wong anguish over son Noah, an idealistic teenager who teeters on both sides of the law. He meets Nina Portfia, his dream girl, and they unwittingly share horrific secrets. Facing a murder charge,

Noah flees and finds himself immersed in a bloody feud between a Chinatown protection racketeer and a crimeland don who, ironically, is Nina's father. Violence targets innocent real estate agents, a Porsche Boxster Spyder, a stolen locket, a petty thief, and an odd pair on a freighter to Southeast Asia. Two mob leaders and the police are pursuing Noah. Torn between loyalty and betrayal, only the boy can unlock his own freedom and bring peace to his family—and Honolulu's Chinatown.

* * * *

There are at least four more books in the hopper waiting to be born. We have published a series of nine "Copper and Goldie" short stories in the online e-zine *Mysterical-E.* A tenth one in the series was published in *Dark Paradise* and there are two more waiting to be submitted. After the twelfth one appears, we will publish the series as a collection entitled: *Copper & Goldie: 12 Tails of Suspense.* I also have written a second draft of *Exploring the Mystery: Eighteen Valuable Lessons on Mystery Writing.* It is currently being critiqued by a colleague from Sisters in Crime. It is based on the mystery course we taught at Anne Arundel Community College in Arnold, MD. I believe, as time goes on, we will have enough individual mystery and fantasy tales to publish another collection. Rosemary is planning a book of her essays.

The two of us are currently doing three or four major craft fairs each year. As a result, our selling technique and setup and breakdown process have been honed to a tee. Instead of barking and hawking our books from our craft fair booth out at the variable stream of shoppers (both window and otherwise), we have turned to a more conservative and efficient form of attracting potential buyers. The whole trick is to catch their eyes and hold their interest with an acknowledging nod. Those definitely not engaged will immediately look away and continue past the booth. The curious will either stop, smile, or change their expression. An efficient "Hi!" will either bring them close enough to the display to make a sales pitch or disengage all communication and they'll continue on their way. On the other hand, there are a lot of lonely people out there who would like to chew your ear off for an hour. Ordinarily, we wouldn't care, but if it interferes with our making sales, it's a definite no-no. I've summarized that annoying part of the process in the following, my humble attempt at poetry.

Catch A Moving Eye

Catch a moving eye while it's roving by,
And bend a listened ear, call the passer near.
Hand them a book and convince them to look,
At front and rear covers—and maybe others.

Hold the line—hoping they won't break the spine,
Flipping pages, maybe spending their wages.
I spin a great spiel I hope seals the deal,
And send the big hook that's selling our book.

Hemming and hawing, still shifting and stalling,
Down and up—reading's really in their cup.
Or get antsy—the book's not to their fancy,
My precious time they spent and away they went.

Now watch for the guy with no intent to buy,
Nor a mind to give, that's his way to live.
So nod and smile and pick with a bit of guile,
For who I hail is the point to my tale.

I believe in denying the potential buyer the option of a negative response by asking: "Do you like to read?" or "Do you enjoy a good mystery? Rather, the question should be: "What do you like to read?" If they respond—all the better. If not, take them through the available categories and then a few of the titles. Any interest in a title—place the book in their hands and encourage them to read the rear cover blurb. I chat and try to be friendly, but if nothing happens in the next five minutes, I do my best to disengage politely. Often we have the opposite pleasure. Someone approaches: "What's your newest book?" I hold it up. "Good!" he says, "I'll take it!"

Chapter 15

Discoveries and Adventures

I believe the many world sights that I've seen in the service of my country and that I've seen thereafter while traveling with my two wives certainly have added new dimensions to not only my store of knowledge, but my personality as well. I further believe that travel has made me more extroverted in my maturing years, releasing me from the shy, klutzy, unsure, and introverted shell of my youth. Hannah and Rosemary were unique, happy, and willing travel companions in sharing some of my life's most thrilling and educational moments. That kind of sharing has lasted me a lifetime and produced a ton of wonderful memories I've never stop revisiting. Now I want to impart some of those memories to you.

Hannah and I had lived in Naples, Italy for awhile in 1957, and that stay in Naples I have already described in Chapter 8. We also ventured into eastern Canada twice, and I related the latter of those two Canadian trips in Chapter 10. That one took place in the mid-Eighties.

Herta joined the four of us in the earlier Canadian trip that took place in 1970. This one proved to be quite disturbing, as we ran into a great deal of prejudice against English-speaking tourists. Our very presence, in fact, had riled French-speaking residents who, at the time, were rebelling against English rule and wanted not only their identity, but their independence. I had no idea what we strangers had to do with their protest and struggle, but that didn't seem to deter their bad behavior toward us.

Our first sour note occurred when we stopped for gas along

one road in the maritime province of Quebec. We had pulled into a full-service bay, so that we might rid ourselves of a bug-splattered windshield and receive an oil check as well as fill the tank. The uniformed attendant stood there watching us with folded arms for almost ten minutes. I wound up pumping my own gas, checking my own oil, and washing my own windshield. When I was through, I was so angry that I left the payment in U.S. dollars on the ground with the squeegee on top so it wouldn't blow away.

Many miles down the road the girls saw a sign for funnel cakes, and there was no silencing them until we pulled into the parking lot of the advertised restaurant. We found an empty booth and the five of us sat down and waited, and waited. Tables and booths all around us were being serviced while we were purposely being ignored. I guess we had U.S. tourist written all over us. We sat for about thirty minutes before leaving. As we made our way out the door, I saw someone else sitting in our both and a waitress standing next to it. Oh well, so much for the rural mentality, I thought, as we drove away. Quebec City will have a more welcoming point of view.

How wrong I was. Hannah had made reservations for us to stay at the Chateau Frontenac, overlooking the old city of Quebec, six months before when we first agreed to the planned trip. She approached the desk with her mailed-back paperwork with a reservation confirmation number that supposedly ensured us two rooms, each with two queen-sized beds. The response was that they had absolutely nothing available. At this point we were tired, hungry, and upset, but we somehow pleaded with the clerk for any room, and that's just what we got. It was a maid's room on one of the top floors with one high window across from a moldy brick wall.

The room had two twin beds. Herta slept in one, Hannah and I in the other, Jackie in the bathtub (lined with blankets), and Myrna between two upholstered chairs pushed together. The only thing good I could say about the room was that it was reasonably clean. By the time we settled into the room the dining room had closed. We ate from the vending machine and Herta's purse that night because we were all too tired to go elsewhere. Herta always kept a banana and some kind of hard, crumbless cookies there for emergencies.

The next day we canceled our nonexistent reservations and left. We moved to a Holiday Inn in the English part of Quebec and spent the next three nights there. We visited the old fort where generals Mountcalm and Wolfe did battle during the French and Indian War. Scaling those tremendous cliffs must have been a major feat for the British. We descended to the old town at the foot of the cliffs and toured the old buildings in the restored seaport on the St. Lawrence River.

The car developed radiator problems just outside of Montreal, so we missed much of what we had scheduled for there. The five of us settled for a mere drive-through of the city and then on to Kingston where we were to spend the following night. On the way we passed the Thousand Islands cutoff and stopped to tour two old forts and the Canadian Naval Academy. The kids liked the motel in Kingston where we stayed because there was a climbable, old-time, train's steam engine parked out back. Our biggest excitement there was the fact that a fire alarm in the middle of the night drove us from our beds to the outside street for almost an hour.

Our next stop was Toronto. Perhaps the highlight of that city was its modern, hands-on museum. The kids enjoyed turning cranks and wheels and pulling levers and watching the consequences of their action. They learned the principles of mechanical advantage through the use of large and small gears intermeshing. There were water pumping and electrical exhibits, and even one that allowed you to modify how the word "coffee" was said. The control enabled you to emit the word as a question, an exclamation, a whisper, or even a shout of joy.

I was impressed with the Boolean logic exhibit where you could connect a slew of logic elements together with switches to ultimately light a lamp for a positive output. I watched two youngsters try to guess their way through the problem for ten minutes and then step back to let me have a try. As a digital engineer schooled in this type of logic, I stepped up and set all of the switches to light the lamp in less than thirty seconds. I proudly explained why to the onlookers. We found the Jewish section of Toronto and ate each night in a different kosher or kosher-style delicatessen.

We reentered the U.S. via the international bridge at Niagara Falls after spending the night in a rundown Sheraton Hotel across from the falls. The four of us put on raincoats and rain hats to visit all the close access points to and under the falls and even took the Maid of the Mist boat ride. Hannah and I found the area fully distasteful and overly commercial. The falls were wonderful. It must have been a gorgeous and magnificent sight when seen unspoiled by the first Frenchman to head upriver. Our family headed across the bridge and south into New York State the very next morning.

On our way back from this Canada trip, we stopped to visit Hannah's aunt, Sig's sister Bertil (or Bertle), who lived with her husband, Louis Guenzburger, on a dairy farm just outside Binghamton, NY. The children got to see the dairy operation and visit with the cows. The cows' names were on their stalls. Myrna noticed the name "Arlene" on one of them and began teasing Jackie because it's her middle name. It was a strange visit; Louis, Bertil's husband, chose not to visit with us. However, Bertil and her older son Peter were more than hospitable to us. That was our last stop on the way home.

* * * *

When the kids were much older, Hannah and I managed to take two trips to resorts in the Pocono Mountains of Pennsylvania. Nanny Hilda sat in as a precaution, but I don't know who was taking care of whom. Call it rest and relaxation (R&R) if you will, but with large heart-shaped hot tubs in every room, I like to think of the other "R" as romance. Besides that, we tried our hand at paddleball, tennis, and even archery while we were there.

* * * *

Retirement and a steady income left Rosemary and me with the time, the means, and the inclination to travel. We had taken many extensive car trips throughout the eastern U.S., mostly to Florida, Pennsylvania, and Ohio to see family, but the two of us did venture into neighboring states and DC to visit Civil War sites, historic landmarks, museums, and theme parks.

At one point in 1997 Rosemary and I latched onto a brochure of a Collette guided bus tour of the national parks out West and decided to try it. That fall the two of us flew to Phoenix, AZ and taxied to Scottsdale, where we spent the night at a DoubleTree Hotel. We had arrived in time the day before the trip started to take a shuttle into Old Town Scottsdale. We saw a magnificent statue of four wild horses and walked along a dirt-covered street lined with stores selling cheap souvenirs and Indian trinkets and pottery. The heat was over 105 degrees, so after an hour and a half of walking, we cried "uncle" and called for the shuttle to take us back to the hotel. The tour guide held a welcome meeting that evening, laying down the rules and perks of the tour.

Bright and early the next morning a luxury-style bus with kneel-down loading features took us north to Sedona, AZ, where, in small groups, most of us took pink jeep rides up into the local rugged mountains. The driver pointed out two rock formations that resembled Charles Schulz's Snoopy and Lucy. Moving on, we saw hoodoos (balanced rock formations)—one in particular, where an immense rock was held up by a much smaller one below it. The tour guide leaned against it to show how perfectly stable the formation

Tough to topple a hoodoo

Rosemary and I at the North Rim

was. The bus traveled north across the Painted Desert and alongside the Vermilion Cliffs, and entered the heavily wooded Kaibab Forest, finally stopping in front of a bunch of duplex log cabins. Night had already fallen, so the sights and surprises of the Grand Canyon's North Rim were denied us until the next morning. Because these accommodations were provided by the U.S. Park Service, they were basically utile and austere. The only complaint that I might have registered was that the triangular shower seemed to be almost form-fitting. Any more so, it would have needed a blip to accommodate my tummy protrusion.

Morning unfolded one of the most magnificent panoramas I have ever seen. Seeking breakfast, Rosemary and I left the cabin and headed for the main rock-lined lodge with its green roof perched high on the North Rim's precarious edge. From the tourist's point of view, the lodge comprised four impressive main areas: the parlor, using its giant bronze burro to greet you as you came in the front door; the dining room, supported by high pitched log beams; the massive picture windows, exposing a generous portion of the canyon; and the spacious rear lanai, unfolding the main exhibit.

Out on the lanai the first thing that hit you was the amount of bright sunlit space that lay before you, the sheer enormity of it all. Then, every earth-tone color imaginable painted the bottom half of your eye's distant canvas—while blue sky, dotted with occasional white puffs, filled out the remainder. Next, you noticed hundreds of thousands of uniquely individual vertical shapes lining the sky's edge and billions of multicolored surfaces separated by horizontal age striations in the near and far. And before that, thick with trees and brush, the greenery at the near top demarcated the sharp rocky slope racing to the canyon floor. Finally, the awed brain put the mind-boggling total array together the way no picture postcard could ever do. The eye was then freed to inspect the individual wonders.

While waiting for the bus to arrive the following morning, the woods around us were alive with mule deer and Kaibab squirrels and the tour group was taking it all in, when the tour guide approached and asked if anyone had seen a jackalope yet.

Some said "No." and others responded with "What's a jackalope? What's one look like, anyway?"

"Well," said the guide, "he looks like a six-foot jackrabbit and can run real fast."

"Aw, you're messing with us," said one of our tourists.

"Don't believe him. He's only kidding," said another.

The guide smiled broadly and held up a picture postcard displaying the creature and captioned Jackalope. "I wouldn't kid you, would I?"

Of course, I just didn't believe such a creature existed, but we managed to pick up the same postcard at the next gift shop we came across. The guide also told us that the North Rim closes for the winter months (October through April) because of deep snows and rough storms. The bus finally came and took us around to the South Rim of the canyon, which we observed was a good deal more commercialized with motels and trinket shops. Then we headed west to Zion National Park, where we rode an open tram through the park. A park guide explained that each of the sheer-cliff rock formations and mountains had a biblical name and a reason for its naming.

The park guide stopped the tram and pointed to a speck on one of the sheer cliffs. He explained that it was a climber asleep in a cocoon-like shelter that clung to the side of the cliff and that the climber would repack the cocoon and take it with him when he was ready to continue up the face. We, however, spent the night in a motel just outside the park and were glad of it.

Our next stop was in Bryce Canyon, where we were allowed to walk among acres of red and white rock formations protruding out of the ground like stalagmites. Some of the formations had recognizable shapes and were appropriately named. We were told the local Indians saw the thousands of natural structures as spirits, ghosts of their ancestors, and some even feared them.

From Bryce we drove east to the Glen Canyon Dam and

on to a motel on the shore of Lake Powell, a manmade lake created by damming up the Colorado River. The next morning a boat ride navigated the expanse of the pale blue lake, revealing the sand-colored mountains and dunes. One mountain in particular was singled out as the substitute Mt. Sinai used in the filming of *The Ten Commandments.* From there we drove north and spent several nights in a plush Salt Lake City hotel.

On the first day, we visited the Mormon compound and saw the great temple with its long lines of decked-out couples waiting to be wed. Not being a registered member of their faith, we were not permitted within that structure, but we did see the inside of the huge Tabernacle and a number of the residences of the leaders and their many wives. The second day we drove up into the surrounding hills to see the historic sights and along the lake shore, stopping only to sample the waters. After scooping up handfuls of tiny shrimp-like creatures, most of the group agreed this was a place none of us wanted to swim in. I was most impressed with two things about the city. The first was a life-size bronze statue of a pioneer man and woman pushing a cart containing their household belongings and their children. It is beyond comprehension how these pioneers covered 1,500 miles across such rough terrain. The second was a system that assisted the blind in crossing most of the downtown streets; it informed them of the color of stoplights via changing audible tones. I had never encountered this before and appreciated the thought that went into this creative kindness.

On the third morning the bus headed due north, crossing the smallest corner of Idaho into Wyoming, passing along the Grand Teton Mountains, and stopping in Jackson Hole, WY, with its town park's fence and gates made of molted deer antlers. We spent a night and a day there soaking up the mountain views. Then, traveling due north, the group spent the night at a motel just outside the gates of Yellowstone National Park. Over the next few days the group explored the upper and lower falls and visited the rustic lodge, with its bundled-stick finish and furnishings. In front of the lodge we witnessed Old Faithful's dependable gushings as well as other geysers and chemically colored, bubbling pools. Even the body of Yellowstone Lake rippled with gaseous emissions. I was suprised to see pelicans flying and diving at the lake so far from the coastal U.S. and was given no explanation for this. We had encountered only one animal inside the park and it was a buffalo tethered outside the lodge. Yet leaving by the east gate, we encountered a whole herd of them crossing the road in front of us.

Continuing east to Cody, WY, the tour was able to take in two famous museums there: the Remington, replete with a fortune in his bronze cowboy and horse statuettes; and an Indian museum. On the road again we passed golden fields of grain and herds of prong-horned antelope, but we weren't sure whether they were wild or being husbanded. The bus drove east into South Dakota, then south into the Black Hills National Forest and Mt. Rushmore in Keystone, SD. Gutzon Borglum's depiction of the four U.S. presidents was magnificent, even from the distant official viewing site. I had no feel for the magnitude of the project until I beheld a copy of Lincoln's eye in the Keystone museum later. It was about six by three by three feet up close.

Then the bus drove deeper into the Black Hills park and four miles north of the city of Custer, SD. The bus pulled into the parking lot of Crazy Horse Monument Park, a park that pays tribute to the Oglala Indian chief who led so many terrorizing campaigns against the U.S. military. Sculptor Korczak Ziolkowski led the project that carved the chief's likeness out of the face of a solid rock cliff with plans to mount him on a horse shooting a bow and arrow, but unless non-Government funds become available, the project remains at a standstill.

We spent the night in Fort Collins, CO, our seamiest accommodation of the trip. The luxury bus tour of the national parks ended in Denver, where we were given a day to tour the city and another on our own. We flew home from there.

* * * *

In 1998 we convinced Rosemary's brother, John, and his wife, Ann, to join us on a fall trip to the British Isles. Behind it all, Rosemary ached to go to Lockerbie, Scotland to see where Miriam had been found and wanted all the support she could get. John and Ann were still working stiffs, so the two of us decided to extend the trip start by two weeks.

Rosemary and I flew to London, England and then on to Edinbrurgh, Scotland on a British Airways Highland Tours package. We were met by a small green 1964 bus outfitted with folding tables and opposing seats. Our tour guide, a tall heavyset Scotsman, drove us, and we started our tour in Edinburgh. The sheer extent of Edinburgh Castle and its armor and warfare museums held us in fascination for nearly a whole day. Still recovering from less than successful arthroscopic knee surgery that previous June, I had no trouble ascending the 300 steps to enter the castle, but leaving, I had to go down backward to alleviate the lingering pain in my knee.

The next day we headed north and west through Trossachs National Park and around Loch Lomand. We stopped in the 2,000-year-old village of Luss for a short walking tour while we viewed homes of loose stone and low doorway transepts. All of us were impressed with the exquisite gardening and landscaping fronting these homes. After lunching in Inverary, we spent the night in beautiful Glencoe Isles overlooking the site where the Campbell clan massacred the McDonald clan in 1692.

Continuing mostly in the same direction we arrived at the Applecross Peninsula and a coastal town where we got a distant view of the Isle of Skye and sampled the local pastries. Then we headed west to Dingwall and spent the night in twelfth-century Tulloch Castle set atop a wooded hill. The bathroom, devoid of a shower, forced me to take a bath in a very deep tub and, because it was so deep and narrow, I had to call Rosemary to help me get out of it—even then a monstrous and scary task. Before dinner I waited for Rosemary in a cozy den just outside the dining room with a

Four travelers stop by the road in Scotland

Laird McCloud and what's left of his breakfast mouse

Larry fireside with Laird McCloud at Tulloch Castle

fire blazing in a stone fireplace with a grand hearth. Settling into a sizeable leather easy chair, I noticed a large black cat lounging on a tartan cushion nearby. We later learned that his name was Laird McCloud. Many years later, the feline laird became the model for Lord Byron in our Dan and Rivka Sherman Mysteries. Dinner that night ended with sticky toffee pudding and, for Rosemary, that became her favorite dessert from then on.

Of course, the castle had its very own ghost story. It seems that the daughter of an earlier castle owner happened in on her father while he was diddling his wife's sister. The daughter ran from the room and tripped down the staircase to her death. Her specter supposedly wanders the castle halls at night and moans. A family grouping in a large oil painting hangs prominently in the dining room—where it is obvious that the father had been painted out of the picture.

The next morning, heading to the bus, we found the castle grounds bathed in a thick fog and, before long, Laird McCloud emerged from it with his breakfast in tow, a large, live "Heeland" mouse. Oh, and we were also shown pictures of the "Heeland coos" which were Scottish Highland cows with extremely hairy faces.

Our next stretch took us a half hour south to Inverness, where we wandered the streets, took in the city's major castle, and lunched in a local pub. Boarding a boat in the early afternoon, it carried us up the Caledonian canal onto Loch Ness. No, we didn't experience a Nessie sighting—the blighter must have had the day off. There were thirteenth- through sixteenth-century castles and castle ruins aplenty while cruising the myth-famous loch for well over an hour. The cruise ended at Urquhart Castle ruins, which were in a little better shape than most. We returned to Inverness for the night.

An hour south of Inverness, the bus parked in front of the Tomatin Distillery, where we were given a tour of the premises and all the steps it takes to produce a quality scotch. We're told that they start with water from a mountain stream and finish with water that's as pure as they acquired it. They add the water to barley to start germination, and then dry the mixture to stop germination in a precise number of days; the result is called malt. Smoke introduced during the drying process controls the flavoring. The dried malt is then ground into grist flour. The grist is then remixed, this time with hot water to brew a mash which, after a measured time limit, is drained as a highly sugared liquid called wort. The leftover mash is used as cattle feed. Yeast is added to the wort to start fermentation and all that remains is double distillation and aging. The eight to ten years of aging is done in oaken barrels. The significant amount of evaporation encountered during the years of aging is called the angels' share.

The remainder of that day we strolled through an elaborate garden whose name, even though it bears remembering, I can't seem to recall. Another day we visited Stirling Castle where the Duke and Duchess of Argyle sometimes live. I immediately dubbed them the Duke and Duchess of Socks. They weren't at home, so I never confronted them with my renaming. The castle was lavishly furnished with a twenty-foot dining table, elaborate service for an army, and numerous ten-foot oils on the walls. One thing I remember is that the silver soup tureens were cast in the form of ships, all Royal Navy men-o-war of centuries past. Sprawling rooms and decorative gardens were explored as well.

We returned to Edinburgh the next day to wait for John and Ann's arrival. They rented a car at the airport and drove to our hotel, only to experience transmission problems. Later, while waiting for the repairs, we four explored the rest of the "Royal Mile," which led past St. Giles Cathedral down to Holyrood Palace, once the residence of Mary Queen of Scots. After exploring the upper floors of the palace, we descended from her bedroom to the main floor via a spiral staircase. Again lavish décor, but this was mixed with extensive religious ruins on the palace grounds.

On our way back to our hotel we stopped off at the Stoplight Pub for supper. Amid many blinking traffic-style stoplights, John and I sampled haggis, a local delicacy consisting of minced sheep's liver, tongue, and suet mixed with toasted dry oats and herbs sewn into a pierced sheep's stomach and boiled for a minimum of three hours. We were told it was one of those things you just had to try while traveling in Scotland. We were pleasantly surprised with the taste and experience and happily ordered it again.

The following morning John drove us south to Lockerbie in Dumfries, one of the main reasons for our trip—to see where Miriam's life had ended. It was just north of the Scottish and English border. We discovered a charming red sandstone town, with a clock-tower town hall, whose triple window glass front displayed the flags of all twenty-one of the victims' countries. Also, we found friendly, thoughtful people who, once they learned we were families of Pan Am 103, were pleased to help us find our way. They pointed out a small strip park that marked the in-town site of the exploded "Clipper-Maid of the Seas" plane that destroyed several homes and took eleven lives on the ground.

Next, the four of us were directed to the Garden of Remembrance just outside of town, where all of the victims' names were inscribed in stone—some on the memorial wall and some on individual plaques in the ground. Miriam's name was on the latter. We took several pictures before heading for the third important site. Quite a few miles out of town we came to a walled-in-stone churchyard. Inside a small stone structure imbedded as apart of the wall, we learned from a map that Miriam's remains had been found in the open field just 400 yards outside this wall. Again we took pictures and signed the guestbook.

The Garden of Remembrance

John, the only driver among the four of us brave enough and willing to venture driving on the left side of the road, took the wheel once more and drove us south through Carlisle and deep into the Lake District National Park—eventually stopping at the Prince of Wales Thistle Hotel in the small, yet famous town of Grasmere.

It was a charming and ram-

Lord Larry, master of my castle (actually our hotel in Grasmere, Lake District)

bling place where any four steps taken horizontally outside the rooms' maze meant you had to either climb or descend another flight of steps. Generous green lawns sprawled to the nearby lake and in every which direction. I wandered to a tempting group of chairs clustered midway to the lake. I actually gave in and sat there, causing Rosemary to muse, "He looks like the bloody lord of the manor."

There was enough sun left in the sky for us to meander into town over the stone bridge to stop at the old Rowan Tree Tavern for a heavenly fully loaded baked potato of enormous proportions. Next came the graveyard behind the old stone church, where the poet Wordsworth and family are buried. The following morning we hired a driver for a day's tour of the lake country's highlights. Gorgeous meadows, clear lakes and beautiful landscapes made the tour worthwhile.

Another day it was south again, on our own, through Manchester, Northwich, and the old walled city of Chester in Cheshire county. After a pub lunch and a short walk atop the surrounding walls in Chester, it was on to Llangollen in the heart of Wales. Our bed and breakfast for the night was an aged stone inn that overlooked the fast-running, shallow, rock-bottom river Dee and a bridge crossing it that dated back to 1345. However, the limited view from our bedroom window merely revealed one side of a blinking red sign of the establishment. As if that on-and-off annoyance wasn't enough, the floors were cockeyed due to the entire building's uneven settling. Conservatively, I'd say the floor dropped twelve to fifteen inches from one wall to the other. I had to hold out my hands in front of me when I crossed the room so I wouldn't trip. Thank goodness, somehow the bed had been leveled out to prevent our rolling out during the night. Who knows where that might have led?

The next morning revealed not only a quaint little Welsh town, but how to pronounce it: "Clan—lock—len," no way near the way Llangollen was actually spelled. As we explored more of Wales, almost nothing there sounded like it was spelled. We encountered several nearby castle ruins and rode the thirty-minute train ride from Llangollen Station to Carrog Station and back. To continue the adventure, a boat ride took us along a raised canal to a spot ending at an ancient aqueduct that originally carried water to the area.

Out of Wales and on our way south again into England, a small detour took us through Stratford-upon-Avon and a drive past Shakespeare's birthplace—a large, three-story, Tudor-style, building with a rock chimney at one end—and past Anne Hathaway's thickly thatched cottage with its three brick chimneys. Back on the main roads again, John pointed us through the low-lying hills of the Cotswolds, where an entrancing pub, claiming to be the oldest in the United Kingdom, provided us with a gourmet lunch. We raved so much about the food that the owner and chef came out to talk with us. Twenty years later, don't ask what we actually ate. Rustic construction and furnishings, along with weapons and shields on the walls, added charm to the meal. Oh, and the huge cold hearth occupied one whole stone wall at one end of the pub's dining area. It was the largest fireplace I'd ever seen. The current season was far too warm for it to have a lit fire.

Pointed southwest through the Cotswolds, the car headed toward the historic city of Bath. Knowing exactly where our King Francis Thistle hotel was on the map wasn't enough. There didn't seem to be a direct path of streets to it, so we stuck to the major roads and pursued an inward spiral path around the city to our hotel. As a result we arrived well after the dining room had closed. Plan B, the hotel bar was sans sandwiches due to a lack of bread, but they fed us heaping bowls of French fries until we quit. For the next five days Bath became our home base for a number of sight-seeing sorties within and outside the city.

The Roman baths, for which the city gets its name, were within walking distance of the hotel, so the four of us spent the day exploring them. The actual baths were below current street levels, and the Sacred Spring and the main pool were fed from a geological fault. The water, heated geothermally from a well under the surface, bubbles up into the spring and eventually into the main Roman pool under the colonnaded roof. The heavy humidity that is generated spreads out and even forms a mist that dampens the surrounding streets. The perimeter of the main pool and a bunch of huge stone blocks, set at various levels, provide the desired seating for the bathers. Discovered over 800 years before the Common Era, the facility furnished the elite with luxury bathing throughout the five centuries of Roman rule and beyond.

On the second day in Bath, John drove us to Salisbury Plain to view the strange phenomenon of the Stonehenge array of stones. History and science may have solved the intended stone alignment and overall configuration by referencing certain stars during the solstices, but who were the builders, and how did they convey this type, size, and weight of stone there from quarries so far to the north? Probably on river rafts, we were told. Tourists were crawling all over the place—some inside and some outside the chained safety areas, but otherwise the stone array was an amazing sight.

The third day took us to the cathedral city of Salisbury itself. A tour of the main cathedral involved too many steps for me to undertake, so I rested on a bench on the grassy grounds just outside.

The others took pictures of one of the first manmade mechanical clocks in English history. It was designed to automatically call the townspeople to church. We stopped in an old inn across the street for high tea, scones, strawberries, and clotted cream. Afterward, we strolled down a brick walkway past a string of good-looking, red-brick homes. One of these belonged to Michael Faraday, a pioneer in the storage of electricity and for whom the unit of capacity, the farad, is named.

A fourth day brought us to historic Wilton House, famous for not only its art, book collections, formal gardens, and park, but for its desirability as a TV and movie filming site. Historically, it was the home of the Earl of Pembroke, a contemporary of King Charles the first. Our docent added another tidbit, telling us that Churchill and Eisenhower met for the D-Day preparations there as well. Both the Milds and Pollacks were impressed with the size and quality of the art collection—also the elaborate wall and ceiling décor.

The fifth day's venture found us amid the Stourhead Estate and gardens. The original Stourton family lived there from the twelfth to eighteenth centuries. The current Palladian style mansion replaced the original in the early eighteenth century. The 2,650-acre gardens were lush with greenery, sunken pathways, statues, and monuments, along with models of the Temple of Apollo and the Pantheon. I took advantage of almost every park bench.

The next morning we packed up and John drove us back to London, dropping us off at our hotel and continuing on to the airport for their departure. Rosemary and I stayed on for a few more days of touring about. The first evening in London, the two of us set out on foot to find a place to have supper. On the street, we encountered a handsome, male shill, undoubtedly from India, who persuaded us to step inside to his restaurant. The two-story establishment had a lavish Arabian Nights décor and musical theme with fluffy gauze-like drapes covering the private alcoves surrounding both floors. The patrons beyond were a faint blur. Dozens of fabric objects hung from the high center ceiling. Not at all what we expected.

We were seated at a tiny table for two in the central open area and a small bowl with celery sticks and sliced raw carrots was set before us. Moments later, I discovered that the table wobbled almost a half-inch back and forth. I selected an appropriately sized carrot slice from the bowl and stuck it under the errant table leg. *There—stabilized—job well done*, I thought. A waiter rushed out of nowhere, crying: "No, no, no!" He removed the slice and replaced it with a full match book. The hazardous matches overcompensated, causing a wobble in another direction. Oh, well, I wasn't about to lecture him on either the hazards or the error of his ways.

Over the next three days we took day tours of Hampton Court and Buckingham Palace; the city and cathedral at Canterbury; and a boat ride up the Thames through waterway locks and gorgeous countryside to Windsor Castle, where the Royals live. The tour through Windsor convinced me that the Brits are paying through the nose to keep the Royals in style. What a waste! On the way back to London the bus broke down, and we had to wait several hours to get seats on other tour buses. We flew back to the States the next afternoon.

A month later Rosemary and I had a polo shirt monogrammed with the title "Master Driver of the British Empire." We sent it to John in appreciation of his willingness and bravery in driving the four of us everywhere during the preceding trip. I usually read the signs while the girls supposedly read the maps. Left-hand roundabouts were bad enough, but indecision upon reaching a flurry of strange directional signs did raise a few voices as we went around a second or more times.

* * * *

In the fall of 1999 Rosemary and I flew to Seattle, WA to take a tour of the Canadian Rockies. Arriving two days before the tour started, we took in a number of local sites. The mere size and variety of products at Pike Place Fish Market were staggering—abounding in beautiful flowers, produce, and seafood. Two clerks were even tossing fish to one another to amuse the elbow-to-elbow crowds. We actually found a good restaurant behind the hundreds of stalls. Rosemary went up in the Space Needle while I enjoyed a cup of coffee down below in coffee city. The two of us took a below-ground, walking-talking tour of the original city and a pleasant ferry ride across the bay to Bainbridge Island and back.

The official Canadian Rockies tour bus loaded over thirty passengers and all their luggage at the hotel, then headed down the steeply inclined street—and scraped bottom at a bump that damaged the bus's transmission. The passengers had to wait several hours in a waterfront park while the bus was repaired. Because of the delay in getting started, the group arrived late at their Spokane hotel. After breakfast the next morning the bus drove east to what I believe was the intended overnight stop, Coeur d'Alene. It was a beautifully serene town overlooking a relatively underdeveloped shoreline and a gorgeous lake.

Moving generally eastward, the bus entered Glacier National Park and the Highway to the Sun, a road that winds through the park but is open only during the summer months. We stopped at the west gate long enough to pick up a park ranger, who pointed out the many glaciers, mountain peaks, lakes, and panoramas. She also informed us about the many disappearing and shrinking glaciers throughout the world due to global warming. The twenty-three glaciers at that park were included in her shrinking predictions. At St. Mary's Gate in the northeast end of the park, the ranger left us, and we drove across the international border into Alberta Province, Canada and over to the upper end of Lake Waterton and the Prince of Wales Hotel, overlooking the beautiful undisturbed international lake and its surrounding forests. We even partook of scones and tea with clotted cream there. We woke the following morning and saw several deer in the fields just beyond the hotel grounds. About half of our group spent the better part of the day exploring nearby hiking trails while the remainder of us relaxed in the serene surroundings.

The bus traveled north to join the Trans-Canada Highway and then west into Banff National Park. With a late start, the bus arrived in Banff in mid-afternoon. The driver stopped for a short while for us to explore one of the downtown streets, but what interested us most was the inclined and terraced park at the end of it that was full of blossoming plants and little trails that allowed us to see more of it. The group stayed that night in the Banff Springs Hotel, a nineteenth-century Canadian grand railway hotel. It was actually a sprawling brick castle with many levels and *beaucoup* turrets. The shops and dining rooms were elegant. At a below-ground level we discovered a labyrinth of springs, Olympic-sized pools, waterfalls, sprays, showering and mineral bathing areas. The geothermally heated spring water appeared in a variety of colors and gave off different but strong aromas due to the richness of a particular chemical found in that location. With more time we would have loved to experience these pools and springs.

Morning found our bus back on the Trans-Canada Highway, now heading north and slightly west through Banff National Park until we encountered Lake Louise. Our route tracked the Canadian Rockies along the way, and although it was still early fall, the snowcapped peaks, worn like white skullcaps, soon would become mounts adorned with full-length white robes. Chateau Lake Louise, our day's destination, turned out to be another massive and sprawling luxury hotel. Built of gray stone in 1890, it was set amidst a full ring of snowy mountaintops overlooking a gorgeous cobalt-colored lake. That picturebook view only improved with an exploding sunset and finally with reflective moonlit images. The dining experience and the rooms were again elegant. Aside from being awed by this and the scenery, many on the tour had the feeling that they were being rushed through these grand hotels without experiencing the luxurious benefits of an extended stay.

So another solo overnight stay, and then it was a long morning's bus ride north on the Ice Fields Parkway to the Columbia Ice Fields, which involved a huge bus terminal. We left our luxury tour bus and, after an hour's wait in the terminal, the group transferred to a monster oversized bus whose wheels had to be at least seven-feet across. This specially designed bus left the paved roads and drove straight onto the flat ice fields portion of this massive glacier for at least a mile. We took a short precarious walk on the ice fields to get a better view of the falling path of the glacier. Returning to the bus station and our own tour bus, we resumed our way north again on the Ice Fields Parkway all the way to Jasper.

Arriving in Jasper, Rosemary and I spent the night in what looked like a log cabin from the outside, yet actually had all of the amenities of most luxury hotels on the inside. In the morning we witnessed a family of elk marching down the street of our log cabin village and taking over the nearby tennis courts. This furry family included a doe, her three offspring, and a buck with a tremendous rack spread. They seemed peaceful enough, but we were warned to steer clear of them, as the bucks are very protective of their families. We spent the rest of our day uncovering moraine blue lakes, cascading waterfalls, and rushing mountain streams. We later encountered a moose almost totally immersed in a stream. Our guide explained that moose necks are so negligible that they have to wade in deep enough to be able to drink.

The following morning our bus left Alberta Province for British Columbia and conveyed us mostly south and westerly to Kamloops for another overnight. Our Hawaii snowbird friends Barry and Joy Huculak, who were Kamloops residents, met with us for dinner and then a tour of the area. They showed us the huge Indian Council Center, where many of the surrounding tribes meet for political purposes and a highly developed, extremely profitable industrial park that was mistakenly (by unimaginative donors) given to the local Indians as a token reservation. We spent the rest of the evening back at our friends' house, where we viewed Barry's wonderful collection of scale-model cars, more than a hundred of them, each about a foot in length.

The following day put us on the road again toward Vancouver Island and particularly the charming city of Victoria. The two of us enjoyed the comfort and convenience of an entire two-bedroom condominium all to ourselves, with kitchen and dining room just a block off the harbor, and four blocks to the center of

A delightful scene from our walking tour of seaport towns in the Netherlands

Rembrandt's *Nightwatch* becomes a Delft tile mosaic in Delft, Netherlands

town. I remember touring a historical, regal-looking hotel and a museum where I learned that the local Indians had a language that sounded very much like the Hawaiian language. Our group had its end-of-tour banquet at beautiful Butchart Gardens. Beforehand, we toured the acres of named flowers, especially the rose gardens, where almost all varieties were named after famous people. The tour ended in Seattle the next day, and we flew to BWI and then taxied home from there.

* * * *

Rosemary and I had traveled to the Netherlands and in particular to the Pan Am bombers' trial at Camp Ziest in the fall of 2000. I described much of that in Chapter 12. Our main purpose in returning to Amsterdam afterward was to connect with our friends from home, Sinjin (St. John) and Ellie Martin, who were visiting Berlin during our trial days. His father, an army colonel, was a military occupation mayor there right after WWII, so Sinjin spent some time there as a youngster. As previously planned, the four of us joined a Collette tour in Amsterdam and became tourists for two weeks more.

Amsterdam is swept away by Rosemary

Amsterdam was a city of gorgeous major art museums, and we sampled a good deal of the cultural fare. We especially enjoyed the Van Gogh museum with more than 200 of his paintings. An ever-cycling trolley system made it easy to move about town; however, just crossing the street you took your life in your hands—heavy traffic and bicycles dominated the scene, surely, thousands of them. In fact, huge numbers of bicycles were heaped next to the railway station for commuters. I also noticed a plethora of very tall blonde women. Our guide also walked us through the red-light district, where pot and ladies of the night were displayed through storefront window glass.

Our tour group walked through the picturesque seaport towns of Marken, Volendam, and Edam—the latter more famous

The guild halls of Brussels' Grand Place

The Martins and Milds waiting for Belgium *frits* and steamed mussels in Brussels for its cheeses. A bus took us to Delft, where a wall-sized rendition of Rembrandt's *Nightwatch* done in blue and white Delft tiles was on display. We had seen the original painting in Amsterdam a few days earlier.

Another ride took us to Aalsmeer and the international flower exchange, where tram-loads of gorgeous flowers were brought into a stadium-like auction room to be bid on in tram-load lots. Once any transaction was completed, the seller's tram car was then connected to the buyer's tram and pulled away. The enormous warehouse behind this auction room was at least two football fields wide by three football fields long.

Our next stop was in Bruges (or Brugge), Belgium where we spent the night. On a walking tour through the area, it was learned that this inland city was once at a major riverhead, making it a seaport. Silt deposits and fill nor longer made it possible for ships to navigate this far upriver. A pleasant boat ride through the city's many canals topped off our day there. Then on to Ghent, Belgium, where the bus stopped off to see a famous Hugo van der Goes religious triptych artwork in oil.

In Brussels, the capital of Belgium, the group took a walking tour through a colorfully and beautifully displayed produce market and wound up in Grand Place, a large open square lined with guild hall buildings of all the major trades, each with its own guild or union emblem prominently displayed atop each hall.

With mussels in Brussels a must, dinner that night comprised a heaping black kettle of steamed mussels and Belgium *frits* which were supposedly invented before their neighbors' so-called French fries. The Belgium version was double fried. Of course, that had to be topped off with local beer—well, almost local. I had a Dutch Amstel Bier. We sat at wrought-iron tables at curbside.

The bullet (high-speed) train to Paris was our next experience. We arrived in Paris faster than the trip from Zeist to Amsterdam. Scenery passed so quickly your eyes couldn't really fix on anything—actually, a bit of a disquieting feeling. That evening a massive elevator conveyed the lot of us up the Eiffel Tower to dine

Aalsmeer auctioneers bidding for flower lots

Massive warehouse of flower carts and trams in Aalsmeer, Netherlands

in a restaurant overlooking the city. Going up in a group allayed my misgivings about high places.

The next day we did whirlwind tours of the Louvre museum in the morning and the D'Orsay museum in the afternoon after crossing over the Seine at the Pont Neuf bridge. On the way to the D'Orsay, the Voltaire Café provided lunch. Apparently, the café got its famous name only because the great philosopher had supposedly died in a room upstairs. Due to the intense crowding around the glass-encased *Mona Lisa* at the Louvre, only a distant viewing from across the room could be had. I was so tired at the end of the D'Orsay trek that I had to sit on the floor for fifteen minutes before tackling the long journey back to the hotel.

The next morning Notre Dame was on the agenda. It would have been easy to envision poor Esmerelda and the hunchbacked Quasimoto while we visited the massive Gothic cathedral. The cathedral was a mob scene, but elaborate, cavernous, and almost sinister. The group was left on its own to rest for the remainder of that afternoon and re-gathered for a large, glittering cabaret evening. We feasted on chateaubriand, but I especially remember a trapeze act that scarily took place right over our heads while we ate and a ventriloquist act that featured a basset hound smoking a cigarette (unlit, of course) out of the side of his mouth that bobbled in sync with what he was supposed to be saying. *Très* cute! The next day was also on our own, so we window-shopped to our hearts' content and visited the Paris opera house of *Phantom* fame. We left for the

U.S. the following morning.

Oh yes, we had bought tulip bulbs in Aalsmeer to take home, but a lot of good that did. When spring finally came, our local squirrels had dug up and feasted on them before they had a chance to bloom. In the years that followed, a solitary spared tulip would break with convention and stick its nose above ground, but never the showy display we'd anticipated. I had lined the flower bed in front of the house with treated two-high railroad ties and filled the beds with rich, fertilized loam. For some unknown reason, both squirrels and rabbits spared the impatiens Rosemary so carefully planted, but the rabbits targeted her Gerbera daisies, so she planted silk flowers where the daisies stood, assuming the rabbits had no taste for silk. And she was right!

Speaking of tulips. Rosemary wrote an essay called "Tulips on Trial" after we attended the trial at Camp Zeist. She had high hopes that the tulips would bloom each year, commemorating our deeply emotional experience. But even she had to laugh at the bulbs' disastrous finale, ending as lunch for the squirrels. Her award-winning essay appeared in *New Lines From the Old Line State*, an anthology of Maryland writers; *Truth Quest;* and *Miriam's World—and Mine*.

Chapter 16

A Whole World To Behold

Early in the fall of 2001 Marty and bobbi (yes, "bobbi") Kogan, our new friends in Honolulu, talked us into taking a trip to China. Because of the time of the year, we had to leave from Maryland and meet them and join our tour at our hotel in Beijing. We flew to Chicago and connected with a fourteen-hour flight that followed the great circle route over Alaska and the Arctic Circle and down over parts of Russia and Korea to Beijing.

An impressive sculpture display welcomed us in the hotel lobby—a temple made from small round mooncakes. The Kogans were also waiting for us when we arrived. The first night we walked across the street to a small fish market, where we saw dubiously fresh fish for sale, lying in open pans scarcely covered in water. A strong odor prevented us from spending much more time there.

Our guide from Grand Circle Tours was a 6'-2" handsome, athletic-looking Han from northern China. There were sixty-four of us in the tour group, so we were split into two groups of thirty-two each with two assigned buses. In tight places it was always difficult to stand close enough to the guide to hear what he had to say. In the morning he walked us from the hotel to the nearby complex making up the massive Forbidden City. We spent a lot of time walking the spacious spread, only to view most of the buildings from the doorways. When it was time to leave, bobbi Kogan was nowhere to be found, and Marty began to panic. We started to retrace our steps when suddenly she decided to show up. We were all relieved.

Our China group tour assembled in Beijing

The Milds and Kogans at the Temple of Heaven

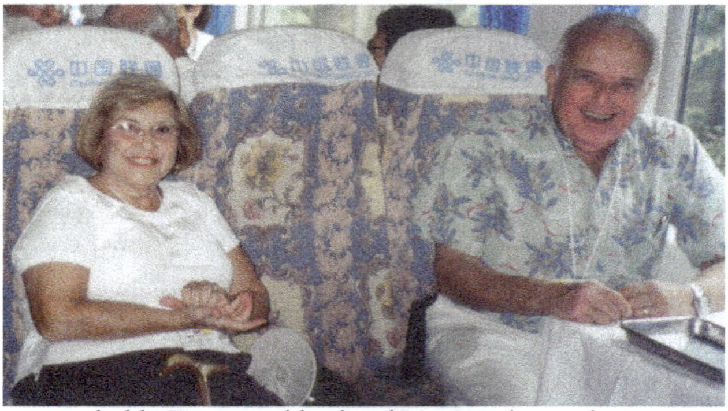

bobbi Kogan and husband Marty in luxury bus

I don't think I could make it as a rickshaw driver

One view of the Great Wall of China

Another similar perspective of the Great Wall

Our next stop was the great hall and gardens commanding Tiananmen Square. Later that afternoon, while visiting a public park, I needed a restroom. When I entered, I saw an old woman sleeping in a chair just inside the door. I went into the next room and discovered two footprints imbedded in the concrete and a shallow trough in the floor as well. A small amount of water trickled through it. Accomplishing my chore, I returned to the first room where the woman had come to life and was extending both arms toward me. In one hand she held out a damp cloth towel and in the other, a collection bowl. I refused the soiled towel and rather than invoke the evil eye, I deposited a paper bill in the bowl to ameliorate my false guilt.

From what we saw of Beijing, it was a mostly clean and modern city with tall buildings and heavy, heavy traffic. Some of the streets were even lined with plants and shrubs. In the high traffic areas there were pedestrian bridges over the busy streets and a few even had continuous escalators on both sides. Our guide informed us that because of the city's hosting of the international athletic games, the local factories had been shut down for the previous two weeks to control air quality. Rickshaws carried us to the *hutongs*, a tightly woven maze of concrete homes where we sipped tea with local resident families. It was in that section of town that we noted miniature (very thin and short) trucks and a number of overloaded, human-powered delivery vehicles servicing this part of town.

The following day the buses took us to a rug factory in the city of Souzhou. The rugs were hand-woven by young adept girls who would spend many years weaving a single rug. The forms were hung vertically and the girls would begin by sitting on the floor, then on a bench; next, standing and then standing on benches and ladders. What a life. A boat carried us back to Beijing along a wide Grand Canal that wound through the poorer residential areas. Children swam in the canal, men relieved themselves there, and women washed clothes there as well—all oblivious to the passing tourists.

On the third day the buses took us inland north and west to the Great Wall of China. The handmade, high winding stone structure stretched from sight over hill and dale. We were informed that the frequent watchtowers were spaced to accommodate twice an archer's normal range of coverage. It was quite a hike just to get on the wall, so I let the others hike a mile or so along the wall, while I soaked up the local scenery and the parade of tourists from near and far. A Great Wall hat and T-shirt bought, and everyone was back on the bus for the ride back to Beijing.

China Air Lines flew us to Shanghai on the fourth day and, during the flight, they favored us with not only the usual drinks and snacks, but dental supplies as well. Shanghai turned out to be another very modern city. Luncheon, after landing, was at a dumpling factory/restaurant where every morsel was shaped like a bird, animal, or other unique figure, a most fun and delicious meal. We began to notice a pattern: that every meal in China ended with watermelon for dessert—never a pastry.

We visited the very fine Shanghai Museum on the fifth day. As a precaution to their relics, the displays are not lit until a sensor detects that you are in proximity. It was an impressive collection displayed well, especially the Asian storytelling screens and dynasty pottery.

One more day brought us to Beihei park and a sheltered concrete path thick with children and adults playing games and vendors pushing their wares while crowds of tour groups and locals plowed through all of them. Crowds were so thick that the tour guides held little flags over their heads to keep their particular sheep in herd. The problem was too many flags and very much confusion. Our group of four, having lagged for photographs and distracted by our immediate surroundings, missed out when our main tour bunch made a detour. Unaware, we saw a similar flag ahead and continued forward past the detour point. On past the wall with nine dragons in relief, reaching the marble boat at the bitter end of the path, only to realize our mistake, and before panic grew too sizeable, we spotted the rest of our companions coming toward us. Whew! I couldn't imagine that this marble boat actually floated, but standing on deck afforded us a perfect view of the Summer Palace across the massive blue-green lake. The day took its toll on me, especially because we had been on our feet for hours.

Yet another day we bused to the Shanghai docks to board long narrow ships designed for river cruising. This would be a five-day Regal China Cruise Line trip up the Yangtze, the world's third longest river. Our stateroom was a matter of approximated inches—a 70" by 30" bunk bed that left my toes in limbo—a 70" by 30" stand-up space next to the bed that had to include your luggage—and a 36" by 60" shower that included a toilet and sink. Size didn't seem to matter that much; we spent most of our cruising outside in a deck chair. We passed through and by beautiful mountain gorges and muddy banks. For the most part, the water looked a murky brownish green.

At the Three Gorges Dam we were lowered to the next river level via a temporary lock, whereas we saw other smaller boats being lowered and raised on tracks by cabling. The unfinished dam was to be China's answer to solving their severe pollution problem as well as tripling their capacity to generate much-needed electricity. Getting rid of China's coal-fired electricity would go a long way toward clearing the air, but there was a price to be paid: when the water upriver of the dam rose 15 meters, the adjoining arable land on either side would be lost to the little-guy farmers all along the river. The river begins high in the Himalayas and carries with it rich topsoil to these lands. Not only farm soil, but homes, schools, and graves would be under water, unreachable.

Stopping at a tiny unknown river port a few days later, we de-boarded our ship for some smaller flat-style boats, allowing us to venture into a much shallower tributary river and its steep-walled gorge. As soon as we left the Yangtze for the feeding tributary, the murky water turned beautifully clear. Our guide pointed high up on the steep rock face, where there were hundreds of tiny caves used as burial crypts. At the tributary's source, we walked, or rather wobbled, on land (actually on smooth fist-sized rocks) for a bit and

WWII P-40 Flying Tiger

re-boarded for the trip back to the river port and our ship. We did stop at one other river port for a few hours to view a local farm market, where live animals and fowl were slaughtered just as they were purchased.

After five days the cruise ended at Chongqing, the Nationalist wartime capital of Chunking during much of WWII. We spent some time the next morning at the local Flying Tigers museum. American Lt. Gen. Claire Chennault led a group of flying mercenaries for Nationalist China prior to the U.S. entry into WWII. They were merged into the U.S. Army Air Corps afterward. They flew P-40s with sharks' teeth painted across the nose of the planes. The photos brought back memories of that war for me.

That afternoon the buses took us north to the city of Xian. Xian was developed about the nearby multiple burial sites and sculpture museum pits of the Terracotta Warriors and Horses. Emperor Qin Shi Huang, responsible for establishing the first Imperial Chinese dynasty, is believed to be buried there, along with terracotta sculptures of thousands of his imperial guardsmen and their horses and chariots, all in neat columns to protect him. The first of three pits was discovered by peasants digging for a well in 1974. Massive buildings for viewing cover and protect the excavated pits and unearthed figures. We found it amazing that anyone would go to these lengths to be protected in his afterlife. I put it on a par with the Egyptians and their giant pyramids. I wondered how many slaves died on this project.

We awoke early on Tuesday, September 11, 2001 from our Xian hotel beds to a pounding on our room door. Marty Kogan stood there telling us to turn on the television: "A plane has crashed into the World Trade Center in New York City." I turned the TV on and flipped through the channels trying to find one I could comprehend. English-speaking CNN was not broadcasting for some reason. I stumbled onto a Japanese-speaking channel where the announcer was translating someone speaking English in the background. The scenes and dialogue described the terrible events going on in New York, Washington, and later Pennsylvania. Four commandeered commercial aircraft were being utilized as suicidal weapons of destruction. At first, all we knew was that one plane and then another had crashed into the Twin Towers of New York's World Trade Center. We later learned that a third plane had crashed into the outer perimeter of the Pentagon in Washington and that a fourth destined for the same target had been diverted and had crashed somewhere in Pennsylvania. The image of the burning towers remains in my head almost two decades later.

We soon found that all commercial air traffic was grounded indefinitely. Here we were, stranded in a foreign nation, wondering whether the U.S. of A. was at war with some unknown enemy. It wasn't long before Islamic extremists took claim for these horrendous attacks. The husband of one in our group worked at the Pentagon, so she spent hours trying to get through to Washington for any news of her spouse. She eventually learned that he was okay. But how long would it be before we could leave China for home? We still had several days of the tour left before our scheduled departure for the States.

The next day our tour bus headed south once more to the Guilin caves on our way to Hong Kong. The caves proved to involve a great deal of walking and climbing, but it was worth it. The stalactites and stalagmites proved to be every bit as magnificent as those in the Luray Caverns of western Virginia. We arrived at our Hong Kong hotel late in the afternoon, so the search for a place to have supper became imminent. The thought of having

Hong Kong's famous floating city

anything, but not another authentic Chinese meal, seemed to be prevalent throughout the group. We were fed well, and deliciously so, throughout the tour; however, three weeks of it was more than enough to elicit cravings for Western food. With that in mind, the group set out independently in smaller groups.

The Milds and Kogans wandered a few blocks from our hotel, shoulder to shoulder and hip to hip, with the most oppressive crowd that I have ever been in. Any movement meant you had to brush against someone else, especially anyone moving in the opposite direction. Those around us didn't seem to mind, but I felt uneasy, almost claustrophobic. In those moments I was glad that I was taller than most people around me—at least I could see my way to navigate the streets. At last we saw the sign for an Italian restaurant and looked in the window. Like a magnet the place had drawn other members of the tour group there as well, and from time to time, we saw others peering in the window at us too. My guess is that at least 80 percent of our bunch showed up there.

The following morning we boarded a local boat of the junk variety to tour the floating city of Hong Kong harbor. We passed by thousands of sizeable boats and barges, crudely tied together, shifting with the tide and rolling hypnotically with the waves in polluted waters. Smaller boats served their transportation needs. The harbor folk went about their lives without paying notice to the curious tourists observing them. Ashore, we could see the tightly knit offices and apartment buildings rising at a seemingly critical angle from the harbor business area to the mountains beyond.

A second day found the group riding an exciting tram up the slope of Victoria Peak for one glorious panorama from the top. There were plenty of shops and arts and crafts booths to explore once we were turned loose at the top, but the sense of crowding never left me, even there.

And then it was time for us to pack and leave. Though the U.S. flight ban had been lifted a day earlier, we worried that the backlog of stranded tourists might affect our departure time. As it turned out we needn't have worried; things went rather smoothly. In fact, we were even able to make minor adjustments in our flight plans. One thing that did strike me about our security was that the Chinese government actually cared about our safety (or at least the continuance of American tourism). Instead of the usual police in tan shorts and nightsticks, we had army men carrying automatic weapons at the ready. We felt safe, and eventually got home to sleep in our own beds for a change.

* * * *

In 2002 we teamed up with John and Ann and flew to Lisbon (Lisboa) Portugal three days prior to the start of our commercial tour. Our hotel was walking distance from the Tagus (Rio Tejo) River, so we found our way to the riverfront park and Belem tower, a one-time prison and fortress guarding the city. An impressive statue to Vasco da Gama, his followers, and the Age of Discovery stood only a few hundred yards away from the tower. The included figures were riding a stone ship. On the city side of the park was an enormous monastery (Mosterio Dos Jeronimos) where da Gama is buried. The four of us explored the entire Belem area pretty well, but when we tried to find sights within the city proper, too much time was spent in map reading with only partial successes. Much of the city's charm appeared through its narrow cobbled streets, electric trolleys, and buildings with walls of multicolored tiles.

We decided to leave the remaining tour of the city to the

Monument to the Great Explorer Vasco da Gama on Tagus riverfront

Belem Tower, a one-time prison and fortress on the Tagus riverfront

A cross-street in downtown Lisboa (Lisbon)

professionals and hired a driver for the day to take us twenty-five miles west of Lisbon to the tiny picturesque village of Sintra. The main attraction there is the Pena Royal Palace, the summer residence of many of Portugal's kings and queens, which is situated on a mountain peak overlooking the Atlantic Ocean on one side and dozens of castles and mansions imbedded in the lush, rolling Sintra mountains on the other side. The Romanesque architecture, arches, domes, and turrets, along with the brightly colored exterior walls, give it a fairyland/Disneyland appearance. The interior construction and décor varied from primitive middle-aged rock walls to elaborately finished halls and rooms. The stairs and miles of walking were well worth the trouble.

We rejoined our driver down the mountain in the village, and he drove us to the ocean at a place called Cabo da Roca, Cape of the Rock. This beachfront rock formation has geographical significance in that it is the western-most extension of the European continent. After returning to the village of Sintra, we made the short trip back to Lisbon to join our organized tour. Because of Portugal's neutrality during WWII, I had always viewed the port of Lisbon as a city of intrigue and spies. It also played an important role in the escape of many Jews from Nazi Europe.

Having been displeased with the size of our China tour group (sixty plus), we had ultimately signed up for Overseas Adventure Travel, a tour group limited to fifteen. Our guide was a youngish man named Carlos, who pronounced his name as Carlosh, explaining that his language, Portuguese, was quite different from Spanish and influenced more by the Germanic tongues of the Netherlands and Luxembourg. Carlos was something of a musician and music lover, especially of the lively Fado folk music genre. Wherever we went on the bus, he had Fado tapes playing.

The group toured the city, repeating a few of our earlier sights, but gaining clarity on them. One of the highlights was the Castle of St. Jorge atop one of the city's seven hills. That night we had supper in one of the nightclubs featuring Fado music and dancing. Rosemary was thrilled with her delicious goat chops. As

The magnificant castle of Portugal's kings and queens at Sintra, Portugal

Another view of the same storybook castle—called Pena Castle at Sintra

Skulls and bones implanted in the walls of the Chapel of the Bones (Capela Dos Ossos) Evora, Portugal

Chapel of the Bones
The monks' warning to all visitors about the inevitability of death

Entrance to our paradore (hotel), a converted Moorish mansion in Carmona, Spain

we waited for our transportation back to the hotel from the nightclub, someone pointed out lettering high on an adjacent wall that spelled "LADINO," the specific language and description of Jews expelled from Spain. Another afternoon we gathered in the hotel kitchen to watch the chefs prepare a Portuguese meal.

The next morning we were off to Evora, a city with a Celtic, Roman, and Moorish past. The Roman Temple of Diana, the great cathedral, the aqueduct, and the Chapel of the Bones (Capela Dos Ossos) were all on the tour's agenda. Rumor has it that monks were supposed to have cleared the local cemeteries of bones to make space for Evora's expansion. The bones wound up in the chapel to remind visitors of the inevitability of death. The place is spooky, with bones piled high everywhere and skulls cemented to pillars, arches, and walls as well. As if that weren't enough, eerie and threatening messages in a number of languages were posted all over the place. We couldn't wait to get out of there. The evening was pleasantly spent in the village square, not too far from our pousadas, a former mansion converted to a hotel.

Shortly before noon the following day, we crossed over into the Andalusia region of Spain and headed for Seville, where we had lunch and toured a former synagogue and then the main cathedral. The most interesting things about the cathedral were the gated crypts within the main area and collective symbols appearing in the stained glass windows. The fact that the artisans installed symbols of all the major religions, including a Star of David, suggested that there may have even been a previous era when people of differing religious beliefs actually got along. On a walking tour of the streets of Cordoba, we encountered a statue of Maimonides, the famous Jewish physician, philosopher, scholar, and poet affectionately known as Rambam, a contraction of his title and name. Strangely, Carlos identified him as a Muslim known for his work in math, science, and poetry in the Moorish world. Rosemary set Carlos straight, telling him that Rambam was actually a world-renowned Jewish physician, philosopher, and scholar, who is buried in Tiberius, Israel. We re-boarded the bus a short while later.

Another hour or so outside Seville, the bus reached the village of Carmona and climbed a dominant hill overlooking flat plains as far as the eye could see. Cresting the hilltop was a sprawling paradore, a former Moorish palace and our lodging for the night. The paradore grounds were surrounded by a high rock wall with an arched gate to the main road. Some of the amenities, the swimming pool and the tennis courts, could be seen outside the wall and at the foot of the hill. The main building furnishings were altogether elaborate, fashionable, and comfortable. We had a pleasant walk down through the village below and yet found it pretty typical.

The following day the bus headed south to British Gibraltar and the Mediterranean Sea. After passing through British customs we were given a few hours on our own to explore, so we took a cab ride to the top of the famous Rock. The slow drive up the steep and winding road enabled the indigenous Barbary apes to climb all over the cab's exterior and attempt to enter via the open, driver-side window.

While the driver seemed to know how to handle them, he cautioned us that they could be both vicious and thieving. At the top of the Rock we had a view of another rock on the Moroccan side of the sea, which our driver told us established the two pillars forming the gateway to the Mediterranean. Later, on foot through the city, we came across a sign supposedly directing us toward a

A spectator on the taxi ride to the top of the Rock

A Barbary ape, resident of the Rock of Gibraltar

Our paradore overlooking the rock gorge of the Guadalevín River at Ronda, Spain

Empty bullring in Ronda

synagogue we never could find. Running out of photo space on the camera, I stopped to purchase a new card at an exorbitant price. We re-boarded the bus after a quick customs check.

The bus moved north and east on to Ronda, arriving at our cliffside paradore/hotel before nightfall. After breakfast the following day we examined the 390-foot gorge created by the Guadalevín River. The Puente Nuevo (new bridge) over the deep gorge separates the two halves of the city. Always seeing the other side as the more interesting, we explored it first and discovered in the old city a large green park, a church, and two storefront museums.

Later in the day we found the bullring in the center of the city. There were no bullfights during our stay, but we were allowed to wander through the empty pens and gates like the star running attractions. A bullfighting museum presented us with historical weapons, tools, and elaborately decorated matador capes and articles of dress.

On our way once more, we crossed flat plains and, then in the distance, we saw a small village of white homes with red roofs nestled in the foothills of nearby mountains. The bus climbed toward the village and, after traveling through groves of olives, turned into the gate of an old olive oil factory. It seemed to be more of an instructional tourist attraction than a functioning factory. There were olive presses and huge storage vats, but when it came to run-off for the oil, there were vee-cut troughs dug into the cement floors—not the sanitary plumbing required of a modern factory. Afterward, in the charming little village, the ladies enjoyed shopping in the boutique shops. Rosemary even replaced a lost rain jacket in the process.

We spent the night in a very large Granada hotel. In the morning, as the bus drew close to the Alhambra—the mountaintop royal palace of Islamic emirs and, later, Spanish kings and queens—we noticed caves in the sides of the mountains. Carlos informed us that gypsies actually lived in them. The Alhambra architecture was definitely Moorish, with Islamic themes and sayings impressed into the walls. Marble pillars, arched entries, patterned inlaid ceramic

One of several pools at Alhambra

Examples of the elaborate architecture at Alhambra Palace in Spain

Statue of Maimonides (Rambam) in Cordoba, Spain

Cathedral ceiling in Toledo, Spain

flooring, walls covered in designed textures and colors, spouting fountains, rippling pools, and panoramic views abounded. One room sprawled to the next, followed by yet another stair flight to more. And alongside the palace, a string of formal gardens added to the display. As tired as we were, the art, craft, and leatherwork in the museum gift shop held us for almost another hour.

Heading north toward Toledo the next day, we stopped at a cork orchard. A local orchard guide explained that a cork tree grown anew takes up to twenty-five years of growing before it can be harvested for the first time—nine to twelve years for the second time and seven to ten years thereafter. If the harvesting of up to two inches of cork bark from the trunk is done correctly, no harm is done to the tree. The region supplies much of the world's cork needs. Carlos added that corks are not only used as bottle stoppers for the wine growers, but are used to make cricket balls, shuttlecocks, and insulation materials.

Arriving at our smaller Toledo paradore, we were shown to our room, which was furnished in sturdy yet elaborately decorated period pieces. Traditional dinner that night was to be roast suckling piglet served whole on a platter with an apple in its mouth. Diners were invited to view the piglet in process over a fire in the kitchen. Seeing and feeling the animal's misfortune turned many of the diners off such a delicacy that evening. John and I enjoyed the feast, but Rosemary and Ann had to be lured into a mere tasting. It was actually a cholesterol collector's delight.

We traveled to Toledo's Jewish Quarter and started our touring with the fabulous El Greco Museum. Although he was Spain's most famous painter, the man was actually born on the island of Crete. The paintings, especially his *View of Toledo*, were exquisite, but the museum proved cavernous and seemed poorly lit for decent viewing. Nearby, we found the Sinagoga del Tránsito, a synagogue noted for its Sephardic (Jewish, Spanish, and Moorish) architecture. The walls were decorated with flowers and geometric designs. This and many other synagogues were converted to churches and mosques when Jews were expelled from Spain during the Inquisition. We visited the Church of Santa Maria la Blanca, one of nine other converted synagogues in the quarter. Walls of white and pillars in bright white, accented with gold pine cones, supported dozens of rowed arches. Strikingly beautiful, but blatantly missing was any kind of furnishings.

The next morning we were off to Madrid, the last stop on our trip, although a few of our compadres would eventually be headed for a post-trip to Barcelona. When I think back to our stay in Madrid, I have to think two things—art and thievery. I had seen art collections in many cities, including Washington, DC, London, and Paris, but I had never seen the quality and quantity offered in Madrid—so many rooms filled with larger-than-life paintings and sculptures. We visited two of the three museums of art comprising the Madrid's Golden Triangle of Art: the Museo del Prado and the Museo del Reina Sofia only a few blocks apart. The Prado offered us works by Hieronymus Bosch, El Greco, Peter Paul Rubens, Titian, Diego Velázquez, Francisco Goya, and Fra Angelico. At the Reina Sofia we saw Picasso's tragic *Guernica* and *Woman in Blue,* as well as many surrealist works by Salvador Dali and Joan Miro. It was impossible to see everything in the amount of time allotted, so we did what we could to cover the proverbial waterfront.

We had heard there was a historic synagogue in the old section of the city and thought it might be worth seeing. It was quite a long walk there and back, but when it turned out to be an empty, unadorned building, it seemed a lot longer.

The second memory of my Madrid experience wasn't quite as exhilarating as the first, but perhaps it was more educational. We were walking back to the hotel from a restaurant on our last evening in Madrid. The sun had gone down hours before, but the streets were reasonably well lit. I wore my camera's leather case belted to my hip and, at the time, gave it little or no thought. The city sidewalks were crowded with people—some lining up for entry to nightclubs along the way, some crossing, and the rest on their way to somewhere else. A turned traffic light caused the moving crowd to quickly solidify into a thick bumper-to-bumper assemblage at one corner. That same light turned again, and the crowd expanded once more like a rubber band, but I didn't sense the loss of weight on my hip until I reached the middle of the next block. I stopped and reeled about. As I reached into the empty camera case, the crowd spilled around me—faces and faces, but none looked guilty, and I dared not stop and accuse anyone even if I had found someone. An expensive camera was gone, but it was replaceable. What wasn't replaceable were the hundreds of pictures residing on the digital photo card inside the camera—many of my travels through Spain. Our trip home was full of mixed emotions.

* * * *

Feeling we had gotten our money's worth out of the Overseas Adventure Travel tour to Portugal and Spain, the Pollacks and the Milds decided to try the OAT twenty-one day tour to Thailand and Cambodia. We met John and Ann in Narita, Japan, where both families changed to connecting flights to Bangkok, Thailand. We spent the night at a hotel there and, after a very early breakfast, we returned to the airport for a much smaller flight into Siem Reap, Cambodia, along with the rest of our pre-tour group. I was very impressed with the elaborately printed individual characters comprising the Thai writing.

Our Siem Reap hotel front was decorated with seven-headed snakes (*nagas*) on either side of the entrance staircase. The room was clean and comfy enough, but the view from the window was a filthy fish pond—murky water and floating trash. A walk down the dusty road out front led us to the local Buddhist temple and surrounding cemetery. Workers were refurbishing the smallish temple—mixing concrete to make building blocks; other workers were climbing on bamboo scaffolding to paint accoutrements high on the building. Out front there were several men and women sitting on the ground mixing sand, mud, and cement to pour into eighteen-inch by eight-inch bas-relief molds. The molds produced fascia blocks with elaborate patterns destined to decorate the temple's exterior sides.

Returning to the hotel, we met our guide, a local named

Fancy rickshaw ride to dinner in Siem Reap

First dinner in Siem Reap

Front and rear gates to Ankor Bayon, Cambodia

Naga, the 7-headed snake
at hotel entrance

Cemetery Shrine at
Siem Reap, Cambodia

Clay workers producing bas-relief décor for temple (at right above)
Siem Reap

Elephant guides waiting for their paying riders

Exploring the Hindu and Buddhist ruins of Angkor Bayon, Cambodia

Exploring more Hindu and Buddhist ruins of Angkor Bayon

Bas-relief Hindu myths at Angkor Thom

Massive roots of the Asian fig tree
Angkor Thom

Rosemary at the root of the matter
Angkor Thom

Asian fig tree roots versus temple buildings at Angkor Thom

Sang who spoke perfect English. At suppertime a fleet of bicycle-powered rickshaws arrived to take us to a restaurant for a nice meal. There were nine of us. After a pleasant local-style meal, we were taken to a nightclub to see native entertainment, that is, Cambodian music and dancers. The most unique feature of these dancers was their ability to bend their fingers backward. It was explained that, in early childhood, their fingers were soaked in hot water for long periods and then bent painfully back until the extension became second nature.

The second day in Siem Reap a bus conveyed us north of

the city to Angkor Thom to see the ancient ninth- through thirteenth-century archaeological ruins. Just before arriving we passed a long stone wall decorated with end-to-end bas-relief elephants. At the gate there were live elephants giving rides to tourists and concession stands selling souvenirs. Even the gates had corncob-like towers with bas-relief faces. In the complex we visited three ancient Hindu temples, complete with fitted stone walls, moats, towers, staircases, raised galleries, and bas-relief images. Many of the images impressed or carved into the walls depicted monkeys, elephants, chariots, and weapons recounting Hindu myths. One in particular depicted a procession of elephants mounted by monkeys

Fish and alligator farming on the Siem Reap River

Real boat basins (actual porcelain tubs)

Fishermen along the Siem Reap River

dressed as warriors and carrying weapons.

We saw a number of Buddhist monks amid the original Hindu surroundings; the group was informed that one of the latter kings had converted to Buddhism, thus leaving his mark on this religious complex. Rosemary ventured close to one of them, and he invited her to sit down. She politely declined.

The most fascinating phenomena of these temple complexes were the enormous roots of banyan and Asian fig trees. They were of such a size and dominance that one had to wonder whether the roots supported the structure of the walls and buildings they appeared to strangle, or did these structures hold up the trees, as they seemed so integral to each other. Many buildings were almost hidden by the draping roots as though they were being swallowed by some creeping gray monster. Some roots were so thick that they dwarfed humans standing next to them.

A twenty-minute bus ride the following morning brought us to the banks of the Seim Reap River. There were boats of every kind lining the river's edge as far as the eye could see. Climbing over a half-dozen of them to reach the outermost one, we settled in for a day cruise in a canvas-covered power boat with forward-facing seats beside the gunnels. Following the river, we actually saw mailboxes and house numbers that indicated how the mail was delivered in these parts. Farther along, we encountered two unattended youngsters, hardly more than toddlers, afloat mid-river in what appeared to be no more than wash basins. We came across fish farms, net frames hung down in the river, and alligator farms, heavy wire frames suspended the same way with trapdoors in the wooden piers topping the frames.

A little after noon our boat left the river mouth, and the waterway ahead broadened, forcing the shores into a vague distant line. Sang broke out the lunches, and while we ate, we cruised around in Tonlé Sap, a rather large lake. Afterward, the boat headed back to the river and upstream. Instead of pulling up where we departed from, we landed at a small pier at the head of a poor village immersed in jungle-like foliage.

Village with houses on stilts along Siem Reap River

Communal cooking in village along the river

Another house on stilts

Almost as soon as we landed, we came upon a communal cooking area inundated with dense smoke and the heavy stench of fish cooked in so many ways. At the river's edge there were men tending their fishing nets and aged boats of questionable sea-worthiness. Between these boats, women beat their laundry clean on the rocks. The village comprised homes built on six-foot stilts with crude wooden ladders out front. Sang took us on a walking tour past several dozen of these homes. The stilts, he explained, were for the flooding during the heavy rain season. The families stared eerily out at us and some even responded to our waving. There were children running about everywhere, none with shoes, and the very youngest without a stitch on. In the middle of the village was a more modern concrete schoolhouse and, at the opposite end, a vendor sat cross-legged selling vegetables and fruit. Several in our group (not us, luckily) purchased packaged chips, choosing from tapioca, potato, and squash. A bridge across the river to the highway led us to a waiting bus back to our hotel. By morning, the bus was crawling with insects due to chips left on the bus overnight.

On our second-to-last day in Cambodia, Sang took us to Angkor Wat (temple city), the largest and most impressive of the Hindu temple complexes. It was originally built to honor the Hindu god Vishnu.

Main entrance to Angkor Wat, Cambodia

A lesser courtyard inside Angkor Wat

Steps to Hindu god Vishnu

Rosemary atempts narrow steps sideways

The Killing Fields Memorial
More than 1.5 million murdered

Buddha's path to enlightenment
on monastery ceiling

The bus deposited the group outside the outer walls. As we approached the steps and colonnaded front facade beyond the wide moat, the corncob-like central tower and four lesser surrounding towers became apparent. Crossing on a path between two ponds, we climbed the steps and explored the colonnaded hallway, which extended farther to the left and right of the five towers, and then to three chambers surrounding the central courtyard, where we saw stone-carved figures, faces, and scenes. There were elaborate carvings on almost every surface.

In the main courtyard the intricacies of the central tower were explained to us. A stone staircase, consisting of narrow treads and steep risers on one side of a pyramiding climb, led possibly thirty feet up to a figure of Vishnu housed in the chambers within the highest of the five towers. The staircase represented Mount Meru, the haven of the Hindu gods. The extremely narrow stairs depicted how difficult it is to reach this Hindu haven. Rosemary sidled up five steps of the strange flight, but then she freaked. "Too scary!" she said, because of her D-width shoes. I stayed at the bottom; my shoes also were too big for the treads.

As we left Angkor Wat, the sunset's rays turned the towers into gold and created the mirror image of the entire temple complex as a reflection in the pond outside the western frontage. The waiting bus conveyed us back to the hotel.

Our last visit in Siem Reap was to the Killing Fields Memorial. In a small concrete shrine lie the skulls and bones of people murdered by Pol Pot and the Khmer Rouge. They were gathered from nearby fields and piled up inside. This was only a sampling of the more than one and a half million slaughtered between 1975 and 1979. Pol Pot was repatriated to Paris, but never punished for his crimes. Within a Buddhist monastery next to the memorial, Buddha's path to enlightenment is elaborately painted on the ceiling in nearly a dozen panels. The next morning we returned to Bangkok—the reverse of the same short flight there.

* * * *

On our first full day in Bangkok the group was taken to the

Royal Barge Museum, Bangkok, Thailand

Royal Barge Museum along the widest point of the Chayo Praya River. Inside were at least fifty of the most ornate ceremonial boats that I have ever seen—all varying lengths and heights and appearances. Each one was uniquely adorned with richly crafted figures, snakes, and dragons, decorated in gold, silver, and ceramic tile. We were informed that these boats were used in processions honoring the king's birthdays, successions to the throne, and other important occasions.

Just before noon, a large speedboat conveyed us up one of many *klongs,* or canals, to a private home where a typical local meal was prepared for us in an open space beneath a large house. The meal was pleasant and informative, but I don't remember what was served. The home abutted the canal with its own wharf, and the only way to reach it was by boat. Outside in front of the home was a small model of the house, affixed atop a post, that served as a "spirit house." Later, we were allowed to roam through the upstairs to see how they lived. The residents were ardent Buddhists who kept a whole room apart dedicated to prayer, and they fed monks who would come to their door every morning for hand-out food.

Returning down the *klong* and then onto the big river, we stopped and visited temples, bells, flower markets, and Buddha statues to round out that day. A bus met us and brought us back to the city along a boulevard lined with topiary elephants and other animals.

Another day our small group of twelve boarded a long-

Temple of the Golden Buddha
Bangkok

Elephant topiary on median strip
Bangkok

Laughing Buddha and others for sale in the night market, Bangkok

Wat Arun on Chayo Praya River
Bangkok

Home hospitality along one of many *klongs*
Bangkok

tailed boat for a trip along one of the other *klongs* to the Floating Market at Damnoen Saduak. Visualize a shallow-draft, thirty-foot boat with a five-foot beam, a canvas cover supported by a number of vertical poles, and a large open, rusty truck engine aft, engaging a fifteen-foot shaft angled to the water and connected to a propeller or screw at its farthest end. The operator sat next to the engine and directly controlled the short carburetor throttle by hand. I learned that this style of boat was specially adapted for navigating the shallow, weed-ridden *klongs*.

The Floating Market consisted of a huge, open-sided, central building supported on pilings with hundreds of flat boats, several deep, tied along each side. Every boat was laden with produce or fish or flowers or trinkets, each vying for customers. Instead of returning us to our hotel, the long-tailed boat brought us to a resort on a lesser branch of the River Kwai. The resort comprised individually detailed, thatched-roof cabins in a jungle setting. Our luggage, packed that morning, had been transferred for us.

The next morning another long-tailed boat took us upriver through thick jungle shores to see kingfishers at work and monitor lizards sunning themselves on the rocks. An hour and a half later our boat pulled to a muddy beach, where we transferred to benches in the back of a pickup truck and traveled overland to the main branch of the River Kwai and the railroad bridge made famous by the Hollywood film. After a short photo stop, the truck conveyed us to Hellfire Pass, where we were given a quick history lesson.

During WWII, Japan had her eyes on capturing India and the British entrenched there, but such an attack required a reliable supply line. Thus, the Death Railway across Thailand and Burma to India was conceived, using forced labor to achieve that supply goal. More than 2,000 Allied prisoners of war and over 300,000 Asian slave laborers died working to that end. Though the toll was great, the project was never completed, despite a cruel and grueling round-the-clock effort. Hellfire Pass was a solid rock obstacle to the rail's right-of-way, so every inch had to be blasted and dug out. A lagging schedule and ruthless taskmasters—torture, filthy

Long-tailed boat ride on the Little River Kwai

Floating Market at Damnoen Saduak

At the bridge over the River Kwai

The cemetery at Hellfire Pass

Rosemary with the original caretaker's widow from the Hellfire Pass Cemetery

Hellfire Pass blasted and dug out of solid rock for the Death Railway

Even elephants get tired

"Look, Ma, no hands" and "Smile"

Milds are back in the saddle again

Whoa! Does this elephant know where she's going?
John and Ann Pollack head off the beaten path

living conditions, rampant disease, and meager rations of food and water—led to over 300 deaths per day. In the center and at one end of the infamous walled passage, a small leafy tree grew out of the solid rock as a symbol of defiance of the horrors perpetrated there. Our group toured the wartime barracks, now a museum stocked with photos and maps.

Then we encountered a beautifully manicured cemetery for the Allied prisoners of war. All of the Americans' remains had been removed and returned home to their families, but their fallen British, Canadian, and Aussie comrades were left row on row there. On our way past the caretaker's house we met a charming Asian woman, possibly in her late seventies, who spoke a broken English. She invited our small group in for a glass of lemon-grass tea. We accepted and soon learned that she was the original caretaker's widow. She informed us that, as a boy during the war, her husband smuggled food to the prisoners and carried messages and letters in and out of the POW camp.

Afterward, we found a small Buddhist temple with dozens of dogs lying about its steps. They were the pets of families too poor to feed them, so the dogs went to the temple to be fed by the monks. A few looked mangy, but the majority seemed to fare well. We returned to the resort via truck, train, and boat in time for our evening meal in the large open dining hall.

The next morning, the twelve of us were bused to an elephant park. While waiting for the next show to begin, we fed bananas to the younger, tamed elephants restrained by chain leashes. The show was designed to demonstrate how strong, clever, and useful they were. Some stood and walked on hind legs, a few played ball games, some played musical instruments, while others carried heavy logs about. Each animal had its own trainer, who carried a three-foot prod to ensure it complied with the assigned task. Sometimes the trainer rode atop just behind the large ears. Upon completion of the show, a smallish female elephant approached the viewing stands in search of tips. She would nudge each person gently with her trunk until they gave up some paper money. She would then transfer the booty to its trainer. I figured what Rosemary had donated was sufficient, but the elephant begged to differ with me. As I grappled for my wallet and then fumbled through it for an appropriate-sized bill, she kept nudging me to the amusement of all those sitting around me. I finally gave up the bill, just as she stroked me one last time.

We were split into pairs and, two-by-two, we climbed up to a platform next to a kneeling very large elephant equipped with a double saddle across its back and a trainer seated behind its ears. Rosemary and I climbed aboard and strapped ourselves in just before we felt this huge sway to one side as the elephant rose to all fours. The animal trotted a few hundred yards to a fueling station, another raised platform well-stocked with bananas. An attendant there accomplished the filler-up function. Satisfied, our mountainous taxi lumbered onto a pre-fixed trail through the surrounding jungle, one thirty yards in front of us, and another the same distance behind us. Every step forward meant a sizeable sway one side or the other. Half an hour later, the trail went uphill. A weird I'm-gonna-fall-off sensation overtook us. But that wasn't as bad as the narrow downhill trek, which really frightened me. The trail itself, was no wider than an elephant's foot—sometimes muddy, other times rocky, leaving me with the conclusion that this was a pretty damn sure-footed animal. Just as the trail leveled out, there was a rapidly flowing river in front of us. Our elephants plunged right in and followed it back until we were adjacent to where we had started. Then we emerged onto dry land.

While we all waited for our turn at a de-boarding platform, another chap in our group had inadvertently dropped his camera to the ground, and his elephant had accidentally stepped on it, crushing it to smithereens. By way of apologizing, the animal backed up, searched for the broken camera and lifted it back up to the owner. Though the camera had seen its last shot, the amazing thing was that the photo card had survived. After our safe arrival, the elephants were stripped of their saddles and herded back into the river to bathe and squirt water at each other. A number of us

Manicured trees on palace grounds

Royal residence of Thai king

Many temples and government buildings on palace grounds

Nope! Too short to be a royal guard

Emerald Buddha in Crystal Palace

52 Golden Buddhas at Marble Palace

Dai Tep Temples at top of mountain near Bangkok

Head of the lengthy Reclining Buddha Bangkok

Nacre images inlaid in soles of the Reclining Buddha

moved closer to the river to watch them play, only to have them squirt water at anyone within range.

Soon afterward, we were herded in a different direction, toward a pier where the twelve of us split to board two separate river rafts. Each raft comprised a dozen or so eight- to ten-foot poles lashed together. A guide used an oar to steer our way out into the current and keep us midstream while the moving river drove us downstream. After about ten minutes on the river we encountered trinket vendors wading out mid-river to meet us. Their wares were balanced on trays atop their heads. Our guides skillfully steered around them and we continued on our way. About forty minutes

Demons guarding the temple gates

later we came to the end of our river journey and docked. While we loaded the awaiting bus, we noticed that the rafts were loaded onto a truck for their return upriver. The bus returned us to Bangkok.

The very next day we spent visiting glorious palaces and

Exploring the ruins at Sukothai Park, Ayutthaya: former capital of Siam (Thailand)

Our group tries rice thrashing

Fancy street sign in Chang Mai

Local water buffalo obeys traffic signal at Chang Mai street corner

Roadside water buffalo herd near Chang Mai

spectacular Buddhas. The Grand Palace, residence of the Thai king and his royal court and home of the Emerald Buddha, turned out to be more like a sprawling college campus with numerous palatial residences, temples, and government buildings; each colored in its own gold, green, and/or red pattern; all arranged on immaculate lawns with manicured ball-shaped trees. Many of the buildings were girded with hundreds of gilded warriors. Within its own temple and attended by many gold figures, the enthroned Emerald Buddha was crowned and clothed in patterned gold. His feminine-like face, one shoulder, and the extremities of all limbs were in a shiny, deep emerald color.

The most remarkable thing about the Marble Palace was its fifty-two gilded Buddhas on the surrounding lanai. It was constructed of Italian Carrara marble. Sheets of gold, gilt, sold in the souvenir shop, were continually being impressed upon the smaller Buddhas to maintain their gold coloring. Next we visited the Wat Tramit and its famous gold Buddha, which is five and a half tons of solid gold and almost 200 feet long. At one point in its history it was covered in thick white plaster to conceal it from foreign marauders. The enormity of the Reclining Buddha at Wat Po made it hard to take it all in at once, as the temple building wrapped so closely around the 150- by 50-foot golden figure. We were told that the reclining position represented the dying Buddha as he entered Nirvana. The soles of Buddha's bare feet were decorated with

Storks by the hundreds nesting in trees at Chang Mai rice farm

Approaching a Hmong hill-tribe village in mountains near Chang Mai, Thailand

108 nacre (mother-of-pearl) images.

Many temples were guarded by giant demons on either side of the main gate or entrance. A code of dress was required to enter, so those of us wearing shorts were issued cloth wraps to cover our legs. Since shoes were not allowed, it was pure faith that you left them in cubbies outside, knowing full well that anyone looking for an upgrade might easily take them. We had no such incident, nor had we heard of any.

A night's sleep, and we were whisked away on a bus heading north toward Chang Mai. On the way we toured Ayutthaya, the ancient capital of Siam, a plethora of wats (temples), and buildings going back at least nine centuries. All of this spread over acres and acres in one big park. On a whim I bought a Thai princess statue through the bus window At lunchtime the group transferred to a spiffy rice barge, a boat with a large, broad-beamed, roundish hull, finished in polished woods. We were fed on board as we cruised downriver for a little over an hour. The bus met us at a predetermined spot, and we were on our way once more.

The only other stops were to tour a former rice processing and packaging plant and to view some farmers thrashing rice stalks with a hinged-pole and paddle. It looked like very hard work, but a few of our group thought they'd give it a try anyway. Entering the city of Chang Mai, the bus stopped for a traffic light. Looking out the window, we saw a man riding a scooter alongside a water buffalo in line with a column of cars and tuk-tuks waiting their turn to go. Though it seemed unusual, it did make some sense.

The highlight of our Chang Mai stay was a trip to a rice farm. We were ushered up to a second-story lanai adjacent to where dozens of open-billed storks nested in overhanging trees. Farmers had installed the storks there to eat the apple snails, a pest afflicting the rice crops. The birds' ease so near to us tourists proved fascinating and fun for both Rosemary and myself. Beyond the trees and birds was a pond used to raise ducks for the marketplace. Later we visited a park with more temples. That evening was spent traipsing through the night bazaar—thousands of booths hawking and sell-

Rosemary with Hmong woman in headdress

Hmong child "Buy my beads"

Hmong woman with child in hill-tribe garb

Border crossing from Thailand into Myanmar (Burma)
The Golden Triangle (at the confluence of Burma, Laos, and Thailand)

My rickshaw ride into Tachilek Myanmar

Temple in Tachilek, Myanmar

ing just about everything one could imagine.

Morning saw us in the bus again as it headed up into the mountains to visit hill-tribe villages. The mostly semi-nomadic hill-tribes—consisting of the Hmongs, Miens, Karens, Lisus, Akhas, and the Lahus—have villages scattered throughout the northern mountains. We walked through a Hmong village where all the locals wore beaded headdresses and necklaces. John traded a few *baht* (Thai cash) for cheap necklaces from a three-year-old, tasked to do so by his family because he was certainly cuter.

At lunchtime the bus carried us to an open-air restaurant on another mountain, where a French expatriot couple prepared a tasty BBQ chicken lunch. Up to now Rosemary had been lunching on rice and dessert, so this was a welcome change for her. Really? No little red and green hot peppers? Afterward, the bus took us to Chang Rai, the northern-most city in Thailand, on the border of Myanmar (Burma) and Laos, forming the so-called Golden Triangle. We stayed in well-detailed cabins at the Golden Pines Resort, which had a luxurious restaurant, pools, and many other facilities. The resort was located in the country amid orchards and grazing water buffalo. In fact, one of them peeked in the bathroom window, startling Rosemary. She never knew she had such a fan club.

In the morning we were taken to the Golden Triangle itself. Rosemary climbed stairs at the side of a mountain to take in a view of the three nations and the mighty Mekong River, while the remaining three of us walked through a narcotics museum—opium being the main agricultural product of the region, apparently started and promoted by former French entrepreneurs. In the afternoon the bus left us off at the gate into Myanmar and, following a brief stop at customs, we walked on through. On the other side man-powered rickshaws carried us to a temple where a Buddhist monk lectured us on the ways of Buddhism and gave us a tour of the temple grounds. Our walking tour ended with a trip to a local tech market, where I bought a bargain camera tripod. Then it was a quick return through the same gate and customs to the bus for the journey back to the resort.

Burmese women sell their trinkets at a community fair

City Hall in Tachilek, Myanmar

Thai elementary school children learn American song from a teacher

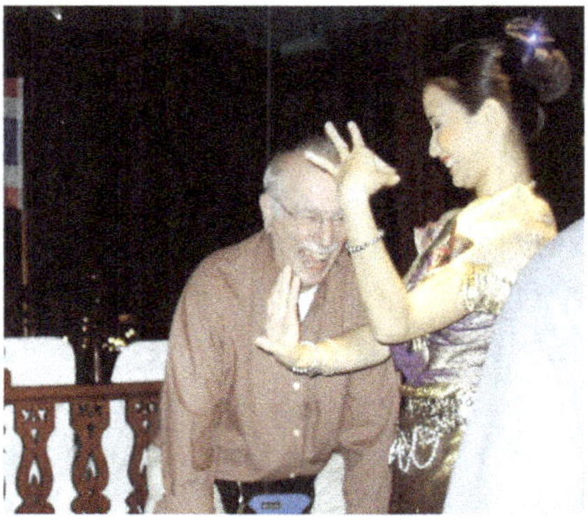

Thai dancer's finger-bending is a laughing matter for John at rice barge banquet

The next morning we toured a local Thai children's school. As the bus pulled onto the school road, youngsters manning every type of hand gardening tool were tending a rather large garden plot, almost a small vegetable farm. Apparently, this was a routine before-school project with not only lessons to be learned, but a very useful one too. On the hour, a loudspeaker called the kids to group exercise, which consisted of in-place calisthenics, followed by a lap around the assembly at a quick trotting pace. A flag-raising ceremony and national anthem singing completed the assembly. Our group meandered through the ongoing classes, trying not to disturb the lessons. At their recess time, a schoolteacher in our group taught a group of younger girls to sing an American ditty. We had all brought school supplies as gifts for the children.

The rest of the day was spent back at the resort packing; we were going to catch the overnight train back to Bangkok. The train accommodations were passable; uppers and lowers with curtains to the main aisle. John awoke in the middle of the night to attend to nature and was informed that the loo was in the next car. He went through the serial double doors to the next car and found what he needed, but when he tried to re-enter our car, he learned that it was locked for the night. After a preponderance of pounding on the door, another person heard him, came to his rescue, and let him back in. Arriving in Bangkok, mid-morning the next day, we were taken to our hotel for a day on our own.

That evening we enjoyed our farewell banquet aboard a large rice barge, complete with a cash bar, a four-piece band, and three lovely Thai dancers. The meal comprised everything from pupus to seafood to pastries. The music proved danceable, and soon the professional dancers were seeking partners from our group. Several of the men, including John, joined them on the dance floor. In the morning, we were bused to the airport for our departures, some back to the States and others off to Vietnam for a post-trip. After eighteen days away, home sounded pretty good to us.

* * * *

Chapter 17

Seasoned Travelers

Having become addicted to the travel bug, especially the limited group size with Overseas Adventure Travel (OAT), the Pollacks and the Milds decided on a trip Down Under. The tour group of twelve united with our tour guide at the airport in Auckland, New Zealand. A minibus conveyed the group to the city of Paihia on the Bay of Islands on the northeast shore of North Island. Following a get-acquainted cocktail hour at our hotel, we were treated to a cook-your-own steak dinner over a preheated hot-stone on an insulated platter—no one else to blame if it wasn't cooked to my perfection. Afterward, a walk through Paihia took no more than half an hour.

The next a.m. fifteen eager tourists boarded a forty-eight-foot covered motor-sailer for an all-day power cruise of the islands in the expansive bay. It seemed like there were hundreds of islands—some large, hilly, and thickly forested green with a scattering of modest homes stuck in between; others barren gray rock, covered in white bird guano, and a wide variety of sizes and shapes. On one large rock, seals lounged, oblivious to their onlookers. The boat made a few short island stops—one to view a small sheep farm and another to hike to a high point of advantage for a panoramic view of the surrounding islands.

The following day we visited the battle site preceding the double-dealing treaty of Waitangi, where the British version of the land treaty differed greatly from the Maori version—to the Brits' great advantage. Then it was across the bay by boat to the restored

Hot-stone steak in Paihia, NZ

Bay of Islands sheep farm, New Zealand

Bay of Islands Rock Island

Cliffs covered in bird guano in the Bay of Islands

Hide-a-way homes on some of the islands in the Bay of Islands

Lush forestation on some of the bay islands

Battle-scarred church, Russell Island

Rosemary and I on Russell Island

Hole in the Rock formation in bay

Ruapekapeka Battlefield, Maori vs British

48-foot motor sailboat *Symmetry*

Auckland Botanical Gardens

historical town of Russell, where we lunched at the Hotel Marlborough. In the afternoon a tour of the local tannery revealed all the processes and tools associated with tanning cattle hides. A small white church, which had suffered the battle scars of a colonizing war, was next on the agenda. Bullet holes could still be seen in its outer walls. Its cemetery sported dates to the late eighteenth century. While waiting for the boat back to Paihia everyone sat on the grass just above the sandy waterfront beach. We were soon inundated with friendly mallard ducks and their ducklings.

On yet another day the group took a boat out beyond the bay to a formation called Hole in the Rock. The boat, with its sixteen-foot beam, aligned itself with the hole's seaside opening and held that position until an ocean swell provided sufficient depth, and then the boat lurched forward and sped into the hundred-or-so-foot natural tunnel in the rock. Three exhilarating minutes later the boat emerged, and the hole got smaller and smaller as we returned to Paihia.

The tour group left Paihia the next morning and headed south through beautiful rolling green hills and wildflowers to Ruapekapeka, yet another battle site between the Brits and the Maori. Again, the Brits defeated the Maoris by bringing cannons from their ships to the fray. The minibus continued south on to Auckland and to our hotel. This unusual hotel was devoid of any grand entrance, as the path in was a narrow passage between two center-of-town storefronts. Once into the lobby, the place took on the visage of a first-class hotel. The rooms met our expectations as well. The rest of the day the group explored on their own—a park high on a hill with a panoramic view of Auckland and the many stores of the business district. One particular store of interest to us sold NZ's soccer team gear. Rosemary had a request from both our grandsons to bring them All-Black team shirts. She happily fulfilled that request.

A new day walked us to the city's huge harbor area, where we boarded a forty-eight-foot motor sailboat called the *Symmetry.* We spent the whole morning motoring about the harbor seeing

Long house at Waitakere Ranges
Regional Park, NZ

Molten steam pots in Rotorua

A plethera of steam vents and noxious fumes throughout Rotorua

The entire tour group (with the exception of the photographer, Rosemary)
Posed at the top of Mount Tarawera

many luxury yachts and ocean-worthy motor-sailers. Afterward, our minibus took us on a tour of the waterfront where many boat/shipbuilders created a competitive class of sleek boats for the America's Cup races. The Auckland Botanical Gardens occupied our afternoon, traipsing through multiple floral gardens typifying those in many diverse countries.

The following day the minibus led us to the Aritaki look-out in the Waitakere Ranges Regional Park. A sign explained that the totem outside the long house represented several Maori ancestors. We took group pictures with everyone standing behind a huge gilded picture frame. From the lookout we took a bush walk down to the Waitakere Sand Dunes, deeply rippled with wind and rain, and strolled along the long empty beach and the stream that runs to it.

Returning to our hotel in the minibus, we stopped long enough for our guide to point out a West Coast Kauri tree, a tree that can live for more than a thousand years. He also told us that many of the pristine forests of these tall straight trees were severely depleted to make ships' masts for the British Royal Navy.

Another day took us to Rotorua, a city teeming with steam vents. Seemingly, it was like the Yellowstone geysers all over again, only twenty times more widespread and maybe ten times more active. There was no waiting for action, as most geysers were continuous and noxious as well. In fact, everywhere you went the steam holes vented sulfur-smelling fumes. The scenery varied greatly, in that some places offered gaping holes, releasing steam amid yellow, grass-like fields. Others had steam escaping through multiple smaller apertures in a lava-like surface. Many bubbled to the surface through lakes of still water and rivers of running water. Even in town, steam burst out of walled well-like structures. At the Rotorua Maori Cultural Center we learned about Maori tattoos, telling matriarchal and patriarchal histories separately on the right and left sides of their bodies. Weapons, fishhooks, and battles won and lost were also on prominent display.

Mount Tarawera was scheduled for the next day. Fore-

Rosemary, John, and Ann, plus another two atop Mount Tarawera, NZ

Awaiting the brave ascenders atop Mount Tarawera, NZ

Long house in Maori Village provided lunch, hospitality, and cultural dancing

With the snow-capped peaks of the Southern Alps in the distance, a ballon soars above our Arrowtown, NZ resort just northeast of Queenstown

Driving overland to Doubtful Sound

Dolphins trailing our boat on Doubtful Sound

Waterfalls as seen from cruising Doubtful Sound

Seals lounging on the rocks as seen from Doubtful Sound cruise

Just above here:
Emperor penguins as seen from Doubtful Sound cruise

Exploring the Dart River Wilderness Park in a jet boat

warned of the cold at the top, we layered on extra clothing. The minibus drove up the side of this extinct volcano as far as a paved road would permit. At this point we were each issued a wooden mosey pole about six feet in length and an inch-and-a-half in diameter. This aided us in climbing the rest of the way to the top.

Once there, the more daring of the group were offered the choice of descending into the crater with the guide. There was no clear path downward, only layer upon layer of round pebble-like lava rocks, which prevented all but the most valiant of us from venturing forth. Rosemary, John, Ann, and one other couple took up the challenge, led by a local guide. I waited at the top near a sign stating the name of the volcano.

The descenders were given special instructions on how to proceed: Plant the mosey pole slightly behind you and take several small shuffling steps. Repeat, but never step unless the pole is firmly planted. We watched and photographed their descent until they were all the way down and then we moved to a new site on the crest to watch and photograph their ascent on a more firm path. I must say that even on this gray and rainy day, the chemical colorings of the various sides of the crater were quite beautiful. Ninety minutes later the group was reunited for the descent to the minibus and the trip back.

That night we returned to Auckland so that we might catch a plane to South Island early the next morning. Imagine going south into a colder climate—experiencing a different phenomenon below the equator. Our plane took us over the snow-capped Southern Alps to the Queenstown airport. From there a bus took us to a resort just outside Arrowtown, a small burg a mile or so northeast of Queenstown. As we checked in, we saw a gas balloon passing overhead with snow-peaked mountains in the background. The group walked off dinner through uneventful Arrowtown.

The next day we set out for Doubtful Sound, which involved three overland bus rides and two scenic boat excursions. While the overland portion provided views of some of South Island's most picturesque waterfalls, sheep farms, rocky streams, and

Sreamship *TSS Earnslaw*
on Lake Wakatipu at Queenstown

Residence at Walter Peak

Restaurant at Walter Peak on
Lake Wakatipu

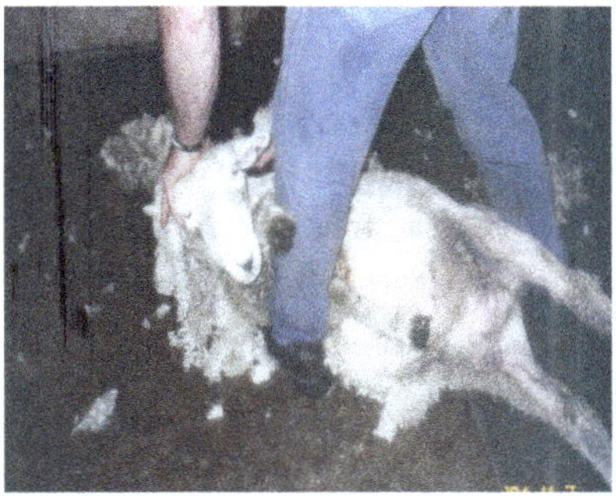

A shear-shocked sheep

Sheep blocking the road

Driving over Hasst Pass: A fence with ladies' bras, apparently a feminist protest mountains; the green scenes used in *Lord of the Rings* were even more magnificent. Crossing Doubtful Sound gave us snow-capped mountains, bottle-nosed dolphins chasing after our wake, dozens of seals lounging on flat rocks, and emperor penguins clapping their flippers at us from their island hideaway. The boat ride ended at Tasman, where Doubtful Sound meets the Tasman Sea. The trip back to Arrowtown was overland and lengthy.

The following morning we skirted north around Lake Wakatipu to the Dart River Wilderness area, passing many expansive sheep farms. We boarded jet boats for a two-hour sightseeing trip up and down the river—sights dense with trees and bush with islands, shores, and shoals of split and rounded rock on either side. The speedy ride proved exciting as well.

That evening we were transported down to the docks in Queenstown on the shore of Lake Wakatipu, where we waited for a river-type steam boat to make a huge U-turn approach, and hug the piers. The group boarded the *TSS Earnslaw* and we headed north again for forty minutes, and this time across the lake to Walter Peak and the large restaurant there. The all-white *Earnslaw*, with its red stack puffing black smoke, had a topless engine room, so the entire antique steam engine and all its exterior parts could be viewed amidships in full motion from any of the three decks above it. The red-roofed restaurant at Walter Peak had three dining rooms complete with fireplaces and homey décor. Of course, the meal was excellent.

Afterward, we were treated to a sheep-shearing show, where a single animal was dispensed in a matter of two or three minutes. It amazed us to see how much of the wool came off in one piece. The sheep was held in an immobile position with one hand while the electric shear, in the other hand, stripped the poor sheep of its woolly coat. Undressed, unharmed, and, possibly embarrassed, the pink-skinned critter scooted across the stage and out the door to the rear of the shearing shed. The moonlit cruise back to Queenstown was a romantic, star-filled interlude.

We left the resort at Arrowhead the next morning, heading

The falls at Thunder Creek

Old Man on a Cane stream formation

The park at Franz Josef Glacier on New Zealand's West Coast (South Island)

Aproaching Franz Josef Glacier
in heavy rainfall

Closeup of Franz Josef Glacier

Pancake Rocks at Punakaiki, NZ

Mural in Greymouth, NZ

north again through Hasst Pass in the Southern Alps. Around one of the bends we encountered a wire border fence with hundreds of ladies' bras hanging from it—most likely a feminine protest of some sort. I'm on their side, but where are they now? The bus continued on to Thunder Creek, where we took a long walk into the bush to see a rushing high waterfall, a bridge over a narrow gorge, some really dense forest, and lots of neat bird life. Then we proceeded to the main sightseeing target for the day, the Franz Josef Glacier. The weather had turned colder and rainy at the higher altitude so we donned our rain jackets and hats. We followed a narrow walkway along a rocky moraine stream for some distance before we saw the actual glacier: a massive river of black rock and dirty white ice blocked from rushing down on us by an invisible wall of ice and captured on either side by mountain slopes.

The bus rambled on to the gold- and coal-mining town of Hokitka on the wild west coast of South Island, where we viewed old-time mining machine artifacts on display. The group learned how both ores were processed and how gold was separated from its ore via the chemical action of mercury and subsequent centrifuging. Then we walked up the hill to the Buck Museum and saw household relics and machines from over a hundred years in the town's past. There was even an old radio with four vacuum tubes and a horn-type speaker on top. From there we went on to the town of Reefton, where we spent the night.

The next morning we headed up the coastline to Punakaiki to see the Pancake Rocks, formations of flat rocks piled such that they looked like stacks of flapjacks ready to be served. Just before we arrived at the site, the heavens quickly turned off the lights and opened up with a miserable downpour. I foolishly continued photographing the formations and the many seals lazing about on them. Even the ocean was angry and raging white over the rocks at that point. Oh, no! My camera suddenly stopped working. That night, where we stayed in Greymouth, I opened up everything that would open on it and laid the camera down next to the blowing room heater. Fortunately, the drowned camera recovered from its infirmities, and I was able to take pictures again. Good thing, too—many of the buildings in Greymouth had huge and interesting murals, painted on brick walls, depicting the town in its earlier years.

The next day the bunch of us were dropped off at the railway station for the trip across the island to Christchurch on the east coast. While waiting for the train I used the public facilities and, on the way in, a man hurriedly bumped into me and stealthfully lifted my wallet, credit cards, and IDs as well. Unfortunately, we didn't discover the theft until we arrived in Christchurch. That evening, while we had supper in some restaurant on a hill, we made calls stateside to report my loss.

We toured the campus of Christchurch University the following morning and listened to a holographic image of Nuclear Nobelist Ernst Rutherford talking about his work. We learned that because of room shortages, he was given an office under the stairs. His classroom upstairs was preserved as it was when he was teaching. The group strolled along the Avon River to spend the afternoon at the city's extensive and beautiful botanic gardens. On the way to supper afterward, we encountered several twisted construction beams stuck into the riverbed. Nearby plaques informed us that this was a thank-you monument to New Zealand's first responders, who came to the aid of New York's 9/11 restoration effort.

The next morning we were bused to the International Antarctic Center. Beginning in the museum, we saw an earlier version of the Hagglund personnel carrier, a large protective vehicle, with quad-pod, tank-style tracks, especially suited to riding over both smooth ice and rough terrain. Later in the tour, the group had the privilege of riding in one over a training obstacle course originally designed to test its capabilities. One building was designated U.S. Antarctica Program. This facility was the staging and jumping off point for most Antarctica expeditions. We were also briefed on the history and preparation for those expeditions.

The tour group had a free afternoon in downtown Christchurch, which everyone found charming. A chess game with

Christchurch University campus in Christchurch, NZ

Christchurch Botanic Gardens

International Antarctic Center, NZ

Hagglund Antarctic ice transporter

Chessmates in downtown Christchurch

Christchurch Cathedral

Touring the city of Christchurch in a trolley, dinner included

three-foot-high pieces and a proportional board laid out on tiled pavement in the large central square. Continuous challengers were in play. We toured the local cathedral and browsed through dozens of stores before surrendering to a trolley dinner tour that circled the central city twice while serving us a *prix fixe* menu. Seatings for two and four were across the main aisle from each other. Unfortunately, much of what we saw that afternoon and evening of downtown Christchurch was destroyed years later in a series of earthquakes, but mainly the 7.1 quake of September 4, 2011. The cathedral and much of the university suffered greatly.

Morning had us in the minibus again, a day trip east to Akaroa, over lovely green rolling hills, viewing more of the same scenery where *Lord of the Rings* was shot. This was indeed sheep country and in some cases they nearly owned the roadways. We slowed and stopped a few times to wait for a herd of the woolies to pass through or by us. The twelve of us boarded a boat in Akaroa and explored the rocky coastline. We were treated to closeup views

Steel beams sent from NYC form the 9/11 Memorial for NZ responders

Penguins from the islands off of the Akaroa Peninsula

of emperor penguins and sea lions on lava rock ledges while bottle-nosed dolphins trailed just outside our wake. We returned to Christchurch that evening and attended a cocktail party at the guide's nearby home. His wife was a gracious hostess.

* * * *

The tour group broke up the next morning with six members returning to the U.S. and six of us and our guide flying across the Tasman Sea to Sydney, Australia. Included were the Milds, the Pollacks, and another couple from Wisconsin. A minibus met us at the airport and drove us to Port Douglas on the northeast coast of Queensland.

Having walked to the nearby piers the following morning, the smaller group of us boarded a boat and were taken out to sea past dozens of half-submerged reef islands belonging to the Great Barrier Reef. After a little over an hour's ride, we arrived. Our destination was a floating station, an anchored base from which we could engage in clothes-changing, swimming, below water viewing, learning (lectures on reef history and preservation), and, of course, fast-food dining. Attached to the base were a few acres of netting hung from floats and securely anchored to the sea bottom to protect swimmers from sizeable predatory fish such as sharks.

We changed into swimsuits and snorkeled, continually re-diving among the many thrilling formations of colorful coral and beautiful species of smaller fish. After an exhausting ninety minutes in the water, we changed back into shorts, had lunch, and took one of the glass-sided submarine rides through a long course of brilliant and unusual coral. Before boarding the boat, a head count was made to be sure that no one was left behind overnight at the base station. The lectures continued on the ride back to Port Douglas.

Walking back to the hotel from the pier, Rosemary pointed out a small, noisy (chirping) bird with rather unusual coloring. She thought it a rare find, but our guide informed her this was a lorikeet and not so rare. An hour later we encountered several hundred of the species dominating the treetops, making a racket en-chorus.

Waiting for ice cream in downtown Port Douglas, Queensland, Australia

Koala bear has lunch at Wildlife Habitat, Port Douglas

Shy wallaby joey jumps in head first

Wallaby joey peeks out of mother's pouch

Wildlife Habitat

Hand-fed baby kangaroo

Rosemary feeds a baby kangaroo

Wildlife Habitat

After dinner that evening we strolled through the town of Port Douglas and found a charming little shop selling ice cream—great flavors and large portions.

The six of us were bused some miles down the coast to a bird and animal habitat. We saw hundreds of species from unfriendly emus to pelicans and parakeets in the heavily forested bird preserve. The paths took us amid the thickets where they lived, so you really had to concentrate on looking. Then, over a small bridge, where alligators quietly nested to blend into the log scenery, we continued on into the land of wallabies and kangaroos. Much of this was in their natural habitat, but then we came upon a petting section. Wallabies and smaller kangaroos fed on appropriate grassy-type food right from our hands. We photographed several jills (kangaroo females) with baby joeys—even one bashful joey with his head in the pouch and his tail sticking out. Apparently there were no jacks (males) in the petting area. We did see some of them in a more heavily forested section later.

The next day the group packed up and boarded a plane for the three-hour flight south to Sydney. We settled into a hotel in the Rock section of town with alleys named Suez Canal Lane and Nurses Walk leading down to the city's famous waterfront. That first night we ate in a small restaurant where we got to physically pick out the piece of meat or fish that we wanted them to cook for us—a fun experience.

The following morning the gang of six set out to explore

Opera House, Sydney, Australia

Harbor Bridge, Sydney

Group of tourists climbing the upper span of Harbor Bridge

the waterfront sights. Almost immediately we came across four didgeridoo players, their seven-foot tubes emitting the deepest and strangest bass sounds in melodies none of us knew. Looking up at the massive bridge spanning Sydney harbor, we saw a line of people climbing the curved truss-work way above the bridge itself. Our guide explained that he could arrange a climb for our group if enough of us wanted it. My brave wife said she was willing, but no one else took him up on it, especially me with my acrophobia, thank God.

The group wandered through the halls of the great opera house, which is said to have over a thousand rooms, including mul-

Unusual rock formations in Ku-ring-gai Chase National Park

Two jack kangaroos in the wilds of Ku-ring-gai Chase National Park

Clock and mini-theater inside Queen Victoria Galleria and Mall

Statue of Queen Victoria in square outside Queen Victoria Galleria and Mall

tiple performing theaters, rehearsal studios, and restaurants. The opera theater can seat over 1,500 people. Thinking that it would be fun to say we'd seen an opera at this venue, we soon discovered that only an obscure ballet was scheduled for the next few days. The Pollacks and the Milds bought expensive tickets for our last day in Sydney anyway. Somehow, it wasn't all that good.

Our group boarded a rather large, high-speed powerboat, along with many other tourists, and headed north to Ku-ring-gai Chase National Park for a day of hiking. We had the opportunity to see the kangaroo and wallaby and exotic birds in the wild from controlled pathways. The park was also full of exceptional geological rock formations and even a few huge petroglyphs.

The six of us returned to Sydney in time for supper downtown. Afterward, we explored the huge Queen Victoria Mall building with its fascinating clocks suspended through four levels of shopping galleries. One of these, the royal clock, trumpeted the arrival of a royal pageant shown in the castle-like box above the four-sided timepiece. In a Walgreens across from the mall, Rosemary and I were able to collect the Cadbury chocolates requested by Myrna's family. We flew back to the U.S. on the day after the ballet.

A year later, in 2005, we heard that Rabbi Ari Goldstein at our Temple Beth Shalom in Arnold, MD planned to lead a tour to

Israel in June. We signed up, and, significantly, fifteen others did the same, so that the number in the group, including the rabbi, totaled eighteen—the lucky Hebrew number *chai*. Our tour began with an El-Al flight to Israel leaving from JFK Airport in New York, so the Milds had to make their way there on their own. The departure lines at El-Al seemed endless. At the end of the first line, we were interviewed by Israeli security for a good twenty minutes, a series of questions that seemed wholly unrelated. Another line ended with checking our luggage and, finally, the last with our boarding passes. In the second line we noticed Hasidic Jews with the largest suitcases ever to fit through any reasonable doorway (probably four-foot by three-foot by two-foot by my estimate). Some had similar-sized cartons labeled as large American appliances—most likely Israelis returning home after major U.S. shopping sprees. And here we were, worried that our luggage was too large or too heavy. Wow! At last, we met the rest of our contingent and took off on our way to the Holy Land.

On June 27th we landed at Ben Gurion Airport in Tel Aviv, but our arrival joy was soon dimmed when we learned that our luggage remained behind. Something in our interview must have triggered the need for Israeli security to dig deeper into our bags in particular. Our classy hotel room looked out over an endless Mediterranean Sea, sandy beach, and wide swirling shades of tan and gray boardwalks. A long rocky breaker reached out to sea, while umbrellas and huts dotted the beach. Dinner that evening required us to have a magnetic wand search before entering the restaurant. Needless to say, neither of us was carrying.

The luggage still hadn't arrived even after a night in the Tel Aviv hotel. However, the bus for our group needed to move on, so we got aboard, sans bags, and headed north to the Roman ruins at Caesarea National Park. The ruins comprised a sizeable amphitheater, a lengthy viaduct, arches, walls, and the remaining columns of buildings long gone, plus statues—headless, armless, and otherwise-less galore.

From there we were driven even farther north to the mod-

Two views from our hotel room in Tel Aviv, Israel

Roman ruins at Caesarea National Park

Roman aquaduct at Caesarea

Bahai Temple at Haifa, Israel
Haifa harbor and city below

British detainment camp for so-called *illegal* Holocaust survivors

Rosemary and I at Haifa overlook

Impressions in the sand at Mount Hermon in Syria's demilitarized zone

The caves at Mount Hermon

American tourists inspect Israeli army tank, Israel Defense Force camp, Golan Heights

Luxurious pool at Kfar Blum Kibbutz near Golan Heights

Entrance to the tomb of philosopher Maimonides (Rambam), Tiberias, Israel

ern seaport of Haifa for an overlook view of that city from the hills high above it. The golden dome of the main Bahai temple and the descending garden grounds were just below us. But on the way, we stopped at a detention camp museum where the British once cruelly held so-called illegal immigrants (even Holocaust survivors) until they could ship them away from what was then pre-1948 Palestine—barbed wire and wood barracks throughout. Remnants of baggage lay on wooden beds, and discarded clothing hung from the ceiling. Another pit stop found us in Safed, the hilltop birthplace of mystical Judaism (Kabbalah) and, according to the Talmud, one of the four holiest cities in Israel.

The tour group spent the night at Kfar Blum, a resort type of kibbutz in the far north of Israel only eight miles below the Golan Heights. Apartment-type accommodations, Olympic-size swimming pool, and sports areas made this kibbutz more of a first-class tourist resort. Since we were still without a change of clothes, Rabbi Ari took us to a cheap department store in a nearby shopping center, where we were able to pick up shorts, T-shirts, and underwear for a few days. Only one hitch occurred there: an embarrassed Rosemary hesitated to buy the larger size underpants she needed, because the rabbi was standing next to her. The missing luggage caught up to us the following morning.

That next morning the bus hauled us along the demilitarized border with Syria to the biblical Mount Hermon on the border between Syria and Lebanon. There we saw more Roman ruins, caves, and locales precious to three major religions. Our bunch encountered a large, heavy conical weight attached to a central pivot point. Its surface protruded with inverse letter fonts. When you pivoted this device in a circle, it wrote (impressed) a biblical message in six languages in the sand beneath it.

For lunch we were taken to a nearby army camp where we chatted with some Israel Defense Force (IDF) soldiers. Afterward, the group got to crawl all over one of their army tanks and collect photos of the experience. An IDF officer lectured us on the need for their defense policies. Later in the afternoon the bus followed the Jordan River a short way south to a place where the rapids were supposed to be more exciting. There we rented rubber rafts and kayaks and lazily drifted along until encountering a huge one-word sign in Hebrew, an unfamiliar word which turned out to be "Waterfall." All twelve of us riding in the rafts managed the major bump without a problem, but the rabbi and congregation president capsized in their kayak with the latter losing a new pair of shoes to boot. We returned to Kfar Blum that evening.

The following a.m. the group headed south again to the ancient city of Tiberias on the shores of the landlocked Sea of Galilee. Initially, we climbed the steps to the memorial for Rabbi Moses ben Maimon, a medieval Sephardic Jewish philosopher commonly known as Maimonides. He is often referred to by the acronym Rambam. The Roman ruins at Tiberias were even more extensive than at Caesarea. A model at the entrance displayed what the ru-

Resort on the Sea of Galilee at Tiberius, Israel

Roman ruins at Tiberius

Walking the stone ramparts of Jerusalem's Old City

The underground Israeli and Arab shops of Jerusalem's Old City

Walking the rooftops of Jerusalem's Arab Quarter

Entrance to the Western (Wailing) Wall of Jerusalem's Old City

A wood fence separates the male and female praying sections at Western Wall

Rosemary at the gates of her namesake restuarant

ined city once looked like and how it was physically laid out. The Roman baths proved to be the most interesting part, as the technical and the functional were quite well explained—the natural heating for bath and steam rooms and the ancillary daily activities. From Tiberias the bus conveyed us to a lookout revealing our first magnificent panoramic viewing of Jerusalem and especially the Old City.

The next day, Friday the 1st of July, we circumnavigated the stone ramparts of Jerusalem's Old City on foot, beginning with the Western (Wailing) Wall plaza and passing gates, towers, and museums on the way. Then, within the walls we explored the Christian Quarter, with its Church of the Holy Sepulchre; the Armenian Quarter, with its plea to recognize the terrible genocide imposed by Turkish rulers; the Muslim quarter, through its tunnels full of Arab businesses; then over Arab rooftops with a mixed view of minarets and satellite dishes; then back to the Jewish Quarter and the Western Wall plaza again. Along the way we encountered an ancient Roman road that appeared to be more like a neatly laid river of flat rock.

The Western Wall plaza was partitioned to separate male prayers from female prayers. The men's section had prayer tables on wheels and stacked chairs for convenience. "Wailing" is the non-Jews' description of the sounds of prayer. Cracks in the wall were stuffed with paper-snippet supplications for the Holy One, and there were Hasidic men all in black continually offering to pray for you—that is, for a fee, of course. That's how they make their living.

That evening the Milds and Singers had supper at Rosemary's Inn around the corner from our hotel. Rosemary just had to have me take a picture of her in front of the sign. In the morning the entire group attended Shabbat services at a local synagogue. From there we had lunch at the famous King David Hotel on a balcony overlooking the pool and gardens. Later that day the group explored the tunnel under the Temple Mount with a view of stone work spanning many centuries at the different levels.

Rosemary and I on the balcony of the King David Hotel in Jerusalem

The memorial statue and logo of Yad Vashem Holocaust Museum

The caves at Qumron where the Dead Sea Scrolls were found

Rosemary celebrates her seventieth birthday at the Dead Sea resort

The tiered swimming pools at the Dead Sea resort as seen from our room

Ascending Herod's fortress at Masada by cable car

Don Singer and Rosemary ride off into the desert on camelback.

On Sunday morning the group visited the Yad Vashem Holocaust Museum at the western end of Jerusalem. We saw the notable statue of gaunt victims standing together, the Holocaust logo, and all the soul-wrenching exhibits. It was very much like the Holocaust museum in Washington, DC, where we are charter members.

That afternoon we were taken just north and west of the Dead Sea to an excavation site at Qumron run by an American university. It had an excellent across-the-gorge view of the caves where the Dead Sea Scrolls were found in 1947. Back then, a Bedouin boy chasing a goat stumbled onto the cave location of seven pottery jars, containing what was left for safekeeping by the Essene culture many millennia before. As a result of the discovery, other nearby caves yielded similar scrolls, revealing parts of biblical tales—some similar, some with different twists. Story has it: when the Bedouin excavators of the caves found they were being paid by the individual piece recovered, they began breaking the pieces further to increase their pay. Leaving this site, the bus moved on to Ein Gedi, where we saw a very green fertile valley amid narrow gorges of desert sandstone.

The day ended with Rosemary celebrating her seventieth birthday, cake and all, at a very posh resort on the Dead Sea. Besides there being a sandy beach at the seashore, there were two tiers of very large, outdoor freshwater swimming pools. Inside there were two more smaller pools—one fresh water and the other salt water and two Jacuzzis. I must add that I took advantage of the lot.

On Monday the group visited Masada, a mountaintop fortress completed in 31 BCE by Herod the Great, a Hasmonean king. The Sicarii, a Jewish extremist group, opposed the Roman garrison in the 66 CE Roman siege of Jerusalem and then retreated to Masada, defeating the small garrison installed there. In 70 CE the Romans pursued a lengthy siege at Masada, resulting in the Sicarii committing suicide rather than be taken prisoners. The site offered two ways to get to the city at the top: a cable car ride and a long

Our group rides off into the desert while I relax in the comfort of a Bedouin tent in the Negev Desert in southern Israel

Longhorn ibexes prance in the tall grass of Sde Boker, Israel, near Ben Gurion U.

We met Helen at the graves of David and Paula Ben Gurion in Sde Boker

Colorful, exotic rock formations on the entrance path to the Silk Road city of Petra, Jordon

Donkey carts provide taxis to and from Petra

switchback climbing path. Not one for heights, I chose to remain below and entertain myself, studying the siege layout for three hours, while the rest went up top and later down in the cable car. The Romans had built a miles-long ramp to get their siege equipment in range. We returned to the resort that night early enough to take advantage of the amenities.

The next morning found us on the road south again. After an hour's ride, the bus stopped at a camel riding attraction, where Rosemary adventurously rode in a two-seater saddle in front of Don Singer. I remained behind in a huge Bedouin tent, because my fragile back cringed at even the thought of repeatedly swaying through a 20-degree angle for the next sixty minutes. Despite their constant spitting and horrid dispositions, these large hairy beasts were actually trained to kneel to facilitate riders getting on and off. While most of our gang braved the blistering sun, desert heat, slippery trails, and narrow cliffside perils while swaying ten feet in the air, I relaxed comfortably atop at least a dozen carpets in the shade of the tent.

Continuing south on the bus again we must have covered about a third of the Negev Desert before arriving at Sde Boker, the sight of Ben Gurion University and where the father of Israel is buried alongside his wife. Prior to the trip, Rosemary had obtained an Israeli cell phone with the intent of connecting with Helen Monias, daughter of good friends and childhood friend of our own Jackie and head librarian at the university. We met her at the Ben Gurion gravesite, and she rode the bus with us for the next two stops in the area while we caught up on our mutual news. The small community was full of long-horned ibexes prancing about in the limited green areas. At the stop where we left her off, we met Helen's husband, a professor of solar engineering at the university.

Traveling more southerly, we passed an Israeli nuclear facility way off in the distance and much more desert, often rocky, sometimes mountainous, and mainly monotonous. A tired group arrived in Elat, a seaport on the Gulf of Aqaba, where we spent the night. In the morning we were bused to the customs facility on the

Treasury building in Petra, Jordon

My rest stop while the others went to see more of Petra

More government buildings in Petra

The square corners inside the Treasury building in Petra

A Jordanian soldier guards the Treasury building

I was just as pooped as this poor animal in Petra

border with Jordon. All eighteen walked through with minimal fuss and boarded another minibus on the Aqaba side. This bus headed about seventy-five miles north through the Jordanian version of the Negev Desert, stopping only once at a wayside for souvenirs and restrooms. The tour stopped for lunch at a hotel on the edge of the more commercial city of Petra. One of our group reacted to a bug or an allergy, likely from the eggplant served there.

Then we began our long trek on foot into the terminal west end of the Silk Road to and from Asia, a virtual shortcut for camel-dependent merchants. Once a wealthy community due to the tolls collected from these merchants, the inhabitants of Petra actually cut a city out of the unusual rocks found there. We followed the low, rock-walled, sandy road in until it became a lengthy, winding canyon with smooth, wavy walls. A waist-high, shallow aqueduct followed the onward passage. We encountered donkey-drawn carts, horsemen, and camels all along the way. Though the horizontal passage varied from twenty down to twelve feet, the floor stayed flat and the sky remained our roof for the most part. Common sandstone turned to brown granite, then a more pinkish color, and next a swirling multiplex of pastel shades only nature could have painted. Soon there were square cuts in the stone, followed by stairs, doorways, crude adobe-like dwellings, and more manmade adornments.

At last, the canyon opened wide onto a plaza of sights, the most prominent of these being the massive Treasury building. Our Jordanian guide explained that this walk-in building, with its considerable set of stairs out front and two-story facade—complete with three columns on each side, a narrow pediment, and many other adornments—was completely hand carved from the top down. Inside, the room was a smooth rectangular parallelepiped, or cuboid, with perfect 90-degree corners. There were other buildings too, but none so elaborate—mostly apartment dwellings. The pink, rock-cut city went on and on beyond my physical capability, so the group went to explore farther sights while I remained behind at a store, alone with a bottled soft drink in hand. The proprietor engaged me for a short dialogue, exploring my origins, and when it was time for his lunch, he graciously invited me to join him. Of course, I politely refused, telling him of our lunch at the hotel.

The group returned in something less than an hour, and we began a trek retracing our steps. Another elder in the group stopped a donkey cart to ride out and offered to share with me. I accepted the ride and as long as the path remained level, the ride went fine. However, when the path became even a mild incline the Arab driver, who walked alongside, began to beat his animal mercilessly. That ended my ride. I complained. He complained. I paid him off and took to my feet. I believe that, even today, I'm still feeling the back pain of that long walk back to the bus. I felt a whole lot of pain at the end of that day—inside and out.

After the second night in Elat we returned over the desert to Tel Aviv and, late in that afternoon, we visited the Palmach Museum in Ramat Aviv. The most impressive museum displays were the dioramas depicting battle scenes of the 1947 war establishing Israeli independence. The male and female figures were without a common uniform and carried nonstandard weapons. Most of what they possessed had been smuggled in to them. Both the Palmach and the pardoned, illegal (terrorist-style bombings) Ergun members, who had been active in smuggling Holocaust immigrants into Israel before the independence war, were eventually united as the Israel Defense Force (IDF).

The group spent the next morning in the old city of Jaffa and particularly in the square with a monument honoring three

Bride and groom in Jaffa, Israel, take off on honeymoon

Jacob's Dream; the Fall of Jericho; and the (near) Sacrifice of Isaac, in Jaffa

biblical events—Jacob's Dream, Isaac's (near) Sacrifice, and the Fall of Jericho. We were able to witness a bride in full regalia (flowing gown) and the groom in tux as they rode off into the sunset on their motorcycle. The tour group returned to the airport that afternoon for the trip home.

* * * *

Ever since the New Zealand and Australia trip in 2004, the Milds and Pol-lacks had been discussing a trip to Japan.

Ginza shopping area of downtown Tokyo, Japan

Storefronts and wires on a Yanaka, Japan street

Haunting statue in streetside Yanaka museum

Manicured trees in Yanaka

When such a trip appeared in the Overseas Adventure Travel catalogue, it suddenly became a reality. Our good friends Joy and Marty Beer, opted to join us on this 2006 trip. We met John, Ann, and the other nine tour members at the Narita Airport in Tokyo. The minibus stopped in downtown Tokyo for a quick look at the busy Ginza shopping area with all of its electrifying signs and skyscrapers. The other half of our hotel was actually a train station, a convenience for getting around the Tokyo vicinity.

The first excursion took us to the Yanaka suburb, a mostly residential area, where we saw how the locals lived—shoulder-to-shoulder shops and homes with very tiny sidewalks, mostly dotted in flower boxes. The tiny streets seemed blanketed in utility wires, lending a mildly claustrophobic feeling. One of these streets led to a private art museum with quality pieces—paintings, statues, busts, and 3Ds, all arranged inside and out in a carefully landscaped garden and pond atmosphere. We continued the walk past many more upscale homes (wood covered by tiled roofs) with manicured grounds behind iron gates and stone walls—to Ueno Park, a local, well-kept cemetery, where we encountered prayer boards. Each of the identically sized boards (five inches wide by a quarter-inch-thick and at least ten feet long) appeared to be either stuck in the ground or leaning against stone rails. The writing and symbols varied from board to board, possibly personal, to the deceased.

A pole outside a nearby temple read in plain English: "May Peace Prevail On Earth." Another sign over the entrance gate to this 1699 Choanji Temple read: "Enshrines Jurogin, the God of Longevity." One of the shrines was the Yanaka Shichi-fukujin, the Seven Gods of Good Fortune. The tomb of Hogai Kano, the Japanese artist, was also located here. Our next stop in Yanaka was Kaneiji (Buddhist) Temple and its surrounding cemetery, where we discovered long, narrow headstones topped with actual stone heads and decorated in bright, coral-colored, flowered bonnets and breastplates.

The following morning we rode the train to Kamakura in Kanagawa Prefecture (south of Tokyo) to see a 121-ton, bronze

Upscale homes in Yanaka, Japan

Cemetery in Yanaka

Choanji Temple in Yanaka

Bathhouse in Yanaka

Shrines and Kotoku-in Temple with Buddha, Kamakura, Japan

Cemetery in Kamakura with doll-like tombs

Forty-foot Buddha at Kotoku-in Temple in Kamakura

Prayer clothesline at Kotoku-in Temple

Kenja Shrine souvenir shop at Kamakura

Kazaridaru barrels at Kenji Shrine park Kamakura

Shinto Gate at Kenji Shrine park

Endless stairs to Kenji Shrine

Ice cream shop in Kamakura

International fish market and auction Tokyo

Examining open tuna flaps for quality at fish market

Amitabha Buddha that stands nearly forty feet tall. This formidable Buddha was also the site of the Kotoku-in Temple and its surrounding parklands, where we found more coral-decorated headstones. The general area was hilly and lush green with foliage, probably due to the amount of rain we were experiencing. We discovered multiple clotheslines under tiny roofs that had paper prayer messages pinned to the lines. Tourists left other messages there as well. John and I even read the few in English. The grounds at Kotoku-in were gorgeous with streams and rocks and floral gardens everywhere. Lunch, served on shiny ebony platters with a paper shield arced across the top, took place in a cute little teahouse inside the park. Shrimp, salmon, dumplings, tofu, pickles, veggies, and dipping sauces were on the menu, as well as sake and water.

Before leaving Kamakura, we visited a Kenji Shrine at another park. A vertical matrix of empty sake barrels, seven feet

View of Tokyo from top of Ginza bldg.

Moat and bridge to Imperial Palace

high by twenty-four wide, lined the entrance to the Shinto shrine park. The individual shiny white barrels, called kazaridaru, were attractively decorated with seldom-repeated red, black, and white characters and arty figures representing the connection between sake (rice wine) and the gods at shrine festivals. Unfortunately for me, the seventy-odd steps up to the actual shrine precluded me, so I waited at the souvenir shop below, while the others went up to the top. Afterward, we explored the bustling town of Kamakura. There was a charming little shop that had three different-colored replicas of ice cream cones standing five-feet tall outside the venue. Of course, we went for it. We returned to Tokyo that night by rail.

Preparing breakfast sushi platters
at Tokyo international fish market

Individual breakfast sushi platter
at Tokyo international fish market

Costumed religious parade and community fair in Asakusa, Japan

Junko, our Japanese tour guide, ladles
holy water at Senso-ji Temple, Asakusa

Prayer messages rolled about incense burn
in caldron at Senso-ji Temple

Kazaridaru barrels at Meiji Shrine park

Shinto wedding at Meiji Shrine park

Up at yawn (five) the next morning, the group headed for the Tokyo Fish Market. The fish, mostly tuna (ahi) sans heads and tails, were aligned in rows and columns on wooden and metal pallets that filled a large warehouse room the size of a football field. Each fish had a lot number tag identifying it. A flap cut in the narrow end of the fish exposed the quality of the flesh for inspection by would-be buyers. At seemingly random times a man would step up on a stool and begin to auction off a particular fish by lot number, followed by a clamor of bidding responses. Hundreds of bidders, representing restaurants and food processors from all over the world, filled the aisles. Each wore a hat and brandished a long-handled gaff. We, the visitors, were kept behind ropes for health and safety reasons. Following a few of the auctions, the group toured the rest of the facility, where sorting, cutting, packaging, and shipping took place. Sturdy two-wheeled carts transported the fish around the market.

Afterward, we shared varieties of eel sushi, strips of smoked salmon, fried tofu squares, and saimin noodles at a nearby shop—a tasty but weird sort of breakfast. Surprisingly, we all liked it. The rest of the day was spent in touring the Tokyo-Edo Museum, a fine collection containing many architectural miniatures of the past.

The following day the tour group headed to Asakusa, an older suburb of Tokyo, where street fairs, food stalls, craft shops, beer bars, and a festival atmosphere surround the ancient Senso-ji Temple. One fountain inside the temple supplied holy water by dipper; a caldron provided a venue for prayer messages rolled around burning incense. Upon leaving the temple we encountered a festival parade with locals dressed in beautiful traditional kimonos and the shorter colorful tunics. Some carried smaller prayer houses with golden figures within and birds atop.

Another day we visited the grounds of the Imperial Palace. A broad moat and high stone walls protected the palace. From there we moved on to the Ginza, where we rode to the top of a building to gain a panoramic view of central Tokyo. Now, we had a bird's eye view of the palace and the green parklands that accompanied it.

2nd Shinto wedding in Meiji Shrine

Craftsman/artist in Hakone wood shop

Next the group went to the Meiji Shrine park, where we came upon a similar sake-barrel entrance and Shinto gateway. Almost immediately, we encountered a Shinto wedding in progress. The bride wore a black kimono with a white flowered print and matching, high headdress. And the groom wore a black jacket and a pinstriped gray skirt. While the couple posed for a professional photographer, we took our own photos. During our tour of the temple and grounds, we encountered a second wedding in progress. There was a long procession following the head priest decked out in white with a tall black hat outlined in white. A second priest and two women with white shawls and red skirts came next. Then came the bride, donned in all white, capped in a white hood. The procession was followed by dozens of attendees dressed in all black—men in Western suits and the women in black kimonos. A large red umbrella hung over the bride's head. Later we lunched in the park at a small eatery.

In the morning we took a train south and west to the small resort town of Hakone in the mountains. The tour group wandered about in the center of town before heading to our hotel. Our guide led us to a small woodcraft shop with all kinds of beautiful laminated and inlaid wood souvenirs: jewelry and puzzle boxes, plates, small furniture, and artwork of every shape and size. To enhance this treat she then led us upstairs to the workshop where these things were created. An artisan there shaved paper-thin sheets of wood of varied origin, color, grains, and texture. He assembled the sheets in interesting patterns and bonded them together. He again shaved the patterned sheets, but this time from the ends, forming a laminate that he bonded to the various objects he made and sold. I purchased a small puzzle box, which I infused into the writing of a short story many years later.

A minibus took us to a local resort hotel with suites that included both Western and Japanese accommodations. We shed our street shoes inside the sliding door to our room and donned room slippers before climbing two tiny steps into the main cham-

We dressed for dinner in kimonos, but I'm not sure if I should be thankful for what I'm about to eat. Everything in Hakone, Japan is traditional.

Nos. 2 thru 6 from the left in the back row: Marty Beer, John Pollack, Rosemary, Joy Beer, me, and just in front of me, Ann Pollack. I don't remember the others.

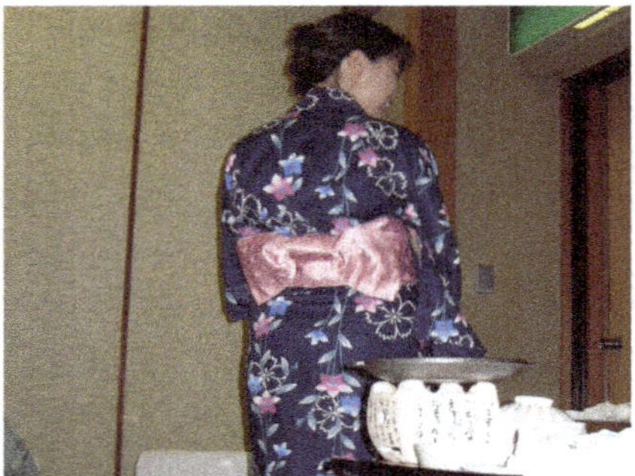

Junko, our OAT tour guide, explains the arts of the kimono and obi

ber. This chamber would have been our Japanese bedroom had we made that choice. Complete with a rattan dresser, tatami mats, and head sleeping pads—this chamber could not provide our usual sleeping comforts, so we chose the Western bedroom beyond with all of the expected accommodations. The bathroom was actually two rooms just off the entranceway. One of these rooms had a toilet with a mind of its own. If you stood for a period in front of it, the seat would automatically rise. If you sat, you had a number of choices from a control panel to your left. You might heat or cool your seat or you could control several exhaust fans or select a number of flush options. The next room had a walk-in tub and multiple shower options.

The following morning we were bused to the Hakone Ropeway (a cable car) on Mt. Hakone and rode across a series of gorges to Gora. The clouds, fog, and rain obscured the view of Mt. Fuji that we had been promised, so our guide held up a picture of it as consolation. The last gorge was actually a mining excavation for sulfur. Eggs hard-boiled black in sulfur water were the supposed treat and souvenir from the establishments at the end of our ride. Rosemary left me to shop in the Gora terminal and somehow came out on a different level and an entirely unfamiliar lineup of buses. After ten minutes of sheer panic in the fog, disconnected from our group, she found her way back to our transportation.

We then rode over to Lake Ashi. where we boarded an old pirate ship for a tour around the lake in a soaking rain. On shore once more, we drove to a Shinto shrine on the old Edo-to-Tokyo stone-paved road. The shrine park was full of statues and smaller shrines amid a wilder sort of garden—less formal and more in tune with the landscape.

That evening everyone dressed in kimonos for dinner. My kimono was the only one in a different pattern and color, as my size wasn't offered in the regular set. We sat on cushions, some with backrests, at tiny individual ebony tables, and after dinner, our guide demonstrated the many steps in putting on a formal kimono with all the accessories.

Eggs boiled in black sulfur water

A pirate ship ride around Lake Ashi

Shrines on the old Edo-to-Tokyo road

Holy water dispenser on Edo-to-Tokyo road

Hakone Open Air Museum's Outdoor Sculpture Garden artwork

Hakone Outdoor Sculpture Garden artwork

Joy and Marty Beer on bullet train to Kanazawa, Japan

Bullet train to Kanazawa

Larry, Rosemary, John, and Ann
in Kenrokuen Castle Park, Kanazawa

The next morning found us in town for a Western brunch at the Hakone hotel and then on to the Hakone/Yumoto train station. We rode the Hakone-Tozan train into the first of three switchbacks as it climbed to another mountain elevation. At each switchback we would stand and flip our seatbacks over to the opposite side and re-sit while the train moved in reverse onto new tracks that climbed to the next level. Upon completing the last of the three, we pulled into Kawakidani station and de-boarded for a short walk to the Hakone Open Air Museum. Although the museum had an indoor component, the vast sculpture gardens, with many hundreds of pieces and artists from all over the world, was far more stirring. The walk was long and tiring, but well worth the effort, as the sculptures were exhilarating We spent the entire day and retraced our train and minibus trip back to the hotel.

The next morning we caught the bullet train northwest to coastal Kanazawa. The platforms for these trains were marked so that everyone knew where to queue for boarding. At the train's high speed, it proved difficult to take any pictures. Our first stop after arriving in Kanazawa was a typical night marketplace. From there we walked through local residential and commercial neighborhoods. The evening meal at the hotel was sumptuous and extremely well presented, especially the fruit and sorbet dessert dish.

In the morning the group headed for Kenrokuen Castle park. A row of immaculate shops lined the road across from the castle moat. For the most part we ignored the great castle and wandered the endless paths through the magnificent wooded gardens and around the many ponds with their arched stone and wood

Kenrokuen Castle Park

Houses in Samurai district dating back to Edo period
Kanazawa

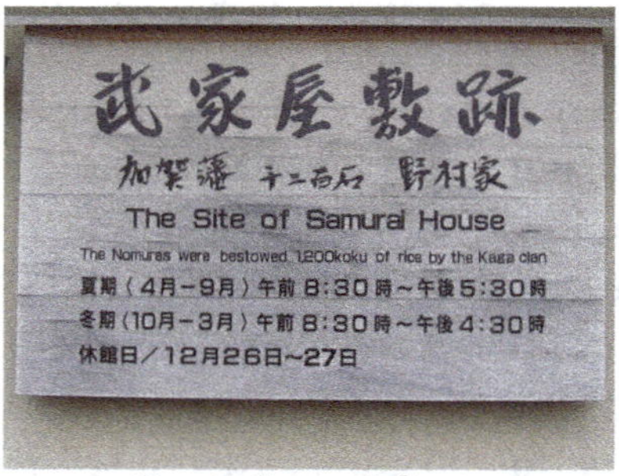

Sign in Samurai district
Kanazawa

Children on lanai of Shigute Teahouse
overlooking koi pond, Kanazawa

Nara Deer Park shrine
Kyoto, Japan

Children at entrance to Nara Deer Park,
eager to try out their English

bridges. Every green bush seemed freshly manicured. Somewhere in the midst of all this greenery was a small Shigure teahouse where we witnessed a formal tea ceremony while squatting on tatami mats. Following the paths once more, we found ourselves amid the Nagamachi ("long town") Samurai houses which dated back to the Edo period. We found this fact on a very unique signpost that carried this message in Japanese, English, and (unexpectedly) Braille—using ivory dots. Our exploration carried us through the long street of Samurai houses and back onto more park paths—on and on until dusk sent us away wanting more of the same.

The next morning brought us back to the park and the Samurai district's more modern houses, where we viewed one of the unused homes to see what it was like—mostly soji screens, mats, urns, and small shrines. A dozen or so elementary school children were sitting on the rear lanai overlooking a koi pond, stone steps leading to it, and a trail through the woods. From there we were bused to a craft market where we witnessed glass blowing and purchased souvenirs—for me, a hand-painted Mt. Fuji tie and cap and T-shirts with Japanese lettering.

Our lunch this day was a home hospitality visit with a thirty-something attractive Japanese couple and a handsome four-year-old son at their upper middle-class home. The Milds, Beers, and Pollacks were chosen for this family. We brought modest gifts from the USA for the hosting family—mine was an Orioles baseball cap. Our host was so thrilled that he immediately went to a drawer and pulled out his baseball glove to show us. The three ladies got to

Prayer nook at entranceway to host home

Rosemary tries on a family kimono

At our host's liquor store, Rosemary examines merchandise. He broke out a bottle of sake.

Our host with glove and Orioles cap, a perfect gift choice

try on kimonos belonging to the lady of the house. She graciously showed us through the home, pointing out her most valued possessions. Afterward, our host took us to his place of business, a liquor store a block away, where he broke out a bottle of sake for us.

Later that afternoon the group was taken to a stylish geisha house where we had ceremonial tea. It was the tortuous tea-at-the-tiny-table again—haunching down on a thin floor pillow for the duration. We viewed paintings of the ritual ceremony and saw musical instruments that geishas play to entertain their clients.

The following day the group truly went to temple—a Ninja temple—in the morning and then boarded a regular train southeast for Kyoto. Our first activity in Kyoto was to tour the grounds of the Nijo Castle in the rain. Next, we moved on to the Ryoan-Ji Temple and the famous rock gardens there. Then we saw the Golden Pavilion, a Zen temple sitting on a pedestal in the middle of a lake. The grounds at the Golden Pavilion occupied a vast piece of real estate, housing many shrines, statues, and buildings of religious significance.

Table setting at stylish geisha house
Kanazawa

Nijo Castle in heavy rain
Kanazawa

Ryoan-Ji Temple grounds in Kyoto

Golden Pavilion, an island in middle of lake at Kyoto

Children and deer mingle freely at Nara Shrine Deer Park, Kyoto

On another day the group bused to the Nara Shrine Deer Park. A rickshaw stand stood just outside the sake-barrel entrance with its Shinto gateway. The many shrines, with their gray-slate tiled roofs, were freshly painted a bright red. Some of these structures were multi-roofed, sustained by many pillars, while others were complete buildings. Message posts loaded with tiny scraps of prayer messages were everywhere. Spotted tan deer roamed the park freely and were as tame and friendly as any I had ever encountered. Local children mingled among the deer, petting them—mostly un-

Todaiji Temple in Kyoto

Warrior stands tall inside Todaiji Temple

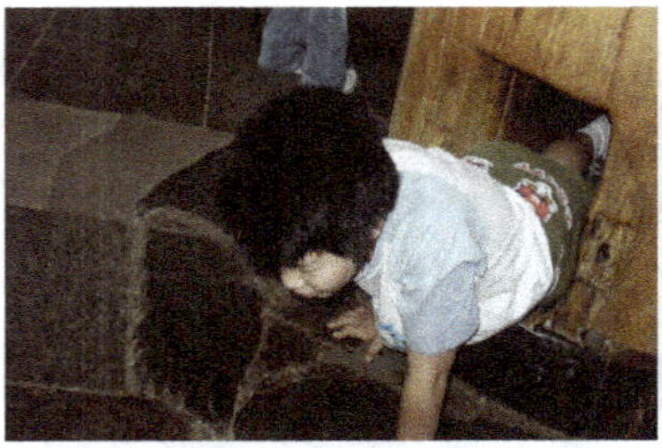

So that's where little kids come from

Rosemary makes a little friend

Inside Todaiji Temple, Kyoto

afraid. At one of the gates a group of preteen children stopped us, so that they could practice their English. We complied. The kids got their practice, and everybody got their photo-shoot.

The next morning the tour group headed for—what else, but another temple, the Todaiji Temple, housing a massive bronze Buddha surrounded by hundreds of smaller gold-leaf Buddhas. The large dual-roof temple was painted brown and white. A table set with candles and a white covering held food and floral offerings for Buddha. Within and at the four corners of the building were huge bronze warriors—ferocious, with their weapons drawn at the ready. One of the large stanchions supporting the building had a square-cut hole through the bottom of it, an attraction for the numerous little kids inspecting and squirting through it.

Later in the day we visited the Fushimi Sake Museum. Most of the vats, kettles, and implements were made of wood. Murals on the wall told how the sake was made. Then it was on to the Fushimi Inari shrine in Taisha, Kyoto. There were two fierce-looking dog statues with red and white bibs guarding the start of

Vats and kazaridaru barrels at Fushimi Sake Museum in Kyoto

Imperial Palace and grounds in Kyoto

Emperor and Empress for a day at palace grounds

Imperial Palace grounds

the Shinto gateway, or torii, entrance to the shrine. I say start, for it was more of a corridor or tunnel of bright red torii as far as the eye could see.

The next morning brought us to the grounds of the Imperial Palace. Although the grounds were deep in well-manicured greenery—dotted with lovely ponds, arched bridges, delicate rock formation gardens, and small stone shrines—for the most part, we looked into empty pavilions with yellow and brown shoji screens. However, some of the pavilion doorways were quite elaborately

On right: Seemingly endless array of Shinto torii (shrine gateways)
On left: Fushimi Inari Shrine Taisha, Kyoto

Fashion show at Nishijin textile factory in Kyoto

Gion geisha district by night in Kyoto

decorated. Of course, there were many areas, mostly pavilions, off-limits to visitors.

Next on the agenda was the Nishijin Textile factory showroom, where we were treated to a fashion show. Young, pretty ladies in their brightly colored kimonos and accessories traipsed across a small stage. Then it was time for a Japanese cooking class at a formal cooking school, a treat for the ladies in our tour group. That evening we had our departure banquet at a small restaurant, preceded by a walk through Kyoto's Gion geisha district and ending with a visit to an operating geisha house. In the morning we were bused off to the Narita Airport for the trip home.

* * * *

In the course of my reading on a broad selection of topics, I have always been fascinated by Egyptology, its history, relics, and related myths, so when John and Ann came up with the idea of a trip to Egypt, we got on board quickly, as did their friends Bruce and Allen Galin. In the fall of 2008 we flew Egyptian Air to Cairo. At

Left to right: Rosemary, Ann, Bruce, me, Allen, and John on Egypt trip

Anwar Sadat Memorial Cairo, Egypt

the airport we were met by our tour director, Mahmoud (sounded Mach-moud). Busing to the Miramics Continental Hotel, we stopped briefly at the memorial to the late Anwar Sadat, an open sandstone pyramid structure displaying his tomb. Guards in full military dress protected the site. A short distance away we saw the parade grandstand where the peace-seeking Egyptian leader was shot. Both of these sites were across from a very large military base. Pulling up to the hotel, security people and dogs examined our bus for explosives and, upon entering the hotel, we passed through magnetometers. Dinner that night was aboard a floating restaurant along the Nile River.

Right after a buffet breakfast the next morning, we boarded a bus for Giza, the site of the largest pyramids in Egypt. We noticed a great number of seemingly unfinished apartment buildings with rebar sticking through the ceilings of the top floors. We were told that this peculiar situation had to do with the authorities not being able to properly tax an unfinished building. As the bus continued, we encountered the slums at the edge of Cairo—drainage ditches with bare traces of running water and heaps of garbage floating around. Children were playing in these ditches and picking though

Three largest pyramids at Giza

The Great Sphinx at Giza

Graduated stones of the pyramids

Step Pyramid at Saqqara, Egypt

the mess. Soon we saw the three largest pyramids in the distance and decided that all the photos we'd previously seen were taken far away from the ugly slums.

I had been forewarned of the arduous walks slated for the Giza pyramid tour and the small associated museum, so I chose to remain close to the bus. Also, my stomach had been acting up. Even from the bus parking lot, I took in the magnificence of these structures. The stones at the base appeared to be taller than a man and diminished in size with elevation. I guessed that each one at the base weighed a ton more or less. Every stone had been roughly cut to resemble a rectangle, although weather and age caused many to erode to other less-describable shapes. The engineer in me began to wonder how these sizeable pyramids were constructed in ancient times, given the tools available. I rejoined the group for a close-up look at the noseless Great Sphinx and the short ride to see more pyramids at Saqqara. A short ride to Memphis revealed more ruins,

The ancient Cairo Citadel

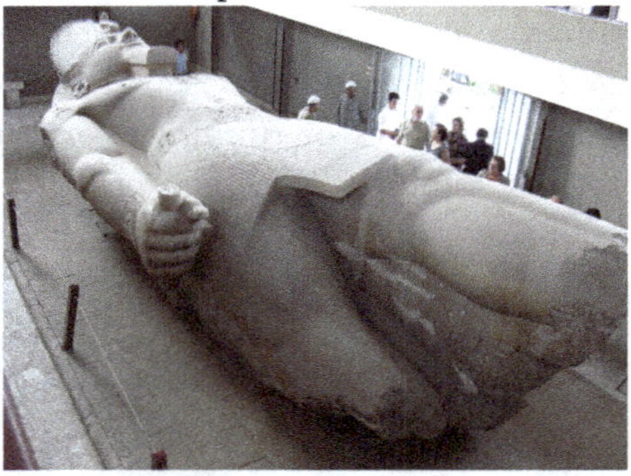

Reclining statue of Ramses II in Memphis, Egypt

Tahir Square, birthplace of "Arab Spring" Cairio

Mosque of Mohammed Ali Cairio

especially the Memphis Sphinx from the nineteenth dynasty.

The next day the group meandered through the domed Mosque of Muhammed Ali, with its alabaster walls and the ancient Citadel nearby. In crisscrossing Cairo, the bus kept passing through Tahir Square, the sight of the mass protests as the Arab Spring revolt emerged a number of years later. Throughout the Egyptian trip many of the people, and especially young girls (late teens and early twenties), were dressed in casual Western garb, but this was mixed in with those dressed in more Arabic traditional wear. Most of those we met spoke both Arabic and English and attempted to be friendly and helpful, but there were exceptions.

While touring the Museum of Egyptian Antiquities that afternoon, we gazed at the six tombs of Tutankhamun and his gold mask. We also encountered an unruly mob of tourists pushing and shoving to see the same exhibits. It was body to body throughout and, at one point, the cane I depended on was knocked out from under me. I was able to recover unharmed, but angry. As for Tut, we found his coal-black shriveled remains under a rectangle of glass, his body reassembled from the myriad of pieces left by the Englishman Howard Carter, his too-curious discoverer, who unwrapped his royal mummified carcass. We finished the day with a visit to the Khan el Khalili bazaar for some local-style shopping and had dinner at another floating restaurant called The Blue Nile.

Another day we were bused to a small village at least an hour southwest of Cairo. As it was outside the city, a cadre of six fully armed Egyptian soldiers accompanied us there. I guess the tourism bureau wanted to protect its bread and butter. The seemingly

Mud blocks laid out to dry in village

Soldier guards his tourist flock from above

abandoned village consisted of dried mud-block buildings and we could witness the blocks being made. Hundreds of them were laid in neat rows and columns to dry in the sun after being ejected from a standard wood mold. While we did our tourist thing, the soldiers took their positions on the high ground surrounding the village. I'm not sure whether that made me feel more or less secure.

A short excursion later brought us to Al Fayyoum (sometimes Al Faiyoum) and three of its many pyramids—Sneferu, Hawarra, and Lahun. The three-tiered Sneferu had steps leading to an entrance that sloped downward inside. Our guide told us about a grave-robbers entrance elsewhere. The mound-like Hawarra, with its stones cut more like cubes, supposedly held the remains of Amenemhet III, while Senuseret II (eighteenth dynasty) resided at Al Lahun. A short distance away, at Crocodilopis, a pyramid in ruins celebrated the crocodile god, and at Karanis, more ruins held the remains of a Roman temple and public baths. Another, more ancient, temple had triple-sized figures with huge elaborate headdresses carved into its stone walls, as well as square-cut recesses outlining the figures. Other interior walls were covered with hieroglyphics. A nearby oasis had many waterwheels pumping water into troughs for field irrigation.

Another day the bus followed the Nile north. Somewhere just north of the Aswan Dam, we boarded the Mövenpick's *MS Prince Abbas* for a luxury cruise around Lake Nasser, the larger body of water created by the dammed Nile. I don't know how we rated it, but the Milds were assigned to one of two first-class spacious cabins on the upper deck—king-size bed, recliners, bureaus,

Ruins of ancient temple at Karanis

***MS Prince Abbas,* our Lake Nasser cruise ship**

Fortunate hilltop ruins survive as islands with the creation of Lake Nasser

sliding glass doors to port and even a window forward. All this plus excellent buffet meals three times daily.

The created lake left islands where hills and mountains once were, and many valued ancient ruins and temples (e.g., Philae and Kalabsha) rest atop these high spots. These were cruise stops, and time was allotted for our exploration of them. There were many figures/statues of humans with bird and animal heads. We were told that a number of additional temples, ruins, and relics still remain below the lake waters beyond rescue. The two temples at Abu Simbel—with their four 50-foot statues of Ramses II and a statue of Hathor dedicated to Queen Nefertari—were actually dragged

Approaching Abu Simbel on Lake Nasser

The four statues of Ramses II hauled from Lake Nasser's former bed

Two separate camel caravans spotted from ship on Lake Nasser

Mahmoud leads way off narrow gangway

Crossing the Nile in a felucca opposite Cairo

from the lake's planned path in multi-ton increments and reassembled on the sandy shores of the lake. The bas-relief figures and hieroglyphics were magnificent. The most amazing thing was that the primitive coloring techniques had lasted with minimal fading for so many millennia. During the cruise we saw crocodiles in the water plus camel parks and caravans along the shore.

The five-day cruise came to an end one morning at the Aswan Dam. Following a tour of the dam, the group took on the Nubian Museum. We spent the evening at a night bazaar before returning to Cairo the next morning. Once there, we walked to the Nile shore to board a sailboat called a felucca, unique for its free-floating boom and sail rigging.

At this point in time I was supported by my one cane and considerably heavy, so when I saw the sagging gangway to our felucca, I became hesitant to go any farther. This gangway consisted of two planks: two-by-sixes twelve feet long and nailed together with one-by-twos every eighteen inches. One end was on the mud-

Feluccas sailing the Nile

Approaching Aswan Botanical Gardens

Lush main path of botanical garden isle

Nubian Crocodile House Café

dy shore and the other was draped over the boat's gunnels—in between about six feet of shallow Nile. Externally, I was cheered on by my fellow travelers; internally, by sheer nerve. I sidestepped slowly and, with every step, the gangway bent deeper and went bouncier. Between steps I had to wait for the bounces to dampen before proceeding farther. Finally, I got across. To this day I wonder how many of those fellow travelers bet on me getting wet. I recovered quickly as we sailed upriver past herds of goats, flocks of egrets and ibises, the Ali Khan Temple, and then across to Aswan Botanical Gardens, an island park in the middle of the Nile. This time there was an appropriate dock for landing.

We learned that a narrow green stretch on the opposite Nile shore edged a desert that ran all the way to the Red Sea. The park turned out to be a tropical paradise. After lunch we re-boarded the felucca and headed upstream for a Nubian village. We then walked to a home labeled Crocodile House. Inside, we found a very colorful décor and a Nubian guide who lectured the group on crocodiles. The next thing we knew he had a baby crocodile in his

Colorful exteriors of Nubian homes

Mural on interior wall of Nubian home

Rosemary braves handling of crocodile

hands about eighteen inches long with its mouth tied shut. Then he passed it around the room, giving everyone a chance to feel the softness of crocodile skin. Then some of the ladies in our group allowed a Nubian woman to pattern tattoo-like designs onto their arms and hands with sienna dye. The sienna tat would only last through a few showers, a matter of days.

Another day the bus took us for a day trip to a Coptic church and monastery, where an English-speaking monk lectured us on the daily life there. On our way back we visited the Temple of Kon Ombo, noted for its hieroglyphics. Upon our return, we boarded Mövenpick's *MS Royal Lily* for a late-afternoon cruise up the Nile to the Temple of Horus at Edfu and a night cruise farther to the ancient city of Thebes (Karnak and Luxor). Buffet dinner that first evening called for a dress-up in Egyptian costumes. It was mostly the ladies, but I'm sure everyone enjoyed it.

Edfu and the Temple of Horus at night was a joy—everything so well lit up. There were columns everywhere, each with its own embossed-like figures in stone accompanied by clean-cut

***MS Royal Lily,* our cruise ship for the Nile**

Columns aplenty at Edfu, Egypt

Columns and figures at Edfu after dark

hieroglyphics. Panels and walls told undecipherable stories. The next morning there was a tour of the ship as the cruise continued upriver. Arriving at Luxor that evening, we found everything well lit again, but far more extensive. Here we saw perhaps the best preserved ruins of our trip, especially the statues. Being able to know what these people looked like and how they dressed millennia past was amazing. And that the applied colors lasted all this time was even more amazing. A promenade with eighteen stone rams facing eighteen stone lions suggested some kind of super-super bowl

Varying columns aplenty at Karnak and Luxor (Thebes), Egypt

Fresco images in lasting colors at Karnak and Luxor

Hieroglyphics at Karnak and Luxor

A row of lions facing a row of rams

Ballons rising over the Nile at dawn

Temple of Queen Hatshepsut in the Valley of the Queens in Egypt

game.

Early the next morning the few braver than the rest of us got up before the chickens to go for a hot-air balloon ride. The remainder of the group got to see them pass our ship hours later as we continued to cruise.

Our next stop was at the Valley of the Queens, and particularly the Mortuary Temple of Queen Hatshepsut of the eighteenth dynasty. This was a magnificent near-perfect, three-tiered, sand-colored structure with endless stairs and a multitude of columns in the shadow of a mountainous cliff. Then we paid a visit to the adjacent Temple of Siti I, where the figures and hieroglyphics were highlighted in vibrant colors painted or dyed at least an amazing 4,000 years earlier.

We then moved on to the Valley of the Kings and their

The many roads and trails of the Valley of the Kings

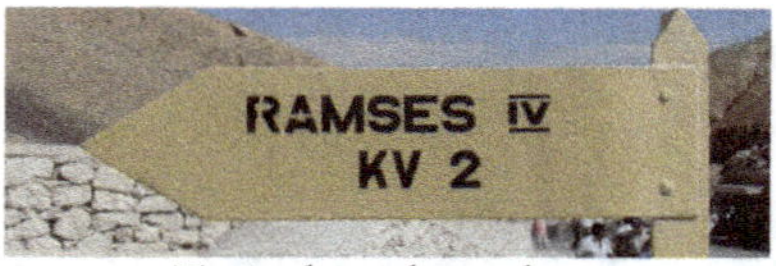

Typical tomb markers in the Valley of the Kings

Column capitals adorned in papyrus petals at Karnak

Columns covered in hieroglyphics at Karnak

supposedly hidden tombs. The entrances to these underground tombs were arranged along a walled roadway, almost like homes dotting a dusty country road. Some were accessible via downward-sloped entrances and stairs leading to multiple levels and dozens of individual and family mausoleum chambers in intricate layouts. The largest of these was KV5, attributed to the sons of Ramses II. Another, KV47, was attributed to Siptah of the nineteenth dynasty. We were told that there were untold numbers of yet undiscovered tombs still waiting to be found.

In a daylight visit to the Karnak temples honoring Amoun Ra's family, we discovered another passageway guarded by rows of stone rams facing stone lions. Here, there seemed to be more high-walled, brick-like structures. The great Hypostyle hall, built by King Seti I and his son Ramses II, was the largest hall in the world, 53 by 103 meters. It was surrounded by 134 towering, forty-foot columns with capitals representing the papyrus flower. The columns themselves were covered with hieroglyphics.

The group returned to Cairo the next day to explore religious sites in another, older, section of the sprawling city. After visiting the elaborate décor of the two main churches, we descended hundreds of stone steps beneath the churches of Ste. Barpara and

Coptic church window mural in Old Cairo, Egypt

A sign outside a group of religious buildings in Old Cairo

Al Montazah Palace, former royal residence in park of Alexandria, Egypt

St. Sergius to the Crypts of the Holy Family, which were smallish caves and hollowed recesses in the walls. Climbing harrowing steps to street level again, we visited the Ben Ezra Synagogue, built on the supposed site where pharaoh's daughter plucked Moses from the Nile in a basket.

The next day we visited the more European-style city of Alexandria, where the view from our Sheridan Montazah Hotel included the Mediterranean Sea and a grand park with a castle-like entrance across the street. We could also see the Al Montazah Palace, a former royal residence, in the distance. In the morning we bused through much of Alexandria to the famous library: a massive, spacious, and extremely modern building (inside and out), containing extensive computers, artwork, and research facilities as well as a vast book collection. A high glass ceiling furnished natural lighting. A tiny moat surrounded the building. Characters, symbols, and words from many languages adorned a round-ish outside gray stone wall.

The afternoon brought us to the circular Roman Amphitheatre and the surrounding ruins. We used the rest of the day wandering through the immense park across from the hotel and got a

Exterior wall and moat of the famous library at Alexandria

Interior work spaces of the library

Interior architecture of the library

Ruins of Roman Amphitheatre at Alexandria

closer look at the Al Montazah Palace. The park was landscaped like a tropical garden. That evening it was dinner at a floating sea-front restaurant once more.

On our way back to Cairo the next morning we stopped at St. Bishoy, a much larger Coptic church and monastery, complete with a small rustic museum. Our first Coptic facility featured a more conventional church design with large and colorful religious murals, elaborate wood carvings, and wood parqueted designs. This monastery featured ceramic domes and clay buildings and a much simpler décor—more Mexican-like. Again, we were shown around the grounds and lectured to by a good-natured monk on stark monastery living. He had glasses hung precariously on the end of his nose, bushy brows, an ear-to-ear gray bristly beard, and a one-piece hooded black robe.

That evening, back at a hotel near the airport, the tour group

Coptic Christian monastery. Its leading monk lectures us on their way of life

held their farewell banquet. Rosemary wrote her usual poem of appreciation for our tour guide, which had the whole group laughing. As Rosemary is well-known for rushing and darting about like a full-grown Tinkerbell, the following morning she tripped over a piece of luggage in our small room and fell into the glass table in front of the window. I rushed to her side and picked her up off the floor. Thank God it was only bruises and not anything broken. The table had slid away from the window, revealing a bullet hole in the bottom of the glass. At this point we were glad to be on our way back to the good old USA in another two hours.

* * * *

The Egypt trip was the last international travel we attempted. My only regrets were that I never got to see the Hermitage artwork in St. Petersburg, Russia, and I would love to have taken a few of the Viking European river cruises and visited the Norse countries. Also, I never went to South Africa or South America. Before that, I did do quite a lot of traveling—enough to satisfy a lifetime. And don't forget all the cities we traveled to for nearly two dozen mystery writers' conventions. I don't have the physical abilities to do more now, but surely I'm satisfied with what we have done. I thank God for the wonderful ride and its tremendous memories.

Chapter 18

On Dealing with Handicaps

As we move through life, we all acquire medical conditions. It's a fact of life that we collect unpleasant memories and scars from them. However, not all of these conditions qualify as handicaps. Most illnesses and conditions are transient—a crutch, few weeks of pills, and/or physical therapy, and we are good as new once more—or almost anyway. A number of these linger and require extended or periodic attention. Even these are not what I would label "handicaps." Advanced age causes us to recognize we can't do the same things we did as youngsters, at least not as well. This, in itself, is not a handicap, for a loss of agility, strength, and endurance is normally expected and accepted with the aging proposition.

A handicap is a permanent condition that forces you to alter the way you live out the rest of your life and severely affects the way you function. I have several such handicaps among my medical conditions. At age eighty-six I need two canes to walk a mere 150 yards. I have lost 85 percent of the sight in my right eye, leaving me with spotty outside peripheral vision there. And I live with a considerable measure of body core and back pain that affects the way I sleep, walk, and even sit.

You may have noticed that I have switched to the present tense to talk about handicaps. While many of the early onslaught symptoms have disappeared, the impact of these handicaps is current and ongoing, leaving me to choose this grammatical tense to emphasize my lifestyle.

The first handicap is my multiple sclerosis. Picture me in

1980. I fall an awful lot, but not so much anymore. In fact, falling down while mowing the lawn and falling down a flight of stairs are among the first of my symptoms. Diagnosis takes four months of tests and spinal taps, and I go through three excruciating exacerbations (episodes). At one point my hospitalizations are reduced to daily overnights and continue through to the following noons for IVs of ACTH, a powerful steroid. I go to work for five hours, have supper at home, and return to the hospital for another night.

Multiple sclerosis is a demyelinating disease, one that strips the myelin, the spongy protective sheathing, from the nerve fibers—like eroding electrical insulation, exposing the conductor it surrounds. If an exacerbation is not curtailed in time, a scar, a sclerosis, forms in lieu of the myelin, thus preventing the precious coating from ever regenerating. MS doesn't always have to be a gargantuan crippler hell-bent on death's path. Fortunately, I am affected only on the sensory side of my nervous system and, thankfully, my motor system continues to function normally. Well, almost. Those inflicted with motor-side damage have a more dismal prognosis and very limited hope.

Though I'm told the actual myelin damage resides somewhere in the region of the neck, the resulting problem occurs in my back and legs. A level of numbness prevails over the entire leg surface that increases in the direction of the toes. During an exacerbation, an intensified numbing sensation progresses up the legs, causing me to feel bands around my legs as though the trouser leg openings are too small to accommodate their contents. I use the word "numb" here not in the sense of feeling less or nothingness—rather as an interfering sensation that keeps me from knowing what I really should feel. A foot fallen asleep best exemplifies the irritating nature and intensity of this interminable numbness sensation. Think of it as static or noise—something one must hear or see through, and in my case, feel and react through.

Once the medical profession gets the disease under control, I have to re-learn the process of walking—something I had taken for granted since toddler days. I find walking largely dependent on balance and the confidence that if you pick up one foot, you can remain upright until it's down again. It takes wheelchairs, walkers, crutches, and canes before I learn to walk "flat footed." This is an expression I use to describe leaving the sole of one foot entirely flat on the floor until the second foot returns to a similar stance. But the method proves useful only temporarily, since painful muscular problems surface as a result of a poor walking posture. A new, more normal step relies chiefly on inertia—and my confidence in the physics of continued forward motion, i.e., my forward inertia.

I understand that human balance depends on at least two of three things—the inner ear, the eye, and the sensing of pressures on the various limb joints. The latter can be demonstrated by bending sideways at the waist while standing. You can feel just enough added pressure at the soles, the ankles, the knees, and the hips to tell you when you have extended too far and that a correction is necessary. The amount of information that I glean through these static-ridden sensors seems to be insufficient to maintain balance. I can't seem to find a way to consciously interact with my inner ear, so I am forced to rely on my eyesight. Here I continually compare and realign my upright position with the vertical lines around me: doorways, room corners, staircase balusters, furniture, and appliances. Out of doors there are plenty of buildings, utility poles, trees, pillars, and trucks to align with.

The process of staying in balance takes a concerted effort, and fatigue does take its own toll. Conversing in a hallway entices me away from concentration. Because the other person usually prefers eye contact, leaning my back against the wall sets me free to give it. On the tennis court I have trouble serving—can't take my eyes off the stabilizing fence-post references. Oh yes, I return to playing tennis for a short while and other things too—though not in the same league. I find that I can freeze a reference image in my mind just before serving, which seems to last long enough to get the job done. (Today, at age eighty-six even tennis is a figment of my long-term memory.)

Getting up and down and in and out of all types of low

or sinking chairs and cars is always a challenge. I constantly keep aware of where my center of gravity lies and how I can use my back and arms to improve mechanical leverage. In other words, I try to use my head before I make a move. For a while I learned to walk without a trace of a limp. Although there is much I can't do, I believe I make a better life for myself and family by attacking this handicap aggressively.

* * * *

To make matters worse, the mounting years deal me yet another handicap. I thank God for sparing me for so much of my life. This second handicap starts with something called stenosis, a so-called calcification of the spine. In addition, there is a progressive deterioration of my spinal disks, or rather nature's padding. Pain increases as time goes on, but the body and brain, working together, can neutralize a portion of it so I can endure and continue to function. The body's job now is to avoid extreme positions or extended periods of fatigue. The brain's job is twofold: maintain a constant sense of physical awareness and fight through the pain to accomplish what I have set out to do. I resist using narcotics, daily or otherwise, in order to keep a clear, sharp head for my writing. It's what I do every day.

Only three of the five spinal epidurals I've had done can be credited with some small relief of my advancing back pain. That precious relief is strictly a matter of where the needle rests when the syringe is discharged. The pain management surgeon tries his best, using a video scan monitor to locate that illusive spot, but it is not always available or evident. What relief I get lasts only six weeks, and I can't have another one for six months, so I disappointingly give up on epidurals.

I wonder how much nerve and padding damage is done when another neurosurgeon takes a drill to my aching spine to grind away built-up stenosis. This has the fancy name of laminectomy. On my first follow-up to this surgery, he announces to me, "The stenosis was so hard I broke three drill bits." This is something I really want to hear.

The years pass. The pain rises. My back hunches over more, causing still more pain. I consult and plead with more doctors, but all they offer is narcotics. I don't want that path. I resort to first one cane and then two to keep me upright. I'm told that more surgery promises little and is considered dangerous. As things worsen, I'm rejected by several more doctors in Honolulu, who respond with the attitude that they wouldn't touch me with a ten-foot pole. I am about to give up, when my pain management doctor recommends a Baltimore surgeon who thinks he can help me. The new surgeon warns me of the risky outcomes: possible improvement with less pain; a strong chance of degradation accompanied by additional pain; and the possibility of death. Wow! I gamble.

The surgery takes ten hours, and I'm told that everything went well. I have no way of knowing—I'm on surgery-associated pain pills and haven't been on my feet as yet. I'm led to believe that after a few more days in the Baltimore hospital, I will be sent home. Wrong. About five in the afternoon the next day I'm sent across town to a rehab facility in an ambulance. Due to a lack of room there, my bed is parked in a first-floor hallway at a wide spot in the corner of the building. I sleep for an hour and wake to another patient screaming bloody murder that someone had cut the nose off his face. His screaming continues through supper and until I fall asleep around one in the morning. At two in the morning he's still screaming, but I learn that they now have a room for me. Since patients aren't generally discharged in the middle of the night I assume that one had passed away in the night, making space for yours truly. Even in the third-floor room I can still hear the screaming in the distance, but the gurney attendant explains that the screamer was a mental patient who had some minor surgery.

The next morning, after I slide off the bed onto my feet and get into a wheelchair, I'm taken to the rehab lab and given a walker. Well, after back surgery, getting up out of a locked wheelchair and onto the walker isn't as easy as it looks. Several tries and even more completion repeats are both difficult and painful. Walking the prescribed path proves much easier, although I tire quickly. By the following day I have climbed a set of six stairs hanging on to a wood railing. At this point I want my two canes, which Rosemary brings to the facility. The therapist refuses me outright, although I counter with "What do I do once I reach the top of the stairs and the walker is still at the bottom?" Still no! I also stopped taking painkillers for the obvious reasons.

I head off to therapy my second full day there, using my canes to propel my wheelchair, and when I manage a pretty fair speed, I encounter a down-ramp between buildings. Now, I've got the chair racing a wee bit faster than I intended. At the bottom of the ramp I take a left on two wheels, a right twenty feet later, and overshoot my way into the therapy lab, whereupon I'm scolded for exceeding the wheelchair speed limits. The scolder is a hefty nurse with folded arms and a problem hiding her smile.

I have a roommate who seems to be a decent chap. On my third night in the room, a nursing aide, called a tech, enters the room and announces: "It's time for your catheter." I tell her I don't have to use a catheter. But she insists: "Doctor's orders." We argue no end about it until I tell her if she comes any closer, I'll throw my pitcher of cold water at her. She keeps on coming anyway, toting all the paraphernalia. I search my side table and come up with the urine bottle instead. I wave it as though I'm about to toss it at her. She hesitates, and I hear this giggling beyond the curtain. My roommate finally admits that the catheter is meant for him. A nurse rushes into the room confirming what he says and remembers that the A and B beds are reversed in this room.

The next morning I announce to the nurse: "I'm going home today." The nurse says: "No, not until you pass certain tests, and the doctor discharges you." The tests were to take a few steps without the walker; climb the practice stairs; traverse the full walking course; stand for five minutes before a counter and complete a game/puzzle; and pull a pair of trousers on. I pass with flying colors, as the expression goes, and wait with Rosemary for the doctor in charge to arrive and sign my escape papers. The doctor in charge finally arrives late in the afternoon, leaving only a small window to cashier out of this chamber of horrors. We argue with her, as she seems to be looking for reasons to keep me at the facility. Finally, with only minutes to spare, I become a free man with two canes to get around.

At the first follow-up to the surgeon, he shows me X-rays of what he's done. I admit the pain is somewhat less, but I have trouble walking correctly without the canes. He tells me it's nothing that a little physical therapy can't fix. After five months of intensive therapy three times a week, home exercises, and a bevy of additional follow-ups, little changes other than I get stronger and more worried. The parallel bars, weights and pulleys, machines, TEMS, and pool work aren't hacking it. The surgeon notices that I walk decently with the canes, but hunched over and, like Frankenstein's Igor, almost sidling my steps without them. He changes my therapist to someone he's sold on in his building. This one uses a set of stainless tools to massage specific nerve centers in my back in addition to all the usual exercises I do anyway. I feel like a beef roast as he saws across my back with dinnerware-like implements. If there is any improvement, I'm not feeling it yet.

The surgeon decides to send me to Mount Sinai Hospital in Baltimore, specifically to their Gait Analysis lab. I'm told some of their techniques come from the Hollywood animation simulation facilities. All of the initial photos and video are taken with and without my two canes to emphasize the differences as I walk yet another prescribed walking course. Then infrared battery-operated bulbs are attached to all my limbs and limb joints. I traverse the course several times more in semidarkness (the lights are out), while I'm being video taped. I logically assume that this wonderful wealth of data is to be crunched into a new diagnosis and a really hopeful prognosis. Wrong again. After months of continually badgering and not hearing from them, the lab finally sends us sheets of raw data without any conclusions. Another prolonged request produces a copy of two videos but still no conclusions. I conclude: interesting, misleading, unhelpful, and irresponsible.

Well, so much for the Hollywood cartooning efforts. I decide to abandon the surgeon and get on with the rest of my life. Because they are going to be with me for the duration, I decide to name my canes Cane and Able. No, not the biblical spellings Cain and Abel. Rather, the rationalization that Cane makes me Able to walk. Able has another task now: to unlock our apartment building's doors, as I have taped an access fob to it. To climb stairs or ride escalators, the canes are held in my left hand as I use my right to grip the moving railing. To open a door, my two friends are easily held in the opposite hand to free the one to attack the knob or handle.

To traverse extended distances I rely on Rosemary to push my transport wheelchair which, by the way, goes by the name of Wally. As I am forced to put my full weight on the two canes, I wear golf and sometimes weight-lifters' gloves to cushion my hands. My arm and shoulder joints suffer varying degrees of soreness on extended forays. But, as the old song lyrics say, "I Get Around."

Much is said about the lack of caring in this modern world. I find a little bit of caring almost every day. Mostly, it's strangers helping with a door, or offering a seat in a crowded room, or aiding at a buffet table. I can accomplish most of these things on my own, but I soon learn to accept good-naturedly when I can. I can't deny them the warm feelings that accompany their good deeds. The nod or smile from someone you don't know works wonders too.

We use what is called a transport-style wheelchair. To make Wally lighter and smaller for car stowage, as well as making it easier to get in and out of, we don't use the foot pedals. With them, my knees are pushed up into my chin. Without them, I must hold my legs up for the duration of the journey. I choose the latter. Sometimes I use Cane and Able and hook the handles under the soles of my shoes to hold them up a while longer. In a museum or at an affair I can slowly navigate Wally backwards, pedaling with my feet. In elevators, Rosemary sometimes forgets that my feet are extended out front and slams me into the rear wall.

I hate the feeling of being dependent. At least when I drive a car I have some control. When I'm in Wally, it's like whirling through space without a steering wheel. Even with a cushion you can feel every last bump. Sitting in a wheelchair looks easy, but it's not. There's a lot of guilt associated with seeing someone you love work so hard to keep you on the go. I am certainly no lightweight (230 lbs) to have to push around. Carpeting, grass, gravel, inclines, and curbs make the task even harder. If the hazard is a heavily sprung door, I stand up and hold the door while Rosemary pushes Wally through it. If it's a high door ledge, I help with my feet.

In a department store, Rosemary sometimes wheels me around the clothes racks like a slalom skier—with all manner of pants and shirts slapping me in the face. If I complain too much, she parks me, on the spot, in a blind, narrow aisle (hopefully not in ladies underwear), while she shops elsewhere for a few minutes. Once, at Macy's, a saleslady offered to hold the heavy glass door for us and Rosemary graciously (with apologies) ran over her sandal. Luckily, the saleslady pulled her foot back in time; her sandal remained but wasn't too squished. Occasionally, when we're walking side-by-side, Rosemary accidentally kicks a cane out from under me, causing me to stumble, but not fall. I forgive her right away, but Cane holds a grudge for the rest of the day. Community service for the traffic offenses are not an option here. All kidding aside, God knows that I love and appreciate my Rosemary. She is an excellent wife, lover, friend, and a caregiver extraordinaire.

* * * *

My third handicap has to do with the loss of sight in my right eye. One evening we go to supper at the Rusty Scupper Restaurant in Baltimore with friends and return home without noticing any difference in sight. I settle into my living room recliner. I turn on the television and something is not right. I blink a few times—no change. I close just my left eye and the room appeared to go mostly dark—sound, but no TV picture. I close just my right eye and the room remains as it was—normal TV picture and sound. I alert Rosemary, and immediately she drives me to the emergency room at Anne Arundel Medical Center. A long line and current triage policy keep us waiting for a doctor from 9:30 p.m. until 12:30

in the morning. A ten-minute examination convinces the doctor that this really is an emergency and an ophthalmologist needs to have a look at my eye.

This ER doctor wakes up an ophthalmologist and makes us a 2 a.m. appointment. Oddly, his office is only a few blocks from our home. If only we'd consulted him earlier and directly—makes us wonder if a different outcome might be realized, but that's pie in the sky nonsense after the fact. He runs a full examination and even drains fluid from the eye to relieve some of the pressure. The result is that I have an occlusion in my central retinal artery, which renders most of the rods and cones in that area useless. Two hours later he tells us that the blockage is contained and the eye is now stable He sends us home with a referral to a retinologist for much later in the day. After another examination and session of multiple mappings of the retina, the ophthalmologist's diagnosis is confirmed, and I return home with the knowledge that I have another handicap to live with.

Amazingly, the effects are not as severe as one might think. The major effect is close-in depth perception. That means that I have to watch out when I pour liquids or add sweetener to coffee or there's a potential spill to contend with. I believe I can still drive effectively, as I have a full range of sight with my left eye, including distant and peripheral vision. The 15 percent sight remaining in the right eye actually aids my distant depth perception, so I can judge distances of twenty feet or more with reasonable accuracy. A new Hawaii driver's license guarantees my driving future. Regardless, Rosemary decides to take over most of the family driving and I am left as the navigator, which she insists I do "brilliantly." I can still spend my five to six hours a day writing at the computer with enlarged type on a wide (27-inch) monitor and an auxiliary 17-inch monitor. And best of all, I can enjoy reading from either my Kindle or a regular paperback with glasses.

* * * *

While I am about my medical conditions, I might as well mention the non-handicap variety as well. The most serious of these has me wearing a defibrillator in an artificial (manmade) pocket inside my chest, very close to my left shoulder. Ventricular tachycardia is responsible for needing this device, which is about two-thirds the volume of a common cigarette pack. It is programmed as a defibrillator, although it can be reprogrammed externally as a pacemaker and can perform a number of other functions. No, it doesn't do windows. Two leads from the device run straight into my heart chambers.

During my regular checkups with my cardiologist, an engineer from the manufacturer checks me, my heart, and my heart device every four months, including a re-estimate of the remaining battery life. The engineer obtains four months worth of data history by wrapping a cable around my neck; a probe that looks like a hockey puck rests like a medallion over my defibrillator. He prints out all the data for the cardiologist to review. He can even tell when I've had a cold, cough, or inflammation during that period. Thankfully, the results are continuing to be good.

But let me go back to Annapolis in August of 2006, when my heart problems started. At a traffic light coming home from Bertolini's Italian Restaurant, I experience sharp chest pains. Being the driver, I turn the corner and quickly pull to the side of the road. Rosemary takes over, and I navigate her to the emergency room at Anne Arundel Medical Center. I rush to the counter in a room full of people awaiting medical attention while Rosemary parks. As soon as I mention chest pain, a nurse rushes me into one of the exam cubicles. I remember being on a gurney surrounded by people in blue and gray scrubs, all talking at once, then nothing.

When I awaken, they tell me: "You had a minor artery blockage." The heart surgeon's attempt to place an expandable stent inside to open the block was unsuccessful. He was unable to reach the spot, because the artery had too many crooks (reversing bends). The blocked artery then disintegrated and disappeared. "However, others will grow in and take their place." After several days of hospital rest, I am sent home with a regimen of pills (including nitro) and a list of exercises, plus a referral to the heart rehab center.

The heart rehab center at the hospital contains machines to exercise just about every part of the human body and some of the nicest people on staff. In the assigned ninety minutes, I take turns on as many machines as I can, keeping records as I go. I wear a heart function transmitter around my neck with leads that tape to my chest, so a head nurse in front of the room can monitor *my* heart functions as well as those of every patient in the room. It's three days a week for the next sixty days and then I graduate—certificate, logo T-shirt, and all. All is fine for the next five years.

While shopping one day in August of 2011, I lift a shopping cart over an aisle curb in Sam's Club parking lot and feel much the same kind of heart pain as with the first heart attack. We have the nitro pills with us, but somehow we don't think of using one. A half-hour later I'm prepped for the OR, and again the surgeons attempt to insert a stent, one much too small, into an enlarged very wide artery. The right size stent or balloon just isn't available. The stent is now in a position that prevents reasonable removal.

They find that the heart muscle is under-functioning, causing me more pain, so they send me to the experts at Johns Hopkins Hospital in Baltimore. Eventually, the artery containing the stent breaks loose and floats away. Corollaries begin to take over the former function. All of this is evident in a video they show me after I recover. More hospital rest at JHH, then I'm sent home with a different set of drugs and a referral to the same rehab center. After a couple of days I return to the center for what I think is routine rehab. It's anything but. After several minutes on one of the machines, the head nurse shouts: "Stop!" My heart rate has climbed to over 150 beats per minute. Paramedics transfer me to ER in the Acute Care Pavilion, where the ventricular tachycardia is diagnosed and the rehab is postponed.

I recover after a few days and I'm sent home with an updated prescription list and another referral, this time with an electro-physiologist. The cardiologist explains: While he is the heart's plumber, this doctor is the heart's electrician. After one office appointment, the electro-physiologist schedules an OR for me. He wants to determine if my heart remains at risk after two attacks. The nurses from rehab show up to wish me luck. In the first hour my heart is stopped momentarily by a less-than-standard amount of chemical stimulus and restarted by an external defibrillator. Being only partially sedated, the shock coming from the two paddles applied to my bare chest feels like an explosion that lifts me off the operating table. Though only an inch or two, it seems like at least a foot. I'm reborn with a new diagnosis. The test proves that I need my very own defibrillator implant. I remain lying there on the operating table while the OR is rescrubbed for full surgery. I'm sedated again and wake an hour later with my trusty new device.

Last year, an arterial fibrillation incident showed up in the defibrillator data, an incident I was not aware of that occurred in the middle of the night. My Honolulu cardiologist (now that we've moved here) explains that my constricted veins need to be thinned with some new drug or I could become the victim of a stroke.

On one of my recent checkups, the defibrillator data that is passed onto my cartiologist indicates that my seven-year-old device is running low on battery. The good doctor calmly says he's going to replace it with a new and improved one first thing Monday morning. It's Thursday afternoon. I tell him that I'm kind of attached to the old one, but he pays me no mind: Monday at 6:00 a.m. it is. I am washed with a special antiseptic liquid twice at home, once more in the prep room, and again on the operating table. I'm put under a tent to prevent me from breathing germs on the open wound. The operation goes so smoothly I don't need any pain medication. The worst of the experience is my shoulders being tied down in an awkward position. My plea for Velcro or a zipper falls on deaf ears.

* * * *

It's not exactly the kind of thing you want to hear. "You're a candidate for a knee replacement," the orthopedist tells me. First of all, I decline the nomination. The X-ray films reveal a mass of osteoarthritis—calcification of joint matter—surrounding some very unhappy left knee bones. The tibia is resting on the femur, with absolutely no cushioning left.

Seeing my reaction to the news, he offers: "We could try arthroscopic surgery to clean out the superfluous matter and see if that would make a difference in your lifestyle. No guarantees, of course." My then-lifestyle: 65, retired, avid walker, tennis doubles in moderation, and lots of swimming. Well, the activities are already curtailed and the continual cracking (bone on bone) promises more restrictions are on the way.

In June of 1998 I agree to the outpatient arthroscopic surgery. Afterward, I spend a few days in moderate pain, groping for the furniture around me as I shuffle through the house. Therapy and diligent exercise (mostly weighted leg lifts) gradually restore my ability to walk with some normalcy. My doctor tells me to go down stairs backward.

Three months later I embark on three weeks of sightseeing in the British Isles. Among the many worthy challenges are: up and down (backward) the endless steps of Edinburgh Castle and the spiral staircase from Mary Queen of Scots' bedroom in Holyrood Palace. By the time of my return, I am anticipating a lower pain level than I'd known before the surgery. But that doesn't happen. In fact, things get worse.

I make the gross mistake of getting down on the floor to eradicate several stains in the rug. The bodily damage is done on the way up. The knee protests most loudly. Cracking and pain increase. Gradually, I revert back to furniture groping to maneuver around the rooms. By this time, we're at our winter home in Hawaii and need to see a second orthopedist 5,400 miles away.

The new doctor seconds the nomination—knee replacement is a must. I tell him that we winter there for only a few months, insufficient time for rehab. Agreeing, he also becomes concerned for my interim lifestyle and suggests a temporary measure: a synthesized lubricant to be injected directly into the knee joint in three doses a week apart. After the second injection of Synvisc, things begin to look up. Seven to nine weeks later, I'm walking more than two miles daily and swimming up to twenty laps. What euphoria!

This too begins to ebb after several additional weeks, and I curtail my activities once more. The literature, even a direct call to the manufacturer, assures me the Synvisc is a one-shot deal. No data, no guarantees on subsequent usage, but thank God, the effects last long enough for me to return home and become disjointed, then rejointed.

The surgery takes place at the Center for Joint Replacement, a unique unit of Anne Arundel Medical Center in Annapolis. The acronym sounds too much like an auto parts store. If I drop off the old joint for rebuilding, I'll get a rebuilt one in its stead, warranty included. It turns out that the center occupies an entire wing of the second floor and specializes in nothing but brand-new knees and hips. The warranty: three to 20 years, with an average lasting more than 10 years. At of this writing I have two years left on the maximum end of the warranty.

In May of 1999, a few days after agreeing to surgery, a huge three-ring binder arrives in the mail. Included are instructions for pre-op exams and blood work, diagrams for pre-op and post-op exercises, and an invitation to attend "Joint Camp."

So my coach (in this case, my wife) and I attend camp beforehand, a session where almost everything is explained to us. I say almost everything—except for the pain, the iron maiden, the sleep deprivation, the vampires, and the rampant black plague that would attack me. I can tell you more about that later. Amid cookies and punch, my fellow campers and I—eight knees and one hip—are briefed on procedures; medications; three weeks of Coumadin blood thinner; frequent blood work for an equal period; antibiotics for any dentistry and/or other invasive body work over the next two years; and thromboembolic deterrent support hose (known as TEDs) for six weeks afterward.

We see models of the joints: a titanium bone cover whose central rod is embedded, cemented, and pinned in the drilled femur; and an oversized golf tee that's similarly embedded in the tibia. A plastic pad in between prevents chafing. Camp concludes with a slide show and the opportunity to view ambulatory patients only a few days post-surgery.

On the day of surgery I fill out a clipboard of hospital disclaimers, surrender my dignity, and climb aboard my gurney to await the ultimate journey to the OR. Two IVs later we clickety-clack our way to a holding area thirteen light fixtures and untold numbers of ceiling squares away. There I'm placed in a queue, second in line, waiting for the operating room to disgorge the prior knee patient. I think better of conversing with the other patient in line. What can I say, anyway? "What are ya in for, pal?" Just before I get to the head of the line, my anesthesiologist drops in for a chat about past experiences with allergies and nausea. When we run out of pleasantries, he subtly releases one of the IVs, and that ends our knockout conversation.

It's 10:50 am. For two and a half hours I remain totally out of it. I recall waking in my room, where my wife welcomes me back to the living. Nurses and medical techs hover around taking temperatures, pressures, and blood samples while physician's assistants gather data and mete out reassurances. The covered wound throbs with just manageable pain. The TED stockings on both legs make me look as though I should be ready to spout Shakespearean verse.

But the biggest shock is yet to come. I spent more than a year lifting leg weights, ten pounds a hundred times on each leg (ordered by the orthopedist to strengthen my quads, the "shock absorbers" for the knees). Now I can't even lift my unweighted left leg a smidgen off the bed. Aided or not, any movement of that leg other than slow-slow-easy proves painful. What a bummer! All that exercise and for what? How low and disappointed could I get? I can only hope that maybe it will pay off later.

This brings me to the subject of canes. I am mildly discouraged from bringing one to the hospital, but if I insist, I should be sure to label it my property. So I bring Cane and Able with me and, boy, am I glad I do. It becomes the most useful tool of my stay there. At that time it has a tee grip as opposed to the Bo Peep curl I use now. The grip fits beautifully under the arch of the bum foot, and I am able to lift and transfer my whole leg with minimal pain wherever it is needed—off the bed, chair, or floor. It also fetches articles of clothing otherwise out of reach, operates the overhead light, and serves as a hard-to-itch scratcher.

I am standing within hours of surgery and otherwise sitting in my gerry chair (for moving *alte cockers* around). Several trips to the john prove really embarrassing. Paying attention to nature's urges and great gobs of pain at the same time is never easy. Since pain usually wins out, I take to using the provided bottle.

Initially, I'm given a small four-legged walker to assist me around the room. It proves to be too small for my width; the pockets of my shorts catch on each swing forward. It's too large to fit in the bathroom and too large to get around the other side of the bed. Really, where else am I going? I do get another walker the next morning when the halls become my thoroughfare. One of the therapists breaks open a brand-new sports model: four-wheel drive, wide chassis, and you could still almost sense the smell of new upholstery.

That first night I'm introduced to my mistress, the iron maiden, with whom I'd be sleeping for the next six weeks. Imagine a stretch of canvas and Velcro lined with miniature rebars to keep my knee joint and leg fully extended and immobilized. The original Egyptian iron maiden is a mummy case lined with spikes. I believe the inventor of this one got his postdoctoral at the U. of Cairo under Ptolemy the Second. Essentially, I spend near-sleepless nights lying hard on my back with only my trusty cane to move the iron maiden about.

Setting aside tears and anger, I embark on a scheme of escape from sleep deprivation. I find that excessive movement causes the swelling within the maiden to painfully press and throb against the binding. I learn that neither leg can support the weight of the other, so sleeping squarely on either side is out of the question. Lying quietly on my back for a while seems to allow the swelling to distribute itself to a less painful state. Surprisingly, this is just as pronounced as the release of a blood pressure cuff. Then, it seems,

I can slowly roll to a near side position, one leg before the other, the free leg offering two choices. In a week or two, when I acquire the strength to lift the iron maiden, the opposite side and two more choices become a reality. Truly, exhaustion proves to be the best path to sleep. Diligent exercise during the day, not only going through the motions, but pushing to do more, longer, and further can help in this regard. Fighting the daytime napping impulse after the first week also contributes to a more restful night too.

On the first night a nurse questions you at bedside. "On a scale of one to ten; ten being the worst pain you've ever experienced and one, a petty annoyance. What are you feeling right now?" Not wishing to be too macho or too much of a sissy either, I respond with: "A seven." She is visibly upset. I couldn't possibly be that uncomfortable. She had been hoping for something like a six or even a five. Not wishing to hurt her feelings, nor her chances for advancement, I negotiate for a six point five.

Actually, my pain is not a static thing worthy of a single number. For the most part, it feels like a heavy, swollen lump pushing and pressing inward and outward. The surface seems to have a burning sensation that defies touching. Something akin to random cramping keeps jolting, yanking, and tugging at my muscle strings, and each new leg position presents its own unique hurting.

The morning after surgery my coach, my walker, and I report to the track for lap duty. The track, calibrated with feet markers, extends down one hallway past patient rooms, turning at the Maryland Room lounge with its view of beautiful Spa Creek, turning right, passing a second set of patient rooms, turning once more at the nursing station, and returning down the stretch to my starting room. It is 440 feet in all. One lap is sufficient for my first try. But lapping is not enough, group therapy class is next, and cutting class is not allowed.

A parade of new joints make their way to the exercise room, while the coaches leisurely drive our exercise recliners after us. A golfing mural dominates the rear wall of the exercise room. One of the depicted golfers sports the stapled leg of the typical knee replacement. Yes, I, like the others, carry thirty-nine brass-colored metallic staples beneath my dressings. It resembles a zipper or the commercial from the popular office supplier, "Staples, we got that."

Seated in the chairs, with both sets of toes pointing skyward, we begin with ankle pumps, quad knee sets, bun (glute) squishes, full leg lifts, short arc leg lifts over a rolled towel, sliding hip and knee extensions, etc. Right up there with the real tortures of our time is the flexion stretch, folding the knee through the ninety degrees to some painfully impossible goal beyond. Twice daily we meet for this ritual and, in between. we are encouraged to lap the measured hallway in our walkers. Coaches accompany their patients everywhere, thus freeing the medical and therapy staff for their specialties. Back in our rooms, another torture: straddling the new knee between two chairs with ice and weights on top, forcing the joint toward full extension.

Delightful luncheons are held on Wednesday and Thursday noon following the Monday and Tuesday surgeries. Coaches as well as patients and staff are invited in appreciation of their joint (forgive the pun) participation. Being that I possess the dominant chow hound gene, I show up for lunch barely twenty hours after surgery, to everyone's surprise. Seeing the group in a social setting leaves me with such a wonderful feeling. I feel that I'm acquiring a cheering section—this despite the continuing pain.

Friday comes around at last, the day for discharge from the hospital. The group is pared down to four as the Monday surgeries left the day before. By Friday I can complete seven Ben Hur laps around the center—a good sign. In addition to completing both therapy sessions, I need to demonstrate two things before I can go home. The first is getting in and out of bed without help. I show off my agility with the cane for that purpose, but I wonder why the belated concern—I've been doing this one since the first night. The second thing is stairs. They produce a five-step mockup complete with railing for practice. No problem, though I explain to the therapist that descending stairs backward is how I do it—for more than a year to appease the old joint. We say our goodbyes and declare that we must stop meeting at joints like this.

It's good to be home again and in my own recliner where multiple positions spell relief. Sofa cushions tailor optimal leg angle. Under no circumstances am I to put any pillow or cushion beneath the joint. I go through two days of home therapy with my coach. On the following Monday I start five consecutive days of physical therapy at a facility near our house.

This facility has a sign on the wall: "It's nice to be kneaded." Well, along with a number of new exercises, kneading becomes a way of coaxing and stretching the leg to its full extension and full flexion limits. Tolerable pain governs the muscle and time of application. I have to admit that mutual fondness and trust must exist before any patient will regularly submit to this kind of torture. Facial contortion and pitiful vocal emissions are acceptable, provided you don't frighten off the rest of therapist Renee's patients. Banshee shrieks and passing out are, of course, in bad taste. Faking pain won't do either. Progress is recorded in the three-ring binder on a day-by-day basis. On the knee's second-week birthday, more X-rays are taken and my staples are removed. Deft hands and a specially designed pair of pliers accomplish the task with hardly any pain and bother. Sterile strips, held in place by a funky-smelling adhesive, replace the bulky dressings. I can now take a full shower—no more sponge bathing.

Because of the blood thinner, I must visit a convenient medical lab, where the resident vampire can draw blood for the purpose of adjusting my Coumadin levels. For her cheerfulness, I'll grant her the Bela Lugosi statuette, but for a 50 percent stabbing accuracy rate it'll have to be a small one—or none. I must admit my veins are rather timid and do have a tendency to hide.

It's ironic to use the term "black plague," as it's probably one of my lesser worries. But just after repelling the constipation brought on by the pain pills of the early post-surgery days, I begin to notice the black fallout of my bodily emissions. Soot-black everywhere, wind and soil—enough to fear a fine from the state emissions police. The culprit turns out to be the iron pills I've been compelled to take with each meal for the past two months. The pills themselves are anal-retentively packaged, in that it takes planning, skill, dexterity, and patience to even get at the little triangular suckers. They come on cardboard flats that must be cut in strips, then row by row. A thumbnail is then inserted into a minute air bubble between paper and plastic. Once the plastic lamination separates, you punch the potent pill through a final layer of paper and pop it into your mouth.

Sitting at the kitchen table for more than fifteen minutes proves to be such a discomfort that I can't stick around for seconds. This silver lining to the cloud allows me to drop two full waist sizes. Lest you think it all silver, I have to make you privy to my secret. Getting out of the car at home, we stop to chat with three neighborhood ladies. Upon completion of the pleasantries, we all turn to go our separate ways—they down the street, me up the path to our house, both hands on my walker. Suddenly, my khaki shorts drop to my ankles—gee! Luckily, my coach is there to literally bring up the rear.

In the fourth week of rehab I add two pounds to the leg lifts and side flexes. Then there are rubber band pulls from both heel and shin positions. The stationary bicycle is an unusual experience in that pedaling backward proves easier than forward. Forcing the knee to bend through the high part of the pedal arc tends to put a real hurting on you. Once started, though, forward soon becomes viable, 100 turns reverse, 400 turns ahead. The unyielding odometer simply wouldn't give credit and, instead, netted the result in miles for only 300 turns. I add to the weights and turns in the succeeding weeks as well as the repetitions. The therapist adds exercises, but she becomes concerned—I'm tackling too much. "I never had a patient I had to slow down before."

I begin walking with a vengeance and soon a mile a day becomes the norm. There are a few longer excursions, mostly confined to a few tenths of a mile more, but a two-miler the third week after surgery leaves me too sore and exhausted. As long as the weather holds, the Baltimore-Annapolis Trail becomes the walk of choice. Not only is it calibrated with half-mile markers, the edges are lined with exquisite waist-high wildflowers. After three months of near-drought, the only twenty-minute downpour coincides precisely with one of our jaunts. On hot and muggy days we do the malls and stores, every aisle a must.

I shed my walker and cane in weeks one and two. At eight weeks I'm simplifying my formal exercises to 100 leg lifts, forty reverse leg lifts and forty knee lifts, all with six-pound weights. Then after forty knee presses and forty shallow knee squats there's twelve minutes of stationary cycling. The weights are increased in measured steps until I reach ten pounds. At eleven weeks I'm at nine pounds. Now that the wounds are healed (no scabs) swimming becomes an excellent adjunct to my total recovery. Two months more, tennis. Nothing competitive or strenuous, mind you, but a chance to just hit balls that happen to pass my way.

The worst aches these days wake up with me. They lessen as I get my tail moving. Other aches and pains remind me of moves I shouldn't have made. I'm told by the Veterans of Foreign Knees that this too shall pass in the next few months, although complete (no-ache) recovery could take as long as two years. At the recommendation and encouragement of the orthopedic surgeon's physician assistant, I continue with 150 reps of the ten-pound leg lifts on both legs for the next five years until the back pains emerged as a problem. Today, I wonder how much of my chronic back problem can be attributed to those excessive lifts. My former pain management doctor felt the leg lifts may certainly have contributed.

Through all of the painful experiences there was this urge to make the time pass, to get beyond it all and not be such a burden to Rosemary, still my coach. This left me with a guilt trip—wishing my finite life away. I decided that life was too short, too precious—I already have more mobility than before. I can still enjoy great moments and fine distractions, even while I hurt. I sometimes forget that I do hurt until I make the wrong move.

In 2011 the right knee becomes a problem. I consult the

same orthopedist about having it replaced. He refuses, saying the problem lies with my back and not my knee. I know this isn't true, because I get temporary relief from localized shots there from my pain management doctor. I arrange to have a replacement in Honolulu, where we winter to be close to family. The years in between have brought improvements. This time I get a custom knee joint made especially for me from a full three-dimensional CT scan.

We moved to Honolulu in July 2013. In November the custom knee is put in place with no adjustments necessary. I'm home after four days and fully functioning after three months of moderate physical therapy. No weighted leg lifts are necessary, only flexing and stretching the joint. The leg pain is far less. I walk the limits that Cane and Able allow me.

Let me digress here to talk about my attitude toward pain in general. I'm sure I can't lay claim to experiencing any higher level of pain than the next person following similar operations. I can't say that I know what agony is like—the nines and tens on the scale of battle wounds and auto injuries. In reality, I do bite the bullet and ride out the postoperative pains without tears and too many complaints, because I'm certain these pains are transient and soon will pass. But there is another kind of pain.

Residual pain is that pain left after all healing is done. There is no expectation that more relief is on the way. Residual pain and I are long-term colleagues, and I assume we are destined to continue for some time to come. The key to sharing the same body with pain is learning to manage and accommodate this relationship sensibly without the use of narcotics. There is no trick to adapting to pain. I must bear the hurting until it no longer becomes a distraction. Any incremental increase in level requires another concerted effort. I must say that it's working for me so far.

What else? Oh, I have this and that: pre-cancer spots removed from various parts of the body from time to time; a major dash of chronic sinusitis; and the usual modicum of dental work done, but I consider these things routine, given my age.

Chapter 19

Aging with Verve, Care, and Finesse

On the Mainland, Rosemary and I had a tight-knit circle of friends and an ever-widening group of acquaintances that we owed return social obligations. We decided to accomplish these favors with a Memorial Day picnic. Unknowingly, we began a tradition that endured for sixteen years, missing only once when I had a knee replaced. The picnics became a big deal—requiring planning, cleaning, and reserving things weeks in advance. Beginning with about three dozen guests, the event soon soared to eighty. We purchased four-foot-round plastic tables and molded chairs for the yard, more chairs for the porch—for which we had to find interim storage, and then retrieve and clean—so we could put them out the next year, weather permitting.

Then there was the food. A small table under the dining room window held a sliced kosher Empire turkey, along with paper plates and plastic utensils. It also held a hot pot full of chili doctored with extra mushrooms, ground beef, and caramelized onions—and don't forget the rice cooker next to it. The main dining room table held a large baked and sliced ham, lox and cream cheese, bagels and rolls, potato salad, and coleslaw. The buffet held an array of delicious desserts. The kitchen table held a few bottles of wine, gin, vodka, and mixes as well as ice and cups. There were three coolers on the porch with beer and canned soft drinks.

All sixteen Memorial Day picnics lasted from ten in the morning until ten in the evening and were a grand success through both rainy and sunshiny days. We had to stop for three reasons.

One, the work got too much for us as we got on in years and accumulated disabilities. Two, several of our closest friends had passed away. And three, as many of our friends aged, they excused themselves to attend events starring their own offspring.

One more thing about the picnic. We originally purchased the baked ham from one of those specialty stores. One year we learned they were fresh out of stock, but the young salesgirl accidentally leaked that they purchased them from Sam's Club fully sliced. Needless to say, we eliminated the middleman after that.

I mentioned the porch earlier. Years before I entered the picture, Rosemary and her ex had purchased a prefabricated, screened-in porch from Sears and had it installed at ground level, requiring three steps down from the kitchen to access it. A second door led outside to the yard. The floor was clay tile set in sand. The screens had been ripped and patched to the point of unsightliness, plus the whole arrangement seemed to be a hazard to our picnics.

One day I noticed a carpenter/handyman putting some finishing touches on additions to the neighbor's house next door and called him over for an estimate. Thus began a whole new porch project. He put in a raised deck with seasoned wood even with the kitchen floor; erected vertical wooden stanchions and studs; raised the roof accordingly; and installed removable screen panels. Everything came out as planned, except for the outside four steps to the ground, which bounced when stepped on, so I reinforced them with heavier wood and added a handrail. At one point we had to replace the columns supporting the front porch roof too.

Some time later I contracted the same man to install a white fiberglass picket fence between the house and the property lines that included a car-wide swing gate. It was then that we contracted out for a new, two-car-wide cement driveway. Another project led me to install two-high railroad ties in front of the house to form flower beds on either side of the front stoop. Each year, I dug through clay, potting soil, and dirt, adding fertilizer and lime while Rosemary planted impatiens and vincas for a glorious display. One year a pair of mature mallard ducks waddled surreptitiously

Aunt Lydia and Uncle Cy Haack

Herta Forsch (Nanny Herta) in better days

up behind Rosemary to watch her plant. I think they approved.

Herta's sister, our Aunt Lydia and her husband, Uncle Cy (Seymour) Haack, lived next door to Herta. Hannah had long since passed away. Uncle Cy passed away a few years before Aunt Lydia, leaving Herta alone in Miami Beach. Jackie generously invited her grandmother to come and live with her and Rodney in Honolulu, and she accepted. Rosemary and I met Jackie and Leah in Miami Beach to help Herta pack her household for the trip. Alena, already in school, stayed behind with Rodney's dad during the day and with Rodney at night. Cousin Jeff Seidenberg came down from New York to join us as well. By the time we got through with the giveaways, throwaways, and takeaways the job was completed. Our last night together, we went out for dinner and reminisced, with sad reminders of better times in Miami Beach. Leah sat in Jeff's lap playing with one of those little coffee-creamer plastic containers. No surprise, Leah squeezed the cup, and the cream squirted all over Jeff's face. It was just the humor we all needed as Jeff wiped his face, laughing as well.

Though things went as well as could be expected for some time, living with Herta was notably hard on all of the Laus. She couldn't walk to a store anymore. In fact, she couldn't walk anywhere anymore because of the steeply terrained streets around the Lau house on Lamaku Place. Jackie couldn't give all of her attention to the girls anymore—some had to be diverted to her grandmother's needs. The family, work, and school schedules left Grandma alone in the house most of the daylight hours. So in time, Herta became argumentative, disagreeable, and justifiably unhappy—but silently grateful, nevertheless. The Lau family tolerated her repeated tirades and interference for a good many years until interactions became more tense and frequent. Sadly, because of this, Rodney stayed at work later and later. Many tears were shed when the situation merited a search for a good private nursing home.

Herta was transferred, kicking and crying, to a very nice four-patient home across from the UH president's mansion. Her private room right next to the kitchen had its own bathroom and shower. She also had access to the refrigerator, a large parlor, and a lanai. Within days, she settled in comfortably and soon saw the benefits of the change. Jackie and the girls visited her often. Once, on one of our own several visits there, Herta heard Rosemary and me talking as we came up the back walkway, and she shouted out my name with such joy that I was deeply moved—she really had loved and missed me. Herta Forsch lived out her days there to the ripe old age of ninety-five and was buried in a cemetery just behind Diamond Head.

Shortly after their big move back to the Mainland, Myrna

Front and rear view of Spurrier home in Foxchase community, Aiken, SC

The pool and guest house in Aiken, SC

Barn and stables in Aiken

All the horses are talking about it

Don't look now, but you're being followed

Leah, Craig, Emily, Alena, and Ben on Huntsman Drive in Aiken

Rosemary has some new pals

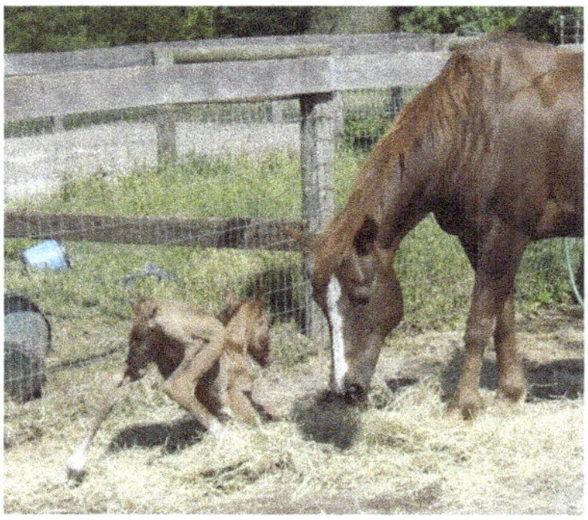

Newborn Hoku tries to stand for first time at Spurrier farm in New Holland, SC

The five Spurriers on Huntsman Drive in Aiken

Myrna is a natural riding Barbi

Emily has horse skills as well

Dinner in the new Spurrier horse farm dining room. From left: Me, Myrna, Craig, Ben, Sydney (Ben's future wife in 2017), Emily, Tim, and Grandma Harriet

and Tim bought a home in an exclusive community called Foxchase on Huntsman Drive in Aiken, SC, surrounded by a horse-trail preserve called Hitchcock Woods—a densely treed and sandy expanse comprising hundreds of acres. Their property consisted of a large house, garage, stable, swimming pool, guest house, gardens, and corralled grazing fields on at least five acres. Even an electric golf cart came with the place. The house was attractive, and the surroundings were landscaped nicely. Rosemary and I visited them twice there and stayed in the guest house.

As time went on, they acquired two additional horses so that the family could ride together. However, Craig rode only occasionally—he had found his niche in computers and even had purchased components online to build one inside an old bread-making machine. At age twelve he had taken the Web Master's exam (in his father's name) and passed it. (Several years later, Craig hosted the Spurrier website through Hawaiian Hosting—a company he started with Julia, an IT consultant, in Waimea, HI.) He also obtained a URL name for our website and I went out and purchased a book on website language (HTML). After a week of study, I put together my first website for Magic Island Literary Works (www.magicile.com) and an email address (roselarry@magicile.com) coupled with it. Thus, Rosemary and I were off and running in cyberspace. Even at this writing, Craig remains my consultant, often reminding me that it's been some time since I worked in the ones and zeros field.

After several years in Foxchase, the Spurriers came to the conclusion that they wanted lower monthly mortgage payments, lower taxes, and fewer land restrictions, so they decided to buy land and build out in rural country. They purchased fifty-five acres of grassland about thirty minutes east of Aiken in New Holland and had a good-sized house erected on a pretty site in the middle of it. Only, choosing the middle meant that a half-mile of driveway, and electricity had to be brought from Sandy Trail, the nearest county road, to the house. The unpaved driveway required constant tractor attention after every rainstorm to ensure decent passage.

Emily enrolled in gymnastics class and did quite well. She proved to be a quick study. Ben resumed his horse riding lessons and soon became proficient at western riding. He began competing at reining and cutting in contests and winning prizes. Actually, his family thought he would make a career of it, so they purchased two more horses, Lady Lena and Nsync, to improve his chances. A successful career as a horse trainer could play off his contest winnings and world ranking in these events. At one point he reached fourth in the world for the eighteen-and-under class of riders.

At the age of nineteen Ben, on One-to-Shine, won second places in Reined-Cow-Horse and Ranch-Reining, and Reining regional competitions. In the world competitions in Stephensville, TX he competed on three horses, finishing in the top five of all

Ben riding in two different competitions

Getting around on the Spurrier farm in New Holland, SC

Rosemary and Emily inspect Myrna's classroom at Aiken Preparatory School

three events. He actually won the world championship in the Cutting event on Nsync at nineteen, competing against adult riders.

It was expensive trailering horses to these events and getting lodging for Ben and at least one parent. We rented an entire bed and breakfast for a whole weekend while attending a competition in Winchester, VA and a block of motel rooms in Ohio for another. The parking lots at these events were full of super-sized horse trailers with kitchen and bedroom built into the opposite end from the horses and tack room. It was the groupie thing all over again, watching Ben manipulating his horses to do figure eights, circles, reverses, and braking after a sprint (reining), then manipulating a horse to work a calf to its ultimate destination, all without verbal commands (cutting).

Upon their arrival in South Carolina, Tim began teaching at Aiken Technical College. Then he left to teach full time at Aiken Preparatory School, which had the additional advantage of free enrollment for their three kids. Some time afterward, Tim left Aiken Prep to become a headmaster at a nearby church school. He eventually tired of that position and found his niche in real estate. For a time, he was quite successful (top listing agent for months on end). That is, until the economic turndown in 2007/8 when the real estate market fell apart altogether.

Initially, Myrna had a teaching job at a nearby charter school. The mismanaged charter school suddenly downsized a year later, leaving Myrna without a job. For a time she joined Tim at Aiken Prep. A few semesters after Tim left there, her job was first reduced to three-quarters, then halftime due to enrollment drops. Because of the decline in the real estate market and Myrna's loss of full-time employment, the Spurriers needed our help. We graciously helped out with their debt and recommended that they sell the farm. They were grateful, but the farm took years to sell.

Myrna quickly found employment at T.W. Josey High, an inner-city high school in Augusta GA, an hour's commute from New Holland where they were living at the time. But she eventually settled into a teaching position she loved at Bel Aire Elementary School just over the border in Evans, GA. All wonderful, except for the commute.

Myrna produced art whenever she found the time; however, she concentrated on print-making and not on her favorite, ceramic sculpture, because it was more portable. She could work on it while waiting for Emily at her gymnastics classes and other activities. She entered her prints and won prizes in local art competitions. On occasion, she taught children's art camps and held evening adult art classes at an art center in downtown Aiken.

In the meanwhile, Tim saw a teaching opening on Molokai, HI and the possibility of a headmaster's position on Oahu. The former was immediate and the latter wouldn't be available for another year. Meanwhile, the two of them saw an opportunity to return to Hawaii, but Myrna would have to remain in her job for at least another year. Tim actually taught school for a year on Molokai while interviewing for the headmaster's position on Oahu. He eventually secured that Honolulu position and has run the (Episcopal) Holy Nativity School ever since.

For the most part things went extremely well for Tim, so they moved everyone—except Ben—and mostly all their household to Honolulu that fall. Ben stayed behind to care for and possibly sell the farm and the fifteen horses in their keep. In order to maintain their worth, the horses had to be continually trained and ridden. Tim, Myrna, and Emily rented a two-bedroom house in Aina Haina near Hawaii Kai on east Oahu. When their lease expired, they relocated to a first-floor apartment in a Kahala house and then moved to their present three-bedroom house in Waialae Iki, with beautiful, expansive views of the Pacific Ocean.

In November of 2017, almost a decade later, the farm finally sold. Fortunately, there were only three horses left, and they were boarded out with the intent to sell. During that ten-year period Craig obtained his bachelor's and master's degrees in anthropology from the University of South Carolina, and a second master's in criminal justice from the University of Cincinnati. He completed his coursework for his doctorate in anthropology and successfully defended his dissertation at Western University in London, Ontario, Canada. Both Tim and Craig received their doctorates; Tim in Summer; Craig in Fall of 2018. We are very proud of both of them. Craig has his own apartment in Waikiki. He is currently employed

Emily dressed for summer

Rosemary and I at Craig's graduation, a BS degree from the University of South Carolina

as an information technology (IT) specialist at Kapiolani Community College, part of the University of Hawaii system. Craig would like to teach anthropology at UH one day. Some years earlier, brother Ben graduated from the University of South Carolina with a bachelor's degree in anthropology. We praised his hard work as well.

In the years prior to 2012 Rosemary and I had been experiencing frequent and sometimes lengthy power and telephone outages at our Severna Park home—sometimes as much as eight to ten days, a major irritation, to say the least. During near-hurricane winds, a heavy branch severed our landline phone on one occasion, and when we made our complaint, we were told that it would be weeks before the phone company could repair it. I took some of my own wire and spliced in a jumper to restore service. When the phone company finally arrived they chewed me out, saying it was dangerous. They had no idea that I was an electronics engineer.

I bought a portable, three-kilowatt Honda gasoline generator and ran extension cords to two refrigerators, the WI-FI, a lamp, and the TV. It all worked fine, but sometimes it was hard to find gasoline stations with electricity to pump the fuel. So in 2012 we put in an automatic, whole-house generator that ran on underground natural gas. It was right outside our kitchen window and we could hear it tested for ten minutes every Wednesday at 8:00 a.m. The generator only kicked in for one emergency while we still lived there. We moved the following July. Perhaps that addition helped to sell the house. We would like to think so, anyway.

Before their marriage, Jackie and Rodney lived in a studio apartment on Sierra Drive in Kaimuki, perched on a ridge above Tenth Avenue, a dozen or so blocks from where they have lived ever since their marriage. Their current four-bedroom home is in Palolo Valley, a suburb just behind Diamond Head—east of Honolulu on the isle of Oahu. They added two of those bedrooms several years after moving in and screened in the area beneath the addition to make an artist's studio for Jackie.

Today, Rodney remains chief financial officer and administrative manager of Hawaiian Home Lands, answering only to a political head appointed by the governor. Rodney testifies regularly before the state legislature on budget and legal matters. His frequent travel to the neighbor islands demonstrates his devotion to his work. He's even talking about retiring in a few years. Doesn't that makes you feel real old when your kids start talking about retirement?

The change from Mainland architecture schools to the one at the University of Hawaii eventually soured Jackie on her prospects in continuing with that profession. At the end of her sophomore year at UH she switched to an art major and got her Bachelor of Fine Arts degree (BFA) even before her divorce from Rick. She continued with art at UH until she got her Master of Fine Arts (MFA) degree. Sculpture and other three-dimensional works proved to be her thing.

Originally, Jackie started work in Honolulu as a draftsman for an architectural firm while still married to Rick. Later she became the art director for the Honolulu Boys and Girls club. Working there she underwent a sort of transition in working with local children. Many natural-born Hawaiians see Caucasians as aliens—*haoles,* in local parlance. One day, while separating two kids from fighting, one local and the other *haole*, Jackie chastised the local child for picking on the *haole*, saying, "After all, I'm *haole* too." The child immediately replied, "No, you local." It was true. Jackie had even begun to pick up some of the speech mannerisms.

Some years later, Jackie had a disagreement with a surly supervisor, who kept butting into art affairs without the necessary art knowledge. Jackie sought new employment at the Honolulu Academy of Art (now the Honolulu Museum of Art) as an art teacher for both adult and children's classes. She remained in that position for many years—until an austerity drive cut her program. By then her reputation as an art teacher and sculptor, working in ceramics and bronze, was well established in Honolulu art circles. Well enough that she could solicit art commissions and fulfill Artist-in-the-Schools sessions.

A birthday party for Alena at our condo pool in Honolulu

Jackie also taught all grades of art at the Temple Emanu-El Sunday school (and still does). After a while, we were pleased to learn that she was taking more of an interest in Temple affairs and Judaism in general. In fact, she was becoming very popular with both children and adults there—so much so that she was asked to run for the board of trustees. She was elected to the board and, by the time we made our move to stay in Honolulu, we learned that she was being groomed for temple president. She was again elected and served three years in that position. She continues to be active and adored at Temple Emanu-El.

Alena and Leah were both schooled in ballet and gymnastics. Whenever Rosemary and I were in Honolulu, it was our pleasure to chauffer them to their practices and competitive events. We

Jackie and I sharing a great smile

Leah (at left) as a toy soldier in *The Nutcracker*

Alena performing hula at Kapiolani Park

Alena practicing the French horn

also went to see Leah when she had a minor part in *The Nutcracker* with Ballet Hawaii. The girls grew up to be bright and beautiful young ladies, each with a special young man in mind. Alena is engaged to marry Zach, and Leah has a live-in also named Ben, a boy she met as a teen at Jewish Camp Newman in California.

Alena seems to have captured the art gene from her mother and won several honors in that field. One of her ceramic sculptures was displayed at the Hawaii Opera Theater (HOT) and another, in a national competition, was displayed at the Corcoran Museum in Washington, DC. We made several trips to the Corcoran to show off her work to friends and relatives. This success motivated her to pursue Art and Psychology, with a double major as her undergraduate degree at the University of Washington in Seattle. Apparently, Alena changed her mind about a career in art-related psychology. She is currently seeking her doctorate in Physical Therapy at Eastern Washington University.

At Roosevelt High School, the lean and muscular Leah excelled in track and field, choosing high hurdles, long jump, and even pole vaulting. Again, her groupies (ooh-ing and wowing away) followed her to the races whenever we could. She began taking a serious interest in sports medicine, assisting her high school sports trainers in treating and bandaging. So she obtained her bachelor's degree in Exercise and Sports Science at the University of San Fran-

Leah in her high school picture

Airborne Leah flying over the high hurdles

cisco. Leah went on to Long Island University in Brooklyn, NY and beame a Doctor of Physical Therapy. She passed her national boards and is currently working in a San Francisco clinic, building a client base. Perhaps the two girls will open a clinic of their own one day. Wouldn't that be wonderful?

In addition to our on-and-off critique groups in both Maryland and Honolulu, Rosemary and I joined the Maryland Writers' Association, Mystery Writers of America, and Sisters in Crime (I am a Mister in Crime). We attended meetings in Mary-

The two of us in our Severna Park work spaces

Relaxing on the lanai in western Maryland during a family wedding weekend

Rear book cover publicity shots taken in Maryland by Craig Herndon

Rear book cover publicity shot taken in
our Severna Park, MD living room

My Honolulu work space
(our second bedroom)

land, Virginia, and the District of Columbia, which kept us pretty busy on a regular basis.

We also started going to mystery writers' conventions and conferences, most notably, Malice Domestic, which was mostly held just over the DC line in Virginia and now in Bethesda, MD. We attended approximately fourteen of the Malice conventions and, each time, we were either on panels with notable authors, or moderated them. We always attended other panels on writing, featuring celebrity authors. And then there were the banquets where the "Agatha" (Christie) Awards (teapots) were given out for the best mysteries in a number of categories. The engraved teapots were like the Oscars for mystery writers. We also attended annual writing workshops at Maryland Writers' Association conferences, during which Rosemary won several awards for her personal essays.

In 2005 Rosemary and I attended our first Left Coast Crime convention on the Big Island of Hawaii and made many new friends. Ironically, it was held at the same hotel where we stayed when the Spurriers lived on the Big Island. I moderated one panel and served on an additional one. Rosemary served on yet another panel. Left Coast Crime holds its conventions in a different city west of the Rockies every year. Their version of the Oscars-for-writers was the "Lefties." For several years after the Big Island convention we coordinated our return from Hawaii to Maryland with stopovers for other four-day Left Coast Crime conventions: in Santa Fe, NM; Colorado Springs, CO; and Phoenix, Az. Each one was memorable in its own way. We also coordinated with John and

Rosemary in our living room

With travel buddies John and Ann Pollack

Ann, who spend their winters in Scottsdale, AZ. They would meet us in these cities for another delightful five-day get-together.

In Santa Fe in 2011, I was on a panel moderated by Rosemary. During the Q and A, Rosemary was asked who wrote the sex scenes for our books, and she quickly replied that I did. A follow-up question redirected at me asked, "Who did the research for those sex scenes?" I replied, "I don't farm that out." Penny Warner, the author sitting next to me on the panel, leaned over with her microphone and asked me, "What's your room number?" The entire audience broke out in roaring laughter. Our historic hotel, La Fonda, was decorated with uniquely painted tiles, but the hotel was so sprawled out that I had trouble getting from one place to another. In the after-trip visit with John and Ann, I remember spicy food, extremely dry air, a trip to the Georgia O'Keeffe Museum, and a visit to a children's museum full of miniature art and toys.

In Colorado Springs in 2013, we received a call from our Honolulu real estate agent that our offer on an apartment had been accepted, but more about that later. It was still cold in Colorado so we had to bring layers of clothes from Hawaii. We requested a room next to the elevator. The three-story hotel complied, only it was in one of their long, long, extended U-shaped buildings across a wide patio. Because of extreme cold, heavy ice, and accumulated snow outside, it was a fifteen-minute walk down endless hallways to the ballrooms where the panels were being held. My aching back. It would have been only a minute's walk across the patio.

Our second night there, we witnessed a near-blizzard. The panels we were on came off without a hitch, and the two of us found great panels to attend. At lunch on the last day we met an author from Oahu, who told us she was angling to get the 2017 convention for Honolulu two years after this one. She asked us, if it came to fruition, would we help and coordinate the panels? Considering it an honor to be asked, and not knowing that it would be a year-long endeavor, a "Yes" escaped from both of our mouths After the convention, we joined with the Pollacks again for sightseeing, including the Air Force Academy and an old mansion's art collection from the late 1800s.

At the March 2016 Phoenix Left Coast Crime convention, I brought Wally the Wheelchair to all the events, and that made getting around a lot easier for me. We met with the chief honchos of the Left Coast Crime (LCC) national committee and set up a line of communication among us. With an eye to possibly hosting LCC in 2017, we began to examine what it took to make each panel a success. Our time with John and Ann was punctuated by a coordinated one-day visit from California relatives of John and Rosemary whom they had not seen since their teens. That day culminated with dinner at a lively, noisy restaurant. By the time dinner was over, it was as though we were solid old friends.

Our local chapter of Sisters in Crime won the bid to host Left Coast Crime 2017. We called it "Honolulu Havoc." The committee expected about 300 avid fans of mysteries and 160 or so authors in the mystery/suspense/thriller genres. As panel co-chairs we examined prior convention programs for subject ideas. The panels themselves would be composed of attending authors. As authors began to enroll, we gleaned information from their applications: which panel they wanted to be on, whether they wanted to moderate one, or whether they even wanted to be a panelist at all.

Rosemary and the convention chair visited a number of beachfront Waikiki hotels, comparing room rates, ballroom pricing, food and drink costs, and tropical ambience. The Hilton Hawaiian Village resort—its Tapa Tower facilities—won the LCC contract. Using the hotel's designated meeting rooms; preparation schedules; the hotel's plan view of the spaces involved; and our list of described panels—we laid out a tentative, six-page master panel chart: a matrix with five venue spaces laid out horizontally and fifty-minute time slots vertically. Each slot was large enough to hold six names: a moderator and up to five panelists. Priority slots were set aside for award nominees, special events, and interviews. Using our past convention experience, we assigned panels on the most popular topics to the larger spaces. Panels sharing a common thread were scheduled at different times. We had to make sure that convention honorees (lifetime achievement honorees; guests of honor; and an international guest of honor) were assigned at least two panels. All in all, there would be 160 authors vying for 310 slots on 62 panels. The convention coordinators sent us enrollee updates every week.

Now came the hard part. Not everyone could be put on the panel of their choice or even a panel matching their particular experience. As long as the assignments remained a committee secret, the only problems were the convention dropouts. Nearly twenty authors dropped out because of personal health, finances, or scheduling conflicts. As soon as the assignments were made public on the convention website, the first wave of proverbial excretion hit the fan. In order to comply with as many author wishes as we could, panelists and moderators were moved about like so many chess pieces, each with their own special requirements. Some national and local chair needs were stirred into the mix as well. And then the week of the convention, a blizzard on the East Coast added its own storm to all our careful planning. Of course, "My plane doesn't land until..." and "I have to leave the convention early to be at the airport by..." didn't help either.

Our own personal schedule wasn't made any easier. (We were also attending the weekly meetings as committee members of the Honolulu Jewish Film Festival that took place the week before the convention.) For Left Coast Crime, I took on the moderating of a panel called "Riveting Suspense: Tales to keep us up at night." I had to read four full-length novels written by my panelists and prepare questions pertinent to their works. Because I wanted to ensure maximal turnout, I put two of the guests of honor on my panel: Dana Stabenow and Colin Cotterill. Rosemary selected a panel to be on called "How Coauthors Cope: Lovey-dovey or strictly business?" All the planning produced one hell of a convention. Dana commented, "Great panel" and Colin said, "You sure did your homework." How could I not appreciate that?

To complicate convention preparation even further, we had been planning a one-month journey to the Mainland in May

Stephanie Sexton

Mitzie Mild, Tom Sexton, Samantha Mild, John Mild, Marsha Mild, Sydney Mild, and Cathy Mild Sexton

and June of 2017, involving forty-two family members—if you include the three live-in boyfriends. For a whole year in advance, we worked on scheduling, reservations, and transportation. Wally the Wheelchair joined our luggage one more time. This was to be "my last hurrah." To start, we flew nonstop to Newark, NJ and took a cab to our hotel in Brooklyn, NY. All of us were there to witness our granddaughter Leah's graduation as a Doctor of Physical Therapy at Long Island U. We also visited with cousin Jeff Seidenberg.

On the third day we rented a minivan and drove to Akron, OH with Jackie and Rosemary doing all of the driving. Rodney, Alena, Leah, and the boyfriends returned home. The three of us spent five days intermittingly visiting sister-in-law Mitzie Mild; nephew John Mild and his wife, Marsha; niece Cathy Mild Sexton, her husband, Tom. and their daughter, Stephanie.

It was a strange feeling, knowing that I might never see these close family members again. I hadn't experienced that queasy a feeling since I was an insecure preteen. Here, I suspected it would become a certainty.

The three of us left Akron and headed south. In Cincinnati we had lunch with a friend of Jackie's and we stopped overnight in Knoxville, TN. The next morning Jackie altered our route to Roswell GA, our next stop, by selecting a road through the Great Smoky Mountains. While the scenery was terrific, I had some anxiety: if I had a health problem, the boonies were not the best place to be. Happily, I came through the Smokies with flying colors. We stopped for lunch at The Pearly Gates café that had a sign above the blackboard: "Eat more bacon." After lunch Jackie stretched her legs next door at some old railroad tracks. She returned with news: she had bumped into a man who graduated from the same high school she did—only a year before her.

That night we stayed in a hotel about two miles from Cousin Go Nodar's house. We took her out to dinner that first night, and she reciprocated the next day by gathering the clan at her house. The clan included Go's brother, Barry Rothberg; his wife, Harriet and their daughter, Sandy; Go's sister, Bobbie Christmas; Go's daughter Susan Saul and her husband, Steven; Cousin Brian Golson and his mate, Michael Gross; and Cousin Cathy Curtis Mild. The following day Brian and Michael held a brunch for everyone at their place about thirty minutes away. Michael's mother, Sylvia Gross, a Holocaust survivor, was also included.

Again, it was hard to say goodbye after such a grand three-day welcome. Jackie wanted to see Savannah, so an overnight and a one-day visit were added to the schedule. We had supper at an Italian, gangster-theme restaurant and Jackie got to see the old town and the home of Juliette Gordon Low (founder of the Girl Scouts). We drove to Charleston, SC that afternoon for another main event: our grandson Ben's marriage to Sydney Turnquist.

We rented one four-bedroom, and one three-bedroom, beachfront condominium in Folly Beach just south of Charleston for one week. Five Spurriers and Emily's boyfriend, Joe, stayed in one and Rosemary and I, Jackie and Rodney, Alena and Zach, Leah and her Ben stayed in the other. The first night Ben, the groom, and his brother, Craig, cooked a BBQ dinner with all the trimmings for the whole crew. The next day we met the Turnquist family at their Folly Beach rental condo and, two nights later, Tim hosted the rehearsal dinner reception at Bowen's Island Restaurant. It was a fun evening.

The sundown wedding was held that Saturday at Wingate Plantation on John's Island, one of many islands surrounding the Charleston shores. They were fortunate to have a clear, balmy evening for the event. The ceremony took place under a large live oak

Sydney and Benjamin Spurrier at their nuptuals

Joe Grandinetti and Emily Spurrier (Maid of Honor)

Alena Lau and Zach Weaver

Leah Lau and Ben Karp

at the Turnquist/Spurrier wedding in Charleston, SC

Craig Spurrier, Best Man

Rosemary and me, happy spectators

at the Turnquist/Spurrier wedding

Alena, Zach, Leah, Ben, and Joe

Jackie and Rodney

At the wedding of Ben and Sydney Spurrier

overlooking a pond with wild birds. Two wide sections of folding chairs reached to the limits of the oak's branches. Sydney's godmother and long-time friend of the Turnquists presided over the couple's vows in a short, but sweet service. We weren't quite sure whether she was some kind of preacher or not.

Following a brief picture-taking period, a buffet dinner was served on a huge covered patio with tables and chairs. A live band and a dance floor occupied the opposite end of the patio, and the festivities lasted for hours.

Rodney, his two girls, and their beaus left for the airport the following day. Tim headed back to Hawaii for a week, only to return to the farm to help take care of chores while the rest of the Spurriers traveled. Mara Gormley Proctor and her husband, Steve, drove up from their new home in Florida to fill the void at the condo. We enjoyed two days with them. On the following Tuesday Emily and Joe headed for the Aiken farm to see friends, while Rosemary, Jackie, Myrna, Craig, and I drove to Rocky Mount, NC for an overnight there.

That evening we walked around a small but pretty lake, complete with with ducks, geese, and bad-ass bugs with an enormous appetite. The bites were so bad that when we got to Annapolis, our last destination, Rosemary needed treatment at a walk-in clinic for a nasty bug-bite rash. We stayed at the Lowes Hotel downtown, close to the City Dock. Myrna, Craig, Emily, and her Joe arrived a day later after dropping Tim off at the airport. They were mainly interested in sightseeing in Washington, DC. to take in a few museums and visit the famed pandas at the National Zoo.

Our long-time, close Annapolis friends Marty and Joy Beer had very recently passed away, so we wanted to visit their graves. It was nice that their daughter and granddaughter met us at the cemetery. Rosemary, Jackie, Myrna, Craig, and I also visited Hannah and Miriam's graves at another time. Sheila and Marty Litzky drove down from Philadelphia to be with us for the day. We had lunch with Sinjin (St. John) and Ellie Martin at their home in Severna Park. They also invited our mutual friends: Donna Brown and Bob and Helene Sachs for a whole afternoon of catching up. Two nights later we had Sinjin and Ellie Martin join our whole gang for dinner at Mike's Crab House on the South River.

An hour's drive to Potomac, MD enabled Rosemary and me to spend an afternoon and evening with Rosemary's cousins Richard and Connie Pokress and their extended families. Jackie had chosen to visit one of her own friends. The upscale woodsy neighborhood rambled in every direction with similar road names, making their place difficult to find. The house was a beautiful gentrified mansion on three floors—one floor per family, as two of their adult children and grandchildren were living with them.

Another day we started to drive to Baltimore to see long-time friends Dr. Mike and Libby Monias. Before we ever left Annapolis, Jackie, suddenly recognized that the minivan was behaving

Rosemary and me in with friends: Evelyn Vaccari, and Joy and Marty Beer

Friends Sinjin and Ellie Martin when they visited us in Hawaii

badly, so we had Rosemary, the driver, pull into a nearby courthouse parking lot. We confirmed that the car had a flat tire and called AAA roadside service. Within fifteen minutes, the man from AAA had re-inflated the tire. We also called the car rental agency, who told us not to have the tire repaired, but to bring the car to a branch of their rental agency, which happened to be only a mile away. The man from AAA followed us there, where we exchanged cars rather than repair the tire—weird. An hour later, the three of us were on our way to Baltimore once more to renew our friendship with Mike and Libby. She served us lunch and we spent a pleasant afternoon with them.

We flew out the next day to Honolulu. Because Jackie had chosen a later flight with a stopover in Seattle, WA to spend a few days with Alena, she kept the car and drove us to the airport. Later that same day she conveyed Myrna, Craig, Emily, and Joe to the airport for their flight to Canada. It was good to get home again and to end "my last hurrah." I was exhausted after a month away from home.

Chapter 20

Changes: The Good and the Worrisome

Two weeks before Rosemary and I left for the Colorado Springs Left Coast Crime convention, a For Sale notice appeared on our condo bulletin board. Unit 1508 was a two-bedroom apartment on the fifteenth floor with a gorgeous 120-degree view of the Pacific Ocean. It had a large living room, covered lanai, modern kitchen, and ceramic tile kitchen floor, and was situated on the side away from street soot. Best of all, six of our family members lived in Honolulu: Jackie and Rodney, and now, also, Tim, Myrna, Craig, and Emily. We had been renting apartment 403 on the street side for twenty years. Using an agent and offering a generous bid, we left town without knowing whether it would be accepted. We gave Jackie power of attorney to act on our behalf just in case the deal went through.

Our bid *was* accepted, and we returned to our Severna Park home knowing we needed to sell it and get rid of excess possessions as quickly as possible. Between us, we had seventy-two years of Stuff to deal with: 3,000 books; power and hand tools galore; a multi-computer network; abundant artwork, and far too much furniture. I had accumulated every manner of nut, bolt, screw, and nail imaginable. All our accumulated possessions in apartment 403, including another computer network, office supplies, and clothes, had to be factored in as well. Our five-bedroom colonial house, with its eat-in kitchen, full dining room, and three-couch, ell-shaped living room, had to be trimmed to fit a two-bedroom apartment. *Squished* is more like it. It took a little over four months and

View from backyard looking left

View from front lawn looking down street

The sad beauty of leaving 120 Kennedy Drive behind

View from backyard looking right at apple tree Miriam planted from a seed at age 5

Even the backyard had color

View looking toward backyard left

View looking toward backyard right

View from front lawn looking up street

View from front lawn looking across street

two potential buyers to sell the house. (The first contract tanked because the buyers lied about their income.) It required twelve-hour days to identify the throw-aways, give-aways, sell-aways, and take-aways—plus the cleanup afterward.

We realized we had too many cars: a gray Honda Odyssey and a red Honda CR-V in Severna Park and a tan Honda CR-V in Honolulu. A young woman who owned a used-furniture shop had just handed us a check for some of ours. On her way out, we told her we also had a minivan to sell. She took one look at it and said, "I have two boys. I want to be a soccer mom. I'll take it!" Our tan CR-V already had handicapped plates, so Myrna wound up with the prettier red one—to Rosemary's minor disappointment.

Meanwhile, returning to Honolulu in July of 2013, we were still living in apartment 403 while we had renovations done in 1508. In the kitchen, the countertops were replaced; the laundry area was extended and enclosed with folding doors; and a useless kitchen half-wall was removed to make room for an eat-in table. The smaller bedroom became our office, so its closet was modified to hold filing cabinets and shelves. The master bath got new everything: plumbing, lighting, countertop, faucets, and handicap rails. The guest bathroom got dressed up with a new countertop, new lighting, and fancy faucets.

The renovations were completed just in time for the delivery of our container from the Mainland. I had marked up plan views of the room spaces, so when the furniture arrived, everything had its proper place. Randy, our contractor, hung some of our heavier artworks. But Myrna's huge ceramic tile depicting the history of ceramics didn't look right. Rosemary was alarmed. "Where's the dragon?" she asked. Randy had hung the piece upside-down.

It's now 2019 as I write this, and I can safely say: through all the sadness and madness of who and what we left behind, the move to Hawaii was for the best. And I have no stairs to climb! The only disappointment we've experienced is the ugly new high-rise building (opposite us) that reduces our 120-degree view of the ocean down to approximately 60 degrees.

No Place To Be But Here

In Honolulu, over the years our religious, communal, and social life has centered more and more around Temple Emanu-El. Perhaps the religious inclination has something to do with aging and self-examination. But, more likely, it has to do with the joyous weekly and holiday services. It's not just us. The entire congregation appreciates Rabbi Ken Aronowitz as our spiritual leader. He's an accomplished cantorial soloist, a Torah scholar, teacher, and a down-to-earth, loving person with a great sense of humor. He leads us in sincere prayer and sermons. We always leave temple feeling uplifted.

As for the communal and social aspects, Rosemary and I are regular members of the Rabbi's Tuesday morning "Jewish Wisdom" class—a participation/discussion group on Jewish values, traditions, and history. On several occasions when the rabbi has been away, I have led the class on pertinent Jewish subjects that I found on the Internet. Whenever there is a guest speaker or lecturer at Temple-E, we make a concerted effort to attend. Once a month we attend a fun "Lunch and Learn" program for the Jewish seniors.

We are also members (for our fifth year) of the annual Honolulu Jewish Film Festival (HJFF) committee. We screen over a hundred films per year and decide which dozen or so make the final list. A few we screen at the weekly meetings. However, we screen the majority at home, using special film links and passwords. In addition, we contribute to the planning, publicity, and hosting duties for the HJFF, always held in March. When the former statistician left the committee, I took over these duties as well. I reorganized the rating/scoring scheme into specific, meaningful ratings, and instituted two new reporting documents. On the alphabetized document the individual films can be found easily, allowing the dozen screeners to enter their ratings. A second document automatically computes the average rating for each film and sorts the most favorable (highest average) films, so they and their scores rise to the top of the page in a prioritizing scheme. I email these reports out to the members weekly, based on incoming scores from the other eleven committee screeners. The contending films rate additional intense discussions on their merits.

* * * *

I have reached that point in my existence where I remain content with my lot, my draw in life's deck of cards. Still, there are a number of national social issues that trouble me. I worry about the recent decline of level-headed governance and the reversal of laws I truly thought were (for the most part) good, essential, and healthy for the majority of the American people and not harmful to the remainder. I fear the blatant callousness of those in power, who woo and trigger economic disaster, environmental doom, foreign relations failures, and, God forbid, even World War III. I tremble at the thought of any in our midst being denied or left behind because of who they are, what they look like, where they came from, or how they believe.

I cringe at the power wielded by the National Rifle Association to stifle gun regulation. We have arrived at a point in history where our Constitution and its amendments have proven to be more than a successful experiment. So where is the need for ordinary citizens to carry automatic and semiautomatic weapons and modification devices to perpetrate arms of mass murder? I believe that—through appropriate licensing—the rights of legitimate hunters and recreational shooters can be upheld without creating fear among the populace. How many weapons are needed by these people? How many are passed on to others illegally? How many get lost in the current system? Why aren't gun show exhibitors/sellers subjected to the same laws as the gun shops? Shouldn't ammunition be limited as well? What is lacking in background checks and waiting periods? Do they consider intended usage, personal gun count, mental stability, and extremist leanings? If not, they should.

I am distressed with the Internet and its social media conduits, which have given rise to speeds that set some actions in motion before giving careful thought about consequences. That such a wondrous and useful idea could be placed into existence without adequate controls is unforgivable. How can we allow privacy violation, identity theft, scams, harassment, and other cyber crimes and annoyances to be perpetrated without a way of tracing their original source?

While I'm on the subject of privacy, I believe my privacy rights belong to *me.* My personal information (and my family's) should *not* be bandied about the digital and paper media without my expressed or writen permission. Inadequate safeguard measures and mal-intended hacking are now everyday occurrences. And once I give that permission, it should not go beyond the entity I've given it to, nor should it be used for anything more than the purposes I have directed. Corporate marketing statistics should not be one of those purposes. Congress has passed privacy laws that have ignored some of these aspects—laws that have created enormous amounts of paperwork that inundate the U.S. mails and laws that endanger our precious resource of trees.

If you don't believe that the bots already have a big foothold in our society, just try to get a human being when you want any customer service; or count how many incoming "robo" calls you've answered; or remember the number of times you've picked up and gotten silence because someone else picked up first in mass dialing. Of all the wasted studies that go on in our Federal Government, isn't this one that deserves some priority? And what have the bot devices, portable/mobile devices, done to our own behavior? Consider the humanoid crossing the street with ear buds, poking at and sliding a finger across a cell phone. Observe a person similarly engaged in a roomful of people, or even seated with others in a restaurant. Contemplate those hours spent oblivious to the surrounding environment and devoid of social contact and exchange. Where are we going and what will we be like in the years to come?

I am troubled at the ineffectiveness of local governments to deal with homelessness. Realizing that there is no one cure that fits all three major groups, at least the willing and capable would be easier to be put on a sure footpath to solvency. The mental and handicapped should be treated at proper facilities at the expense of the taxpayers. Lastly, the alcohol- and drug-dependent, along with the unwilling, might be provided with individual low-cost shelters and sanitary conditions in self-governed camps off the beaten path. As for low-cost shelters, Rubbermaid sells a sizeable, easily assembled shed for about $300. An especially modified design of twice the size from any manufacturer might be considered affordable by most metropolitan areas. After decades of pushing the homeless from one place to another, isn't it time to find fit places for them to live?

Another thing. I am dumbfounded by the general prospects of modernization. While our politicians are busy shrinking the middle class through unfair taxation, robotics are stealing blue-collar jobs. In the midst of all the wonderful advancements science and industry have wrought, we find their leaders remiss in creating new jobs for the semiskilled and nonskilled among us. In fact, huge numbers of jobs have been shipped overseas to avoid the unprofitable tax laws. Let those firms be the ones to pay tariffs. Once robotics move from the factories to drive our vehicles, where do taxi- and truck- and even Uber-type drivers look for employment? When catalogue companies, department stores, and even grocery chains turn to drones for delivery where do those people get jobs?

Chapter 21

Dealing with Hate

Let me begin by saying it is frightening to learn that anti-Semitism is on the rise worldwide: for instance, in France and Germany, and with Poland's declaration of Holocaust innocence, where it takes a presidential order to even investigate an action as a hate crime. The continuing excuses—"just a slip of the tongue" and "My words were taken out of context"—by persons of national prominence reflect that anti-Semitism lies just beneath the surface, even in our own country. Anti-Semitism takes many forms and it's not always easy to recognize. Cruel words can be intended to hurt or merely be ingrained in habitual speech patterns and cultural history without intent toward malice. Nonetheless, such words harm and can proliferate. Cruel actions such as bias and exclusion, whether visible or not, take hate a step further. Harm escalates even more viciously with beatings, kidnapping, and disfigurement. Murder is the ultimate hate crime.

I am an earnest and sincere advocate of free speech and freedom of the press. I have always believed in freedom of expression. Growing older, I have come to think of free expression as a privilege to be safeguarded rather than an absolute right. I believe that we earn that privilege by pledging to neither demean nor abuse nor treat others in a hateful manner, nor promulgate that hate in any inciting way.

Professional newspaper and broadcast journalists wield powerful tools to report news, opinions, beliefs, and events in our communities and the world in general. Now many individuals have glommed onto similar tools with the advent of the Internet. Their power exists in the sheer numbers of individuals they reach. Most of the empowered wield those tools responsibly and with care and forethought. They also criticize constructively and with respect. I appeal to them to take one more step.

We tend to make celebrities and, in some cases, martyrs of those who create the most heinous hate crimes. How? By disclosing their full names, complete with photographs, in print in all the media, even if they are still only suspects. In essence, the media is lionizing these perpetrators, who are, most probably, looking for two things: notoriety and a deed to bring about that notoriety. The successes of their predecessors goad them to instigate a crime even more spectacular. Seeing their name and likeness in print, on screen, and/or hearing their names and deeds gives them that desired notoriety. Just suppose print journalists, TV reporters, op-ed authors, etc. eliminate, substitute, or even demonize the perpetrators' names. Let's see if this doesn't reduce the number and severity of hate crimes. All the facts of the crimes can still be reported effectively. But let's take away the credit and publicity these evil-doers don't deserve.

Hate suggestions coming from celebrities and role models are onerous and especially dangerous. The media can just report that something hateful was said without actually repeating the hateful statement. I am not a proponent of Big Brother watching, but neither am I for turning our heads away from impending disaster. Although law enforcement cannot act until an actual crime is committed, what if a watchful eye and ear are turned toward the hatefully outspoken. Without invading their privacy, only their inflammatory words would be surveilled. Knowing such statements are incendiary and ignoring them is almost as criminal.

Whether it be in jest or with pure evil intent: if you directly link words and phrases to any of the religions, races, ethnicities, or nationalities (politics excluded), you have actually created hateful speech. If such speech is published, or promulgated over the airways or cyberspace, couldn't the use of these denigrating phrases be construed as inciteful, even unlawful? Most of us understand what is defamatory; all that would be needed would be a special dictionary of such words and phrases. We already have laws against inciting a riot. Why not a law against inciting a hate crime?

The victims' loved ones do need to know they are not alone and the world is not made up of only evil-inclined minds. We all try in our separate ways to build community, education, and love, but today the hate problem is building as well. Overheard hateful messages in family and peer conversations extend the problem to the next generation and beyond. The messages abound even where peer acceptance is sought and hate is not intended. Counter-messages need to be delivered by the school systems, religious communities, families—and all of us folks.

These same thoughts occurred to me more than thirty years ago when I included them in an op-ed piece I published in the *Baltimore Sun:* "Six Ways To Prevent Airline Terrorism." I wrote it because Rosemary and I ourselves had become victims of hate and terror. We lost our dear daughter, Miriam Luby Wolfe, in the terrorist bombing of Pan Am Flight 103 over Lockerbie, Scotland on December 21, 1988. One of my "six ways" was to stop printing and broadcasting the names and pictures of the suspected/convicted bombers. U.S. Senator Barbara Mikulski (D) of Maryland came across my op-ed piece and was so impressed with its message that she read it into the *Congressional Record.*

In dealing with hate, how much has the world learned since?

Chapter 22

When I Bow Out of Here

I can't imagine leaving here without some sort of bureaucratic snag. First of all there's all that estate planning I've done to prevent confusion after I'm gone—to provide for the ones who'll miss me most—*and* all those things one needs to do to make sure there's something left after taxes. Then, of course, there's setting right all those things I've done wrong and those things I've neglected. I've honestly tried to do all those things. But now the powers-to-be tell me I absolutely cannot leave this life without filling out my End-of-Life Exit Form (Form EX1346502.3a). What are they going to do—stop me from moving on? Oh-oh! Is there any way to keep my expiration date pending?

Since I'm one who likes to be prepared, I've obtained this required exit form, and now I need help with some of the responses. I'd call the Help Line, but why should I give up precious living time to wait for the next available outsourcee? He or she probably wouldn't speak American-English anyway, and I can't stand their "Please hold. Your call is important to us" music selections. The online FAQ (Frequently Asked Questions) and Help sites offer questions no one in their right mind would ever ask, and answers that must have been written in legalese, a language devised by lawyers to justify their own existence.

Anyway, there's a category on my End-of-Life Exit Form that I'm pretty concerned about. It's the one marked AFTERLIFE. What concerns me most is that it's multiple choice! HEAVEN, OBLIVION, REINCARNATION, and OTHER. I need to have these profound selections explained before I can make a sensible choice. So I'm asking you:

1. If I choose Heaven, is it really up? If so, how far is this up? Should I take lunch?

2. If I choose Heaven, will it spoil my chances at being reincarnated at a later date?

3. If I choose Reincarnation, will it ruin my chances of getting into Heaven? Will I need to re-file?

4. If I mark both, or don't mark any, am I left in limbo? And in what direction is limbo?

5. Why would anyone choose Oblivion? Don't even shlemiels deserve another chance?

6. Will I be issued an exit visa instead of a death certificate? Will it endure the trip?

7. How can I be identified if I don't have any fingerprints or features with me?

8. Is Other only intended for Christians and Islamics, who have Hell pretty well defined?

9. What's a Jew to do with Other? Don't we deserve a better definition? Aren't we the chosen ones?

10. What gelatinous, gaseous, or spirit form will I be traveling in? Is it fashionable?

11. How much actual room does a soul take up? Are souls custom made? Will I fit?

12. Where are souls kept? Is there a storage charge? Is there a bargain "Keep" or cloud online where they are stored?

13. Does Heaven really have a gatekeeper to exclude the riffraff and the sinful?

14. If St. Peter guards the Christian gate, who guards the Jewish gate? The Messiah?

15. If the Messiah is so busy at the gate, is this why he (or she) hasn't come to us yet?

16. If we are to receive our reward in the afterlife, what form will it be? How big is it? Will I like it?

17. Is Oblivion complete? Is there anything left? Will I feel pain or anything?

18. Can Oblivion be reversed if I change my mind?

* * * *

Oh-oh! I marked Reincarnation and I did it with a pen, so I can't erase it. Good grief! Now I'll have to fill out page two of the form. But that raises a whole new batch of questions I'll need answered.

1. Will I have to get all new passwords, usernames, numbers, and apps in the next life?

2. Am I entitled to pick and choose any preferences in my next life? Is there a catalogue, or at least a menu?

3. Can I get an upgrade for all my good deeds, or do I have to re-accumulate them?

4. Will I be punished for my prior sins in my new life or only the newly acquired ones?

5. Do I have to make the same mistakes in the next life or can I get credit for the ones I already made?

6. Does someone with more prior lives have more priority in the next life?

7. Can I bring anyone or anything with me or is there an excess baggage charge?

8. Can I leave some of my excess bulk behind when I move on? Is there a weight limit?

9. Does my current vasectomy work in the next world? Or will I have to get another one?

10. Will I begin as a baby in the next world or will I continue from my current age?

11. Can I leave all my aches and pains behind in this life? Should I expect new ones?

12. Will I come back as the family's favorite pet in the next life?

13. Will I need a toothbrush, a Milk Bone, or catnip in my next life?

14. Do I have to take the driver's test again in the next life?

15. Will I have to befriend everyone all over again in my new life?

16. Will I be bigger than a breadbox in my new life? How will I recognize myself?

17. Can I sit down while I wait for my new assignment or is lying down required?

Thanks. I knew I could count on you for answers.

* * * *

Seriously, although I feel a strong belief in God, I can't imagine there is any such thing as an afterlife. What would God do with such a collection of souls that's been accumulating since the so-called Big Bang or, rather, the beginning of man's evolution, unless He plans to reuse them in some sort of reincarnation plan. While reincarnation is a definite major issue in some Eastern religions, I am left with two possibilities: to speculate about my ultimate disposition or to joke about it as I have done in the earlier lists. By the way, several passages in the Torah and Haftarah seem to imply that the wicked man's soul can only return three times, whereas the righteous man's soul can return a thousand times (Exodus 20:5, Job 33:29, and Amos 2:6). Hmm, three strikes and you're out. What then?

I suppose the more relevant question is: where does all my belief in God come from? There are two sides to consider here: the logical explanation for the pragmatist, for which I must claim to be a member; and the emotional explanation for the idealist whom I aspire to become.

First, I'll lay out my logical explanation. Science tells us the universe is in an ever-expanding and decaying mode ever since the Big Bang. I see any growth or even transition implying at least a beginning and an ending. If I'm thinking about the seed and the flower or the chicken and the egg, the question is not which came first, but where did the first one come from? Evolution, you say? Ah, but that is not without progression either.

Humankind continually uncovers hard and fast rules governing most physical phenomena—mechanics, solids, fluids, gases, heat, light, sound, and electricity. The mathematical formulas abound on these subjects. With the passage of time, more and more is learned about the hard, fast, and grim rules governing living things—the flora and fauna around us and the multitude of procreation methods sustaining the continuum of life's phenommena. And don't forget the hazards. All of us can agree to the miraculous nature of these things. Miraculous, but whose miracles are they? Who laid down these rules by which the universe and all things, living or not, behave? I believe it all began with the chaos and disorder of the Big Bang—a virtual scrambling of all the elements, molecules, atoms, and subatomic particles therein, as well as the behavioral rules that govern each of them. I find it difficult to believe that so much repetitive order arrived through randomness, survival, development, and natural rejection, even given the hundreds of billions of years that have elapsed since that event. Even once is statistically off the charts. But twice? A male and a female in each species? That's random tandem—so much worse than having enough monkeys and enough typewriters to result in a great novel. P.S. I don't believe that one either.

Instead, I believe that an indescribable spirit I call God is responsible for all that order. I've assigned God no specific form, or appearance or solitary place to reside. As I see it, there's a most complete lack of genderless and formless properties assigned to God.

The emotional explanation is a little harder to present. Those who have come before us have always wanted to worship what they could not explain, e.g., the sun, moon, mountains, fire, water, and so forth. Earlier, many bowed to multiple gods and even invented exciting tales to fulfill their myths. Those poor souls needed someone to blame for all their misfortunes, someone to thank for their prosperity, someone to fear for their misgivings, and someone to plead with for all that they lacked. One might concede that any positive response to their requests was certainly fortuitous. And, of course, those powerful gods must appear in forms that resemble humans and live somewhere in the enormous ill-defined space above us. I can only assume this is what led to all the misconceptions about being "created in God's image" and "heavens above."As I understand what is intended here: it is to behave in a God-like manner and not really to presume any resemblance to God's likely appearance.

As far as where God resides, I like to think that He is a distributive God, dwelling in those positive attributes in all mankind that we label "goodness and righteousness." When that goodness assembles in one place to pray, it takes on a power—the more participants gathered, the greater that power. As long as collective goodness exists, it is passed on from generation to generation, making God not only eternal, but omnipotent and ubiquitous. If each of us knew we carried a precious portion of God within us, wouldn't we take better care of how we lived our lives? A distributive God is more than just worthy of all the respect and adoration we can deliver.

Perhaps Dr. Leon Lederman, the renowned Jewish physicist (1922-2018), was on the right track. He hinted that there might be a hyperintelligent, omnipresent, superpowerful, subatomic particle or plasma out there, so tiny that it defies discovery, and yet it contains all the secrets and algorithms of matter, force, and all of life existence. He called the Higgs boson subatomic discovery "The God Particle." Are we looking in the wrong place for God when we look to the heavens above? Isn't it just as plausible that God looks up at us from within the multitudes of such particles and/or plasmas? Regardless, I still think we should look within ourselves to find our Godliness.

On the one hand, most of us offer sincere prayer and, incidentally, wonder whether God will intervene. We pray that He will grant our wishes and pleas, guard us from all harm, forgive our sins and iniquities, enable our healing, or even keep tabs on our daily living. On the other hand, we fill our worship with tons of praise and glorification without any personal feedback. Are we being heard? Is our plea credible? Will it help our cause? It is difficult for me to conceive that even the Most Omnipotent/Omniscient-of-All-Time would intervene in a lowly individual's daily affairs. So I, personally, ask for nothing but God's blessings for me, mine, and those in need and thank Him for doing so.

The *Unetanah Tkef* prayer speaks of who shall live and who shall die once the vows of Yom Kippur have been sealed. To me, this prayer proposes the ultimate punishment for any and all our crimes—the ultimate form of intervention. I believe that this prayer is poorly conceived. How many in any congregation have sinned in such magnitude and deserve so severe a punishment? Perhaps it is God's plan, but I believe mankind certainly has an ugly hand in it when the young, the good, and the innocent are taken well before their expected time.

I have found that prayer, in itself, has healing and feel-good qualities that soothe the soul no matter who or what you pray to. Mostly, I can sense the good and evil in those around me and presume that others can do the same. I'd like to think the good in humankind is God-like, even Godly. I guess that someone else thought so too when you consider the spelling similarity between God and good, but alas, that comparison just might be a bit of language chance.

This leads me to an important question: Do I believe in the Torah? Of course, I do. It not only provides the basis for all righteous behavior, but is the basis for all communal living rules. Do I believe every word, every interpreted meaning per se? Do I think it is absolutely historical and precisely correct? Of course not. Even setting aside its inconsistencies, misconceptions, and ancient perceptions, the Torah has stood the test of time as the greatest teaching instrument ever assembled. And as an anthology of sermon-like short stories, there has never been a piece of literature quite equal to it.

So what do I think about the holy Torah? Do I consider it holy? It certainly is holy and worthy of everyone's full respect when you consider what it has accomplished for mankind. It is the perfect reference for how to live a righteous life once you learn how to glean those precious gems and are willing to apply them. Is it all truth? In one sense, it is all truth, if you interpret all the intended meanings and nuances and don't dwell on literal accuracy. While it is morally correct, the details were conveyed in a manner easily understood by an existing culture at the time of its writing.

Take the creation story, for example. Science tells us that it took many millennia to accomplish, yet the Torah tells us that it all took place in a matter of six days. What can be said about earlier man's concept of time? He lived and worked by the sun and the moon and the harvest. It comprised his total clock and calendar. At some point man might have wanted a regular daylight time off—a day's cycle of the sun was too short, and the twenty-nine and a quarter days of the moon's cycle were too long, so he might have settled on some concept approaching a week. The idea of the work-and-rest combination was something he could live with and apply to other phenomena he didn't quite understand. If Methuselah lived to be 900 years, what was the meaning of a year or even a day? So why not use metaphoric days in the creation story as eras, ages, or some other partition of time? After all, the concept was symbolic and God can still be seen as omnipotent.

Can the Torah really be called the history of our people? I can only suppose that some of it is historically true, and the rest is there to appeal, proselytize, teach, and connect the proverbial dots. In all our personal writing I've come to appreciate the value of creative nonfiction. It is necessary in the truest and most well-meaning of documents. I must admire those original rabbis who collected the multiple versions of these moralistic tales, sermons, anecdotes, and rules for righteous living and edited them into one brilliant literary masterpiece that has been the staple of our people and Judaism.

Whether Torah and tablets were actually and historically given at Sinai doesn't really matter so much. Such a wonderfully described gift and event gives us a cause for appreciation and supreme celebration. The concept of orderly communal living and its designed language must have been divinely inspired to captivate the masses over the ages. Again, this might be the collective Godliness of mere men with divine motivation and inspiration.

The rabbis who collected, assembled, recorded, and edited the original Torah were indeed wise and thoughtful men. However, I should think that much of their times and surroundings were rural, simpler, and devoid of any perception of what future civilizations, so many millennia ahead, might entail. Even so, man's behavior toward his fellow man essentially has not changed, and a good many of those rules, laws, stories, and *mitzvot* endure and still bear meaning today.

I was raised as a Jew in a Jewish family because it was expected of my parents. "And you shall teach them (His words) to your children." Mom and Dad were good, believing people, working hard to survive in the Great Depression. The family attended High Holy Day services at Temple Mishkan Israel in New Haven and loosely observed most of the other holy days at home. We adhered to the Passover seder and abstained from bread for eight days, but we did not keep kosher. Also, it was extremely rare for us to attend a weekly Shabbat service. They sent me to religious school, and I was confirmed as a Jew. It seemed the right thing for them to do. But unfortunately, Hebrew School was never included, so I never became a Bar Mitzvah (Son of the Covenant). Looking back, I have to believe they had considered it an excessive expense in tight times. I've regretted that omission even to this day, though I must confess, I'm somewhat of a coward when it comes to languages. I've tried several times to learn Hebrew on my own, and this *alte cocker* has been too embarrassed to take a formal class. At least I was determined enough to see that my children learned Hebrew and and were properly B'nai Mitzvahed.

Regardless of my linguistic failures, my Jewish identity is ever-present, and I've never been without it. I've learned so many prayers by rote and sing out with the rest of the congregants. Transliterations fill the remainder of the void, as I have been attending weekly Shabbat services more and more for the past few decades.

Each Friday night I feel moved and satisfied, as if it's the most joyous Friday night service I have ever experienced.

Growing up, I was beaten up, disqualified, excluded, ignored, and insulted for being a Jew. So I figure I've earned my right to be Jewish. Despite all those disadvantages of being Jewish, as I matured, I eagerly reaffirmed my faith in Judaism for several reasons. No, it didn't happen all at once. I can't claim to have had an epiphany. It happened one reason at a time over many, many years.

One, I have this great legacy of belonging to the first religion to ever recognize one God. Two, I can claim a heritage that first gave recorded law and order to all communal living, i.e., the Ten Commandments. Three, my ancestors assembled the most powerful guides to moral and righteous living ever written, namely the Torah and Haftarah. Four, my religion allows me room to question, reason, assume, and analyze any aspect of my religion as long as it is done with respect. In fact, I might reference countless commentaries that take advantage of this aspect of Judaism, e.g., the Talmud. I am not expected to follow rites, rituals, and beliefs beyond my ability to reason their soundness as many other religions do, e.g., beads, wheels, idols, kneeling, etc. Five, I can take comfort that I have a loving God and not One to be constantly feared. I believe we should do the right thing just because it *is* the right thing and not because we fear punishment for doing the wrong thing. Six, I admire the fact that Reform Judaism has taken steps to achieve gender equality in all religious matters. Seven, I can very much appreciate the universal outlook of Judaism in its obligation to recognize and repair what is wrong with the entire world—not just our own person, our own house, and our own people. Eight, my religion teaches me to respect what others believe in, even though I might not believe in those things myself. Nine, I admire the attention to education and study that comes with being a Jew. Ten, I am comfortable being Jewish, and enjoy the literature, humor, music, holidays, camaraderie, and food that accompany it. Eleven, I can't help being proud of the contribution in every field of endeavor that Jews have made to improving this world.

So, after eighty-six years of opportunity and practice, have I been a good Jew, a good person, a good husband, a good father, a good son, a good neighbor, a good citizen, and a role model in my community? I think so. Most likely I could have accomplished more, tried harder, and done better, but I must believe that I was never really that bad at any of these things. My intentions were always the best, but petty excuses often got in the way of complete fulfillment. How much would I change, given the opportunity to relive my life? Probably not much. I've seen and experienced some wonderful things—and still do every day. I've never stopped appreciating the daily miracles that surround me. I've loved my life so far and all those who have loved me back. My regrets are minimal, and I am genuinely happy with my lot.

Hey, wait! I'm not done yet! My engine is still humming. I still have more stories to write, more love to dole out, and more kindnesses to perform. With all my preparations and declarations, am I ready to die? Nope! Will I ever be ready? Of course not! Every day that I am privileged to live is filled with gorgeous miracles, continuous love, and contiguous quests that require my completion. Will I still fight to endure, to live on? You're darn tootin'! Do I fear dying? Not really—where is the sense in fearing the inevitable? Has it ever changed the outcome or even the timing? So, why waste the effort? Of course, there isn't one among the living who doesn't dread a prolonged and painful illness. I've been there, witnessed that. God forbid!

If I have my way, my current life will pass at some distant instant with my face squished down on the computer keyboard, a growing string of z's continually filling the wide-screen monitor in front of me, and a blissful smile on my lips. Get the image? Hopefully, this won't occur until I've finished my last attempted project. I do so hate leaving things undone or in the middle. And if there's any unfinished business, I'm counting on Rosemary to tie things up for me.

No place to be but here? Well, there's no place I'd rather be but here—and now too. Meanwhile, I have my family, my friends, my daily joys, and my work. I thank God for being here, my family for loving me, my muse for being kind to me, and you for your patience in paying attention to my story.

§

www.ingramcontent.com/pod-product-compliance
Lightning Source LLC
Chambersburg PA
CBHW070521010526
44118CB00012B/1045
* 9 7 8 0 9 9 0 5 4 7 2 1 1 *